Mediation and Law in China II

As the second volume of a two-volume set on mediation in China, this book examines the development of a diversified dispute resolution regime and other major types of mediation in China.

Grounded in traditional dispute resolution practices throughout Chinese history, mediation is born out of the Chinese legal tradition and considered to be "Eastern" in nature. This second volume focuses on eight types of mediation prevalent in China in terms of its formation, development, challenges, and achievements: people's mediation, court mediation, administrative mediation, industry mediation, commercial mediation, lawyer mediation, online mediation, and a combination of arbitration and mediation. In analyzing these diversified forms of mediation, the authors explain the necessity of integrating emerging forms of mediation with historical ties and traditional practice and thereby reshape a mediation system that incorporates diversified approaches, changing contexts and various dimensions including history and reality, theory and practice, state and society.

Mediation and Law in China, Volume II, will serve as a crucial reference for scholars, students, and related professionals interested in alternative dispute resolution, civil litigation, and especially China's dispute resolution policy, law, and practice.

Liao Yong'an is Professor in the Law School at Xiangtan University, China, and Vice-President of the China Civil Procedure Law Research Association. His main research interests are dispute resolution and civil litigation.

Duan Ming is Associate Professor in the Law School at Xiangtan University, China. His main research interests are dispute resolution and civil litigation.

Zhao Yiyu is Lecturer in the Law School at Xiangtan University, China. His main research interests are dispute resolution and civil litigation.

Mediation and Law in China II
Development and Integration

Liao Yong'an, Duan Ming, and Zhao Yiyu

LONDON AND NEW YORK

First published in English 2023
by Routledge
4 Park Square, Milton Park, Abingdon, Oxon OX14 4RN

and by Routledge
605 Third Avenue, New York, NY 10158

Routledge is an imprint of the Taylor & Francis Group, an informa business

© 2023 Liao Yong'an, Duan Ming, and Zhao Yiyu

The right of Liao Yong'an, Duan Ming, and Zhao Yiyu to be identified as authors of this work has been asserted in accordance with sections 77 and 78 of the Copyright, Designs and Patents Act 1988.

All rights reserved. No part of this book may be reprinted or reproduced or utilised in any form or by any electronic, mechanical, or other means, now known or hereafter invented, including photocopying and recording, or in any information storage or retrieval system, without permission in writing from the publishers.

Trademark notice: Product or corporate names may be trademarks or registered trademarks, and are used only for identification and explanation without intent to infringe.

English Version by permission of China Renmin University Press.

British Library Cataloguing-in-Publication Data
A catalogue record for this book is available from the British Library

Library of Congress Cataloging-in-Publication Data
Names: Liao, Yong'an, author. | Wang, Cong (Legal researcher), author. | Duan, Ming, author. | Zhao, Yiyu, author.
Title: Mediation and law in China.
Description: Abingdon, Oxon [UK] ; New York, NY : Routledge, 2023. | Includes bibliographical references and index. | Contents: v. 1. The past, present, and future / Liao Yong'an, Wang Cong: Re-discovering of legal principles of mediation in China – Transformation and remolding of China's traditional mediation idea – New ideas and new thinking of China's modern mediation – Transformation and changes of mediation model in China – Road for professionalization of mediation in China – Practical exploration of mediation procedural prerequisite in China – Basic conception for formulation of mediation law in China – Structuring of mediation discourse system with Chinese characteristic – v. 2: Development and integration / Liao Yong'an, Duan Ming, Zhao Yiyu: Changes and transformations in people's mediation – The rise, fall, and reform of court mediation – The history and revival of administrative mediation – The dilemma and the way forward for industry mediation – The challenges of internationalizing commercial mediation : analysis based on the Singapore Convention on Mediation – Paradoxes and crackdowns in lawyer mediation – The rise and regulation of online mediation – The practice and development of the combination of arbitration and mediation – Reinventing and integrating the mediation system. |
Identifiers: LCCN 2022053948 (print) | LCCN 2022053949 (ebook) |
ISBN 9781032473499 (v. 1 ; hardback) | ISBN 9781032478319 (v. 1 ; paperback) |
ISBN 9781032473529 (v. 2 ; hardback) | ISBN 9781032478302 (v. 2 ; paperback) |
ISBN 9781032472713 (hardback) | ISBN 9781032478326 (paperback) |
ISBN 9781003385882 (v. 1 ; ebook) | ISBN 9781003385776 (v. 2 ; ebook)
Subjects: LCSH: Mediation–China. | Dispute resolution (Law)–China. | Conciliation (Civil procedure)–China.
Classification: LCC KNQ1758.S47 L54 2023 (print) |
LCC KNQ1758.S47 (ebook) | DDC 347.51/09–dc23/eng/20230403
LC record available at https://lccn.loc.gov/2022053948
LC ebook record available at https://lccn.loc.gov/2022053949

ISBN: 978-1-032-47352-9 (hbk)
ISBN: 978-1-032-47830-2 (pbk)
ISBN: 978-1-003-38577-6 (ebk)

DOI: 10.4324/9781003385776

Typeset in Times New Roman
by Newgen Publishing UK

Contents

List of Figures		vi
List of Tables		vii
Preface		ix

1. Changes in and Transformation of People's Mediation — 1
2. The Rise, Fall, and Reform of Court Mediation — 47
3. The History and Revival of Administrative Mediation — 81
4. The Dilemma and the Way Forward for Industry Mediation — 110
5. The International Challenges of Commercial Mediation: Analysis Based on the Singapore Convention on Mediation — 130
6. Paradoxes and Crackdowns in Lawyer Mediation — 152
7. The Rise and Regulation of Online Mediation — 178
8. The Practice and Development of the Combination of Arbitration and Mediation — 214
9. Reinventing and Integrating the Mediation System — 250

Index — 287

Figures

1.1	Workflow chart of the Dispute Resolution Center	18
1.2	The generalization of people's mediation	22
6.1	Chinese lawyers' mediation	155
7.1	Online mediation flow chart of the Baoji Online People's Mediation Committee	182
7.2	The design process of Sina's online dispute resolution platform	184
9.1	The typical civil litigation construct and the mediation construct	262

Tables

2.1	The change in China's court mediation rate (1980–2016)	54
6.1	Data on mediation work by lawyers in the sample courts, December 2017–June 2018 (in units)	161
6.2	A sample of market-based lawyer mediation practice in China	166
8.1	Mediation followed by arbitration models and their main forms	217
8.2	Arbitration followed by mediation models and their main forms	219
8.3	Settlement of arbitration cases by arbitration and mediation nationwide (unit: pieces)	223
8.4	Provisions of the CIETCA Rules on the combination of arbitration and mediation	225
8.5	Provisions of the BAC Rules for combining arbitration and mediation	228
8.6	BAC's Case Closure Table, 2013–2018 (Number of cases; proportion in percent)	231
8.7	Independent mediation cases since the establishment of the BAC Mediation Center	232
8.8	Combination of arbitration and mediation in the FTZ Arbitration Rules	233
8.9	Combination of arbitration and mediation in the Xiangtan Arbitration Commission Rules	235

Preface

After the demystification of the world, human society has entered the modern society of "the struggle of the gods." Modern society is a typical pluralistic society, with multiple values, concepts, institutions, and cultures. After the reform and opening-up, Chinese society has gradually bidden farewell to the traditional society and embarked on the path of pluralism, which has been embedded in every aspect of Chinese society. In the field of social governance, the subject of governance has changed from a single subject in the past to a plurality of subjects, and the mode of governance has also changed from one-way coercion in the past to pluralistic shared governance. As an important part of social governance, dispute resolution is also unable to resist the tide of pluralism, and the construction of an organically connected and coordinated pluralistic dispute resolution mechanism has become an important goal of social governance in China.

Mediation, as an important part of China's pluralistic dispute resolution mechanism, has also undergone a development process from traditional to modern, and from relatively homogeneous to increasingly diverse. Since ancient times, Chinese society has focused on the use of mediation to resolve disputes and maintain order, and has accumulated a long and rich mediation culture, which has been hailed by the Western world as the "Eastern experience." Before the reform and opening-up of China, due to the single social structure and governance model, mediation in China was mainly based on people's mediation, administrative mediation, and court mediation. In practice, these types of mediation were always intertwined with the influence of administrative power, and were therefore called "policy-led" mediation and labeled as "traditional mediation."

Reform and opening-up has provided the historical ground for the conceptual innovation and institutional reshaping of mediation in China. Since November 2013, when the Communist Party of China put forward the goal of modernizing the national governance system and its ability to govern, the concept of "co-construction, co-management and sharing" has profoundly changed the development of mediation in China. Chinese mediation has changed from its previous image of being administrative, closed, and lagging behind, to one of being diversified, socialized, open and intelligent.

Commercial mediation, mediation by lawyers, and industry mediation have emerged, and there is a sudden breeze of spring, and thousands of pear trees have blossomed.

While mediation is flourishing in China, we are soberly aware that both traditional people's mediation, court mediation, and administrative mediation, as well as the emerging commercial mediation, lawyer mediation, industry mediation, and online mediation, are facing their own development challenges. Traditional mediation is mainly faced with the problems of "transformation" and "renewal," while emerging mediation is mainly faced with the problems of "regulation" and "protection." Specifically, people's mediation faces the problem of how to pass on and innovate. Court mediation faces the problem of how to handle the relationship between litigation and mediation. Administrative mediation faces the problem of how to move from decline to revival. Commercial mediation faces the dilemma of marketization and internationalization. Lawyer mediation faces the problem of conflicting roles of agents and mediators. Industry mediation faces the problem of the autonomy of industry organizations and the lack of mediation capacity. Online mediation faces the problem of how to reconcile flexibility with certainty. More importantly, how to promote cooperation and interaction between traditional mediation and new mediation while promoting the development of mediation pluralism, and how to achieve organic integration within the mediation system, are also important challenges facing the development of mediation in China.

It is for this reason that we have attempted to explore the codes of the pluralistic development and systemic integration of mediation in China, from the perspective of traversing history and reality, blending East and West, combining theory and practice, and linking state and society. Of course, this is not the only purpose of writing this book. As we all know, mediation is the most oriental form of dispute resolution, and it is also an excellent window to China and its understanding. Therefore, through this book, we hope to tell the story of Chinese mediation, so that the Western world can get to know Chinese society, understand Chinese culture, and embrace the Chinese system through mediation.

This book is the result of years of contemplation by me and my students around the Chinese discourse system of mediation. As this book goes to press, I would like to thank Dr. Duan Ming, Dr. Zhao Yiyu, Dr. Wang Cong, Dr. Zhang Qinglin, Dr. Hou Yuanzhen, and Dr. Lv Zongcheng for their hard work in writing this book. Despite our commitment to excellence in the writing process, the world of mediation is so vast and profound that omissions and inaccuracies are inevitable. All such shortcomings must be remedied by subsequent research, and we would be grateful for your criticism.

Liao Yong'an
Mao Zedong's hometown Xiangtan, Hunan
November 9. 2020

1 Changes in and Transformation of People's Mediation

As a method of dispute resolution and social governance, mediation, which carries the cultural and ethical value of "harmony," is internationally renowned as an "Eastern experience." People's mediation, born out of traditional Chinese folk mediation, originated during the Soviet period, formed during the Shaanxi-Ganjiang-Ningxia Border Region Government, and was formally institutionalized after the founding of the People's Republic of China, following the battles of the Anti-Japanese War and the Liberation War. During the period of socialist construction and reform and opening-up, people's mediation played an extremely important role in social governance and became the first line of defense in China's social governance. The 19th National Congress of the Communist Party of China has proposed to create a social governance pattern of "co-construction, co-management, and sharing," which has put forward new requirements for the innovative development of people's mediation in the new era, as well as a new vision and task for academic research. This chapter attempts to provide a panoramic analysis of the past, present, and future of the people's mediation system, to sort out its historical genealogy and analyze its practical dilemmas and explore its improvement path.

1.1 Historical Changes in People's Mediation: Continuity and Rupture

1.1.1 The Historical Origins of People's Mediation

Mediation has a long history in China. During China's long social development, mediation has been widely used as a form of dispute resolution and has become an important resource of traditional Chinese legal culture. It is based on traditional Chinese folk mediation and people's mediation was formed, developed, and perfected during the New Democratic Revolution and socialist construction.

DOI: 10.4324/9781003385776-1

1.1.1.1 Traditional Chinese Folk Mediation

The traditional civil mediation system in China from the Western Zhou Dynasty to the late Qing Dynasty and the Republic of China was characterized by the following features: First, there are various forms of mediation. China's traditional mediation consists of three basic forms: governmental mediation, civil mediation, and government-approved civil mediation. Governmental mediation is mainly conducted by state and county officials and the judiciary, while civil mediation is mostly conducted by respected people such as clan elders and grass-roots officials specializing in mediation. Government-approved civil mediation is between government mediation and civil mediation, and is semi-official in nature. The official refers the petition to the chief of the clan, the village bailiff, etc. for mediation, and if the mediation is successful, the official dismisses the case.[1]

Second, the scope of mediation is wide. The scope of cases to which China's traditional mediation applies includes almost all civil disputes and a portion of minor criminal cases. Most of the disputes dealt with by mediation are over household, marriage, land, and money debts, in addition to disputes over water resources, service, and taxes. These disputes are collectively referred to as "minor civil matters," in other words, they are regarded as minor by the government and do not threaten the very essence of the rule, but there are so many of them that the local state and county officials want to resolve them as much as possible at the grass-roots level, and one of the most important ways to solve this problem is through mediation.[2]

Third, mediation carried a certain degree of coercion. After the Han Dynasty, disputes were first mediated at the family or township level, and towns had petty officers such as elders and village officials who were specifically responsible for mediating civil disputes and minor criminal disputes. Mediation was even a compulsory procedure for civil disputes in general, and parties who went to the government without mediation were considered to have "overstepped" the law and were punished for doing so. In addition to the compulsory conduct of mediation, the compulsory nature of traditional mediation was also reflected in the compulsory nature of the outcome of mediation. In traditional Chinese society, which was a patriarchal family society maintained by the three cardinal principles and five constant virtues, the parties to a dispute were not on an equal footing and could not bargain. In addition, the mediator always acted as the spokesperson for the values and norms that were accepted by the society at the time, whether it was a civil or official mediation. As a result, it was difficult for the parties to reject either the mediator's value judgment on the merits of the case or the mediator's proposed solution to the dispute. "Even when the parties appealed for a settlement, they had to state that it was 'in accordance with the order' and was clearly a 'peace settlement'."[3]

Fourth, the way of mediation is based on moral edification:

> If the people were guided by law and decree and restrained by criminal law, they would only seek to be spared from punishment for their crimes, but they will lose their sense of integrity; if they were guided by morality and regulated by decency, they would not only know shame but would also be disciplined.[4]

The Chinese "rule of etiquette" emphasizes the use of virtue as a complement to punishment and the use of rite and law. Kangxi's "sixteen sacred oracles" said: "I believe the most important thing for governance is not to make decrees urgent, but to educate. The law governs for a while, while the indoctrination lasts." The process of traditional mediation is in fact a process of indoctrination, and there are numerous historical accounts of disputes being resolved through indoctrination. For example, in the Tang Dynasty, when Wei Jingjun was a magistrate in Guixiang, there was a mother and son who had a lawsuit against each other. Jingjun said to the son:

> I was an orphan, and every time I saw someone raising a relative, I hated myself for not having this blessing in my life. You are fortunate to be in a place where filial piety and obedience to parents are taught, so why do you have to do this? It is the fault of the county magistrate that filial piety cannot be carried out.

He sobbed and took the Book of Filial Piety and gave it to the son to study and read. So, the mother and son were enlightened and each asked to repent. This is called filial piety and kindness.[5]

1.1.1.2 People's Mediation during the New Democratic Revolution

It is generally believed that the people's mediation system sprang from the workers' and peasants' movement during the First Civil Revolutionary War in the early 1920s, and was formed and developed in the revolutionary base areas during the War of Resistance, with the people's mediation system in the Shaanxi-Ganjiang-Ningxia Border Region in particular being typical.

In the peasant movement during the First Civil Revolutionary War, "all power was vested in the peasant associations," and "even minor matters such as quarrels between two in-laws had to be settled in the peasant associations."[6] Mediation activities in the workers' movement are represented by the "refereeing" activities of the "Referee Committee" of the Anyuan Road Miners' Club. The "Anyuan Road Miners' Club Rules" formulated in September 1923 stipulate: "All disputes between members of the Ministry, or between members and non-members, shall be handled by the Referee Committee," and "an inquiry office shall be set up within the Ministry to receive all disputes." In the workers' and peasants' movement during the First Revolutionary War, civil disputes were no longer mediated by clan elders and gentry, but by new organizations such as the Peasants Association and the Workers' Club, whose mediators were representatives elected by the workers and peasants, and whose judgments were based on the Communist Party's revolutionary program and the rules and prohibitions laid down by the workers' and peasants' movement, as well as by progressive and good customs. This can be said to be the prototype of the people's mediation system. For example, in the peasant movement in Guangdong Province, the Chishangyo Farmers Association, under the leadership of Pengpai, set up an arbitration department to mediate disputes over marriage, money debts, tenancy, and even property. Notice of the Peasants Association:

> Any dispute between the members must first be reported to the Association, otherwise if it is first reported to the gentry and the government, he or she is to be declared expelled from the association, no matter how justified he or she is, to assist the opposing party to the dispute with all our strength. In the event of a dispute between a member of the Association and a non-member, the member shall also report to the Association first. If a dispute arises between a landlord and a member, the Association shall not be held responsible for any failure of the dispute settlement if it is not reported.

During the Second Domestic Revolutionary War, Article 17 of the *Provisional Regulations on the Organization of Soviet Local Government*, adopted by the First Plenary Session of the Central Executive Committee of the Chinese Soviet Republic (November 1931), stipulated that "the village soviets have the right to settle all kinds of disputes that do not involve the issue of crime." In accordance with this provision, the practice in some Soviet areas, such as Sichuan and Shaanxi provinces, was as follows: village soviets were directly responsible for settling disputes among the masses; disputes that could not be settled by the soviets at the village and township levels could be referred to the district soviets for mediation. Villages, communes, and wards all had the right to lodge complaints with the county revolutionary courts on major issues. Strictly speaking, this is a kind of mediation under the auspices of the government, but it is different from court mediation because it had a broad mass base and was in fact also in the nature of people's mediation.[7] According to the summaries of scholars, the characteristics of people's mediation in the Soviet Union at that time included: the form of mediation was mainly government mediation; mediation was practiced at different levels; the scope of mediation was limited to civil disputes that did not involve crimes; and in case of major problems in mediation, the grass-roots soviets had the right to file complaints with the judicial organs. In short, although mediation during this period did not form a set of definite and complete principles and procedural regulations, nor was it universally practiced in the soviet, it provided favorable conditions for the formation and development of the people's mediation system later.[8]

During the Anti-Japanese War and the Liberation War, people's mediation entered a new stage of development, where the organizational form, content, and procedures of mediation were further developed and perfected, and mediation work was initially standardized and institutionalized. Among them, the development of the mediation system in the Shaanxi-Ganjiang-Ningxia Border Region is typical. The implementation of the mediation system in the Shaanxi-Ganjiang-Ningxia Border Region can be roughly divided into three stages.[9]

> *The first stage: from 1943 to the first half of 1944.* This was characterized by an emphasis on mediation mainly within the judicial system and faced uneven development in different parts of the country. Mediation was introduced as early as the mid-1930s, just after the establishment of the border district government, but the results were unsatisfactory, mainly because judicial personnel did not attach enough importance to it and were not used to it. The main impetus for the introduction of the court mediation system in this period came from the border district government from the beginning to the end. Under extreme pressure from the government, mediation was somewhat better than before, but there were still some judicial personnel who were careful to keep the necessary distance from it, so it still did not achieve the desired results.
>
> *The second stage: from the second half of 1944 to the end of 1945.* This was characterized by the beginning of the full-scale development of mediation in the border areas, from court mediation to people's mediation. As the introduction of mediation within the judicial system did not yield satisfactory results, the border district government pushed the mediation movement from within the judicial system to the private sector and all government departments, and even social groups. With the promotion and encouragement of the governments at all levels, the people began to participate in mediation and rediscovered some of the traditional techniques of mediation, and created many fresh approaches and experiences. Mediation in this period was undoubtedly a great success.
>
> *The third stage: after 1946.* The most significant feature of this period was the withdrawal of the government from the field of mediation and the fact that the main form of mediation was civil mediation. In the second half of 1946, the Border Region Government also amended the *Regulations on Civil and Criminal Mediation in the Shaanxi-Ganjiang-Ningxia Border Area.* Some of the original practices were rejected, and the principles that mediation must be voluntary and not forced, that trial is the mainstay and mediation is secondary, and that mediation is not a compulsory procedure for litigation were re-established.

From the implementation and development of people's mediation in the Shaanxi-Gan'ning-Ningxia Border Region, we can see that the forms of people's mediation there include civil mediation, mediation by mass groups, and government mediation. The principles of mediation include the principle of voluntary will and the principle that mediation is not a necessary procedure for litigation, and mediation is based on government policies and decrees, and takes into account the good customs of the people.

1.1.1.3 People's Mediation in the Socialist Planned Economy

The founding of the People's Republic of China marked the beginning of a new historical period, which also meant that people's mediation entered a new stage of development. During the period of socialist planned economy, the system of people's mediation went through two stages of legal establishment and subsequent ups and downs.

At the beginning of the founding of the People's Republic of China, in order to meet the needs of peacetime economic construction, exploring how to extend the people's mediation system applied in the rural areas during the New Democracy to urban areas became the main task of this period. According to incomplete statistics, by the end of 1953, there were already 46,000 people's mediation committees in Eastern China, accounting for 80 percent of all township formations; in Shanxi and Hebei in Northern China, about one-third to one-half of the counties had established district and village mediation committees or joint village mediation stations; and most of the regions in Central and Southwest China were at the stage of large-scale typical experiments. These practical explorations laid the theoretical and organizational foundations for the unification and establishment of a nationwide people's mediation system.

On March 22, 1954, the State Council of the Central People's Government promulgated the *General Rules for the Provisional Organization of People's Mediation Committees* (hereafter referred to as the General Rules). The General Rules, consisting of 11 articles, comprehensively and systematically set out the nature, tasks, organization, principles of activities, working system, working methods, and discipline of people's mediation committees, so that the work of people's mediation committees could be governed by rules and regulations, and that people's mediation committees would acquire a clear legal status.[10] The promulgation of the General Rules was an important milestone in the history of the development of China's people's mediation system, marking the formal establishment of the people's mediation system as a legal system in China.

In April 1954, the Ministry of Justice issued the *Explanation on the Provisional General Rules for the Organization of People's Mediation Committees*, which elaborated on four aspects of the organization and leadership of people's mediation: (1) the tasks of mediation committees; (2) working principles; (3) working methods; and (4) systems. Among them, the working principles that the mediation committee must abide by are: (1) it must act in accordance with the policies and decrees of the people's government; (2) it must obtain the consent of both parties; and (3) mediation is not a compulsory procedure for litigation.

The promulgation of the General Rules and related laws and regulations gave a great impetus to the development of people's mediation work. By December 1954, there were more than 155,100 conciliation committees throughout the country.[11] By the end of 1955, 170,400 people's mediation committees had been established in 7,096 townships and streets throughout the country, and the number of mediators had grown to millions.[12]

After the promulgation and implementation of the General Rules, people's mediation work developed rapidly and played a good role in the cause of socialist transformation. However, from the second half of 1957 onwards, under the influence of the "leftist" ideology of expanding the class struggle, mediation organizations were gradually replaced by reconciliation organizations, and mediation work gradually evolved into reconciliation work. However, mediation and reconciliation belong to two different categories, and there is no necessary historical connection or origin between them. Reconciliation was not a "new development in mediation," nor was it a "great innovation in the socialist revolution," but rather a change of mediation organizations and mediation work into tools and measures of dictatorship under the guidance of "leftist" ideology. After the transformation of the people's communes in 1958, in many areas the reconciliation committees and the security committees were combined into one, collectively known as public security reconciliation committees. The nature, tasks, and powers of the mediation organizations were very different from those set out in the General Rules. First, the task of the reconciliation organizations is not to resolve civil disputes, but to restrain, deal with, and rehabilitate the so-called "undesirables" who "do not break the major laws, but often break the minor ones."

Second, the mandate of the reconciliation organizations is not merely to persuade and educate the parties to reach an agreement to settle the dispute, but has a wide range of coercive powers. For example, the "Provisional Measures on the Establishment of Patriotic Conventions and Mediation Committees (Draft)" of the Henan Provincial Committee of the Communist Party of China, which came into effect on September 12, 1958, provide that those who violate the conventions and do not repent after persuasion and education may, in addition to being ordered to self-criticize, apologize and pay damages, be subject to coercive measures, ranging from confession and repentance, organized debates to re-education through labor, depending on the circumstances. This shows that the mediation organization is no longer a mass organization and the disputes it settles are not only civil disputes, which is a setback for people's mediation in its development.

From 1961 onwards, the General Rules were re-implemented in accordance with their provisions, and people's mediation organizations and mediation work began to take the path of recovery and development. By 1963, people's mediation organizations had regained greater popularity, and many regions placed great emphasis on training mediation cadres, emphasizing mediation disciplines, improving the quality of mediation, and attaching importance to the summing-up of mediation experience, thus making mediation work more standardized.[13]

In the ten years following the start of the Cultural Revolution in 1966, socialist democracy and the rule of law were severely trampled upon, and while the public, prosecutors, and the law were completely smashed, the people's mediation system was also treated as a product of the "class reconciliation" line and a "revisionist" product. The people's mediation system was completely abolished as a product of the "revisionist" line and "revisionist" goods, and the people's mediation organizations and teams were disbanded and the people's mediation system was severely damaged.

1.1.1.4 People's Mediation after the Reform and Opening-Up

After 40 years of development since the reform and opening-up, people's mediation has achieved a prosperous system and elevated legislative status, with its legal sources including the Constitution, relevant norms scattered in other laws, administrative regulations and departmental rules, judicial interpretations, local regulations and the single act law, the *People's Mediation Law*. As the first law in China that specifically and systematically regulates people's mediation, the *People's Mediation Law* is also a reorganization of the existing provisions, and the relevant provisions that previously contradicted it automatically become invalid. According to the *People's Mediation Law*, the main contents of the people's mediation system are as follows.

In terms of the form of mediation organizations, in the mid-1980s, in line with the institutional reform of separating government and society, the network of grass-roots mediation organizations consisted of three levels, namely, leading mediation teams in townships (streets), people's mediation committees under villagers' (residents') committees, and mediators (mediation teams) in villagers' (residents') groups. The *Regulations on the Organization of People's Mediation Committees*, promulgated in 1989, stipulate that, in addition to continuing to retain the People's Mediation Committees under village and neighborhood committees, enterprises and institutions may set up People's Mediation Committees according to their needs, thus allowing the form of mediation organizations to expand and develop. With the development of the market economy and in order to meet the diversified needs of dispute resolution, the Ministry of Justice issued the *Certain Provisions on People's Mediation Work* in 2002, which further expanded the organizational form of people's mediation to regional and industrial people's mediation committees. Article 8 of the *People's Mediation Law*, issued in 2010, stipulates that villagers' committees and residents' committees will establish people's mediation committees. Enterprises and institutions will establish people's mediation committees according to their needs. In addition to reiterating the forms of people's mediation organizations, the *People's Mediation Law* provides in its by-laws that townships, streets, and social organizations or other organizations may, in accordance with their needs, set up people's mediation committees to mediate civil disputes with reference to the relevant provisions of this law.

In terms of the attributes that people's mediators must have, the *People's Mediation Law* stipulates that people's mediators must be fair and decent, enthusiastic about people's mediation work, and have a certain level of education, knowledge of policy, and legal knowledge. The work of grassroots mediation is tedious and demanding, and the initiation of mediation procedures and the conclusion of mediation agreements must be based on the parties' willingness, so personal charisma becomes an important resource for mediators to successfully promote mediation. Mediation is a legal and policy-oriented task, which requires a certain level of legal knowledge and knowledge of policy. With the development of society and the increased demand for mediation work, it is imperative that mediators have a certain level of education, but education here does not simply mean academic education.[14] At the same time, mediation is an experience and art born out of practice and is closely related to the mediator's personal experience, ability, and charisma. Therefore, the *People's Mediation Law* does not set uniformly high requirements on the education and professional background of mediators, in order to adapt to the vernacular, mass, and pluralistic nature of people's mediation.

Regarding the scope of people's mediation, Article 20 of the *Certain Provisions on People's Mediation Work*, issued by the Ministry of Justice in 2002, stipulates that the civil disputes mediated by people's mediation committees include all kinds of disputes involving disputes over civil rights and obligations between citizens, and between citizens and legal persons and other social organizations. Article 22, on the contrary, excludes two types of disputes that cannot be accepted by the people's mediation committee, namely, those that can only be handled by the jurisdiction of special organs as stipulated by laws and regulations, or those that are prohibited by laws and regulations from being settled by means of civil mediation; and those that have already been accepted or settled by the people's courts, public security organs, or other administrative organs. The *People's Mediation Law*, which was enacted in 2010 and implemented in 2011, stipulates that people's mediation is an activity to resolve "civil disputes," but does not provide a further definition of "civil disputes."

Regarding the working principles of people's mediation, Article 3 of the *People's Mediation Law* stipulates that mediation should be conducted based on the voluntary will and equality of the parties; should not be contrary to laws, regulations, and national policies; should respect the rights of the parties, and should not prevent the parties from defending their rights through arbitration, administrative or judicial means in accordance with the law as a result of mediation. Accordingly, the working principles of people's mediation can be summarized as the principles of voluntary will, equality, legality, and respect for the parties' right to redress.

Articles 17–27 of the *People's Mediation Law* provide general provisions on the mediation procedure. According to the law, there are two ways of initiating people's mediation: (1) mediation by application of the parties; and (2) mediation on the initiative of the people's mediation committee. A dispute may be mediated by one or several mediators. There are three ways in which the mediator of a dispute can come into being: (1) appointed by the mediation committee; (2) chosen by the parties; and (3) with the consent of the parties, the people's mediator may invite relevant persons to participate in the mediation of the dispute.[15] In the process of mediation, the people's mediator may adopt a variety of ways to mediate according to the different circumstances of the dispute and help the parties to reach a mediation agreement voluntarily. If mediation fails, the mediation will be terminated and the parties will be informed, in accordance with the relevant laws and regulations, that they may seek redress through administrative, arbitration, or judicial means.

Regarding the form of the mediation agreement, Article 28 of the *People's Mediation Law* stipulates that if a mediation agreement is reached through the mediation of the people's mediation committee, a mediation agreement may be made. If the parties consider that it is not necessary to make a mediation agreement, they may adopt the form of an oral agreement. The people's mediator will record the contents of the agreement. In other words, there are two forms of mediation agreements: in writing and orally. The *People's Mediation Law* clearly stipulates that people's mediation agreements are legally binding and provides that the validity of mediation agreements can be established through judicial confirmation procedures.

1.1.2 Comparison of People's Mediation in Different Periods[16]

1.1.2.1 Fractures and Changes in the Concept of Conflict Resolution

"The ancient Chinese sought order and harmony throughout the natural world and saw this as the ideal for all human relationships."[17] Confucianism, which dominated traditional Chinese political thought, believed that "heaven and man are one" and advocated ritual and music in order to match heaven and earth, thus achieving harmony between man and nature. "Rites are a set of rules that define the behavior of individuals in their social relations and in specific situations," and their function is to "distinguish between nobility and inferiority and to rank them." The concepts of order, responsibility, hierarchy, and harmony are at the heart of the rites. Music is used to harmonize people's relationships, and rites are used to distinguish between the superior and the inferior. When music reaches the hearts of the people, resentment is eliminated; when rites are carried out, strife is eliminated. In the ancient Chinese view, all disputes and conflicts were a disruption of the existing order and a manifestation of the breakdown of rituals and music, so dispute resolution aimed at repairing damaged social relations and seeking reconciliation became the logical thing to do.

During the early years of reform and opening-up, people's mediation was revived and played a great role in the resolution of civil disputes; in the 1990s, with the advance of the socialist legal system, people's mediation tended to be depoliticized and its function declined as people's mediation agreements were not legally binding. In the twenty-first century, China entered a critical period of reform and development, under the concept of building a harmonious society, "maintaining the harmony and stability of the social order" was conceptualized, and conflicts and disputes were once more regarded as unstable factors affecting social harmony and were forcibly suppressed. The Third Plenary Session of the 18th Central Committee of the Communist Party of China put forward the reform objective of "innovating social governance," bringing the mediation and resolution of conflicts and disputes onto the track of legal governance. On October 23, 2014, the *Decision of the Central Committee of the Communist Party of China on Several Major Issues in Comprehensively Promoting the Rule of Law*, adopted at the Fourth Plenary Session of the 18th Central Committee of the Communist Party of China, proposed

> to strengthen the authority of the law in safeguarding the rights and interests of the masses and resolving social conflicts, to guide and support people to rationally express their demands and defend their rights and interests in accordance with the law, and to solve the most direct and realistic problems that the masses are most concerned about.

It is clear from this that the state's understanding of disputes in the new era has been transformed into one in which disputes are a way for people to express their demands and defend their rights and interests, and mediation is a mechanism for safeguarding the rights and interests of the public and resolving disputes.

1.1.2.2 Turnover and Succession of Mediation Organizations

One of the characteristics of traditional Chinese society is that people live in villages and "they are geographically restricted in their scope of activity, have little contact between regions, live in isolation and maintain their own social circles."[18] Due to local constraints, people are born and die in the same place, so it is a "society of acquaintances" where there are no strangers. In a society of acquaintances, the resolution of civil disputes relies heavily on the mediation of relatives and neighbors, which is usually carried out first and foremost through "middleman." The "middleman" here refers to the "introducer" or "matchmaker" in the case of loans, land leases and land sales, as well as the "matchmaker" in the case of marriage relationships. When there is no intermediary to turn to for marriage, family, and neighbor disputes, villagers usually use a third party to resolve the dispute. These include older and more virtuous members of the clan and community, as well as those who enjoy credibility, and sometimes some of the heads of grass-roots administrative organizations, such as chief of the *bao*, *jia* or village.[19] When civil mediation did not work, the dispute went to an official hearing as the parties filed a complaint, but most disputes were resolved before the formal hearing. In other words, there is an intermediate stage between the informal mediation of the village community and the formal trial at the Prefecture and county offices, where civil mediation and the official trial meet and interact. At this stage, the formal system and the informal system intermingled and dialogued, and there was an established procedure, namely, the government approved civil mediation, which Professor Huang Zongzhi refers to as the "third domain." Huang Zongzhi's study of the litigation documents of Ba County, Baodi, and Tanxin led him to conclude that civil litigation in the Qing Dynasty comprised three distinct stages. The "initial stage" was when the magistrate received a petition from a party, and his initial reaction was to refuse to accept a suit that did not meet the requirements or was found to be false, based on the statements of the party and the relevant laws and regulations, while other cases that were considered worthy of consideration but did not require personal attention were handed over to grass-roots officials, such as the village bailiffs, or sometimes with the assistance of magistrates. At the "intermediate stage," the government will summon the parties to the dispute to confront each other and witnesses to testify in court. If the dispute cannot be settled out of court at this stage, the civil dispute proceeds to the "final stage," where it is adjudicated by the magistrate in court.[20] In short, in traditional Chinese society, the people who presided over civil mediation and government-approved civil mediation included not only the elders of clans and communities, the gentry and the "middlemen" in contractual relationships, but also the heads of grass-roots organizations below the county level, such as townships, neighborhood, village, clans, village communities, and guilds. However, there is a slight difference between government-approved mediation and civil mediation. First, the mediators in government-approved mediation are basically the heads of established grass-roots organizations; second, the government has already filed a record of such mediation, and in some cases has even given a principled proposal for its resolution. "Although the mediation is located outside the public hall, it has an official overtone."[21]

In the workers' and peasants' movement during the First Civil Revolutionary War, civil disputes were no longer mediated by clan elders, squires, and gentry, but by new types of organizations such as "peasants' associations" and "workers' clubs." During the Second Civil Revolutionary War, mediation was mainly conducted by the government. During the Second Civil Revolutionary War, mediation was mainly conducted by the government, i.e., by soviets at the village, township, and district levels. During the Anti-Japanese War, mediation was mainly conducted by the government, mass organizations, and civil activists. Since the founding of the People's Republic of China in 1949, the Communist Party of China has consolidated its rule through economic reconstruction and comprehensive social change, integrating a society that had been divided and weakened a century earlier and subsequently undergone decades of war. According to the *Provisional General Rules for the Organization of People's Mediation Committees*, promulgated in 1954, the mediation committees established in each commune and street are organizational networks made up of activists through which state power is extended to the grass-roots. Mediators need to have a certain level of political awareness, political quality, be aware of policy, and possess the language, means, and tactics used in mediation to serve the Party's governance. After the reform and opening-up, there has been a new development in the construction of mediation organizations, namely the multi-layered nature of mediation organizations and the emergence of professional and industry-specific mediation committees. Compared to the planned economy period, after the reform and opening-up, people's mediation has shed its previous strong politicization and the political literacy and policy level of people's mediators are no longer an important consideration.

A glance at civil mediation and semi-governmental and semi-people mediation in various periods in China reveals a significant difference in that the relationship between the mediator and the state and society was not the same in all periods. In traditional China, where imperial power did not rest with the county, dispute resolution was mostly outside the scope of the county officials' activities. Except for folk such as elders, gentry, and highly respected individuals, the heads of grass-roots organizations such as villages, clans, guilds, townships, *bao*, and *jia* were not regular members of the closely woven state apparatus. They also acted as auxiliaries to the formal state apparatus in resolving disputes and participating in the propagation of Confucian ideology. However, these dispute resolvers were not formally accountable to the prefectural officials, but sought to protect and deepen their own interests, even sometimes being in conflict with official interests, and, in part, villages, clans, and guilds resolved disputes between their internal members with the aim of increasing their autonomy from the government. In socialist China, the relationship between the state and society is much closer, and state control over society is deeper and more comprehensive than in the past. Mediators in the early years of the People's Republic of China were cadres of government agencies or activists from their branches, who represented the state in resolving disputes, were expected to propagate and convey Party policies, and were subject to the leadership and supervision of the grass-roots government. During the period of reform and opening-up, the politicization of people's mediation faded and people's mediation organizations were positioned by law as self-governing organizations of a mass nature.

1.1.2.3 The Alienation and Return of the Mediation Function

Mediation is a peaceful and inexpensive form of dispute resolution, and its original function is to resolve disputes:

14 *Changes in and Transformation of People's Mediation*

Mediation is intended to maintain public order and the orderly functioning of economic activity by suppressing and settling disputes. Mediation is also intended to put an end to bad feelings between individuals in a quick, effective, and highly informal way.[22]

In China, mediation is a form of dispute resolution that is highly compatible with Confucianism, with its concept of "harmony" and its emphasis and advocacy of the spirit of "rite," "concession," and self-reflection. The mediation system in China also has another important function, namely to educate. In short, mediation provides a low-cost and widely acceptable solution to disputes, based on Confucian ethics. Moreover, because of its emphasis on conflict avoidance and the observance of appropriate rules, mediation also disseminates and transmits Confucian ethics and values while maintaining social order. In traditional Chinese society, the functions of mediation include dispute resolution, edification, and the maintenance of social order.

After the reform and opening-up, the primary function of mediation has returned to a non-politicized approach to resolving civil disputes. The depoliticization of mediation means that mediation focuses on the dispute itself and proposes solutions or alternative solutions according to the issues raised by the parties to the dispute. In addition, China's current network of "vertical and horizontal" mediation organizations not only provides the public with an economical and convenient way to resolve disputes, but also has the function of understanding social and public opinion and collecting information on governance, so that disputes can be prevented, investigated, and resolved through "mass prevention and treatment." Therefore, mediation at this stage is also a means for the state to improve social governance and to achieve comprehensive governance and governance at source, and has a function of social governance in addition to dispute resolution.

Looking back at the trajectory of the people's mediation system since its formation during the revolutionary war, its consolidation during the people's commune period, and its adjustment since the reform and opening-up, from the dualistic perspective of "state and society," although the strong political color of people's mediation has gradually diminished, and the social significance of people's mediation has moved from the periphery to the center, it has on the whole assumed a semi-official character, becoming an "advisor and assistant to the party committee and government in resolving conflicts and maintaining social stability." This makes people's mediation a "third sphere" of dispute resolution and a "minimalist governance" of state power between the traditional folk mediation and official trials.[23]

1.2 The Real-Life Dilemma of People's Mediation: The Drawbacks of the Phenomenon of Generalization

According to the Chinese Constitution and the *People's Mediation Law*, the organizational attributes of people's mediation are positioned as mass, civil, and autonomous. However, judging from its historical genealogy and operational practice, people's mediation is more of a government-driven mechanism for resolving disputes, and there is a tendency for both academics and officials to generalize the concept of people's mediation, putting new types of mediation organizations such as commercial mediation, industrial mediation, and mediation by lawyers into the bag. The "path dependence" caused by this generalization of people's mediation has seriously restricted the development of the people's mediation system in the new era.

1.2.1 People's Mediation in the Diversified Dispute Resolution Mechanism

In recent years, along with China's rapid socio-economic development, deepening changes in the economic system, and continuous adjustment of social interests, the numbers of social conflicts and disputes have risen, and these are characterized by diversified subjects of disputes, complex demands for interests, and diverse types of disputes. In order to provide parties with diversified, low-cost and convenient dispute resolution services, under the guidance of regulations and policies such as the *People's Mediation Law* (2010), the *Guidance on Furthering the Work of Grand Mediation of Conflicts and Disputes* (2011), the *Opinions on Improving the Mechanism* of *Diversified Dispute Resolution* (2015), the *Guidance on Promoting the Work of Industry-based and Professional People's Mediation* (2016), these various practical explorations and innovations have been carried out to resolve disputes and maintain social order according to local specificities and in accordance with the logic of pragmatism. In the construction of a diversified dispute resolution mechanism, although different models have been developed in different places, the people's mediation among them still has some common features.

1. *The "vertical" and "horizontal" expansion of the network of people's mediation organizations.* Article 8 of the *People's Mediation Law* stipulates that villagers' committees and residents' committees will establish people's mediation committees, and enterprises and institutions will establish people's mediation committees according to their needs. In addition to reiterating the form of people's mediation organizations, the *People's Mediation Law* also stipulates in its by-laws that townships, streets, and social organizations or other organizations may, in accordance with their needs, establish people's mediation committees to mediate folk disputes with reference to the relevant provisions of this law. Through such an authoritative and open institutional design, the *People's Mediation Law* not only clarifies the positioning of people's mediation committees as autonomous organizations of the masses, but also responds to practical needs and provides room for the development of a diversified pattern of people's mediation organizations. The "vertical" expansion of the network of people's mediation organizations refers to the multi-level expansion of

people's mediation organizations, i.e., in addition to village and neighborhood people's mediation committees, there are also township (street) mediation committees and county (city and district) people's mediation committees at the upper level, and mediation groups in villages, groups, and buildings at the lower level. The "horizontal" expansion of the network of people's mediation organizations refers to the emergence of specialized and sectoral people's mediation organizations.

2. *The fundamental nature of people's mediation in the pluralistic dispute resolution mechanism.* First, people's mediation organizations are fundamental in the pluralistic dispute resolution mechanism because people's mediation committees are grass-roots organizations that mediate civil disputes. In the Grand Mediation system, apart from the traditional village and neighborhood mediation committees, there are mediation information officers in villagers' groups and buildings, and these people's mediation organizations rooted locally are the basis of the Grand Mediation system. Second, the disputes handled by people's mediation are fundamental in the overall social conflicts and disputes. Many disputes that can be handled by people's mediation are "trivial" civil disputes.[24] These small disputes are not only numerous and account for most social conflicts and disputes, but if not handled properly, they may also intensify under certain conditions and even turn into mass incidents or criminal cases. People's mediation organizations, rooted in the front line of daily life, not only mediate, and resolve conflicts and disputes, but also undertake the function of identifying and preventing conflicts and disputes, which has a fundamental role in maintaining social harmony and stability. Finally, the approach of people's mediation is also fundamental. The purpose of people's mediation is not to declare the rules and uphold the mainstream values of the state, but to settle the dispute appropriately and properly without violating the state laws. The purpose of people's mediation determines that people's mediation is justified on the basis of the parties' voluntary will and the parties' consent as a guarantee of authority; at the same time, it also determines the comparative advantages of people's mediation and public remedy, namely the calm and non-confrontational nature of the mediation process.[25] In the process of mediation, mediators can flexibly use judgmental, bargaining, correctional and therapeutic mediation methods according to the type and characteristics of the dispute, the character traits of the parties and their relationship with each other,[26] integrating emotion, reason, and law, which undoubtedly has a role in resolving conflicts and disputes and maintaining social order that cannot be replaced by other mediation.

3. *The pivotal role of people's mediation in the coupling of various dispute resolution mechanisms.* Based on empirical research and the findings of others, we believe that, in general, mediation in China currently consists of two workflows in opposite directions: bottom-up and top-down. The

bottom-up workflow means that disputes that cannot be mediated by the mediation committee at this level or that are considered likely to intensify are reported up the hierarchy and finally mediated by the county (city or district) mediation body in coordination with the relevant administrative and judicial departments. The top-down workflow generally includes the following steps: First, the case window of the county (city or district) conflict and dispute mediation work platform accepts disputes in a unified manner. The sources of conflicts and disputes include disputes applied for mediation by the parties concerned, disputes assigned for mediation by higher authorities, and disputes reported by various administrative departments and lower-level mediation committees. Second, after the case window has received the disputes in a unified manner, the disputes are triaged according to the type and characteristics of the disputes. There are four types of triages: (a) for major and difficult disputes that cross regions and industries, they are reported to the work leading group, which organizes joint mediation by relevant departments and specifies the subject of responsibility; (b) disputes are referred directly to the relevant administrative department; (c) disputes are assigned to the township (street) mediation committee for mediation; and (d) disputes that are suitable for judicial resolution are triaged to the court. Third, the relevant administrative departments handle the transferred disputes: by administrative mediation or by directing people's mediation for disputes that can be mediated, and by administrative adjudication or by directing parties to the court for disputes that the parties do not want to mediate. Fourth, the township (street) mediation committee handles the assigned disputes in accordance with the relevant provisions of the *People's Mediation Law*. Fifth, the court handles the referred disputes: for disputes that do not meet the conditions for filing, the parties are guided to conduct people's mediation. For those that do meet the conditions for filing, the parties are informed that they can choose pre-litigation mediation. For disputes that are filed, mediation is conducted in the case, and if mediation fails, they are tried according to law. Sixth, for disputes referred to the county (city or district) conflicts and disputes mediation work center for triage, the subjects are required to feed back information to the center after processing.[27] See Figure 1.1.

As can be seen from the workflow of the Dispute Resolution Center, people's mediation ranges from the identification, prevention, and mediation of disputes by mediation organizations rooted at the grass-roots level, to mediation by township (street) mediation committees and mediation by professional and industrial people's mediation committees, and even mediation by some administrative-related departments, all of which fall within the scope of people's mediation. In other words, in practice, people's mediation is used in a generalized way.

18 Changes in and Transformation of People's Mediation

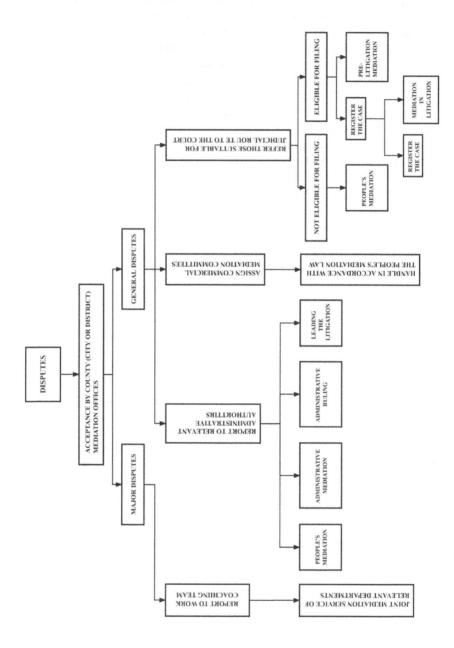

Figure 1.1 Workflow chart of the Dispute Resolution Center.

1.2.2 The Creation of a New Type of Mediation Organization: Mediation in "the Name of the People"

During the drafting process of the *People's Mediation Law*, there had been significant differences in the organizational positioning of people's mediation. In response to the current pluralistic mediation situation, the leading view of the legal profession, especially the judicial administration system, was to transform people's mediation into a professional and judicial dispute resolution mechanism, so that it would be free from the dependence and shackles of grass-roots self-government organizations and attract the participation of a large number of legal professionals. However, this option is contrary to the positioning of people's mediation as a mass self-governance organization under the Constitution. Therefore, the *People's Mediation Law* finally compromised on this issue by stipulating in the by-laws section that "townships, streets, and social organizations or other organizations may, in accordance with their needs, establish people's mediation committees to mediate civil disputes in accordance with the relevant provisions of this law," thus leaving room for the development of new mediation organizations. In practice, these new mediation organizations have already exceeded the organizational form and characteristics of people's mediation in the strictest sense, but due to the lack of a legal organizational basis, they have to operate in the name of the people, using the shell of people's mediation, in order to gain a basis for legitimacy. The most typical forms of operation include the following:

1. *Government-purchased social mediation.* One type is the mediation studio set up by individuals. For example, since 2003, individual mediation studios have been set up, named after chief mediators. In Shanghai, the most influential of which are the "Li Qin People's Mediation Studio" and the "Yang Boshou People's Mediation Studio." Another type is mediation organization set up by NGOs. For example, in 2004, a volunteer organization in Beijing specializing in assisting migrant workers defend their rights set up the "Little Bird" Mediation Committee, which became the first mediation committee set up by an NGO in China. In terms of organizational attributes, both types of mediation organizations are not part of traditional people's mediation committees, nor are they subordinate bodies of the government, let alone subject to government guidance. Rather, they are non-profit civil associations with a high degree of autonomy, thus weakening the role of government officials in people's mediation. The government contracts these individual "mediation workshops" or social organizations to resolve social conflicts and disputes with a high degree of professionalism, and their operations are mainly funded by the "government's purchase of services."
2. *Commercial mediation.* As market interactions become more frequent, various types of private commercial mediation organizations have

emerged to provide commercial mediation services in areas such as investment, finance, securities, and futures, insurance, e-commerce, intellectual property rights, and international trade. For example, independent third-party commercial mediation organizations, such as the China Council for the Promotion of International Trade (CCPIT) Mediation Center and the Shanghai Economic and Trade Commercial Mediation Center, follow internationally accepted mediation rules and operate in a professional and vocational manner, employ senior experts and legal professionals as mediators, These organizations are funded by mediation fees and donations, providing fast, efficient, economical, and flexible services for international and domestic commercial disputes.

3. *Industry mediation.* Industry mediation is based on industry organizations and is set up for disputes in specific industry sectors, such as medical services, property services, consumer protection, road traffic accidents, insurance, and intellectual property. With the implementation of the "decentralization service" reform, industry associations are transforming from administrative to autonomous beings. These industry and professional mediation organizations are basically set up and promoted by administrative authorities with the participation of industry representatives, experts, and other specific subjects, thus forming an interactive interface between litigation and mediation, civil mechanisms, and administrative mechanisms. For example, in 2016, the People's Mediation Committee for Intellectual Property Disputes in Hunan Province was initiated and established by the Hunan Intellectual Property Association as an independent third-party platform and filed by the judicial administrative department, with IPR expert mediators from different nature sectors such as IPR administrative organs, universities, intermediaries, and enterprises respectively, specializing in resolving disputes in the IPR field.

4. *Lawyer mediation.* In countries where the rule of law is well developed extraterritorially, such as the United States, the United Kingdom, and Japan, lawyers have become the backbone of the development of the mediation market. In recent years, lawyer mediation has begun to receive attention in China. 2006 saw the establishment of the first lawyer-led social mediation organization in Qingdao, Shandong Province, China, which has lawyers acting as mediators to preside over the mediation of foreign-related commercial disputes and promote pre-litigation and in-litigation settlements. in September 2017, the Supreme People's Court and the Ministry of Justice jointly issued the *Opinions on the Pilot Work of Lawyer Mediation*, through the mediation studios or mediation centers set up by courts, public legal service centers (stations), bar associations, and law firms. Lawyers act as neutral mediators to facilitate parties to negotiate and settle disputes.

5. *State-society cooperation type of mediation.* One type is mediation organizations attached to the courts in cooperation with the judiciary. At

present, many grass-roots courts in China have set up people's mediation windows or people's mediation studios or litigation mediation docking centers, and employ invited mediators or invited mediation organizations to assign mediation before filing a case or entrust a case to mediation after filing a case.[28] Another type of mediation organization is one that cooperates with administrative organs, such as the joint mediation rooms for public security and civil disputes set up in police stations across the city of Beijing, with two to three retired personnel from the public, prosecution, law, justice and neighborhood committees serving as mediators in each police station, working together with police officers in police stations to resolve social conflicts.[29] The creation of these two types of mediation organizations, the selection of mediators, and the mode of operation of mediation are all different from traditional people's mediation, but are still included in the framework of people's mediation.

It is obvious that the above-mentioned types of mediation are beyond the scope of the traditional system of people's mediation, both in terms of organizational form and operational concept, and are professionalized, vocational, and market-oriented social mediation. Some of these are far from the public product of people's mediation, which is a free service. Some scholars have interpreted these new types of mediation organizations from a sociological perspective as "the socialization and re-organization of people's mediation."[30] Rather than the socialization and re-organization of people's mediation, it is the socialization of mediation, and rather than the transfer of power between the state and society, it is the shift of the state's support from traditional mediation to new types of social mediation.

The *People's Mediation Law* does not establish a pluralistic social mediation system that is tailored to the characteristics of different types of disputes. This has led to relevant policy documents being expressed in the name of the people, with all the new types of mediation organizations that have emerged in practice being labeled as "people's mediation" or put into the "bag of people's mediation" (as shown in Figure 1.2). This conceptual generalization conceals the institutional characteristics of pluralistic forms of social mediation, such as commercial mediation, industrial mediation, and professional mediation, resulting in the unclear legal positioning of these unofficial mediation types, making mediation legislation lag behind new mediation practices, and seriously restricting the coordinated development of pluralistic forms of mediation, to the detriment of international exchange and cooperation in dispute resolution.

1.3 The Rightful Origin of People's Mediation: Sticking to Its Position and Returning to Its Original Spirit

The generalization of people's mediation is due both to sectoral interests in the legislative process and to the influence of path dependence in historical

22 *Changes in and Transformation of People's Mediation*

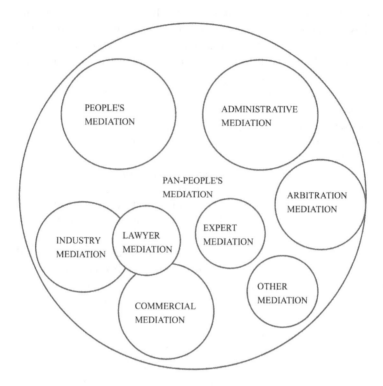

Figure 1.2 The generalization of people's mediation.

tradition. The current decline of people's mediation or the lagging behind of new types of social mediation is certainly constrained by the institutional mechanism, but the generalization of the concept is also an important reason. In order to put people's mediation back on the right track, we should stick to the original position of people's mediation and not forget the original intention of the people's mediation system.

1.3.1 New Social Mediation Cannot Be Equated with People's Mediation

The so-called "new type of social mediation" is not a strict legal concept, but is used to refer to mediation conducted by social organizations or social forces other than village (residence, enterprises) people's mediation committees and township (street) people's mediation committees. Depending on the type of dispute being mediated and the needs of the parties to the dispute, we believe that people's mediation cannot cover new types of social mediation, in other words, it is not appropriate to put new wine into old bottles.

First, the main types of disputes resolved by the two types of mediation are different. People's mediation deals mostly with disputes over "household, marriage, land, money, and debts" and some minor criminal cases such as fights and minor injuries, which generally come from the society of acquaintances and have more emotional elements. In many cases it is a matter of "face." The new types of social mediation are mainly new types of disputes arising from the development of the market economy, such as construction disputes, house sales and leases, intellectual property rights disputes, etc. These disputes generally come from the society of strangers or semi-acquaintances, and the interests of the disputes are more directed.

Second, people's mediation and new types of social mediation have different requirements for mediators. People's mediation is rooted in the local level and settles mainly social disputes among acquaintances, and the legitimacy and authority of mediation usually come from a combination of factors based on the personal charisma of the mediator. For new types of disputes, the parties to the dispute tend to seek legal judgment results through mediation, which is faster and more convenient than litigation, and this requires mediators with a higher level of legal or other expertise.

Finally, the functional focus and working mechanism of the two types of mediation are different. Since its inception and formation, people's mediation has carried the political functions of ideological reform and social control. Today, people's mediation still must carry the party line, identify and prevent conflicts and collect information on governance. Therefore, in the new era, people's mediation has the function of social governance in addition to dispute resolution. In terms of working mechanism, people's mediation should adhere to the combination of mediation and prevention, so that all disputes can be properly resolved in accordance with the law and *in situ* in a timely manner. Conflicts and disputes that are not suitable for mediation or cases that cannot be mediated should be promptly introduced into the rule of law. Conflicts and disputes that may lead to mass incidents, cross-level petitions and other illegal and criminal activities found in the process of investigation and mediation, should be promptly warned and actively reported to the public security organs of the district and the local party committee and government. The social governance function of the new type of social mediation, on the other hand, is attached to its dispute function, i.e., through resolving disputes and maintaining social order, thereby achieving the goal of social governance. Therefore, the focus of the new type of social mediation is the standardization of mediation and the appropriateness and acceptability of the mediation in this case.

To sum up, as the disputes to be mediated have different characteristics, mediation models and mediation mechanisms will differ. If new types of social mediation are put into the "old bottle" of people's mediation, this will, on the one hand, blur the nature and advantages of people's mediation and, on the other hand, limit the space for the development of other social mediations, so that new types of social mediation cannot be equated with people's mediation.

1.3.2 People's Mediation Cannot Converge to a New Type of Social Mediation

Faced with the declining effectiveness of people's mediation in resolving disputes and the innovative development of various types of mediation organizations, there is an extremely attractive view in academia that the exogenous and government-controlled institutional barriers to mediation are the key reason for the low performance of the people's mediation system, and that the only way out of the dilemma is to transform people's mediation from government-promoted control to social autonomy and from semi-official mediation to genuine civil mediation.[31] In the process of promoting people's mediation, the distinction between people's mediation and civil mediation should be diluted, and there should be no need to distinguish between the two, as people's mediation is itself a form of civil mediation, and all civil mediation is, in a sense, "people's mediation."[32]

This viewpoint provides insight into the current problem of the unclear positioning and generalization of the concept of people's mediation, but the redemptive solution is to dismantle the concept of people's mediation itself and seek legal support for all unofficial mediation organizations. Some scholars are aware of the "highly subjective value proposition" of this view from the perspective of historical continuity, and argue that the promotion of a purely endogenous dispute resolution mechanism relies on a high degree of autonomy and space for self-government in grass-roots societies.[33] However, for a long time since the formation of people's mediation, China's traditional social self-governance organizations have been severely damaged by the disintegration of the "cultural network of power," and the capacity for social self-governance has fallen to a low ebb. Since the reform and opening-up of China, social organizations, despite their diversity and number, have failed to play a role in dispute resolution and are in fact "functionally absent." As a result, some scholars have described the current situation of social organizations in China as one in which government-run social organizations are loaded with officialdom, private social organizations have limited resources, and grass-roots social organizations are struggling to survive.[34] This makes the idea of the autonomy of people's mediation too idealistic. More importantly, this conflation of the nature and objectives of people's mediation with those of civil mediation will result in an infinite generalization of the concept of people's mediation, which will affect and constrain the development of other mediation organizations and blur their legal status. It is by confusing "people's mediation, which is based on grass-roots autonomy, with other dispute resolution mechanisms established by the Constitution, that it gradually loses its own character and vitality."[35]

It is a theoretical misconception to equate people's mediation simply with civil society mediation. Traditional folk mediation is generally done by community authorities such as clan chiefs, elders, and gentry within families, clans and villages, and individuals such as neighbors, elders, and friends can participate in mediation,[36] which is often an ad hoc, random, and non-institutionalized community mediation.[37] Modern civil mediation, on the other hand, is mainly a standardized mediation conducted by autonomous organizations established by various market players as a neutral third party in the process of frequent interactions. As such, folk mediation is more of an endogenous social order with spontaneity, which is clearly different from people's mediation supported by state constructs. Traditional people's mediation, on the other hand, was cadre-based mediation in which members of the (village) neighborhood committee also acted as mediators. The most important feature of traditional people's mediation was that it was supported by the Party and the government and had a semi-official, semi-formal overtones: "it was embedded in the power network woven by the Party and the government and served the Party and government's governance goals." Therefore, it can be said that the key to the effectiveness of people's mediation in its heyday was the importance attached to it by the local party committee and government. It is for this reason that some scholars have perceptively pointed out that "if people's mediation becomes completely civil mediation and no longer receives any resources from the Party and the state, then people's mediation will be dead," and that people's mediation should now be repositioned as "a public good provided by the state to the general public free of charge with the participation of the people." Therefore, the responsibility of the state for people's mediation should still be clarified, to guarantee the healthy development of people' mediation.[38] It should be said that this is a viewpoint that respects history and is in line with objective reality.

The new type of social mediation cannot be equated with people's mediation, nor can people's mediation simply converge with the new type of social mediation. Only by distinguishing between people's mediation and the new type of social mediation, by taking spontaneity and autonomy as the direction of development of the new type of social mediation, and by strengthening government support and protection, guidance and supervision of people's mediation as the direction of development of people's mediation, and by making the connotation and extension of people's mediation pure, can the gap between expression and practice of people's mediation be bridged. As for the "mass nature" of people's mediation, it can be reflected through the democratic nature of the selection of people's mediators, the realization of democratic elections in villages and communities, so that people's mediators arise from grass-roots cadres who have the trust of the voters, while employing traditional social authority and maintaining the minimum autonomy required by the Constitution.

1.4 Practical Innovation of People's Mediation: Insights from the "Fengqiao Experience" in the New Era

The year 2018 marks the 55th anniversary of Comrade Mao Zedong's instruction to study and promote the "Fengqiao Experience" and the 15th anniversary of Xi Jinping's instruction to adhere to the development of the "Fengqiao Experience." The conference emphasized the development of the "Fengqiao Experience" and the writing of a new chapter of people's mediation in the new era.

1.4.1 Origin and Development of the "Fengqiao Experience"

In February 1963, the Central Committee of the Communist Party of China (CPC) decided to launch a socialist education campaign in the country's rural areas, and in May, Mao Zedong chaired an enlarged meeting of the Politburo in Hangzhou and proposed that the vast majority of the "four categories" should be transformed into new people. The Zhejiang Provincial Committee of the CPC chose Zhuji, Xiaoshan, and Shangyu counties as the pilot sites for the social education campaign, and followed the instructions of the Central Committee and Mao Zedong to basically adopt a "no-killing, no-arresting" approach to the "landlords, kulaks, counter-revolutionaries and bad elements," stipulating that in the rural socialist education campaign and the urban "five antis" campaign, no arrests were to be made except for current offenders; in the later stages of the campaign, if arrests had to be made, they had to be reported to the provincial committee for approval. From June to October 1963, the political and legal team of the Fengqiao Task Force of the Zhejiang Provincial Committee carried out a pilot socialist education campaign in seven communes in the Fengqiao area, resolutely implementing the instructions of the Central Committee and the provincial party committee, implementing the principle of not beating people, not arresting them, and not handing over conflicts, and fully mobilizing the masses to carry out reasoned struggles to subdue the "four types of elements" who were considered to be those who were inevitably arrested. This approach was recognized by Mao Zedong and was summarized as the "Fengqiao Experience" of arresting fewer people, not handing over conflicts, relying on the masses, and using reasoned struggle to transform the majority of the "four types of elements" into new people on the spot. In November, in a conversation with the Head of the Ministry of Public Security, Mao Zedong again stressed: "From the experience of Zhuji, after the masses have risen up, they have done no worse or weaker than you have. You must not forget to mobilize the masses; if the masses work well, you can reduce counter-revolutionary cases and criminal cases." In January 1964, the Central Committee of the Communist Party of China issued the *Instruction on Relying on the Power of the Masses, Strengthening the People's Democratic Dictatorship, and Transforming the Majority of the "Four Categories of Elements" into New People*, taking the "Fengqiao Experience" to the whole country.

The "Fengqiao Experience" has a strong historical adaptability and historical creativity. The needs of the times arise and change, and the development and continuous transformation, enrichment of the needs of the times change also. Over the past 50 years, the development and evolution of the "Fengqiao Experience" can be roughly divided into three stages.

The first stage is the experience of political struggle and social reform, including the experience of how to correctly fight the enemy in the socialist education campaign launched in 1963; the experience of local rehabilitation of roving criminals, and the help and education of delinquent youths in the mid-1970s. Also the system of evaluation and removal of labels for the "four types of elements" created by the cadres and masses of Fengqiao in practice after the "Gang of Four" was smashed.

The second stage is the experience of extensive participation of the masses in the comprehensive management of security in society. After the reform and opening-up, with the shift of the party's work focus, the Fengqiao cadres and masses had time to adhere to the "Fengqiao Experience" focus on maintaining security in society. They focus on strengthening the construction of rural security councils, adhere to regular training, effectively improve the political and business quality of security cadres, set up a few security councils to solve cases on their own, relying on the masses to do a good job of security provision. They also carried out socialist education on the rule of law among the masses and worked to raise the people's awareness of the rule of law, thus achieving the requirement of "fewer arrests, better security and higher productivity." Since 1980, Fengqiao has relied on the masses to absorb many conflicts and disputes and general law and order problems, basically following the requirement of "small matters do not go beyond the village, big matters do not go beyond the township, and conflicts are not handed over."

The third stage is the experience of villagers' autonomy and the construction of democracy and rule of law at the grass-roots level. After the 16th Party Congress, the Zhejiang Provincial Party Committee, with Xi Jinping as its Secretary, actively implemented the scientific outlook on development and the grand blueprint for building a harmonious society, and the "Fengqiao Experience" became an important spiritual, historical, and practical resource for implementing the "Eight Strengths and Eight Measures" Strategy[39] and building "Safe Zhejiang." In 2003, Xi Jinping gave instructions to the Zhejiang party committees and governments at all levels to attach great importance to the study and promotion of the "Fengqiao Experience," to adhere to the "Fengqiao Experience" and to develop it. During this period, the main practices included:

1. promoting grass-roots democracy and villagers' autonomy in rural areas;
2. focusing on the provision of public goods in rural areas (e.g. implementing road hardening, planting trees, brightening and purification projects, vigorously strengthening cultural construction, setting up medical insurance for major diseases, etc.);
3. democratic management and supervision in rural areas, and reform of the financial system;
4. charitable assistance for poor farmers;
5. strengthening security of society and mediation at the village level;
6. carrying out the new "Fengqiao Experience" mediation;

28 *Changes in and Transformation of People's Mediation*

7. development of new rural areas, village construction, democratic management, and group defense;
8. provision of guarantees for privately-run enterprises;
9. service management for foreign populations;
10. rehabilitation of released prisoners.[40]

The core of the "Fengqiao Experience" is to deploy the masses. At the time of the socialist education campaign, the "Fengqiao Experience" took the form of reasoned struggle, while the context of the change from resolving conflicts between the enemy and us to resolving internal conflicts within the people provided the conditions for the intervention and even integration of people's mediation. After the reform and opening-up, Zhuji's "Fengqiao Experience" on the comprehensive management of security in society gradually took shape, and the "Fengqiao Experience" called for relying on the masses to resolve conflicts and general public security cases locally. People's mediation was integrated into the "Fengqiao Experience" and rapidly developed.

From the 1990s to the beginning of the twenty-first century, contrary to the national downturn in people's mediation, Zhuji's people's mediation was flourishing and innovating due to the "Fengqiao Experience." During this period, according to the "Fengqiao Experience," the comprehensive management of security in society required the establishment of a mechanism of departmental coordination and village/township linkage to prevent conflicts and to resolve them through people's mediation. Zhuji then carried out the standardization and institutionalization of the people's mediation committee and its work, and innovated many mechanisms and methods of mediation work according to local conditions. In 1996, Zhuji took the opportunity of the "Year of Grass-roots Construction" to set up a "People's Mediation Assistance Center" to strengthen the standardization of grass-roots mediation committees and to standardize the management of mediation work in towns and villages. In 2000, Zhuji established mediation centers in all 35 townships, forming a vertical and horizontal network of mediation organizations with mediation centers in townships, mediation teams in offices, mediation committees in villages and liaison officers in villagers' groups, extending the tentacles of mediation organizations into the people's grass-roots life, deep and internal, and forming a mediation coordination network with comprehensive coverage and leaving no dead ends. In 2003, Zhuji carried out a work inspection based on the criteria of "five haves and four implementations" (have signage, seal, logo, procedures, and documents; implementation of organizations, personnel, remuneration, and systems).

After 2008, with the development of the "Fengqiao Experience," the mediation mode of Zhuji's people's mediation committee also entered a period of innovative development, along with the innovation of working mechanisms and methods. Especially after 2010, as one of the 35 pilot units for social management innovation, Zhuji began to explore and actively build a "Grand Mediation" system. On the one hand, it has consolidated the basic role of the people's mediation committees in the Grand Mediation system, and formed a three-level people's mediation network at the city, town, and village levels under the leadership of the leading group for the construction of the Grand Mediation system for social conflicts and disputes and under the guidance of the municipal people's mediation work center. Horizontally it has established and improved the municipal joint people's mediation committees as well as various professional and industry-specific people's mediation committees. On the other hand, it has further improved the articulation and interaction between the people's mediation committee and judicial mediation, administrative mediation, procuratorial work, as well as arbitration and petition work. In 2015, Zhuji strengthened the construction of social mediation organizations based on sound grass-roots people's mediation organizations, promoted the participation of diverse forces such as village volunteers, the media, and arbitrators in people's mediation, and carried out socialized operations, such as the purchase of services by the government and the incubation of mediation-type social organizations. The construction of a volunteer team for people's mediation was also strengthened in 2016.[41]

1.4.2 New Upgrade of the "Fengqiao Experience"

1.4.2.1 Building a "People's Mediation +" Model[42]

In 2017, the Zhuji Municipal Bureau of Justice set out to build a "people's mediation +" expert, a brand, using volunteers, with linkage, and an internet model, based on people's mediation, with the participation of government, society, and professional forces.

First, people's mediation + experts. People's mediation + experts, i.e., professional mediators "sit and consult." They have creatively introduced the "consultation" system into the field of professional conflict resolution, and established ten professional mediation committees for medical disputes, marriage and family, traffic accidents, etc., using the identity of a neutral third party to integrate professional strength and efficiently resolve conflicts and disputes in professional fields. Since 2017, a total of 3,987 disputes have been accepted by the ten specialized investigation committees and 3,839 have been successfully mediated, with a success rate of 96.28 percent and a subject matter of RMB 112 million.

Second, people's mediation + brand, i.e., branded mediation "leading the way with a point." This means selecting mediators with rich experience in grass-roots mediation and the trust of the masses, and carefully building branded mediation rooms. For example, the experience of "Lao Zhu Mediation" in Juanshan Town, which resolves conflicts at source in exchange for the happiness of ten thousand families, was published and promoted by the central "Party Building" magazine. Fengqiao town brand mediator Lao Yang won the award of "Zhejiang top ten rule of law figures." As a result, Zhuji City has taken an important step in its mediation "branding" strategy by cultivating branded mediators and mediation rooms with regional influence, to achieve the effect of fanning out from a point to an area, and ultimately achieving one town, one brand.

Third, people's mediation + volunteers, i.e., through volunteer mediation to achieve "group prevention and governance." That is, to explore the establishment of a city, town, and village three-tier mediation volunteer team, the municipal level to establish a team of 1,000 expert volunteers, the town (street) to establish mediation volunteer squadrons, including the well-known Fengqiao Mediation Volunteers Association, the town of Paitou's sage help group, Jiangzao town's "Sister Zhan help group," and the village (community) to establish a mediation squad composed of village cadres, legal advisers, sages, etc. Zhuji has recruited 1,396 people's mediation volunteers, and since 2017, a total of 2,607 disputes have been mediated, thus truly achieving the goal of "group prevention and group governance."

Fourth, people's mediation + linkage, i.e., to achieve one-stop, multi-tuning linkage to facilitate mediation. That is, to establish the large-scale mediation operation mechanism of "multi-departmental linkage" to achieve an effective interface between police mediation, litigation mediation, and prosecution mediation. Specifically, this means directing the establishment of people's mediation rooms in grass-roots police stations to resolve grass-roots security disputes; establishing pre-litigation people's mediation rooms in court cases and grass-roots courts to persuade parties to modulate; and importing people's mediation work into town and village procuratorial offices to achieve interaction and mutual progress between procuratorial and people's mediation work. Through the collaboration of departments, a one-stop system of entering one door to solve all problems can be achieved, realizing the facilitation of mediation in one stop.

Fifth, people's mediation + internet, i.e., in order to break the limitations of different groups of people applying for mediation in time and space and to facilitate the masses, Zhuji City has implemented a multi-channel application for people's mediation. In addition to on-site applications, parties can also apply for mediation through the "Ping An Tong" "Online Court." Relying on the "Online Court" platform, the ten specialized mediation committees and 50 professional mediators have been successfully established, and mediation is officially online. As of June, the platform has assigned 39 online mediation cases to mediation organizations, 27 of which have been successfully mediated and 9 have been judicially confirmed. Through the mobile internet terminal, the time of people's mediation work is greatly shortened, allowing mediation efficiency.

1.4.2.2 Creating a "Four-In-One" Working Method[43]

The development of the "Fengqiao Experience" is of great significance in maintaining security and stability in society and in comprehensively promoting the rule of law. After the 19th National Congress of the Communist Party of China, China entered a new era of socialism with Chinese characteristics. Regarding social governance, the 19th CPC National Congress proposed to create a pattern of "co-construction, co-governance, and sharing," by doing the following:

> Strengthen the construction of social governance system, improve the social governance mechanism led by the party committee, responsible by the government, coordinated by the society, with public participation and guaranteed by the rule of law, and improve the level of socialization, rule of law, intelligence, and professionalization of social governance. Strengthen the construction of mechanisms for preventing and resolving social conflicts [and] bring into play the role of social organizations to achieve a positive interaction between government governance, social regulation and residents' autonomy.

This has put forward new requirements for the innovative development of the "Fengqiao Experience" of people's mediation. Focusing on the objectives and tasks of the 19th Party Congress on social governance, Zhuji City has been striving to build a new system of diversified conflict resolution work at a higher level and with a wider scope with new concepts, new approaches, and new methods. This is manifested in the following areas.

It has integrated and optimized various types of mediation resources, vigorously promoting the management combination of the Municipal Mediation Guidance Center (government) and the Municipal General Mediation Council (social organization), and strengthening their operational guidance capacity for mediation work. In other words, based on the upgraded Municipal Public Legal Service Center, it has integrated mediation organization, such as the Municipal Traffic Accidents Mediation Center, the Municipal Medical Accidents Mediation Committee, the Municipal Commercial Mediation Commission, the Municipal Property Mediation Commission, the Municipal Family Mediation Committee, and the Municipal Labor Dispute Mediation Commission. It has established municipal joint mediation centers, unified office space, and standardized mediation processes and window services. At the same time, it has built a network of diversified conflict resolution with the city's Joint Mediation Center as the leader, 27 town and township (street) joint mediation centers as the backbone, and 13 municipal specialized mediation committees as the supplement. Through the establishment of an organic, coordinated, efficient, and convenient mechanism for the diversified resolution of conflicts and disputes, a synergy has been formed to resolve disputes and facilitate the one stop mediation service.

It has made the professional organization of mediation bigger and stronger. That is, in response to the changing characteristics of conflicts in the new situation, Zhuji City continues to deepen the construction of specialized mediation committees, forming industry mediation committees in emerging conflict-prone areas such as finance, e-commerce and agricultural products as needed, taking the form of government purchase of services, vigorously promoting the recruitment of full-time people's mediators, carrying out professional grading, and realizing the full-time management of mediators. At the same time, it has also created a high-quality branded mediation room to highlight the power of individual brands. Relying on the opportunity of branded mediator Yang Guangzhao being awarded the "CCTV 2018 Top 10 People of the Year in the Rule of Law," the city's branded mediation has continued to expand its regional influence by effectively improving the quality of the mediator team's capabilities through mentoring.

The "Online Fengqiao Experience" has been consolidated and enhanced, i.e., the Zhuji Online Public Legal Service Platform has been established to provide online intelligent consultation on conflicts and disputes, self-help applications, and online mediation functions. At the same time, relying on the "12348 Law Network," the latest mediation cases are released in real time, gradually forming a database of mediation cases, automatically generating legal opinions and other services, forming a case-based mediation model, and providing online access for mediators or parties to disputes. By deepening the "online platform for the diversified settlement of conflicts and disputes," training for mediators has been strengthened and the usage rate of the platform has increased, realizing online mediation, online agreements, online judicial confirmation, and online litigation filing as a one-stop service.

It has further improved the mechanism of conflict resolution screening and diversion, clarified the scope of dispute acceptance, opened the channels of rule of law, and strictly transferred the conflicts and disputes outside the scope of people's mediation to relevant administrative departments and judicial departments for disposal according to the law, effectively bringing conflicts and disputes on the track of handling according to the law. It also does a good job of combining mediation work with the popularization of law and governance in accordance with the law, i.e. through lectures about the law, analyzing the law in the middle of the matter and clarifying the law afterwards, so that parties to conflicts and disputes can learn the law, understand the law, and abide by the law while undergoing mediation.

1.4.3 Inspiration from the "Fengqiao Experience"

The "Fengqiao Experience" in the new era is a major achievement of Xi Jinping's ocialist thought with Chinese characteristics in the new era. It is a set of effective and typical grass-roots social governance mechanisms and methods that have been created and developed by the people of Fengqiao and other places under the leadership of the Party to resolve conflicts, promote harmony, lead the way, and guarantee development.

> The "Fengqiao Experience" consists of five core elements, including the Party's building leadership, the people's mainstay, the combination of self-governance, rule of law and moral governance, common construction,

shared governance, peace, and harmony. These five elements constitute the distinctive features and contemporary connotations of the "Fengqiao Experience."

Among them, the Party building is the fundamental guarantee, the people's mainstay is the value of the core, the combination of "three governances" is the core meaning, common construction and shared governance are the basic pattern, peace and harmony is the goal effect.[44] The development of the "Fengqiao Experience" is an important theme of people's mediation in the new era. The "Fengqiao Experience" developed and innovated by Zhuji City has the following characteristics:

1. Under the leadership of the party committee, it is a joint effort of government promotion, social collaboration, and public participation. People's mediation is a system that relies on the power of the masses to resolve civil disputes, and is based on social coordination and public participation. At the same time, the Chinese people's mediation system is a "government-run" system, and the leadership of the party committee and the government of Zhuji City have clearly played an important role in the formation of the "Fengqiao Experience" of people's mediation.

    In terms of policy guidance, since 2008, Zhuji has issued several important normative documents on the construction of a people's mediation system, which were mainly issued jointly by the Zhuji Municipal Party Committee and the Municipal Government or by the Zhuji Municipal Government. For example, the *Opinions on the Establishment of the Linkage Mechanism between People's Mediation and Civil Litigation* in 2008, the *Notice on the Establishment of the Leading Group for the Construction of "Great Mediation" for Social Conflicts and Disputes in Zhuji City* in 2012, the *Opinions on Further Strengthening the Work of People's Mediation in the New Situation* and the *Opinions on Strengthening the Construction of Socialized Mediation System* in 2014, and *Opinions on the Implementation of Strengthening the "Great Mediation" System to Effectively Resolve Social Conflicts and Disputes* and *Opinions on Establishing and Improving Mechanism for the Interface of Administrative Mediation and People's Mediation* in 2015, and *Opinions on the Implementation of Establishing People's Mediation Volunteer Teams and Vigorously Carrying Out Volunteer Service Activities* in 2016, etc. In addition, the Mediation Office of the Leading Group for the Construction of the "Great Mediation" System for Social Conflicts and Disputes in Zhuji City, the Zhuji Judicial Bureau, the Procuratorate, the Court and the Public Security Bureau have also jointly issued many important normative documents concerning the mode and operation of people's mediation. Under the guidance of these normative documents, the relevant departments have actively organized and vigorously promoted the formation and operation of the people's mediation system in Zhuji.

In terms of the construction of the people's mediation system, the Zhuji Municipal Party Committee and Municipal Government set up a leading group for the construction of a "Grand Mediation" system for social conflicts and disputes in 2012 and set up a special office for the group. At the same time, the Zhuji Municipal Bureau of Justice set up a fully funded institution, the Municipal Mediation Guidance Center, which is responsible for the day-to-day work of the Leading Group's office, as well as guiding and managing the construction of municipal people's mediation organizations and providing operational guidance to the Municipal General Mediation Council and organizing the investigation and handling of conflicts and disputes. All towns (street) and villages (streets) and relevant departments (units) are also required to establish corresponding organizational bodies, with the head of the Party and government acting as the first person in charge of the "Great Mediation" work, guiding and coordinating the resolution of major conflicts and disputes. These initiatives have ensured that the plan and specific tasks of the Zhuji Municipal Party Committee and Municipal Government for the construction of the people's mediation system, mechanism and work can be effectively implemented, enabling the construction of the people's mediation system to move forward rapidly.

In terms of funding and provision of facilities, Zhuji City requires that, in addition to the financial implementation and protection of funds for the guidance of people's mediation work, and subsidies for people's mediation committees and for people's mediators, townships (streets), villages (dwellings and communities), enterprises and institutions and other organizations must also solve problems such as workplaces and office facilities for people's mediation committees.[45]

2. Mediation by traditional village (residence) people's mediation committees as the basis and backbone. The "Fengqiao Experience" is the experience of grass-roots social governance, with its emphasis on the grass-roots and grasping the foundations, and its basic requirement that "small cases do not go beyond the village, big cases do not go beyond the township, and conflicts are not handed over." Therefore, it is important to consolidate and improve the construction of village (residence and enterprise) people's mediation organizations to ensure that they can carry out their work effectively. Under the leadership of the party committee, the government's responsibility, social coordination, and public participation, Zhuji has formed a network of mediation organizations consisting of people's mediation committees at the village (residence and enterprise), township (street) and city levels, as well as professional and industrial people's mediation committees. In the mediation system of Zhuji City, 533 village (residence) people's mediation committees and 149 people's mediation committees of enterprises and institutions have been established. In order to solve the problems of larger administrative villages or small communities, more conflicts and disputes, and more

complicated situations, Zhuji also actively explores the establishment of people's mediation teams or the staffing of people's mediators in rural villages or small communities in order to carry out the investigation, acceptance, and mediation of conflicts and disputes.[46]

While building a network of people's mediation organization, Zhuji City has not neglected the construction and training of people's mediation teams at the village (residence) level. After 2012, Zhuji City started to build and strengthen its people's mediation team, hiring full-time people's mediators and including some retired cadres and lawyers in the mediation team to cope with the new, complex, and specialized nature of social conflicts and disputes. In addition, the Zhuji Judicial Bureau and its judicial offices also actively carry out training for people's mediators at the village (residence) level. In addition to explaining in depth the principles, procedures, and techniques of mediation, they also focus on common conflicts and disputes such as neighborhood relations and marriage and family, to continuously improve the mediation ability and level of village people's mediators and better play the role of the first line of defense.

3. Continuous innovation and development according to the needs of practice. Over the past 55 years, by relying on persistent development and innovation in the changes, the "Fengqiao Experience" has been able to endure and flourish for a long time. According to the problems of social governance at different times, Zhuji has constantly innovated and developed its mediation methods and working mechanisms to meet practical needs. Without innovation, Zhuji's people's mediation would not have developed, let alone become the "Fengqiao Experience." For example, Zhuji City has promoted the "four-in-advance" working method of people's mediation, which means that "organizational construction comes before work, forecasting comes before prevention, prevention comes before mediation, and mediation comes before planning." Another example is the "sit-in" method of specialized mediation, in which a neutral third party makes use of his or her professional strengths and provides objective assessments to efficiently resolve conflicts and disputes in his or her area of expertise. In terms of working mechanism, for example, around the 19th National Congress on the goals and tasks of social governance, Zhuji City put forward the concept of "a network and three transformations" to create a new pattern of diversified settlement of conflicts and disputes in the new era. The so-called "one network" is to build a three-dimensional dispute resolution network, based on the network of mediation organizations, to realize the integration and coordination of multiple mediation links, such as police-mediation docking, procuratorial-mediation docking, and litigation-mediation docking, and promote online mediation models. The so-called "three transformations" refer to the rule of law, specialization, and socialization of people's mediation. For example, mediation work should be combined with rule of law

publicity and legal services, so that parties to disputes can learn the law, understand the law, and abide by the law while undergoing mediation. In terms of specialization, it means expanding the construction of professional mediation organizations, forming professional people's mediators, and developing standardized mediation processes. In terms of socialization, this means decentralizing the management of mediation by social organizations, guiding social organizations to participate in mediation, and exploring the establishment of volunteer mediation teams, etc.[47]

These innovations and developments are not only a reflection of the "Fengqiao Experience," but also are a response to the requirements of the times. Of course, as innovation is exploration, it is impossible to completely avoid the fact that there will be problems. Similarly, in the exploration and practice of people's mediation in Zhuji, such as the rule of law of people's mediation, one of the important aspects is the standardization and normalization of people's mediation organizations and mediation work. However, the "Fengqiao Experience" is dedicated to relying on the masses to prevent and resolve conflicts, while people's mediation is an extra-judicial dispute resolution method for civil disputes, whose subjects, mediation methods, and bases are necessarily diverse. Will the rule of law and standardization undermine the "Fengqiao Experience"? For example, if the mediation provided by professional, industrial, or social organizations is free of charge and the government provides the funding for mediation, it will increase the financial burden of the government, on the one hand, and, on the other hand, due to subsidies provided by the government, it will be difficult to attract talented people to join the people's mediation team, which will inevitably affect the overall quality of the mediators and the effectiveness of the mediation work. Therefore, it is necessary to think rationally about the generalization of people's mediation.

1.5 The Path to Perfection of People's Mediation in China: Also, on the Integration of China's Social Mediation System

It is worth noting that the 2016 *Opinions of the Supreme People's Court on the People's Courts Further Deepening the Reform of the Diversified Dispute Resolution Mechanism* juxtaposed people's mediation with administrative mediation, commercial mediation, and industrial mediation. In a sense, this indicates that the Supreme People's Court is aware of the problem of the generalization of the concept of people's mediation. In a fundamental sense, mediation, regardless of the type, is based on the consensual agreement of the parties to resolve a dispute. If the dispute has not yet entered the litigation process, whether it is pre-litigation court mediation, administrative mediation, or civil mediation hosted by various other entities, the objective of resolving the dispute is the same and is by nature an alternative dispute resolution mechanism (ADR). As administrative mediation is backed by administrative power and judicial mediation is guaranteed by judicial coercive power, these two types of mediation mechanisms need to be regulated separately. Therefore, the most pressing issue now is how to rationalize the relationship between people's mediation and other forms of civil mediation (social mediation) and reshape China's social mediation system in the light of the contemporary challenges faced by the people's mediation system in the new era. In general, it is important to stick to a "two-legged approach."

1.5.1 Taking the Path of Legal Governance and Enacting the Social Mediation Act

"Social mediation" refers to socialized mediation other than judicial mediation, administrative mediation, and other public mediation, including people's mediation, industrial mediation, commercial mediation, lawyer mediation, arbitration mediation and other types of mediation. At a time of social transformation when the division of labor is becoming more and more refined and the interest demands are increasingly diversified, only by developing social mediation, expanding the field of mediation, and innovating mediation vehicles can we make up for the narrow positioning of mediation in the current *People's Mediation Law*, better adapt to the requirements of the new era, and improve the mechanism for the diversified resolution of social conflicts and disputes. The state should enact a unified *Social Mediation Law*, which clearly regulates the qualifications of mediators, the setting-up of mediation institutions and various types of civil mediation activities other than court mediation and administrative mediation.[48]

The *Social Mediation Law* should give all social mediation agreements the same legal effect and improve the docking mechanism, establish a unified judicial confirmation system for social mediation agreements, and the mediation agreements or mediation letters formed by social mediation subjects should have the same legal effect as people's mediation agreements. For the parties, it does not matter who presides over the mediation if it can lead to the formation of a consensual agreement and the conclusion of the case. Therefore, the legislation should treat the mediation agreements formed by all types of social mediation subjects equally, without any distinction. The parties have the right to choose the appropriate mediation subject to resolve their disputes according to their own circumstances. In this sense, "the institutional model of people's mediation as the mainstay, supplemented by other mediation, should be abandoned, so that mediation can become a socialized dispute resolution mechanism."[49] The focus of developing other forms of social mediation is to strengthen new types of civil mediation, such as commercial mediation, professional mediation, lawyer mediation, and individual expert mediation, clarify their legal status, highlight their neutrality and autonomy, give full play to the advantages of social mediation in terms of pluralism, specialization, and professionalism, improve the "social capital" of social mediation, and activate the institutional vitality and credibility of social mediation.

1.5.2 Taking the Path of Comprehensive Governance and Consolidating the Status of People's Mediation

The mainstream view of the current academic community is to promote people's mediation toward full social autonomy, which, as pointed out earlier, is an idealized solution influenced by Western centrist thinking. The Western countries have long pursued the dichotomy of "state and society," "either the government or the people," and the concept of "minimal government," advocating "governance without government." In contrast, the traditional experience of Chinese social governance focuses on the interaction and cooperation between the state and society, the government, and the people, and adheres to the social governance concept of "shared governance by all," which is led by the Party and the government, coordinated by comprehensive governance, and shared by multiple governance. The "Fengqiao Experience" is effective precisely because of the political advantage of the central government and the active promotion of the party committees at all levels, especially by adhering to the organizational network and mass route with grass-roots party organizations at the core and the participation of the whole society, so that "conflicts are not handed over and are resolved locally."

Local practices like the "Fengqiao Experience" prove that giving full play to the role of the party committee in the overall situation and coordination of all parties in the allocation of resources for people's mediation are the key to enhancing the effectiveness of people's mediation. Where the Party and government attach great importance to people's mediation, the role of people's mediation is well played; where the Party and government do not attach importance to it, people's mediation will fall into organizational paralysis and become virtually useless. Through bottom-up mass participation and top-down government mobilization, local resources should be effectively mobilized to build an organizational network for group prevention and governance, so that people's mediation can be closely integrated with the entire comprehensive social security management network to resolve social conflicts locally and realize that "small matters do not go beyond the village, big matters do not go beyond the town and conflicts are not handed over."[50] The *Opinion of the Six Central Ministries and Commissions on Strengthening the Construction of People's Mediator Teams* further requires that party committees and governments at all levels should strengthen the financial support, operational training and organizational leadership for people's mediation. The opinions, while clarifying the specific guiding responsibilities of the judicial administrative organs in strengthening the team of people's mediators, also require the judicial administrative organs to take the initiative to report to the party committee and government on people's mediation work, actively seek the attention and support of the relevant departments, and require the Political and Legal Affairs Commission, the people's courts, the finance department, the civil affairs department, the human resources and social security department and the competent industry department to clarify their respective responsibilities, strengthen coordination and cooperation, and work together to do a good job in people's mediation. Party committees and governments at all levels and all relevant departments should prioritize the building of a team of people's mediators, strengthen the responsibility for their work, form a synergy for their work and strive for effective work, pay unwavering attention to, support and promote people's mediation, actively and extensively mobilize social forces to participate in people's mediation, remove the bottlenecks that plague the development of people's mediation, and ensure that people's mediation is always vibrant and dynamic. This idea of the Central Government reflects the idea of comprehensive governance of people's mediation under the leadership of the party committee. The reason for relying on party committees and governments to promote mediation is not to rigidly adhere to the historical organizational attributes of people's mediation, but more realistically because the governance capacity and mechanisms of Chinese social organizations are still imperfect, and the ineffective operation of people's mediation in the "village and residence committees" requires the state to inject legitimacy resources into it and enhance its authority. Therefore, at present and for a long time to come, Chinese people's mediation cannot and should not escape from the path of "government-driven" mediation. Of course, in the long run, with the increasing improvement of social autonomy, especially grass-roots autonomy, and the increasing ability of society to self-regulate, self-develop, and self-manage, socially autonomous people's mediation is bound to be the trend of the times, and people's mediation will tend to evolve into a new type of community mediation, which, together with other forms of civil society mediation, will jointly construct a "third sphere" for the state and society to participate in dispute resolution.[51]

1.5.3 Taking a Differentiated Path to Promote Mediation Specialization

In the development of a pluralistic dispute resolution mechanism there is inevitably a diverse mix between public interest (non-profit) and market-based (for-profit), as well as between private, social, and public remedies.[52] The reshaping of China's social mediation system means that people's mediation and other civil mediation should be treated differently according to their respective characteristics and follow a differentiated path of development. The reason for taking a differentiated path is that China is a large country with inadequate and unequal development in eastern, central, and western China, in urban and rural areas, thus, these factors are intertwined, and the types of disputes and mediation needs are very different; therefore, we should not adopt a monolithic mindset and "consider mediation practice in China as a unified and homogenous whole, considering mediation as a dispute resolution practice to be the same in different parts of China."[53] In providing a uniform legal regulation of the mediation system, it is important to focus on the flexibility and plurality of mediation and not to obliterate the vitality of the mediation system itself with a monolithic model of professionalism.

Since its inception, people's mediation has been positioned as a non-remunerated, public good, mainly supported and guaranteed by the state treasury. However, due to the limited public resources of the state and the lack of economic incentives for social mediation, the Six Central Ministries' *Opinions on Strengthening the People's Mediator Team* proposed that the basic principle of "combining both specialization and guidance" should be adhered to in strengthening the people's mediator team. The differentiated path means that a mediation system should be developed in which part-time and professional, public interest and market-oriented categories co-exist. In the context of China's rapid socio-economic development and increasingly frequent civil and commercial transactions, the market mechanism is an important path to nurture social mediation toward maturity. Market-based mediation means providing mediation services to parties for a fee, with the demand, supply, and price of the service regulated by the market. Parties must pay a certain fee for mediation services, and mediation organizations must obtain market recognition by enhancing the professionalism level of their mediation services, promoting a balance between supply and demand in the dispute resolution market. In the field of commercial disputes, parties often have a high ability and willingness to pay; and commercial mediation, professional mediation and lawyer mediation charge reasonable fees, which is also in line with the market law of "whoever uses it, pays." The *Opinions of the Ministry of Justice of the Supreme People's Court on the Pilot Work of Lawyer Mediation* is beginning to explore the marketization of lawyer mediation services, which clearly stipulates that "mediation studios set up in law firms that receive direct applications from parties to mediate disputes may charge mediation fees to both parties in accordance with the principles of compensation and low price."

Of course, the current market for social mediation services in China is still in its infancy, and local governments should, in accordance with local conditions, promptly introduce preferential and supportive policies such as simplified procedures and tax exemptions, and encourage social forces to participate in dispute resolution by actively purchasing mediation services from social mediation organizations.[54] In this way, a pluralistic mediation system can be formed in which administrative mediation, judicial mediation, people's mediation, and other social mediations, such as commercial mediation, industrial mediation, and lawyer mediation are promoted by the state, with limited competition among mediation organizations regarding the quality of their mediation, ultimately improving the specialization, professionalism, and standardization of social mediation.

Notes

1 Chen Ruilai and Xiao Buwen: A Political Analysis of the Qing Dynasty Government-Approved Mediation System: An Examination of the "Huang Yan Litigation File," *Journal of Guangdong Education College*, 2009 (2).

2 Liu Junping: On the Reconciliation and Settlement in Traditional Chinese Sentimental Trials, *Journal of Xiangtan University (Philosophy and Social Sciences Edition)*, 2014 (6).
3 Hu Xusheng and Xia Xinhua: A Study of the Chinese Mediation Tradition: A Cultural Perspective, *Journal of the Henan Provincial Academy of Political and Legal Administration*, 2000 (4).
4 Zhang Yanying: *The Analects of Confucius* (Beijing: China Bookstore, 2007), p. 13.
5 Liu Lian et al.: *The Old Book of the Tang Dynasty* (Beijing: China Books, 1975), p. 4797.
6 Mao Zedong: *Selected Works of Mao Zedong* (Vol. 1) (Beijing: People's Publishing House, 1991), p. 14.
7 Jiang Wei and Yang Rongxin (Eds.): *An Introduction to People's Mediation* (Beijing: Law Press, 1990), p. 29.
8 Zhang Xibo and Han Yanlong (Eds.): *A History of the Chinese Revolutionary Legal System* (Beijing: China Social Science Press, 1987), p. 500.
9 Hou Xinyi: *From Justice for the People to the People's Justice* (Beijing: China University of Political Science and Law Press, 2007), pp. 274–279.
10 Article 1 of the General Rules clearly stipulates that people's mediation committees should be established in urban and rural areas throughout the country; that they should be mass mediation organizations working under the guidance of the grass-roots people's governments and the grass-roots courts; and that they should mediate general civil disputes and minor criminal disputes.
11 Han Yanlong: Thirty Years of People's Mediation in China, *Studies in Law*, 1981 (2).
12 Peng Furong and Feng Xuezhi: *Rethinking and Reconstructing: A Study of the People's Mediation System* (Beijing: China University of Political Science and Law Press, 2013), p. 45.
13 Hong Dongying: *A Study on the Changes of the Mediation System in Contemporary China* (Shanghai: Shanghai People's Publishing House, 2011), p. 73.
14 Fan Yu: Review of the People's Mediation Law of the People's Republic of China, *The Jurist*, 2011 (2).
15 Article 20 of the *People's Mediation Law* stipulates that: according to the needs of mediation of disputes, the people's mediator may, with the consent of the parties, invite the relatives, neighbors, and colleagues of the parties to participate in the mediation, and may also invite people with expertise, specific experience or people from relevant social organizations to participate in the mediation.
16 Hou Yuanzhen and Liao Yongan: On the Changes of the Chinese People's Mediation System: The View of Dispute Resolution, Mediation Organization and Mediation Function, *Journal of Shihezi University (Philosophy and Social Sciences Edition)*, 2016 (2).
17 Joseph Lee: *The Collected Works of Joseph Lee* (Shenyang: Liaoning Science Press, 1986), p. 338.
18 Fei Xiaotong: *Vernacular China* (Beijing: People's Publishing House, 2008), p. 6.
19 Huang Zongzhi: *Society and Culture in the Qing Dynasty: The Expression and Practice of Civil Law* (Shanghai: Shanghai Bookstore Press, 2001), pp. 51–74.
20 Ibid., pp. 107–130.
21 Zeng Xianyi: A Study of Some Issues Concerning the Traditional Chinese Mediation System, *Chinese Jurisprudence*, 2009 (4).

22 Lu Sili: *Mao Zedong and Mediation: Politics and Dispute Resolution in Communist China*, trans. Xu Xu and ed. Wang Xiaohong, in Qiang Shigong (Ed.): *Mediation, Legal System and Modernity: A Study of China's Mediation System* (Beijing: China Legal Publishing House, 2005), p. 79.
23 Huang Zongzhi: *Past and Present: Explorations in Chinese Civil Legal Practice* (Beijing: Law Press, 2009), p. 78.
24 Both in Chinese legislation and in practice, the scope of civil disputes has been broadened in line with the development of society. At this stage, civil disputes that can be subject to people's mediation in China include civil disputes, minor criminal disputes, private criminal prosecution cases, and civil disputes incidental to criminal matters.
25 Liao Yong'an and Hou Yuanzhen: The Relevance of Developing Social Mediation, *Guangming Daily*, July 6, 2014, p. 13.
26 Tanase Takao: *Dispute Resolution and the Trial System*, trans. Wang Yaxin (Beijing: China University of Political Science and Law Press, 2004), pp. 53–69.
27 Hou Yuanzhen: *A Study of the People's Mediation System in the Period of Social Transition: Focusing on the Administrative Turn of the People's Mediation as an Analysis* (Xiangtan: Xiangtan University Press, 2016), pp. 31–32.
28 Wu Aibin: Court-attached People's Mediation and its Operation, *Contemporary Law*, 2012 (2).
29 Shen Zhimin: Mediators "Live" in Police Stations to Resolve 60,000 Disputes, *Xinjing News*, September 13, 2012, p. A38.
30 Xiong Yihan: The Socialization and Reorganization of People's Mediation: A Case Study of Yang Boshou's Workshop in Shanghai, *Society*, 2006 (6).
31 Wu Aibin: The Chinese Experience of People's Mediation, in Xu Xin (Ed.): *Justice* (Xiamen: Xiamen University Press, 2010), p. 48.
32 Xu Xin: Towards Socially Autonomous People's Mediation, *Learning and Exploration*, 2012 91).
33 Ze ng Lingjian: The Changing Meaning of Government-Promoted People's Mediation (1931–2010), *Xiamen University Law Review*, 2016 (1).
34 Ma Changshan: The Rule of Law Turn from State Construction to Shared Construction: An Examination Based on the Relationship between Social Organizations and Rule of Law Construction, *Juridical Studies*, 2017 (3).
35 Fan Yu: *The Theory and Practice of Dispute Resolution* (Beijing: Tsinghua University Press, 2007), p. 570.
36 It is noteworthy that Article 9 of the *Xiamen Special Economic Zone Regulations* on the Promotion of Pluralistic Dispute Resolution Mechanism, China's first local regulation on pluralistic dispute resolution, affirms "individual mediation" as a separate type for the first time, and places it alongside people's mediation, industrial mediation, and commercial mediation.
37 Fan Yu, Shi Changqing, and Qiu Xingmei: *The Mediation System and the Code of Conduct for Mediators* (Beijing: Tsinghua University Press, 2007), p. 34.
38 He Yongjun: Rural Social Transitions and Changes in the People's Mediation System, *Legal System and Social Development*, 2013 (1).
39 The "8-8 Strategy" refers to the eight initiatives for future development proposed at the Fourth Plenary (enlarged) Meeting of the 11th CPC Zhejiang Provincial Committee held in July 2003, namely to further develop the strengths and promote the initiatives in eight areas.

40 Wang Shirong: *Fengqiao Experience: The Practice of Grass-Roots Social Governance* Beijing: Law Press, 2018), pp. 1–6.
41 Wang Shirong and Zhu Jiping: *The "Fengqiao Experience" of People's Mediation* (Beijing: Law Press, 2018), pp. 17–18.
42 The Bureau builds "People's Mediation+" to create an upgraded version of the "Fengqiao Experience," in Zhuji City Judicial Bureau. Available at: www.zhuji.gov.cn/art/2017/6/20/art_1382713_12625745.html (accessed January 18, 2019).
43 Zhuji Municipal Bureau of Justice: The "Four-In-One" Working Method of the Municipal Bureau of Justice to Create a New Pattern of Diversified Conflict Resolution in the New Era. Available at: www.zhuji.gov.cn/art/2018/12/28/art_1 382711_28618687.html (accessed January 18, 2019).
44 Zhang Wenxian: The Theoretical Proposition of the "Fengqiao Experience" in the New Era, *Law and Social Development*, 2018 (6).
45 Wang Shirong and Zhu Jiping: *The "Fengqiao Experience" of People's Mediation* (Beijing: Law Press, 2018), pp. 23–24.
46 Ibid., p. 36.
47 Zhuji City Judicial Bureau: The City's "Network of Three" Is Meant to Create a New Pattern of Diversified Settlement of Conflicts and Disputes in the New Era. Available at: www.zhuji.gov.cn/art/2018/2/27/art_1382711_15654184.html (accessed January 18, 2019).
48 Tang Weijian: Reflections on the Development of Social Mediation Law, *Legal and Commercial Studies*, 2007 (1).
49 Zhao Xudong: *Disputes and Dispute Resolution Protology: An In-Depth Analysis from Causes to Concepts* (Beijing: Peking University Press, 2009), p. 128.
50 The "Fengqiao Experience" of Zhejiang in the 1960s and the "Ma Xiwu Trial Method" of Yan'an in the 1940s both adhered to the mass route and focused on resolving conflicts and disputes through mediation. The former was approved by two generations of Party and State leaders, Mao Zedong and Xi Jinping, and the latter was highly appreciated by Comrade Mao Zedong. Both are far-reaching socialist legal traditions created by the Communist Party, and both are models of social governance with Chinese characteristics. The "Fengqiao Experience" is also being innovated and upgraded in the new era. See Chen Hongguo, The "Fengqiao Experience" and the Rule of Law Generation Model with Chinese Characteristics, *Legal Science*, 2009 (1).
51 Song Ming: The Modern Positioning of People's Mediation: The "Third Domain" in the Dispute Resolution Mechanism, *Legal System and Social Development*, 2008 (2).
52 Fan Yu: People's Mediation in a Transitional Society: The Experience of Reforming People's Mediation Organizations in Changning District, Shanghai as a Pilot, *China Justice*, 2004 (10).
53 Xiong Hao: On the Transformation of the Legal Regulation Model of Mediation in China, *Legal and Commercial Studies*, 2018 (3).
54 Liao Yong'an and Jiang Fengming: New Ideas F=for Developing Social Mediation in China in the New Era, *China Social Science Journal*, January 18, 2018, p. 1.

References

Chen Ruilai and Xiao Buwen: A Political Analysis of the Qing Dynasty Government-Approved Mediation System: An Examination of the "Huang Yan Litigation File," *Journal of Guangdong Education College*, 2009 (2): 83–87.

Fan Yu, Shi Changqing, and Qiu Xingmei: *The Mediation System and the Code of Conduct for Mediators*, Beijing: Tsinghua University Press, 2007.

Fan Yu: People's Mediation in a Transitional Society: The Experience of Reforming People's Mediation Organizations in Changning District, Shanghai as a Pilot, *China Justice*, 2004 (10): 55–62.

Fan Yu: *The Theory and Practice of Dispute Resolution*, Beijing: Tsinghua University Press, 2007.

Fan Yu: Review of the People's Mediation Law of the People's Republic of China, *The Jurist*, 2011 (2): 1–12+176.

Fei Xiaotong: *Vernacular China*, Beijing: People's Publishing House, 2008.

Han Yanlong: Thirty Years of People's Mediation in China, *Studies in Law*, 1981 (2): 44–50.

He Yongjun: Rural Social Transitions and Changes in the People's Mediation System, *Legal System and Social Development*, 2013 (1): 76–90.

Hong Dongying: *A Study on the Changes of the Mediation System in Contemporary China*, Shanghai: Shanghai People's Publishing House, 2011.

Hou Xinyi: *From Justice for the People to the People's Justice*, Beijing: China University of Political Science and Law Press, 2007.

Hou Yuanzhen and Liao Yongan: On the Changes of the Chinese People's Mediation System: The View of Dispute Resolution, Mediation Organization and Mediation Function, *Journal of Shihezi University (Philosophy and Social Sciences Edition)*, 2016 (2): 44–50.

Hou Yuanzhen: *A Study of the People's Mediation System in the Period of Social Transition – Focusing on the Administrative Turn of People's Mediation as an Analysis*, Xiangtan: Xiangtan University Press, 2016.

Hu Xusheng and Xia Xinhua: A Study of the Chinese Mediation Tradition: A Cultural Perspective, Journal of the Henan Provincial Academy of Political and Legal Administration, 2000 (4): 22–35.

Huang Zongzhi: *Society and Culture in the Qing Dynasty: The Expression and Practice of Civil Law*, Shanghai: Shanghai Bookstore Press, 2001.

Huang Zongzhi: *Past and Present: Explorations in Chinese Civil Legal Practice*, Beijing: Law Press, 2009.

Jiang Wei and Yang Rongxin (Eds.): *An Introduction to People's Mediation*, Beijing: Law Press, 1990.

Lee, Joseph: *The Collected Works of Joseph Lee,* Shenyang: Liaoning Science Press, 1986.

Liao Yong'an and Hou Yuanzhen: The Relevance of Developing Social Mediation, Guangming Daily, July 16, 2014, p. 13.

Liao Yong'an and Jiang Fengming: New Ideas for Developing Social Mediation in China in the New Era, China Social Science Journal, January 18, 2018, p. 1.

Liu Junping: On the Reconciliation and Settlement in Traditional Chinese Sentimental Trials, *Journal of Xiangtan University (Philosophy and Social Sciences Edition)*, 2014 (6): 21–25.

Liu Lian et al.: *The Old Book of the Tang Dynasty*, Beijing: China Books, 1975.

Lu Sili: Mao Zedong and Mediation: Politics and Dispute Resolution in Communist China, trans. Xu and ed. Wang Xiaohong, in Qiang Shigong (Ed.): *Mediation, Legal System and Modernity: A Study of China's Mediation System*, Beijing: China Legal Publishing House, 2005, p. 79.

Ma Changshan: The Rule of Law Turn from State Construction to Shared Construction: An Examination Based on the Relationship between Social Organizations and Rule of Law Construction, *Juridical Studies*, 2017 (3): 24–43.

Mao Zedong: *Selected Works of Mao Zedong* (Vol. 1), Beijing: People's Publishing House, 1991.

Peng Furong and Feng Xuezhi: *Rethinking and Reconstructing: A Study of the People's Mediation System*, Beijing, China University of Political Science and Law Press, 2013.

Shen Zhimin: Mediators "Live" in Police Stations to Resolve 60,000 Disputes, Xinjing News, September 13, 2012, p. A38.

Song Ming: The Modern Positioning of People's Mediation: The "Third Domain" in the Dispute Resolution Mechanism, Legal System and Social Development, 2008 (2): 148–155.

Takao, Tanase: *Dispute Resolution and the Trial System*, trans. Wang Yaxin, Beijing: China University of Political Science and Law Press, 2004.

Tang Weijian: Reflections on the Development of Social Mediation Law, *Legal and Commercial Studies*, 2007 (1): 59–64.

Wang Shirong: *Fengqiao Experience: The Practice of Grass-Roots Social Governance*, Beijing: Law Press, 2018.

Wang Shirong and Zhu Jiping: *The "Fengqiao Experience" of People's Mediation*, Beijing: Law Press, 2018.

Wu Aibin: The Chinese Experience of People's Mediation, in Xu Xin (Ed.): *Justice*, Xiamen: Xiamen University Press, 2010, p. 48.

Wu Aibin: Court-Attached People's Mediation and its Operation, *Contemporary Law*, 2012 (2): 19–26.

Xiong Hao: On the Transformation of the Legal Regulation Model of Mediation in China, Legal and Commercial Studies, 2018 (3): 115–125.

Xiong Yihan: The Socialization and Reorganization of People's Mediation – A Case Study of Yang Boshou's Workshop in Shanghai, *Society*, 2006 (6): 95–116+ 210–211.

Xu Xin: Towards Socially Autonomous People's Mediation, Learning and Exploration, 2012 (1): 87–89.

Zeng Lingjian: The Changing Meaning of Government-Promoted People's Mediation (1931–2010), Xiamen University Law Review, 2016 (1): 1–16.

Zeng Xianyi: A Study of Some Issues Concerning the Traditional Chinese Mediation System, Chinese Jurisprudence, 2009 (4): 36–46.

Zhang Wenxian: The Theoretical Proposition of the "Fengqiao Experience" in the New Era, Law and Social Development, 2018 (6): 2.

Zhang Xibo and Han Yanlong (Eds.): *A History of the Chinese Revolutionary Legal System*, Beijing: China Social Science Press, 1987.

Zhang Yanying: *The Analects of Confucius*, Beijing: China Bookstore, 2007.

Zhao Xudong: *Disputes and Dispute Resolution Protology: An In-Depth Analysis from Causes to Concepts*, Beijing: Peking University Press, 2009.

Zhuji City Judicial Bureau: The City's "Network of Three" Is Meant to Create a New Pattern of Diversified Settlement of Conflicts and Disputes in the New

Era. Available at: www.zhuji.gov.cn/art/2018/2/27/art_1382711_15654184.html (accessed January 18, 2019).

Zhuji Municipal Bureau of Justice: The "Four-In-One" Working Method of the Municipal Bureau of Justice to Create a New Pattern of Diversified Conflict Resolution in the New Era. Available at: www.zhuji.gov.cn/art/2018/12/28/art_1382711_28618687.html (accessed January 18, 2019).

2 The Rise, Fall, and Reform of Court Mediation

Court mediation is a concept prone to ambiguity in the Chinese jurisprudential context, with related expressions such as "judicial mediation" and "litigation mediation." In order to avoid confusion between court mediation and the Western out-of-court settlement system, some scholars also use the term "tribunal mediation."[1] In many cases, these three concepts are often used interchangeably in a narrow sense, referring specifically to the court's mediation activities during a case to facilitate the parties to reach a mediation agreement and thereby resolve the dispute. In a broader sense, the scope of court mediation is broader than litigation mediation or judicial mediation, and includes both mediation within and outside litigation proceedings; it includes both mediation activities conducted by the court as the subject of mediation and various forms of mediation facilitated by the court as a participating body. This chapter uses the concept of "court mediation" in a broad sense, and court mediation is an extremely important part of the "map" of mediation in China. The mixture of court mediation and court trials has become both an enduringly controversial part of the modernization of China's civil judicial process and the most characteristic part of socialist justice. Court mediation itself is in the process of being adapted in the context of a pluralistic dispute resolution mechanism. This chapter attempts to explore where court mediation should be in China. Where exactly did court mediation come from? What changes are taking place? And where should it go in the future? Should court mediation be abolished in China? The answers to these questions are as much about the modernization of China's civil procedure as they are about the process making China's mediation system scientific.

2.1 The Historical Genealogy of Court Mediation: From Folklore to Statehood

It is well known that civil disputes were more often settled through mediation than litigation in ancient China. The expression and practice of the mediation system were heavily influenced by Confucian moral ideals and suited the needs of a society of acquaintance under the conditions of a traditional smallholder economy. Before the birth of the modern court, the ancient government also used mediation to settle "minor matters," using morality to educate the people. The Japanese scholar Shiga Hidesan argues that the ancient Chinese civil trial was essentially a "parental litigation," in contrast to the Western "competitive litigation," and that the ancient Chinese civil trial was essentially an "oratorical mediation" rather than a verdict.[2] However, with the excavation and use of judicial archives, these traditional views have been challenged. The American scholar Huang Zongzhi argues that the practice of litigation in the Qing Dynasty shows that the ancient government rarely mediated in the hearing of lawsuits, but mostly ruled according to the law, and that there was a "third sphere" of government-public interaction and government-approved civil mediation between official trials and civil mediation. Professor Huang uses the concept of "civil mediation trials" to express this interactive relationship.[3] Chinese scholar Zhang Qin argues that mediation and adjudication played an equally important part in the way disputes were handled in the Qing Dynasty.[4] The debate between Shiga Hidesan's "mediation" and Huang Zongzhi's "trial" shows that in ancient Chinese civil judicial practice "mediation" and "trial" went hand in hand, and that the convergence of the two in practice was much greater than the differences in expression. In the face of the conflict between a low degree of grass-roots permeable power and a high degree of autocratic power, dispute resolution in the Qing Dynasty adhered to the concept of "simple governance," and mediation was mainly civilized, i.e., civil mediation conducted by clans, neighbors, middlemen, and village guardians, and semi-civilized government-approved civil mediation. When these methods did not work, the government mainly ruled according to the law, although a small amount of government mediation was not excluded.[5]

During the Republican period, after the initial establishment of a unified national regime, the Kuomintang set up special modern courts to strengthen the judicial system, following the example of the Western countries. At the same time, the Kuomintang government retained the ancient tradition of mediation, setting up a "Civil Mediation Division" in the courts to mediate civil cases that came before them and enacting a special *Civil Mediation Law* to "put an end to disputes and reduce litigation."[6] The organized, institutionalized, and bureaucratic construction of the mediation system during the Republican period signified the strengthening of the modern state's involvement in dispute resolution, but due to the frequent wars and political instability during the Republican period, the National Government's attempt to strengthen the penetration and control of state power over grass-roots society through the regulation of the mediation system did not materialize. Practice has shown that mediation by the courts of the Republic of China has had little effect, while civil mediation has operated more effectively.[7] Despite this, it is easy to see from the establishment of the Litigation Settlement Council, the District, Village, Township and Square Mediation Committee, and the Civil Mediation

Service of the courts that mediation has become increasingly nationalized during the establishment of the modern nation-state.

What the Kuomintang government failed to achieve was achieved by the Communists. In the border areas of Shaanxi, Gansu, and Ningxia, outside the control of the KMT sphere of influence, the Communists took a popular route to justice that was closer to the grass-roots than the Western-style justice system transplanted by the Nationalist government. Court mediation, which combined the tradition of mediation in rural communities with court trials, became a new practice[8] created by the Communist Party and was eventually symbolized as the "Ma Xiwu trial style," characterized by in-depth investigation by judges, reliance on the masses, the combination of trial and mediation, and the simplicity of the proceedings.[9] In the social context of the time, divorce disputes became the predominant form of dispute and formed the most significant arena for court mediation. Professor Huang Zongzhi brilliantly analyzes how court mediation was born out of a unique history of divorce practice. In the early days of the revolution, the Communist Party supported the freedom of divorce in order to break up feudal marriages in order to win the support of the peasants, but marriage was a costly affair in the countryside, and support for arbitrary divorce aroused strong resentment among the peasants. The Communist Party eventually tried to find a middle way between radical promises and reality, and the court mediation system, characterized by "reconciliation" through the concept of sentimentality, became a legitimizing tool, with the courts actively mediating in divorce cases rather than simply deciding, thus creating a balanced compromise between ending feudal marriages and easing peasant opposition. It is in this communist revolutionary practice of divorce law that we find the true origins of mediation in contemporary courts.[10] The "Ma Xiwu trial style" and the people's mediation system that developed during this period shaped the new tradition of socialist law after the founding of the People's Republic of China.[11]

At the same time, Hou Xinyi's research shows that the main impetus for the introduction of mediation came from the frontier government rather than from the judicial system itself, and that the frontier government was motivated both by the need to overcome popular dissatisfaction with the "bureaucratic" judicial status quo in order to adapt to the political struggle and by the need to explore a new judicial system. The border government first introduced mediation within the judicial system (1943–the first half of 1944), and only later extended the mediation movement to the private sector and all government departments (late 1944–1945).[12] In this process, with the extension and penetration of state power, informal civil mediation was squeezed, and the "troika" of people's mediation, administrative mediation, and court mediation came together and took the stage in history, with mediation shifting from the initial duality of civil and state to the monolithic dominance of the state. With the changing socio-economic conditions, we will see the ups and downs of the three types of mediation.

2.2 The Rise and Fall of Court Mediation: The Policy Transition of the Mediation-Trial Relationship

After the Communist Party of China established the new nationally unified regime in 1949, court mediation, an important legacy of the revolutionary era, was logically continued. As an important part of comprehensive social governance, the changing status of court mediation in civil trials can be roughly divided into six stages.[13]

> *Phase 1: "Mediation-oriented" (1949–1981).* In 1958, Mao Zedong proposed at the Beidaihe Conference that it was better to settle civil cases in the same way as Ma Qingtian (Ma Xiwu), that is, to investigate and research, to settle mainly through mediation, and to settle on the spot. In 1963, the Supreme People's Court held the First National Conference on Civil Trial Work and formally put forward the 12-character policy of "investigation and research, local resolution and mediation as the mainstay," and pointed out that this was the fundamental working method and style of civil trial work. In 1964, the Supreme People's Court developed this 12-character policy into the 16-character policy of "relying on the masses, investigation and research, local resolution, and mediation as the mainstay." In 1979, the Supreme People's Court formulated the *Provisions on the Procedural System for Hearing Civil Cases in the People's Courts (for Trial Implementation)*, which reaffirmed the 16-character policy.
>
> *Phase 2: "Emphasis on mediation" (1982–1990).* It was established in Article 6 of the first *Civil Procedure Law* promulgated in 1982, which corrected the previous emphasis on "mediation as the mainstay." At the same time, Article 100 stipulated that "mediation must be voluntary and not forced," but mediation still took precedence over judgment.
>
> *Phase 3: "Voluntary and lawful mediation" (1991–2002).* The principle of "emphasis on mediation" was finally replaced by "voluntary and lawful mediation" when the *Civil Procedure Law* was amended in 1991. The background to this change was the reform of China's civil judiciary since 1988, a period in which academics made profound criticisms of the shortcomings of court mediation. The rise of partyist reform measures that strengthen the evidence of the parties, the one-step presence in court, the "sitting of the case" and the reinforcement of judgment, resulted in the increasing marginalization of court mediation.
>
> *Phase 4: "Mediation should be carried out, when possible, adjudication should be made when appropriate, mediation should be combined with adjudication" (2003–2008).* The year 2002 marked a turning point in the reform of the civil trial system. The General Office of the Central Committee of the Communist Party of China and

the General Office of the State Council forwarded the *Opinions of the Supreme People's Court on Further Strengthening People's Mediation in the New Era*, and the Supreme People's Court subsequently issued the *Several Provisions on Hearing Civil Cases on People's Mediation Agreements*, which, although directed at people's mediation, heralded a new revival of court mediation. Article 4 of the *Regulations of the Supreme People's Court on the Trial of Civil Compensation Cases Arising from Misrepresentation in the Securities Market*, which came into effect in January 2003, provides that the people's courts shall "place emphasis on mediation" when hearing such cases. Article 14 of the *Regulations of the Supreme People's Court on the Application of Summary Procedures in Hearing Civil Cases*, which came into force in December 2003, stipulates that the people's courts should "first mediate" when hearing certain types of disputes such as marriage and family, inheritance disputes, and small disputes. In 2004, the Supreme People's Court issued the *Provisions on Several Issues Concerning Civil Mediation in the People's Courts*, which stipulates that courts may mediate in the first, second, and retrial instances, relaxes the requirements on the applicable trial limits for mediation, and provides that courts may invite social forces to participate in mediation. The introduction of this series of judicial interpretations attempts to reverse the declining trend of court mediation in civil trials. In 2005, Xiao Yang, the then President of the Supreme People's Court, made his work report to the National People's Congress, and for the first time, he clearly stated that "mediation should be carried out, when possible, adjudication should be made when appropriate, mediation should be combined with adjudication, and the case should be settled" as a working policy for civil trials, and this 16-character policy was written into the work report of the Supreme People's Court for four consecutive years. In 2007, the Supreme People's Court issued *Several Opinions on Further Bringing into Play the Positive Role of Litigation Mediation in Building a Harmonious Socialist Society*, which clearly proposed that we should obey the overall situation and make full use of litigation mediation to "maximize the harmonious factors and minimize the disharmonious factors," to further reverse the situation of "emphasis on trial over mediation."

Phase 5: "Prioritizing mediation and combining mediation and adjudication" (2009–2013). Since the national leaders put forward the governing philosophy of "building a harmonious socialist society" and the requirement of "three supremacies" in political and legal work, the judiciary had been gradually adapting to this new situation and in 2008, at a national seminar on political and legal work, the principle of "mediation first" was first put forward. The year 2009 was a crucial year for the full recovery of court mediation. In response to the impact of the global financial crisis on the domestic economy and social development, the Supreme People's Court, under the leadership of the Central Committee of Political and Legal Affairs, put forward the concept of "dynamic justice" and promoted the trinity of "people's mediation, administrative mediation, and judicial mediation" and the "judicial-led" "Great Mediation" campaign, emphasizing that judges should not passively sit on the bench to handle cases, but should give priority to mediation to resolve disputes and pursue the unification of the political, legal, and social effects of handling cases. In 2009, the Supreme People's Court's work report clearly stated that the "Ma Xiwu trial style" should be inherited and carried forward, and the judges should "attach great importance to the use of mediation to resolve conflicts and disputes," to change the concept of trial and adhere to the principle of "giving priority to mediation and combining mediation and trial." Since then, until 2013, the principle of "giving priority to mediation and combining mediation and trial" had been written into the work report of the Supreme People's Court for five consecutive years. This period saw a mediation boom in the nation's courts, with many local courts putting out satellites of ultra-high mediation rates. The year 2009 was positioned as the "Year of Mediation" by many local courts, with a "Zero Judgment Competition" being launched around the country, giving the courts a picture of a "disappearing trial."[14]

Phase 6: "Legal and voluntary mediation" (2014–the present). The "Great Leap Forward" in the pursuit of "zero verdicts" in mediation made court mediation deviate from the right track, and the blind "mediation rate" numerical assessment indicator deviated from the original intention of the mediation system and undermined the independence of the trial. Officials were clearly aware of this problem and in 2014, the new President of the Supreme People's Court, Zhou Qiang, proposed in his work report to the National People's Congress to "adhere to the principle of legality and voluntariness and regulate judicial mediation" to return to the original judicial law of mediation and trial. In the same year, the Supreme People's Court decided to abolish the assessment and ranking of the higher people's courts across the country, except for some necessary binding indicators such as the completion rate of cases within the trial period, which were retained in accordance with the law, all other assessment indicators set were all used as reference indicators for statistical analysis and as data references for the analysis of the trial operation situation. The mediation dismissal rate, which had been an important part of the court's trial quality, was also no longer a binding indicator, and justice returned to its rational face. In the same year, the Outline of the Fourth Five-Year Reform of the People's Courts proposed to "continue to promote the organic interface and coordination between dispute resolution mechanisms such as mediation, arbitration, administrative adjudication and administrative reconsideration and litigation, and to guide the parties to choose the appropriate dispute resolution method." The *Decision of the Central Committee of the Communist Party of China on Several Major Issues in Comprehensively Promoting the Rule of Law*, adopted at the Fourth Plenary Session of the 18th Central Committee of the Communist Party of China, clearly proposed that "a diversified dispute resolution mechanism with organic articulation and coordination among mediation, arbitration, administrative adjudication, administrative reconsideration and litigation should be improved." In a series of official documents of the Supreme People's Court since then, the expression "mediation takes precedence" no longer appears, but attempts to build a systematic and scientific system of diversified dispute resolution are made. In 2016, the Supreme People's Court, in order to further implement the decision and deployment of the Central Government, issued the *Opinions on the People's Courts' Further Deepening of the Reform of the Diversified Dispute Resolution Mechanism*, and proposed for the first time:

Promoting the appropriate separation of mediation and adjudication, establishing a mechanism for the appropriate separation of mediation and adjudication of cases in terms of personnel and procedures, with judges engaged in mediation at the filing stage in principle not participating in the adjudication of the same case, and that judges engaged in adjudication may mediate in cases where the parties still have a desire to mediate in the course of the case.

Looking back at the six stages that court mediation has gone through from 1949 to the present, mediation and trial have presented different contrasting power relationships in the political, social, and economic contexts of different historical periods, and the status of court mediation in civil trials has gone through a course of negation, and this orientation of judicial policy is also reflected in the court mediation rates over the years (see Table 2.1).

Among the ways of closing cases in court, withdrawal is a relatively special event. Dismissals may be the result of court-organized mediation or the result of a unilateral expression of intent on the part of the plaintiff. As the proportion of such cases is relatively small (in 2016, the withdrawal rate was 22.9 percent in the first trial, 12 percent in the second trial and 3.7 percent in the retrial) and until 2015, the *Interpretation of the Supreme People's Court on the Application of the Civil Procedure Law of the People's Republic of China* provided that, except for the plaintiff's withdrawal in the second trial and retrial, which cannot be repeated, the party can still sue again after withdrawing the first trial. Therefore, it is impossible to accurately determine whether the plaintiff's withdrawal was based on court mediation, but the rate

Table 2.1 The change in China's court mediation rate (1980–2016)

Year	First instance mediation rate (%)	Mediation rate at second instance (%)	Retrial mediation rate (%)
1980	69.1	–	–
1981	68.9	–	–
1982	68.2	–	–
1983	71.9	–	–
1984	72.9	–	–
1985	75.3	17.4	–
1986	74.8	16.3	–
1897	73	15.2	–
1988	73.8	–	–
1989	71.3	–	–
1990	65.7	–	–
1991	59.6	–	–
1992	62.4	12.1	4.8
1993	59.8	12.2	5.9
1994	58.8	11.8	5.2
1995	57	11.6	7.4
1996	53.9	10.7	5.3
1997	50.5	9.7	4.9
1998	45	8.5	4.8
1999	42.1	7.9	5.1
2000	37.7	7.8	4.8
2001	35.1	7.5	5
2002	30.3	7.3	7
2003	29.9	7.6	7.2
2004	31	8	8.2
2005	32.1	8.5	9.6
2006	32.5	9.4	10.7
2007	33.4	10.9	12.9
2008	35.2	12.4	12.5
2009	36.2	15	12.7
2010	38.8	15.9	14.4
2011	40.6	13	14
2012	41.7	13	13.9
2013	37.9	11.9	11.7
2014	33.3	9.8	9.8
2015	28.7	7.3	8.6
2016	25.9	6.6	8.6

Source: *China Law Yearbook, Bulletin of the Supreme People's Court.*

of retrial withdrawal is most indicative of whether the withdrawal may have been based on court mediation, but such cases are rare.

After more than 60 years of history, from the 1950s and 1960s when almost all civil cases were settled by mediation, to the 1980s and 1990s when more than 80 percent of civil cases were settled by mediation, to around 2002 when the mediation rate dropped to 34 percent, to 2009 when the mediation rate returned to 60 percent during the period known as the "renaissance of mediation," to 2016 when the first instance civil mediation rate was only 25.9 percent, and the total mediation rate for first, second, and retrial trials was only 40.8 percent, it indicates that mediation no longer occupies a dominant position in civil trials. Meanwhile, in terms of types of disputes, in 2016, the mediation rate at first instance for matrimonial and family inheritance disputes (38.5 percent) > disputes over rights infringement and other disputes (25.3 percent) > contractual disputes (22.8 percent), but none of them exceeded 50 percent. This long period of observation provides us with temporal and spatial data for distilling the basic structure of civil trials in China.

2.3 The Realistic Movement of the "Ideal Type" of Civil Trial Structure: Between Mediation and Adjudication

How does one view the ups and downs in the fortunes of court mediation that have befallen it in different historical periods? Why have mediation and adjudication been combined in Chinese civil judicial practice? What are the difficulties faced by the combination of mediation and adjudication? How should we view the "moderate separation of mediation and adjudication" in the context of the return of mediation to judicial rationality? Does the combination of mediation and adjudication inevitably mean that mediation is strengthened and adjudication is weakened? Does the way out of the dilemma necessarily mean the complete separation of mediation and adjudication? These questions are directly related to the direction of the modernization of Chinese civil justice.

In order to provide a clearer picture of the procedural features of dispute resolution and to provide a comprehensive explanation of the relationship between mediation and trial in the courts over a period of more than 60 years, it is necessary to introduce a basic "structural model of the civil trial" as a theoretical presupposition. Wang Yaxin was the first to examine the relationship between mediation and adjudication from this perspective and although he focuses on the "relationship between mediation and adjudication" between the second and third stages, the two theoretical models he proposes for Chinese civil trials have been influential in Chinese civil litigation jurisprudence and still have strong explanatory power to analyze the relationship between mediation and adjudication. Wang Yaxin abstracts the procedural structure of civil trials in China into "judgment-based" and a "mediation-based" model. In the "mediation" model, the primary objective of the judge's trial is to bring the case to an end by obtaining the parties' agreement, and therefore mediation is the primary means of dispute resolution, and the judge has a duty to proactively mediate, and only if, after repeated and patient mediation, agreement cannot be obtained does judgment become the last resort. In the "adjudicative" model, the immediate objective of the judge's trial is to reach a decision, so that adjudication is the main form of dispute resolution in the proceedings, and obtaining consent is not a duty that the judge must fulfill. Mediation is only a procedural right of the parties and the judge is not required to be proactive, but is in a passive position to respond to the parties' request. There are clear differences between the two models: the principle of legitimacy in the "adjudicative" model is that the burden of proof is shifted to the parties, who present evidence in opposition to the judge in order to obtain a decision in their favor, and that the decision is the result of the parties' own responsibility. The process of litigation focuses on safeguarding the legitimacy of the judgment through irreversible and programmatic due process. In the "mediation" model, the principle of due process lies in the active authority of the judge to investigate and educate and persuade the parties, who form the correct solution and persuade them to accept it, with the litigation process being carried out in a more flexible and informal manner by the judge, depending on the circumstances. Wang Yaxin reminds us that both models have their own advantages and disadvantages, and there is no difference between the lower and higher levels. Both are historically adapted approaches to the practice of dispute resolution in different social conditions and cultural contexts, and both are theoretical tools formed by the abstraction of the procedural elements and conditions of the real litigation process. The trial is often a mixture of two models of compromise, and the transition between the two models is only relative, rather than a total exclusion of one or the other. In fact, there is a trend toward self-correction and partial importation of "mediation" procedural elements in the Western "adjudicative" procedural structure.[15]

Xu Yun, on the other hand, takes the link between the phenomenon of "informal sessions" in judicial practice and the Ma Xiwu trial style as a starting point, and proposes a theoretical model of "Ma Xiwu trial style + formal sessions" through an empirical study of the structure of civil trials in China from the first to the fourth stage. The Ma Xiwu trial style represents one pole of the civil trial structure that emphasizes substantive justice, non-proceduralism, focus on mediation, people's satisfaction and the mass line, while the formal court session represents the other pole of the civil trial structure that emphasizes procedural justice, focus on judgment, negative neutrality of judges, and regulation of courtroom operation, and there are structural conflicts and tensions between the two. At the same time, Xu Yun links the changes in the structure of civil trials to changes in national political and legal policies, arguing that the "political + legal" model of the political and judicial system constitutes a higher-level context for changes in the structure of civil trials. Whether the structure of civil trials moves to the pole of the Ma Xiwu trial style or to the pole of formal court sessions depends on the political and legal changes in the judicial system, while the direct cause of the political and legal changes is the political decisions of the Party and the State, and the deeper cause is the resolution of the conflicts and problems in the process of social transformation; therefore, the external cause of the change in the relationship between mediation and judgment lies in social transformation.[16]

Wang Yaxin's "mediation + judgment" model and Xu Yun's "Ma Xiwu trial style + formal court session" model are similar in that they both distinguish between mediation and judgment by the process of procedure. The difference is that Wang Yaxin named his model after a process-oriented outcome, while Xu Yun named his model after the operation of the process itself. In contrast, Wang Yaxin's model is more abstract and universal, while Xu Yun's model is more concrete and local, and it might even be said that the latter is a concrete rendition of the former, which is less clear, concise, and extensive in its interpretation and application. Both Wang Yaxin and Xu Yun have conceptualized the "Ideal Type" from the practical experience of specific civil trials, and this awareness of the problem is essentially derived from the classical framework of the German sociologist Max Weber on the "ideal type" of Western law, with the modern Western civil trial structure as a reference.

From the perspective of the structural model of the civil trial, the changing status of court mediation in civil judicial practice has been influenced by social transformation and institutional change. In particular, the most significant impact on Ma Xiwu's approach to trial was the reform of the civil trial system that emerged in the 1980s and continued until 2002, when the reform of the civil litigation system shifted from the previous supra-authoritarianism to clientelism, and from an emphasis on "field investigation" to "sitting in on cases." "The emphasis on the parties' burden of proof and the adjustment of the interrelationship between mediation and judgment became important elements of the reform."[17] The space for mediation in the courtroom was drastically shrunk, and the civil trial process was transformed from "mediation-based" to "trial-based,"[18] and the weakening of court mediation and the strengthening of legal judgment became important features of theoretical research in civil litigation during this period. During the period 1991–2002, court mediation suffered an unprecedented low point.

It is worth noting that the decade of accelerated reform of the civil trial method was the decade of judicial specialization reform of the Supreme People's Court (1998–2008). Although the reform of the civil judiciary has encountered a number of litigation-related petition problems during the transition period since 2002, and in 2008, the Supreme People's Court also put forward the 16-character policy of "mediation should be carried out when possible, judgment should be made when appropriate, mediation should be combined with judgment, and the case should be settled," the professionalization and specialization of the judiciary have led to judges basically embracing the modern concept of the rule of law and developing a basic sense of procedure, returning to a judgment-based approach in the adjudication of cases and de-emphasizing the centrality of mediation. From 2008 to 2013, the judicial reform policy of the Supreme People's Court shifted toward "dynamic justice" and "Grand Mediation," from emphasizing court hearings and sitting on cases in the past to emphasizing the use of mediation as a means of resolving conflicts and disputes. An inescapable background to this turn is that, with the dramatic transformation of society, the division of interests, the upsurge in disputes, the prominence of conflicts involving lawsuits and petitions, and the decline in judicial credibility, court mediation had enjoyed a resurgence in a situation where stability had to prevail. In 2009, against the backdrop of the global financial crisis, the Supreme People's Court clearly put forward the dynamic judicial concept of "giving priority to mediation and combining mediation and adjudication," and mediation once again gained the status of being "equal" or even given priority to adjudication.

The revival of court mediation in this period has given rise to a new wave of research in the academic world. The denial theory is represented by Zhang Weiping and Zhou Yongkun. Zhang Weiping believes that this revival of mediation is essentially a return to the Ma Xiwu trial style, and that a single-minded emphasis on the results of mediation will inevitably obscure this concrete role of adjudication and dilute people's awareness of the norms of behavior, and the function of the court as a judicial organ will inevitably be gradually mutated and alienated into a non-judicial organ.[19] Zhou Yongkun argues that mediation is the dominant dispute resolution system in under-developed societies and that the authority of judgment is the hallmark of a society governed by the rule of law, while the developed mediation system in the East is part of a society governed by the rule of man and is therefore not an advanced culture, but rather an important institutional reason why the East lags behind the West. The popularity of mediation in post-1949 China was the result of China's society of the rule of man, and the short-term strength of adjudication after the reform and opening-up was a product of the social impulse to rule of law. Compulsory mediation constitutes an undermining of the fundamental values of the rule of law. Therefore, since China has chosen the path of the rule of law, we have no choice but to opt for a judgment-driven dispute resolution system.[20]

The relatively moderate critical view is that the revival of court mediation is, on the surface, a passive submission of the courts to the demands of a "harmonious society," but in the context of social transformation, it cannot be ruled out that the courts have taken the initiative to put forward the slogan of "harmonious justice" in order to benefit from the new redistribution of resources, power, and legitimacy. While the critics are relatively objective in their view that the significance of such a policy for the "closure of cases" or the social effects of justice cannot be denied, overall, they still hold a negative view. They argue that such a policy blurs judicial boundaries and leads to a convergence between courts and social-type mediation institutions, and that this one-sided pursuit of mediation is inconsistent with the intentions of policy-makers, and that the root cause of this phenomenon lies in the coupling of justice and mediation and the failure to separate mediation and trial in the litigation system.[21]

Professor Wu Yingzhi, who holds a "sympathetic understanding," starts with an analysis of the reasons behind the revival of court mediation, which justifies the existence of court mediation in contemporary China, including the unsatisfactory effectiveness of social dispute resolution mechanisms such as people's mediation, the low capacity of society to dissipate disputes on its own, and the intertwining of real and non-real social conflicts during the transition period. She pointed out that court mediation has not escaped the fate of becoming a tool of social governance, and that court mediation still carries a specific political mission and social function. The rationality of court mediation is also demonstrated by the fact that it has a significance that cannot be replaced by judgments in terms of the complete settlement of disputes and the maintenance of harmony in social relations between the parties, and that, in a sense, court mediation also plays a role in bridging law and society and helping law and justice to gain legitimacy. In response to the current shortcomings of court mediation, she believes that the system should be improved as far as possible through the design to limit its "negative function" and play on its "positive function." A mechanism should be constructed to constrain the power of litigation to the power of trial and to enhance the institutionalization of court mediation, because the improvement of the system not only can better play the role of the mediation system and realize its social function, but also can promote the modernization of China's judicial system.[22] At the same time, however, Wu Yingzhi, after a practical investigation of one court, argues that the judicial structure under the "mediation first" policy is characterized by a "mediation-judgment" dichotomy, with inherent tensions and fluidity and room for rent-seeking. In addition, the mediation priority policy lacks the support of external resources, and the pre-litigation diversion is not effective; while the two-way push type of reform is not as effective as it could be due to the tendency to go to extremes and to be detached from the needs of society. Therefore, legislation is needed to further clarify the meaning of the first mediation rules, as well as to supplement and safeguard the parties' right to procedural objections.[23]

While most scholars have been critical and negative about the revival of court mediation around 2008, some have taken a positive view. Professor Fan Yu criticized the jurisprudence for questioning the legitimacy of mediation from principles and logical reasoning rather than from empirical experience:

> Faced with the revival of mediation, some jurists have habitually questioned the legitimacy of mediation based on some traditional theories or universal values, asserting that mediation is a system of less-developed societies or a product of the rule of man and planned economy, placing mediation and trials, judicial mediation and civil mediation in absolute opposition to each other, presuming that the courts encourage mediation solely out of self-interest and inevitably lead to coercion of the parties. These judgments are almost completely at odds with the actual effects of court mediation and the true reflections of the parties, showing a lack of understanding by scholars of judicial practice, trial experience, and the development of the doctrine itself.

Starting from the identification of the relationship between trial experience and jurisprudence, she argues that judicial practice should not be bound by traditional rule of law principles, and that contemporary society's recognition of the legitimacy of mediation has in fact transcended and sublimated traditional rule of law principles, especially by moving away from state-centric and litigious fetishism. The judicial policy of "giving priority to mediation and combining mediation and adjudication" is a choice made by the judiciary in response to the current system and judicial environment in China, and in response to the need for social disputes and solutions.[24] According to Fan Yu, the judicial policy of "giving priority to mediation" does not mean that "mediation is everything," but that it is meant to further promote the role of mediation in civil litigation and to adapt to social needs by introducing a consultative element in the criminal and administrative fields. In civil litigation, the "priority of mediation" is in line with the principle of private law autonomy, i.e., the dispositive rights of the parties take precedence over consideration of the public interest. Except for cases expressly prohibited or restricted by law, mediation and consultation and conciliation are the rights of the parties and the duties and responsibilities of the judge, and generally cannot be denied or restricted because of considerations of public interest. The basic principles of China's civil procedure law, institutional constraints, the combination of the parties' right to dispose and the court's authority, and the corresponding relief mechanisms can ensure the legitimacy and effectiveness of mediation.[25]

2.4 Reconfiguration of Court Mediation: Integration or Separation of Mediation and Trial

Although the majority of scholars in the legal profession agree that mediation as a form of dispute resolution is reasonable and justified, they also reject the rationality of the priority of mediation in the courts, as they are concerned that the integration of mediation may lead to violation of the rules of law and infringement of the principle of voluntariness, especially under the unreasonable assessment index of the mediation rate, which may lead to the compulsory mediation of "pressing mediation by judgment" and the one-sided pursuit of "zero judgment" which will erode the principle of rule of law.

Since 1991, court mediation has been marginalized. It was against this background that some scholars began to question the legitimacy of court mediation, which was "united with the trial," arguing that it was inappropriate to provide for mediation and judgment as different ways of exercising the people's court's power to adjudicate in civil proceedings, and that the process of mediation should be separated from the process of trial, and the court mediation should be separated from the civil litigation. The most representative scholar who advocates the separation of mediation and trial is Li Hao. He argued from the different nature of trial and mediation, and proposed that "mediation should return to mediation and trial to trial." In his view, there are at least 12 differences in the nature of mediation and adjudication: compulsory versus voluntary, fact-finding versus not necessarily fact-finding, based on the law versus not contrary to the law, strict adherence to procedure versus no strict requirement for procedure, obtaining a judgment versus reaching a consensus, declaring the rules versus resolving the dispute, limiting oneself to the facts of the claim versus being flexible about the facts of the claim, public versus private, facing the past versus facing the future, setting the record straight versus settling the disputes, and fixed versus varied methods. He believes that the separation of mediation and trial is conducive to: (1) effective implementation of the principle of voluntariness; (2) implementation of the principle of confidentiality; (3) maintenance of judicial impartiality; (4) maintenance of judicial authority; (5) clarification of the relationship between mediation and trial; (6) regulation of the proper exercise of judicial power; and (7) elimination of criticism of the weak protection of civil rights.[26] The disadvantages of unifying mediation and trial are: (1) that the aforementioned fundamental differences in the nature of the two cause tension and conflict in their relationship in civil proceedings, i.e. the unification of mediation and trial brings about structural conflicts in civil trials. The current state of court mediation not only breaks with the legislator's expectations when setting up the mediation system, but also leads to the mutation of the litigation system, softening the constraints of both substantive and procedural law on trial activities, and making the operation of Chinese civil litigation deviate significantly from the intended goals of the civil litigation system. (2) Because of the differences in procedural principles between mediation and trial, mediation in civil trials should be proceduralized separately and not mixed with judges' trial proceedings in order to avoid the rigidity of full legalization.[27] Based on this, Professor Li Hao distinctly proposed that "mediation should not be used as a mode of action of civil judicial power," but should transform and reset the operation of civil judicial power in accordance with the concept of trial by law, separating mediation from the trial process and making it an independent system of dispute resolution different from the trial. However, it is possible to establish a system of settlement in litigation based on the essential objective of settling disputes by mutual consent.[28] Professor Li Hao's views are shared by most scholars in the academy. According to Professor Hao Zhenjiang, the unification of mediation and trial will cause an inherent conflict between mediation and trial procedures, which seriously restricts the modernization of mediation and trial procedures and affects the performance of the multiple functions of the trial. However, he differs slightly from Professor Li Hao on the specific scheme of separation of mediation and trial, suggesting that the current path of separation of mediation and trial procedures in China is mainly the construction of certain special principles and systems of mediation procedures, and does not address the homogeneity of mediation procedures and trial procedures. He argues that the idea of the removal of litigation of mediation in Japan should be borrowed, and that attempts should be made to transform the adversarial structure of the mediation process, so that it is built on a non-adversarial structure, and to focus on the self-sufficiency and systemic nature of the process, in order to form an independent court mediation process, so that the process is not only "separate" but "discrete."[29]

At the same time, some judges have also reflected on some of the problems that have arisen in the reform of the separation of mediation and trial by examining the practice of exploring and piloting the "moderate separation of mediation and trial." Through his examination of the practice of the Nanjing courts, Judge Wang Yaming found that there were four models of moderate separation of mediation and trial conducted by the Nanjing courts at two levels: the first model is the separation of mediation and trial at the filing stage. The second model is the separation of mediation and adjudication at the pre-trial stage, whereby the trial court judges are divided into a mediation team and an adjudication team, and the case is first mediated by the mediation team judges, and then transferred to the adjudication team judges if mediation fails. The third model is the separation of mediation and trial in the pre-trial stage, i.e., the judges are divided into mediation and adjudication teams in the operational division, and the mediation team is assigned to the court division to be responsible for all mediation work before the trial, and if mediation fails, then the judges are transferred to the adjudication team. The judges of the mediation team are in principle not involved in the handling of cases, while the judges of the adjudication team are responsible for mediation in-court and afterwards, and if conciliation fails, judgment is then handed down according to the law. The fourth model is the separation of the whole process of mediation and trial, i.e., the division of judges into mediation and adjudication teams within the operational division. The judges of the mediation team are responsible for the preparatory work before the trial and assume all mediation duties before the conclusion of the case, i.e., they follow the case through mediation before the judges of the adjudication team decide, while the judges of the adjudication team are only responsible for deciding and in principle do not participate in mediation. The judges of the city's grassroots courts generally agree with the first model, namely, the separation of mediation and trial at the filing stage, specifically, pre-litigation mediation by the litigation service center set up in the filing division, and timely transfer to trial (both mediation and adjudication) if mediation fails. The latter three models of mediation and trial separation are unpopular because they suffer from the following four deficiencies: (1) they are not in line with the laws of trial, because whether a case can be mediated needs to be determined after a trial, and it is difficult to operate an artificial division between mediation and adjudication groups for case separation. (2) Separating mediation from trial within the trial chamber would waste trial resources, as it would result in duplication of effort and exacerbate the situation of too many cases. (3) Repetition of labor is against the subjective wishes of the parties. (4) The distinction between mediation and adjudication groups within the trial division is not conducive to the improvement of the judges' professional competence.[30]

The opposite of the separation theory is the integration theory, which is represented by the scholars Fan Yu and Tian Pingan. Starting from an analysis of foreign practice, Fan Yu points out that judicial practice and trial experience in both the East and the West have challenged the principle of "separation of mediation and trial," and that the taboo of "separation of mediation and trial" has been loosened in common law countries, while civil law countries have largely broken this taboo. The typical conciliatory element in civil law systems is the role of the judge in facilitating the settlement. The activity of facilitating a settlement occurs in the trial court and the judge responsible for the settlement is the same judge who later hears the case. She argues that a purely theoretical level of institutional construction is not conducive to a solution, and that

> the ability of trial judges to conduct litigation mediation and play a proactive role does not depend on the rationale, but rather on the type of case, its complexity, the needs of the parties, the mode of litigation and other specific factors, on the premise of which mediation is established pre-litigation, pre-trial and throughout the litigation process, respectively.[31]

Professor Tian Pingan believes that, although "separation of mediation and trial theory" is intended to overcome the disadvantages of a unified system of civil mediation and trial, such as the use of judgment to suppress investigation, to achieve the value of litigation justice, and to take the ideal picture of litigation mediation back to the rule of law, the previous experience of the "Economic Dispute Mediation Center" and the "reform" attempt of "moderate separation of mediation and trial" have negated the feasibility of separation of mediation and trial from a practical level. At the theoretical level, the contradictory nature of the theory of the separation of mediation and trial, the ambiguity of the concept and the misjudgment of the laws of mediation, as well as the unrealistic choice of the path of "reform" at the practical level, have led to the ideal being celebrated as a utopia. Thus, the doctrine of the separation of mediation and trial suffers from a double backlash of lack of theoretical self-sufficiency and falsification of practical feasibility. In the face of mediation chaos, such as misalignment of dynamic justice, lack of mediation priority, outrageous mediation targets, and intensified dependence on mediation, the "reform" idea of separating mediation and trial is undoubtedly not a remedy to suit the case. The solution proposed by Professor Tian Pingan is "three musts" and "three should nots" while adhering to the judicial concept of integration of investigation and trial: First, we must remove the priority in mediation, and let the combination of mediation and judgment return to the basics; Second, we must abandon dependence on mediation and let mediation return to normalcy; Third, we must overcome compulsion of mediation and let mediation return to voluntary and legal. At the same time, mediation and trial should go hand in hand and not be biased; mediation and trial should co-exist and not be replaced; mediation and trial should be united and not separated.[32]

We believe that court mediation is a technique of social governance by the state at the macro level, and at the micro level, it is a form of dispute resolution that combines the exercise of the parties' right of disposition with the exercise of the people's courts' power of adjudication. As a system of dispute resolution with Chinese characteristics inherited from the revolutionary period, this institutional structure is almost unique in courts around the world. Such a judicial system, which has a deep cultural and political foundation, has undergone decades of practical accumulation and is deeply embedded in the judicial practice of the people's courts, becoming an indispensable means of dispute resolution. Nevertheless, we must face up to the drawbacks of court mediation in the "unification of mediation and trial."

First, "unification of mediation and trial" may indeed lead to the hidden emergence of forced mediation phenomena such as "press mediation with judgment" and "forced mediation by procrastination," which seriously infringe on the parties' right to litigation, while "separation of mediation and trial" can avoid the occurrence of this phenomenon. Second, the laws governing the two judicial activities, mediation, and adjudication, are completely different. Mediation aims at forming a consensus, while adjudication aims at discovering the truth; the former seeks cooperation, while the latter seeks confrontation; the former seeks confidentiality, while the latter demands openness; the former requires the mediator to intervene and propose a solution in due course, while the latter requires the judge to maintain a neutral role. The professional requirements of judges are different. The "unification of mediation and trial" will lead to a misalignment in the ethics of judges' roles, especially when mediating judges continue to act as adjudicators after the failure of mediation, which may lead to preconceived perceptions being formed and thus violating the requirements of judicial neutrality. Third, a judge cannot refuse to adjudicate, and when faced with major, difficult, complex, and sensitive cases, the public especially expects judges to be able to determine the ownership of rights and stop disputes through a clear adjudication orientation. However, in a professional environment where judicial job security in China is not yet sound, and Chinese judges are faced with multiple risks such as a system of accountability for wrongful cases, the maintenance of stability through litigation-related petitions, and public opinion hype, mediation has become an excellent means of shifting the risks of adjudication, which allows judges to no longer expend energy on adjudication reasoning, nor do they have to worry about cases being changed on appeal, without being tied to trial limits. Therefore, the "unification of mediation and trial" provides institutional space for judges to avoid the risk of adjudication,[33] and thus tends to lead to the emergence of "muddling along" justice, as exemplified by the second trial of the "Peng Yu case" in Nanjing.

In the face of the shortcomings of "unification of mediation and trial," does it mean that we should abandon court mediation altogether, as most scholars advocate, and choose the German and Japanese "settlement in litigation" of civil litigation as the direction for the modernization of Chinese civil litigation?[34] In this regard, we disagree, because the genealogy of court mediation in China is different from that of the Western system of "settlement in litigation." The former has been embedded in Chinese civil trial practice from the very beginning and has become a way for judges to exercise their judicial power, while the latter was derived from the adversarial litigation system in order to alleviate the procedural rigidity brought about by adversarialism. The former is a product of the culture of judicial concord, while the latter is a product of the culture of judicial athleticism. The former is a product of judicial governance in the tradition of political law, while the latter is a product of judicial autonomy and the protection of the parties' procedural options in the tradition of the rule of law. Therefore, the two should not be identical, let alone directly transplanted and "grafted." If the procedure is designed only for the sake of the rational design of the procedure itself, the abolition of court mediation and the establishment of a separate mediation procedure will inevitably lead to complication and over-consumption of the procedure, which will raise the cost of justice and inconvenience the parties in using the procedure, with the result that it will not be conducive to facilitating dispute resolution. Therefore, we believe that in order to avoid the drawbacks of the "integration of mediation and trial" and to mitigate the inefficiencies and high costs associated with the complete separation of mediation and trial, court mediation in China should take a third path between the "integration of mediation and trial" and the "separation of mediation and trial," that is, the "moderate separation of mediation and trial." Some scholars, in light of the actual judicial situation in China, suggest that mediation should not be used as a basic principle of civil litigation throughout the litigation process, but rather as a system design that the parties can choose to use in civil litigation, without changing the basic structure of the litigation process. Specifically, a limited separation of the mediation pre-procedure could be introduced, moving the mediation process forward to pre-trial, and establishing a "mandatory mediation process" based on the type of case, with the court initiating mediation *ex officio* for specific disputes such as family cases.[35] We agree with this view, because in pre-trial proceedings, the parties have not yet entered into a substantive confrontation and their antagonism may be eased, thus avoiding the procedural tensions associated with the non-adversarial structure of conciliation proceedings and the "adversarial" structure of trial proceedings. At the same time, for marriage and family disputes, adoption disputes, custody disputes, inheritance disputes, upbringing disputes, alimony disputes, disputes for provision for the elderly parents, disputes over residential bases, disputes over neighboring relations and other specific types of cases, to implement pre-litigation mediation pre-procedure has gradually become a new trend in the world of civil litigation and Germany, Japan, and even Taiwan, China have special provisions for this. The specific institutional arrangements for pre-mediation procedures will be developed in detail in the following chapters.

It is worth noting that Article 30 of the *Opinions of the Supreme People's Court on the People's Courts' Further Deepening of the Reform of the Diversified Dispute Resolution Mechanism* proposes that, in principle, judges engaged in mediation at the filing stage will not participate in the adjudication of the same case, and that judges engaged in adjudication may mediate if the parties still have a desire to mediate during the trial of the case. This is in fact a theory of "moderate separation of mediation and trial," opting for a limited separation of the mediating judge from the adjudicating judge. Of course, according to the authoritative interpretation of the authorities, the so-called "moderate" here also contains another layer of meaning, that is, in speedy cases or small litigation cases, because of the simple legal relationship and the small amount of litigation, the strict implementation of the principle of "separation of trial" is not conducive to the rapid resolution of disputes and the principle of saving judicial resources, so unless the parties expressly opposed it, the mediation judge can still participate in the trial of subsequent cases.[36]

If you choose a limited "separation of trial," a consequential problem is, if the parties in the case go into the trial process, that is, in the process of the case still have the desire to mediate, then how to implement the "separation of trial" principle? Of course, at this point, the judge can tell the parties to reconcile themselves, but the judge cannot ignore the parties' need for mediation to resolve their disputes on the grounds that the case has already entered the trial process. In this regard, a realistic and feasible institutional interface is to appoint a full-time mediator to the court to mediate outside the trial proceedings or to be appointed by the court to mediate, and if mediation fails, then to proceed to trial proceedings, and the latter involves the socialization of court mediation.

2.5 New Trends in Court Mediation: Socialization of Court Mediation

The introduction of court-commissioned mediation into the institutional design of "separation of mediation and trial" is a practice being experimented with in Chinese judicial practice, behind which lies the jurisprudential proposition of the socialization of court mediation and even the socialization of justice.

2.5.1 Forms of Socialization of Court Mediation in Practice

At present, in the wave of reform of the diversified dispute resolution mechanism, courts across the country are making innovations in the practice of court mediation. The most important ways are the following: (1) let conflicts and disputes "go out" and entrust or assign other mediation organizations or mediators to mediate; and (2) invite mediation subjects "in" and invite mediation organizations or mediators to the court for mediation. For both types of dispute resolution outcomes, litigation mediation is then eventually dovetailed by way of judicial confirmation:

1. *Court-attached people's mediation.* That is, people's mediation in which a dedicated office is set up within the people's court and a resident people's mediator is assigned to that office by the Bureau of Justice to conduct pre-litigation mediation. For example, in 2003, the Changning District Court in Shanghai set up the country's first professional people's mediation institution, the "People's Mediation Window of the District Joint Mediation Committee," and carried out the exploration of "moderate socialization of litigation mediation under the leadership of judges," pioneering the "people's mediation into the court." Subsequently, the "People's Mediation Window," the "People's Mediation Studio," and the "People's Mediation Workshops for dovetailing litigation and mediation" were set up in courts across the country, and were promoted by the Supreme People's Court.[37] Article 17 of the *Opinions of the Supreme People's Court on the People's Courts' Further Deepening of the Reform of the Diversified Dispute Resolution Mechanism* of June 28, 2016, on the other hand, provides for the admission of qualified individuals such as deputies to the National People's Congress, members of the Chinese People's Political Consultative Conference, people's assessors, experts and scholars, lawyers, arbitrators and retired legal workers as special invited mediators, fully reflecting the socialization of court mediation.
2. The system of assigned and commissioned mediation. On June 28, 2016, the Supreme People's Court issued the *Provisions on Invited Mediation by the Peoples Courts*. Article 1 of the Provisions specifies that "invited mediation" refers to the acceptance of qualified mediation organizations, such as people's mediation, administrative mediation, commercial mediation, and industrial mediation, or individuals as invited mediation organizations or invited mediators, who are appointed by the people's courts before filing a case or entrusted by the people's courts after filing a case to conduct mediation in accordance with the law. Here, there are two forms of mediation: assigned and commissioned. The term "assigned mediation" refers to the screening and triage of civil and commercial disputes brought to the court by judges or other staff of the court's filing division before the registration of the case. For cases suitable for mediation, with the consent of both parties, they can be assigned to an invited mediation organization, an invited mediator, or an organization with mediation functions to mediate first, and if the parties do not agree to mediate, the people's court will then register the case. The term "entrusted mediation" refers to the fact that, after the registration of a dispute or during the trial process, cases suitable for mediation may also be entrusted to an invited mediation organization, an invited mediator, or a full-time court mediator for mediation with the consent of the parties. In the case of mediation agreements reached through assigned or

commissioned mediation, the subject of the mediation will, in accordance with the requirements of the work, explain to the parties in due course that they may apply for judicial confirmation of the mediation agreement. For parties applying for judicial confirmation, the court will review and confirm the application in a timely manner through the litigation and mediation docking platform in accordance with the law, to provide a strong judicial guarantee for the non-litigation mediation work. Some scholars have likened the practice of entrusting mediation to the ancient practice of government-approved civil mediation, arguing that it is in the nature of "litigation mediation" and should ensure the dominance of the courts over entrusted mediation.[38]

3. The system of full-time court mediators. In addition to "inviting in" and "going out," the Supreme People's Court has also attempted to set up special mediators within the courts. Article 18 of the *Opinions of the Supreme People's Court on the People's Courts# Further Deepening of the Reform of the Diversified Dispute Settlement Mechanism* stipulates that the people's courts may have full-time mediators in the litigation service centers and other departments, who are judges or judicial support staff who are good at mediation to engage in mediation guidance and entrusted mediation work after the registration of cases. If a mediation agreement is reached under the auspices of a judge, a mediation letter shall be issued in accordance with the law. If a mediation agreement is reached under the auspices of a judicial support staff, a mediation letter shall be issued in accordance with the law after examination by a judge. This system provides a good institutional interface for the "moderate separation of mediation and trial" and facilitates the smooth operation of court-commissioned mediation.

2.5.2 Jurisprudential Basis for the Socialization of Court Mediation

Huang Zongzhi, a renowned historian, argues from legal history that there is a semi-formal "third sphere" between the state and society in China's dispute resolution system. "In this intermediate stage, the formal system and the informal system have some kind of dialogue and have their established procedures, thus forming a semi-governmental and semi-people dispute processing zone."[39] In the case of "minor matters" (civil disputes), the state generally does not intervene directly. Only when the society and the "third sphere" where the state and society intersect and cannot resolve it, does the state intervene, what he calls the "centralized minimalist governance" model.[40]

Court-commissioned mediation (also including assigned mediation, see the same below) precisely reflects the above-mentioned thinking. The practice of entrusting mediation across the country shows that, after a civil dispute has been brought to court, the parties can be appropriately guided to choose mediation depending on the timing, i.e., before a case is filed, before a trial is held after acceptance, and before a judgment is rendered during the trial.

Specifically, based on respecting the parties' right to choose the procedure, the case is entrusted to a social mediation organization for mediation, and the parties can apply to the court for judicial confirmation of the mediation agreement after the mediation is successful, and if the mediation fails, the case is transferred to litigation proceedings. So, the delegation of disputes that go to court is a minimalist governance strategy adopted by the courts in response to the pressures of a large caseload. First, given the scarcity of justice as a public good provided by the state, delegating cases can save the state's limited resources; Second, it also shows the new idea of polycentric governance. After realizing the limited nature of the state as a single governing force, the judicial-centric dispute resolution mechanism must also be changed. Because the intersection of real and non-real disputes makes it more difficult to deal with cases, the "black-or-white" approach in many cases does not make things easier, and the judiciary (in a narrow sense, trial) faces many limitations due to its "adversarial and adjudicative" litigation structure, and, as American jurisprudence expert, Fowler pointed out when arguing the limits of justice, the judiciary is not good at dealing with "polycentric problems."[41] Once again, minimalist governance makes the self-management capacity of social organizations increasingly prominent in social development, which is conducive to the cultivation of the ability of society to dissipate disputes and practice self-governance, while "inviting in" and "going out" help to bridge the distance between judicial specialization and society, reflecting the spirit of judicial democracy.

Although entrusted mediation has only received attention in judicial practice and attracted academic attention in recent years, as far as the design of the system is concerned, it is provided for in Article 3(2) of the 2004 *Provisions of the Supreme People's Court on Several Issues Concerning Civil Mediation in the People's Courts*, that is, the system whereby the court, with the consent of both parties, entrusts the cases already accepted by the court to relevant units or individuals for mediation, and confirms the mediation agreements reached in accordance with law. At the same time, paragraph 1 of this article also provides for a system of assisted mediation, i.e., the people's courts may invite relevant units and individuals to assist in mediation, thus bringing in social forces to participate in the mediation process.

Some scholars have attributed the rationale for the socialization of court mediation to the social nature of judicial power.[42] We believe that the explanation of the political-philosophical progression of entrusting mediation leaves something to be desired in terms of persuasiveness, as it ignores the key question of whether it is the case or the judicial power that the court entrusts to the society. Some scholars have argued that entrusting mediation to the courts is a delegation of judicial power, and therefore the socialization of court mediation conflicts with the legal principle that "judicial power can only be exercised by the people's courts,"[43] which in effect confuses the power of mediation with judicial power. There are fundamental differences in the structure and power structure of mediation and adjudication, and therefore the adoption of a "separation of mediation and adjudication" is a model that is in line with institutional principles. Since the birth of the state, as its power has grown stronger, public remedies have gradually replaced private remedies, and judicial power has gained an exclusive position in this historical evolution, based in essence on the coercive power of the state and the finality of dispute resolution that it obtains. Therefore, even if we give judicial power a broad understanding so that it includes the power to judge and the power to mediate in litigation, it cannot be considered that the courts are delegating judicial power, but at best they are delegating cases to social forces for mediation. This is because mediation is essentially a process whereby a neutral third party guides the parties to resolve their dispute on their own, thereby reaching a consensus and forming a mediation agreement. The reason why litigation mediation has the same validity as judgment is not because the subject of mediation is a judge and thus gains certainty, but because the mediation agreement reached during the litigation process, which is itself subject to judicial review and confirmation and ultimately consumes the judicial resources of the state, is based on the integration and stability of the legal order, the effectiveness of dispute resolution, and the finality of judicial power, thus giving it *res judicata* power. In other words, the power to adjudicate belongs exclusively to the courts, but the power to mediate disputes has never been monopolized by the courts and mediators are allowed to mediate if they meet certain conditions. Further, in the case of delegated mediation, the outcome of the mediation reached by the social forces is not a fully autonomous and final resolution of the dispute, as the final review and confirmation remain with the court, and judicial power is not delegated throughout the dispute resolution process, but rather the case is entrusted to a social organization that already has the power to mediate the dispute. This has greatly expanded the social resources at the disposal of the courts, extending the reach of the courts' involvement in social governance in terms of breadth and enabling them to focus on more complex and important cases in terms of depth.

Thus, the commissioning of mediation as a form of socialization of court mediation is, in a broader sense, a form of socialization of justice, based not on the "social nature of judicial power" but rather on the extension and development of the state's minimalist governance strategy. In this process, the court does not relinquish control of dispute resolution, as it is up to the court to decide whether to delegate, to whom to delegate, and whether it is appropriate to delegate, depending on the circumstances, and in the process of mediation, the court may give some opinion guidance, and the outcome of the mediation must be confirmed by the court to be enforceable. This suggests that the socialization of mediation in civil proceedings is a strategy of action by the courts in the context of both "stress reduction" and "stability maintenance," with the courts entrusting social forces such as people's mediation to be integrated into the formal "network of power organizations" of the state, becoming part of the overall governance system of the state.[44]

2.5.3 The Limits of Socialization of Court Mediation: A Social Capital Theory Perspective

Whether or not court-commissioned mediation is able to bring about a comparative advantage that judgments do not have, so that the case can be settled, is subject to several conditions. In terms of internal conditions, it depends on whether the dispute is suitable for mediation, and only disputes suitable for litigation mediation have the need to be entrusted to mediation. In terms of external conditions, the effective functioning of commissioned mediation depends on the ability of social forces to resolve disputes. In the case of the latter, we introduce an important sociological concept, namely the level of social capital.

Social capital theory was introduced by French sociologist Pierre Bourdieu and has been developed by scholars such as James Coleman and Robert Putnam, making it an important and inclusive concept in sociology, economics, political science, and management. This chapter focuses on the sociological meaning of social capital, which, according to Putnam, consists of three main components, namely social trust, reciprocal norms, and civic engagement networks.[45] From the perspective of social capital theory, the ability of the entrusted social forces to resolve disputes depends first and foremost on the trust of the parties, because only if the social forces are trusted and recognized by the parties can they constitute a mutually effective communication mechanism between them and provide the legality/legitimacy basis of entrusted mediation. Therefore, from the established practice of entrusted mediation, the organizations or individuals who are entrusted with the task are usually of the following categories (taking the Shanghai Pudong Court as an example): highly respected retired cadres (e.g. retired judges, retired cadres); grass-roots cadres with rich experience in working with the masses (e.g. village committee cadres, street office cadres, NPC deputies, CPPCC members); people or organizations with expertise or skills in a certain area (e.g. consumer associations, industry associations, mediation workshops, lawyers), etc. One thing these people have in common is that they all have a certain authority by virtue of their profession, experience, expertise, etc. and are therefore able to gain the trust of their clients. Second, the social nature of the mediation subject can make up for the professional paranoia of professional judges formed over a long period of time, because the social force entrusted with the mediation is able to deal with the deviation between legal rigidity and social norms in a more flexible manner, using local knowledge such as morals, customs, and local feelings to bridge the gap between the two, and these norms are more in line with the common code of conduct of the region to which the parties belong and are easily accepted. In addition, such norms, which have a natural affinity with mediation, provide an institutional guarantee for the operation of delegated mediation. Finally, in terms of the effective functioning of the whole system of commissioned mediation, it also requires the active and enthusiastic participation of those entrusted with the mediation of disputes, as without the active participation of citizens, commissioned mediation cannot operate smoothly. In the final sense, therefore, the effective operation of commissioned mediation is governed by social capital. If the social capital of a society declines, the original society turns from a "society of acquaintances" to a "society of strangers," as there is a lack of trust between people, and citizens are less enthusiastic about participating in public affairs, so the effectiveness of delegated mediation will be less significant. Only by building a mature civil society and strengthening the bonds and trust between citizens through the construction of a network of civic participation can the social foundation for entrusted mediation be laid.

An examination through the lens of social capital theory reveals the limits that commissioned mediation currently faces because of the external conditions to which it is subject. This is because, as far as societies in transition are concerned, due to the disintegration of traditional social structures, the absence of the concept of community integration, i.e., the weakness of social self-integration, the low level of social autonomy and the fact that a mature civil society is far from being established. Social capital in China is currently not high, resulting in the ability of social forces to resolve civil disputes not being high. In the face of this reality, the courts must adhere to the principle of gradual and orderly progress in entrusting mediation, starting with some relatively simple civil cases at the initial stage, in order to achieve the purpose of triage. For major, complex, and difficult cases, the court must adopt a cautious and restrained attitude, as it is doubtful whether the commissioned mediation organization is competent to mediate such disputes, and if it fails to do so effectively, it may intensify the disputes between the parties, resulting in a waste of social resources and an increase in dispute resolution costs (time, energy, etc.). More seriously, the courts may be challenged for avoiding justice by "throwing the hot potato out of the window" and thus become the target of greater discontent.

2.6 The Future of the Socializing Court Mediation: Toward Contractual Governance

Prior to the reform and opening-up, social governance in China was on the whole dominated by the state, with "big government and small society," which led to the underdevelopment of social organizations and their functional "absence" in the process of building the rule of law.[46] As China's social autonomy is still insufficient and the social capital on which mediation relies is poor, the entire mediation system in China is government-led and government-driven, and the current people's mediation has a clear state intervention and government orientation, with a high degree of reliance on the party committee and government. Some scholars have pointed out that the "Grand Mediation" system is essentially the use of administrative power to intervene in disputes, and the adoption of "social mobilization" to promote mediation by social forces is not only very costly, but also ineffective and unable to establish a long-term mechanism.[47] This is also a common problem faced by social mediation in the courts at present. Since the 19th Party Congress, with the establishment of a new concept of social governance based on the core concept of "building, governing and sharing by all," the transition from state-building to sharing has become a major trend, so the government-driven governance strategy during the transition period must be transformed. With the maturity of civil society and the abundance of social capital, the capacity for social autonomy is increasing, and autonomous mediation, with its focus on fostering the capacity of society to resolve disputes on its own, is bound to be the trend of socialized mediation. In this process, the government or the courts can no longer "fight alone," but must update and change their governance philosophy to guide various social forces to self-manage and self-resolve disputes, to achieve a benign common governance and "good governance." So, how to change the concept of governance? First of all, it is necessary to break the long-standing traditional mindset of a dichotomy between the state and society and between the public and private sectors in the governance of public affairs, and to "transplant the conceptual model, operational model, and strategic techniques of the contract into the governance of public affairs," emphasizing the introduction of market mechanisms into the operation of public service organizations with the contract as the centerpiece, and the "marketization of public services."[48] This is the core idea of the contractual model of governance that has emerged since the 1980s. Contractual governance is particularly prevalent and evident in the field of social security services in developed Western countries. For example, private detectives, private police (security service companies), private prisons, private judges, and private debt collection companies in the United States all operate in a market-based mode of operation in practice and operate extremely effectively, competing with the public goods provided by the state.[49]

So, can contractual governance be incorporated into the practice of socializing court mediation in China? We believe that the socialization of court mediation is in line with the concept of contractual governance, and that once integrated into the market mechanism, it can provide an incentive to those trustees and give rise to more professional mediation organizations. With the increase in social autonomy and the accumulation of social capital, autonomous socialized mediation can be integrated into market-based mechanisms, which can effectively alleviate the problems of insufficient supply, inefficient operation, and poor quality of judicial public goods. Since the ability of social organizations to play a role in dispute resolution depends on market demand and their ability to produce marketable "public goods," market incentives can increase the efficiency and improve the effectiveness of mediation by social organizations, thus establishing a long-term stable mechanism for mediation. In economically developed regions, many parties to commercial disputes can choose to mediate with trade and business organizations that have a better understanding of the industry's habits, so that they not only can obtain a quicker, more convenient and less costly product, but also maintain a long-term business relationship if necessary. The marketization of mediation means that "it is neither possible nor necessary for the state to determine the market share of various types of dispute resolution organizations," but rather "to allow different levels of legal service intermediaries to position themselves in the dispute resolution market and provide diversified ways of resolving disputes," thereby ultimately stimulating society's ability to resolve disputes on its own.[50] At the same time, in the face of the problem of insufficient supply of public goods in less-developed rural areas due to market imbalances, the state can encourage mediation organizations with local knowledge to provide affordable and reasonable dispute resolution products to rural society through tax breaks, subsidies, and other preferential policies. In order to overcome the failure of the market-based dispute resolution mechanism, the state should set up a "public interest mechanism" for the settlement of disputes involving vulnerable groups and the public interest, based on the externalities of public goods, such as extensive legal aid, the establishment of special funds and support for social groups and individuals to engage in public interest dispute resolution. In some economically developed regions, the government's purchase of private dispute mediation services reflects this concept. One of the successful examples in recent years is the Futian model, which was developed in Shenzhen, a city at the forefront of reform and opening-up. Shenzhen Futian District makes use of the rich resources of lawyers' services in the district, purchases legal services from qualified law firms through bidding, introduces legal professionals as people's mediators, sets up people's mediation offices in units with more conflicts and disputes, and assigns them to various public security police stations, traffic police brigades, courts, sends letters and calls, employs comprehensive governance, public transport, subways, industry associations and other units under Futian's jurisdiction to engage in people's mediation work as mediators of the people's mediation committee, providing legal services and mediating conflicts and disputes for the local people around the clock and actively promoting the resolution of social conflicts.[51] The advantage of the Futian Model of People's Mediation is that the government is no longer the direct subject of mediation, but has been transformed into the author of mediation norms and the supervisor of mediation behavior, thus promoting the development of people's mediation in the direction of socialization and autonomy, which is therefore a social governance practice with profound theoretical implications. Fundamentally, whether this model can operate effectively in the long term requires the government to fundamentally change its concept of governance and move from management-based governance to contractual governance, so that the "Futian model" becomes a regular governance technique, which is the key to the effective operation of the socialization of court mediation, and the key to freeing the courts from the "litigation explosion." Only in this way can the crowded litigation doors be unblocked and a "multi-door court" be opened, so that disputes can be effectively resolved through multiple channels.

Notes

1 Huang Zongzhi: *Past and Present: Explorations in Chinese Civil Legal Practice* (Beijing: Law Press, 2009), p. 191.
2 Shiga Hidesan, Terada Hiroaki, Kishimoto Misao, and Fuma Jin: *Civil Trials and Civil Contracts in the Ming and Qing Dynasties*, trans. Wang Yaxin (Beijing: Law Press, 1998), pp. 98–99.
3 Huang Zongzhi: *Past and Present: Explorations in Chinese Civil Legal Practice*, p. 8.
4 In a statistical analysis of the civil disputes received by the governor of Kuandian County, Fengtian Province, between the 28th and 32nd years of Guangxu in the late Qing Dynasty, the author found that out of a total of 114 cases, 39 (34 percent) were settled by judgment, and 35 (31 percent) by settlement. This shows that the importance of mediation in dispute resolution has not been denied. See Zhang Qin: *A Study of the Transformation of Civil Justice in Modern China: The Case of Fengtian Province* (Beijing: The Commercial Press, 2012), p. 99.
5 Liang Zhiping also argues that in ancient China, when settling civil disputes, mediation took various forms: it could be carried out by the people's close neighbors or by the village bailiffs themselves, or by the government with the approval of the village bailiffs or clan chiefs, or directly by the government. After the Song Dynasty, as family organizations became more and more complete, direct mediation by the government became less and less frequent, and mediation by the people themselves gradually became the norm. See Liang Zhiping: *The Search for Harmony in the Natural Order* (Shanghai: Shanghai People's Publishing House, 1991), pp. 212–213.
6 In the early years of the Kuomintang regime, they set up committees of settlement of litigation and committees of settlement of disputes throughout the country, which were not fully autonomous but rather bureaucratic in character. After the initial establishment of the unified regime, district and township mediation committees were set up in an attempt to replace civil mediation, which was scattered throughout grass-roots society and involved clan chiefs, neighbors, and middlemen, with mediation committees that had a hierarchical and bureaucratic character. See Luo Jinshou and Yu Yang: The Mediation System and its Operation in the Republican Period, *Journal of Jiangxi Normal University (Philosophy and Social Sciences Edition)*, 2016 (3).
7 Huang Zongzhi: *Past and Present: Explorations in Chinese Civil Legal Practice*, pp. 198–201.
8 Ibid., pp. 191–228.
9 Zhang Xipo: *Ma Xiwu's Way of Trial* (Beijing: Law Press, 1983), pp. 22–25.
10 Huang Zongzhi: *Past and Present: Explorations in Chinese Civil Legal Practice*, pp. 88–124.
11 Qiang Shigong: The Organizational Network of Power and the Governability of Law – Ma Xiwu's Trial Approach and the New Tradition of Chinese Law, *Peking University Law Review*, 2000 (3).
12 Hou Xinyi: *Justice for the People to People's Justice: A Study of the Popularized Judicial System in the Shaanxi-Ganjing Border Region* (Beijing: China University of Political Science and Law Press, 2007), pp. 274–278.
13 Shao Liuyi: Paradox and Necessity: The Return of Court Mediation (2003–2012), *Journal of East China University of Political Science and Law*, 2013 (5).
14 Zhang Jiajun: An Empirical Study of the Settlement Rate of Civil Lawsuits by Mediation, *Legal Studies*, 2012 (1).

15 Wang Yaxin: On the Reform of Civil and Economic Trial Methods, *Chinese Social Sciences*, 1994 (1): 9–15.
16 Xu Yun: The Dilemma of Combining Judgment and Mediation: A Framework for Analysis of Civil Trial Structure Theory, *Open Times*, 2009 (6).
17 Zhang Weiping: Reflections on the Return of Ma Xiwu, *Modern Law*, 2009 (5).
18 Wang Yaxin: On the Reform of Civil and Economic Trial Methods.
19 Zhang Weiping: Reflections on the Return of Ma Xiwu; Zhang Weiping: Litigation Mediation: Analysis and Reflections on the Current Situation, *Jurisprudence*, 2007 (5).
20 Zhou Yongkun: On the Impact of Compulsory Mediation on the Rule of Law and Equity, *Legal Science*, 2007 (3).
21 Chen Hangping: Social Transformation, Legalization and Court Mediation, *Legal System and Social Development*, 2010 (2).
22 Wu Yingzhi: The "Revival" and Future of Court Mediation, *Legal System and Social Development*, 2007 (3).
23 Wu Yingzhi: "Mediation First": Reform Paradigm and Legal Interpretation – A Sample of Municipal Court Reform, *Chinese and Foreign Law*, 2013 (3).
24 Fan Yu: Litigation Mediation: Trial Experience and Jurisprudence, *Chinese Jurisprudence*, 2009 (6).
25 Fan Yu: "Judgment When It's Right" and "Combination of Mediation and Judgment" – An Analysis Based on Practical and Operational Aspects, *Law and Social Development*, 2011 (6).
26 Li Hao: Mediation to Mediation, Trial to Trial: The Separation of Mediation and Trial in Civil Trials, *Chinese Jurisprudence*, 2013 (3).
27 Li Hao: The Separation of Mediation and Trial in Civil Trials, *Legal Studies*, 1996 (4); Li Hao: On the Double Softening of Procedural and Substantive Law Constraints in Court Mediation: An Analysis of the Contradiction between Preference for Mediation and Serious Law Enforcement in Civil Litigation, *Legal Studies Review*, 1996 (4).
28 Li Hao: Mediation Is Not Appropriate as a Mode of Operation of Civil Trial Power, *Legal Science*, 1996 (4).
29 Hao Zhenjiang: On the Procedural Separation of Mediation and Trial in Chinese Courts, *Jinan Journal (Philosophy and Social Sciences Edition)*, 2017 (9).
30 Wang Yaming; Separation of the Investigation and Trial: Problems and Paths, *Journal of the Party School of the Nanjing Municipal Committee of the Communist Party of China*, 2012 (5).
31 Fan Yu: Litigation Mediation: Trial Experience and Jurisprudence.
32 Tian Pingan and Yang Chengliang: The Theory of the Separation of the Trial and Regulation: The Ideal Picture and the Double Backlash – and a Discussion with Professor Li Hao, *Hunan Social Science*, 2015 (5).
33 Cao Yunji: Trial Risk and Court Mediation, *Journal of the National Academy of Public Prosecutors*, 2015 (9).
34 Some scholars believe that mediation in Chinese courts should not only be separated from trials in terms of procedure, but also "separate" from trials, and form an independent mediation procedure by drawing on the non-litigation procedure of Japanese mediation. See Hao Zhenjiang: On the Procedural Separation of Mediation and Trial in Chinese Courts.

35 Tang Li: Between Compulsion and Consent: The Dilemma and Way Out of China's Litigation Mediation System, *Modern Law*, 2012 (3); Tang Li: A Study on the Mechanism of Inducing Consent in Litigation, *Law Business Research*, 2016 (4).
36 Li Shaoping (Ed.): *The Understanding and Application of the Opinions on the Reform of the Diversified Dispute Resolution Mechanism of the Supreme People's Court and the Provisions on Specially Invited Mediation* (Beijing: People's Court Press, 2017), p. 279.
37 Gou Aibin: Court-Attached People's Mediation and Its Operation, *Contemporary Law*, 2012 (2).
38 Liu Jialiang: The Original Theory of Delegated Mediation, *Journal of Henan University (Social Science Edition)*, 2011 (5).
39 Huang Zongzhi: *Society and Culture in the Qing Dynasty: The Expression and Practice of Civil Law* (Beijing: Law Press, 2014), pp. 91–111.
40 Huang Zongzhi: *Past and Present: Explorations in Chinese Civil Law Practice*, pp. 74–87.
41 Lon L. Fuller: The Forms and Limits of Adjudication, *Harvard Law Review*, 1978 (92): 395.
42 Liu Jialiang: The Basis, Principles and Limits of Socialization of Civil Litigation Mediation, *Legal Science*, 2011 (3).
43 Yang Xiuqing: Rethinking the Socialization of the Subject of Court Mediation, *Social Science Forum*, 2008 (2).
44 The author's main ideas on the socialization of mediation in the courts were developed in 2011. Eight years later, the current situation of the socialization of court mediation in China has improved, but the basic problems are still similar to those faced eight years ago. For this reason, I have included the article published eight years ago in this chapter, with some modifications. See Wang Cong and Qin Chuan: Practice and Reflection: A Sociological Analysis of Delegated Mediation, *Commercial Mediation and ADR*, 2011 (3).
45 Zou Dongsheng: *Contracting for Policing in the Context of Contractual Governance* (Beijing: China Procuratorate Press, 2009), pp. 155–156.
46 Ma Changshan: The Rule of Law Turn from State Construction to Shared Construction – An Examination Based on the Relationship between Social Organizations and Rule of Law Construction, *Juridical Studies*, 2017 (3).
47 Wu Yingzhi: The Functions and Limits of "Grand Mediation" – Institutional Provision and Social Autonomy in Dispute Resolution, *Chinese and Foreign Law*, 2008 (2).
48 Zou Dongsheng: *Contracting for Policing in the Context of Contractual Governance*, pp. 22–60.
49 Xu Xin: *On Private Remedies* (Beijing: China University of Political Science and Law Press, 2005), pp. 223–261.
50 Wu Yingzhi: The Functions and Limits of "Grand Mediation" – Institutional Provision and Social Autonomy in Dispute Resolution..
51 Wang Shirong et al.: *A Study of the Futian Model of People's Mediation* (Beijing: Peking University Press, 2016); Feng Jiang et al.: *An Effective Exploration of Modern Social Governance System: People's Mediation Research on the "Futian Model"* (Beijing: China Social Science Press, 2017).

References

Cao Yunji: Trial Risk and Court Mediation, *Journal of the National Academy of Public Prosecutors*, 2015 (9): 118–132+175.

Chen Hangping: Social Transformation, Legalization and Court Mediation, Legal System and Social Development, 2010 (2): 101–111.

Fan Yu: Litigation Mediation: Trial Experience and Jurisprudence, Chinese Jurisprudence, 2009 (6): 128–137.

Fan Yu: "Judgment When It's Right" and "Combination of Mediation and Judgment" – An Analysis Based on Practical and Operational Aspects, Law and Social Development, 2011 (6): 49–56.

Feng Jiang et al.: An Effective Exploration of Modern Social Governance System: People's Mediation Research on the "Futian Model," Beijing: China Social Science Press, 2017.

Fuller, Lon L.: The Forms and Limits of Adjudication, Harvard Law Review, 1978 (92): 395.

Gou Aibin: Court-Attached People's Mediation and Its Operation, Contemporary Law, 2012 (2).

Hao Zhenjiang: On the Procedural Separation of Mediation and Trial in Chinese Courts, Jinan Journal (Philosophy and Social Sciences Edition), 2017 (9): 28–37+129.

Hou Xinyi: From Justice for the People to People's Justice – A Study of the Popularized Judicial System in the Shaanxi-Ganjing Border Region, Beijing: China University of Political Science and Law Press, 2007, pp. 274–278.

Huang Zongzhi: Past and Present: Explorations in Chinese Civil Legal Practice, Beijing: Law Press, 2009.

Huang Zongzhi: Society and Culture in the Qing Dynasty: The Expression and Practice of Civil Law, Beijing: Law Press, 2014.

Li Hao: Mediation Is Not Appropriate as a Mode of Operation of Civil Trial Power, Legal Science, 1996a (4): 68–74.

Li Hao: The Separation of Mediation and Trial in Civil Trials, Legal Studies, 1996b (4): 57–68.

Li Hao: On the Double Softening of Procedural and Substantive Law Constraints in Court Mediation – An Analysis of the Contradiction between Preference for Mediation and Serious Law Enforcement in Civil Litigation, Legal Studies *Review*, 1996c (4): 11–16.

Li Hao: Mediation to Mediation, Trial to Trial: The Separation of Mediation and Trial in Civil Trials, Chinese Jurisprudence, 2013 (3): 5–18.

Li Shaoping (Ed.): The Understanding and Application of the Opinions on the Reform of the Diversified Dispute Resolution Mechanism of the Supreme People's Court and the Provisions on Specially Invited Mediation, Beijing: People's Court Press, 2017.

Liang Zhiping: The Search for Harmony in the Natural Order, Shanghai: Shanghai People's Publishing House, 1991.

Liu Jialiang: The Basis, Principles and Limits of Socialization of Civil Litigation Mediation, Legal Science, 2011a (3): 151–159.

Liu Jialiang: The Original Theory of Delegated Mediation, Journal of Henan University (Social Science Edition), 2011b (5): 67–72.

Luo Jinshou and Yu Yang: The Mediation System and its Operation in the Republican Period, Journal of Jiangxi Normal University (Philosophy and Social Sciences Edition), 2016 (3): 149–156.

Ma Changshan: The Rule of Law Turn from State Construction to Shared Construction – An Examination Based on the Relationship between Social Organizations and Rule of Law Construction, Juridical Studies, 2017 (3): 24–43.

Qiang Shigong: The Organizational Network of Power and the Governability of Law – Ma Xiwu's Trial Approach and the New Tradition of Chinese Law, Peking University Law Review, 2000 (3): 1–61.

Shao Liuyi: Paradox and Necessity: The Return of Court Mediation (2003–2012), Journal of East China University of Political Science and Law, 2013 (5): 112–124.

Shiga Hidesan, Terada Hiroaki, Kishimoto Misao, and Fuma Jin: Civil Trials and Civil Contracts in the Ming and Qing Dynasties, trans. Wang Yaxin, Beijing: Law Press, 1998, pp. 98–99.

Tang Li: Between Compulsion and Consent: The Dilemma and Way Out of China's Litigation Mediation System, Modern Law, 2012 (3): 86–96.

Tang Li: A Study on the Mechanism of Inducing Consent in Litigation, Law Business Research, 2016 (4): 121–130.

Tian Pingan and Yang Chengliang: The Theory of the Separation of the Trial and Regulation: The Ideal Picture and the Double Backlash – and a Discussion with Professor Li Hao, Hunan Social Science, 2015 (5): 53–59.

Wang Cong and Qin Chuan: Practice and Reflection: A Sociological Analysis of Delegated Mediation, Commercial Mediation and ADR, 2011 (3): 18–26.

Wang Shirong et al.: A Study of the Futian Model of People's Mediation, Beijing: Peking University Press, 2016.

Wang Yaming: Separation of the Investigation and Trial: Problems and Paths, Journal of the Party School of the Nanjing Municipal Committee of the Communist Party of China, 2012 (5): 94–98.

Wang Yaxin: On the Reform of Civil and Economic Trial Methods, Chinese Social Sciences, 1994 (1): 3–22.

Wu Yingzhi: The "Revival" and Future of Court Mediation, Legal System and Social Development, 2007 (3): 34–45.

Wu Yingzhi: The Functions and Limits of "Grand Mediation" – Institutional Provision and Social Autonomy in Dispute Resolution, Chinese and Foreign Law, 2008 (2): 309–319.

Wu Yingzhi: "Mediation First": Reform Paradigm and Legal Interpretation – A Sample of Municipal Court Reform, Chinese and Foreign Law, 2013 (3): 536–555.

Xu Xin: On Private Remedies, Beijing: China University of Political Science and Law Press, 2005.

Xu Yun: The Dilemma of Combining Judgment and Mediation: A Framework for Analysis of Civil Trial Structure Theory, Open Times, 2009 (6): 98–115.

Yang Xiuqing: Rethinking the Socialization of the Subject of Court Mediation, Social Science Forum, 2008 (2): 39–42.

Zhang Jiajun: An Empirical Study of the Settlement Rate of Civil Lawsuits by Mediation, Legal Studies, 2012 (1): 31–45.

Zhang Qin: A Study of the Transformation of Civil Justice in Modern China: The Case of Fengtian Province, Beijing: The Commercial Press, 2012.

Zhang Weiping: Litigation Mediation: Analysis and Reflections on the Current Situation, Jurisprudence, 2007 (5): 18–27.

Zhang Weiping: Reflections on the Return of Ma Xiwu, Modern Law, 2009 (5): 139–156.

Zhang Xipo: Ma Xiwu's Way of Trial, Beijing: Law Press, 1983.

Zhou Yongkun: On the Impact of Compulsory Mediation on the Rule of Law and Equity, Legal Science, 2007 (3): 11–24.

Zou Dongsheng: Contracting for Policing in the Context of Contractual Governance, Beijing: China Procuratorate Press, 2009.

3 The History and Revival of Administrative Mediation

A person may not have anything to do with the courts in his or her lifetime, but a person will have contact with the executive from birth to death. "We all live in an administrative state, which is shaped by policies universally implemented and explicitly adopted by a vast set of administrative agencies."[1] The administrative organs have the widest involvement in social life through the exercise of administrative management and governance, yet their responsibilities in dispute resolution are easily overlooked. How to enhance the enthusiasm and effectiveness of the administrative organs in dispute resolution is an important element in deepening the reform of the diversified dispute resolution mechanism and improving the modernization of the state's governance capacity and system. In the framework of the current legal system, the administrative organs can resolve disputes through administrative mediation, administrative reconsideration, and administrative adjudication, of which the weakest link is administrative mediation. Administrative mediation refers to a system whereby administrative organs, in accordance with their statutory duties and procedures, resolve civil disputes between citizens, legal persons or other organizations, as well as administrative disputes between administrative organs and administrative counterparts, by means of explanation, communication, persuasion, facilitation, and consultation on a voluntary and equal basis. This chapter will therefore focus on the system of administrative mediation. By going back in history, it can be found that administrative mediation has taken different forms in various historical periods. It is difficult to match the contemporary forms of people's mediation, litigation mediation and administrative mediation with the traditional meaning of mediation and conciliation in ancient times. In different historical periods, administrative mediation has had different political positions, procedural designs, and presentation, and has played different roles. This chapter will introduce the historical origins and development of administrative mediation according to the historical stages of ancient, modern (1840–1949), modern (1949–), and contemporary China.

DOI: 10.4324/9781003385776-3

3.1 "Administrative Mediation" in Ancient Times

China has a culture of harmony that has been built up over two thousand years. The idea of harmony is the essence of Chinese culture and has been used as the basis for the establishment of rules and regulations throughout the dynasties, shaping the concept of dispute and dispute resolution from the highest rulers to the common people. The idea of "harmony is precious" has also become an important basis for the emergence of mediation. It is commonly believed that mediation in ancient China can be divided into folk mediation, semi-governmental mediation, and governmental mediation. Folk mediation includes clan mediation, neighborhood mediation, etc., semi-governmental mediation, i.e., township mediation, and "governmental mediation, i.e., litigation mediation, refers to the mediation conducted by officials of the judiciary when hearing a case."[2] Institutionalized mediation arose as early as the Zhou Dynasty in a slave society. The Rites of the Zhou record more than 380 officials in the Western Zhou, of which

> the magistrates, who oversaw the land and the people, were responsible for the edification of the country. The head of the magistrates was called Dasitu, also known as Situ, who oversaw the education of the country and assisted the king in stabilizing the states.

Among the 79 "earth officials," there was a "mediator" who was responsible for "reconciling feuds" and whose duty was to "harmonize the difficulties of all the people."[3] According to Western Zhou bronze inscriptions, the magistrate was to inform the defendant of his or her legal liability in the proceedings and to mediate, and then to pass judgment if mediation failed. The main process of mediation is that the person at fault admits the wrong to the other party and proposes a compensation package which, if accepted by the other party, concludes the case; if it is not accepted, the case is decided by a judicial officer.[4] If the concept of "administration" is understood in its broadest sense, the system of "mediators" of Western Zhou can be seen as a prototype of administrative mediation.

During the Qin and Han Dynasties, there were records of official mediation of civil disputes. For example, *the Hanshu*, Wu You's biography contains:

> Wu You, called Ji Ying, was a native of Chang Yuan, Chenliu ... Wu You was later promoted to the rank of Marquis of Jiaodong. He strove for kindness and simplicity in his administration and led by example. When he encountered people who came to the government to file lawsuits, he always closed his door and blamed himself first, before adjudicating the lawsuits and enlightening them with reason. He would also go to the place where the people lived to mediate and reconcile the two sides. After his appointment as Marquis of Jiaodong, Wu You often visited the people in person, mediating disputes and bringing about reconciliation.

According to the litigation system of the Han and Tang Dynasties, for civil cases, especially family property disputes, the magistrates mainly adopted an educational approach, presenting themselves and mediating to settle the case. The Li Zheng and Fang Zheng, set up in the Tang Dynasty, would first mediate disputes in the countryside.

In the Song Dynasty, the settlement of civil disputes by mediation was known as "peace and reconciliation." *The History of the Song Dynasty* contains cases of mediation by officials, such as

> When Lu Xiangshan was governor of Jingmen, he would hold court for any complaint from the people, whether early or late. Lu Jiuyuan (Lu Xiangshan) also ordered those defendants to take their own pleadings retrospectively and set up deadlines for them, all of whom returned as promised, and Lu Jiuyuan immediately dealt with them at his discretion, and most were persuaded to mediate.

This historical record shows that Lu Jiuyuan was an honest and incorruptible official, who not only accepted lawsuits from the people in person, no matter how early or late, but also used mediation and persuasion. There is also a Song Dynasty verdict that reads:

> Besides, what can be gained from a lawsuit? It costs you money and delays your work. Why bother yourself to have a trial when you must be humiliated in front of the magistrates, frightened in the official's hall, tied up and beaten with a cane, and whether you win or lose, the lawsuit will depend on the official's decision?

When hearing civil cases, local officials make it their main objective to "put an end to the litigation" and try to persuade the parties to settle the case through mediation. For example, the Ming Gong Shu Collection recorded that two families, Shen and Fu, who were originally close neighbors, were involved in a lawsuit over a land boundary dispute. After finding out what was right and wrong, the official admonished both parties that "harmony between neighbors is important" and settled the dispute. After the Song Dynasty, mediation became an important civil dispute resolution system.

In the Yuan Dynasty, the government's mediation of civil disputes further developed and was seen as a form of political achievement for the officials, and thus was valued in trial practice. The government set up societies in the countryside, and one of the duties of the president was to mediate disputes. Usually, the magistrate mediated in court, based mainly on the laws of the court and the ethics of the time, and for the conclusion of civil proceedings, both mediation and trial have the same legal effect, and a case settled by mediation cannot be submitted again for litigation by the parties on the same grounds and facts. Furthermore, the magistrate's mediation scheme had an enforcement effect.[5]

The rulers of the Ming and Qing Dynasties placed greater emphasis on mediation and governance, and only disputes that failed to be mediated were to be adjudicated by the government. For example, the laws of the Ming Dynasty providing specific and detailed provisions for the mediation of disputes by the officials of villages and towns, contained such provisions that "for minor disputes such as family, marriage, or land, the official of the village or patriarch was allowed to settle it at the judicial venue (*shenmingting*) through persuading." Only if the case cannot be resolved after mediation by the village is it referred to the government, and only after the government has accepted the case is it still subject to mediation.[6] By the Qing Dynasty, mediation was divided into state and county mediation and civil mediation, and became an important form of trial in the state and county offices. According to the Qing Law, the village magistrate could mediate family disputes and some "minor matters" involving real estate, while other disputes that could not be resolved were referred to the county magistrate, "who was the local chief executive and the presiding judge of the entire jurisdiction."[7] Although the Qing law did not make mediation by village elders a compulsory procedure or a prerequisite for civil trials, as was the case with Japanese shogunate legislation of the same period, in practice, "disputes were still usually settled by mediation conducted by influential figures in the community, neighbors of the litigants or members of the government, even after the dispute had been brought before the government offices."[8] The Archives of the Shuntian Prefecture record 244 cases heard at the Baodi County Court between the 15th and 25th years of the Jiaqing era, nearly 90 percent of which were settled by mediation.[9] It is evident that mediation was an important means of state rule and social management in the Ming and Qing Dynasties. However, an important criterion for the examination and assessment of officials in feudal society was the "clearing of lawsuits and the conclusion of prisons," and the government often carried out forced mediation with the aim of settling lawsuits, forcing the parties concerned to submit to the will of officials and sacrifice their own interests. Some scholars have pointed out that "underneath the warm veil of mediation to settle lawsuits, a harsh class oppression was concealed."[10]

In ancient China, there was no clear division between judicial and administrative power. "Judicial power in ancient times was not only controlled by the supreme ruler, but was subordinate to the executive from the local to the central level, and the judiciary was not independent."[11] Since the Yuan Dynasty, the administration and the judiciary have gradually merged, with the judiciary being subordinate to the administration, and administrative intervention in the judiciary thus having an "institutional" basis. In this sense, the mediation of civil disputes by officials of the state and county government agencies in feudal society could be called both litigation mediation and administrative mediation.

It should be noted that the main function of the feudal local government was to help the supreme ruler to rule over the people, and its function of adjudicating cases was also closer to the administrative act of maintaining local social security and maintaining the ruling order, thus it is more reasonable to understand the ancient governmental mediation as the historical origin of administrative mediation. Of course, in the ancient times of Chinese history, i.e., before a clear distinction was made between the judiciary, which had jurisdictional powers, and the executive, which had administrative powers, all official and semi-official mediation could in fact be defined as public (power) mediation, and these institutions and traditions constitute the cultural deposits and indigenous resources common to modern judicial and administrative mediation.

3.2 Administrative Mediation in the Modern Era (1840–1949)[12]

After the Opium Wars, Western civilization of the rule of law was introduced to China as a foreign product, a civil litigation system with judgment and enforcement as the cornerstone gradually took shape, and the concept of separation of judicial and administrative powers began to influence the political structure of China.

> But the penetration of this litigation system into Chinese society was limited due to the impact of the war of aggression and the conflict with Chinese socio-economic conditions and traditional legal culture ... in the settlement of civil disputes, and due to its profound adaptation to the local economic culture, the legal culture of Western countries' impact, not only has it not atrophied, but overall, it has shown a new development trend.[13]

During the Republican period, the government actively promoted organizations such as the "Lawsuit Settlement Association" and the "Dispute Settlement Association" in the private sector, merging the various organizations of traditional society to gradually establish a standardized and unified civil mediation organization, and the tradition of settling disputes through the mediation of kin, neighbors, gentry, and various social organizations was continued. Since the late Qing Dynasty and the early Republic of China, although the modern judicial system was initially established, the status quo of county governors as administrators who also administered justice still prevailed, and the lack of judicial resources continued to plague those in power. As a result, it became a priority for the government to make active use of existing social organizations and resources to build a functioning civil mediation mechanism. In Jiangxi, for example, the Bin Hing Society, the Qing Ming Society, the Cha Shan Society, the Cao Society, the Zong Society, the Ancestral Hall Society, and the Hetian Society were all organized as clubs. Although their specific historical mission had come to an end by the early years of the Republic, they still played a mediating role in rural society by adjudicating matters and settling lawsuits, and the village "talkers" became the central figures in settling disputes. By 1928, Jiangxi was implementing the system of the "Dispute

Settlement Association" in all counties and towns, and Article 4 of the charter clearly stipulated its purpose was "specially designed for the settlement of people's disputes." "Those who are literate and upright" would be elected as "arbitrators," specializing in mediating daily disputes within their jurisdiction. The extension of "Dispute Settlement Association" to the villages, which was transformed by the organizations of various clubs, allowed for more uniform and standardized mediation.

Yan Xishan's "Lawsuit Settlement Association," which he introduced in the construction of village rule in Shanxi, was representative of the standardization of civil mediation in the same period. Yan Xishan believed that the essence of administration lay in the village, and promoted "village-based politics." He also promoted "people-based politics," which actively used the role of the people and advocated the development of people's morality, wisdom, and wealth. He promulgated the "Instructions for the People" and the "Instructions for the Family," preaching feudal ethics and morality with Confucianism at its center, organizing village administration, promulgating the Village Prohibition Covenant, and setting up village offices, litigation settlement committees, supervisory committees, and people's meetings. This series of ruling measures led to a temporary period of social stability and productive development in Shanxi, which was awarded the title of "model province."[14] In 1927, the Shanxi Provincial Charter for the Litigation Settlement Association required each village to establish a Litigation Settlement Association, electing three to five reputable members of the village as umpires, and relying as much as possible on experienced and established members of the village who had experience in mediating disputes. The Litigation Settlement Committee also established a system of regular reporting by observers and roving inspections by inspectors, and rewards and punishments were given to umpires according to their performance in mediation.[15]

In Shanxi and Jiangxi, while litigation and dispute settlement committees were being implemented, other places also gradually established similar civil mediation organizations, for example, on March 21, 1929, the Hebei Provincial Government published the Statutes of the Village Litigation Settlement Committees, stipulating that "those who have been mediated by the counties and districts will have their cases dismissed immediately after the mediation, but if they are not convinced, they will still ask the counties and districts to handle the case."[16] In addition, the counties of the capital also had a lawsuit settlement committee. The litigation settlement committees in Linchuan, Jiangxi, extended the organization to neighborhood, and thus there were two types of neighborhood litigation and district litigation settlement committees. The Provisional Regulations of the Linchuan Experimental District Lawsuit Settlement Society set out detailed mediation procedures and principles of mediation, such as the prohibition of bribery, the prohibition of private meetings with parties, and the system of recusal. The Constitution of the Village Lawsuit Settlement Society in Hebei provided for a system of recusal, the principle of open mediation, and the principle of combining majority decision and chief umpire decision.[17]

The ability of folk mediation organizations, such as the Litigation Settlement Association and the Dispute Settlement Association, to develop the role and function of mediation between kinsmen and villagers in traditional societies into a stable system and institution for grass-roots society at the time was due to the advocacy and support of the government, backed by deep administrative power resources, which also enabled them to help the rulers reduce the troubles of civil litigation and maintain the ruling order.

During the Republican period, a mechanism was also established to link judicial mediation, civil mediation, and administrative mediation in a complementary manner, i.e., according to the *Civil Procedure Law* of 1935, the court may conduct mediation *ex officio* or upon application of the parties after receiving a civil case and before making a judgment. Mediation may take place in court, or the parties' relatives or the mediation committee of the township or village where they live may be entrusted to carry out out out-of-court mediation. And the parties can apply to dismiss the case if they agree and sign on the mediation results, which will have legal effect.[18]

During the Republican period, administrative mediation had begun to take on the basic characteristics of modern administrative mediation. The tentacles of state power extended from the county level to the district, township, and even village levels, and the administrative system of local self-government organizations had special dispute mediation organs, which in essence carried out administrative mediation. The Nanjing National Government enacted and amended the *Law on the Implementation of Township Self-Government* and the *Law on the Implementation of District Self-Government* around 1930, which explicitly provided for the establishment of conciliation committees in township offices and district offices to carry out civil conciliation. In 1941, the Local Self-Government Implementation Programme was promulgated, and the basic ideals of the new life included "mediation of disputes and reconciliation of neighbors." In 1942, the Ministry of the Interior promulgated 34 "Matters to Be Done for Township Security," including "mediation of disputes." With regard to the regulation of the powers and procedures of the mediation committees set up within the autonomous bodies at all levels, Article 4 of the *Regulations on the Powers of the Mediation Committees of Districts, Villages, Townships and Squares*, dated April 3, 1931, stipulates that "the mediation committees may handle the following criminal cases: offenses against decency; offenses against marriage; injury; offenses against freedom; offenses against honor and credit; offenses against secrecy; theft; misappropriation; fraud and breach of trust; destruction and damage." After 1940, it was amended and refined into the "Rules for the Organization of the Township Mediation Committee." Subsequently, various counties also set up mediation committees to accept and mediate disputes that could not be mediated in each district, and practiced administrative mediation, for example, in 1942, Yu

Gan County in Jiangxi Province set up a county mediation committee at the Dongshan Chanlin Observatory. The committee "aimed to assist the county government and the Judicial Division in mediating local disputes, trying to settle disputes and reduce litigation," and elected 37 mediators and 15 standing members to take turns to mediate at the meetings, as the last administrative mediation procedure before the county Judicial Division accepted civil lawsuits. On June 3, 1943, the Ministry of Justice and Administration of the Nanjing National Government issued a directive requiring the introduction of a mediation system everywhere. The development of specific rules for administrative mediation gave local self-government bodies at all levels a legal basis for mediation, while the use of autonomous administrative organizations and networks enabled mediation to expand its scope of action and strengthen its social base. However, the administrative mediation in the Republic of China was attached to the mediation committees of autonomous bodies at all levels, and "in order to pursue the performance of administrative mediation, the parties were often forced to mediate by means of administrative power, resulting in the settlement of disputes and the conclusion of grievances."[19]

During the revolutionary base period, the Soviet regime under the guidance of Mao Zedong's thought established and developed a revolutionary legal system that embodied both distinct class and revolutionary characteristics and carried the characteristics of the times. This was reflected in the settlement of civil disputes, in which the democratic nature of the Western rule of law civilization was absorbed and borrowed, while at the same time critically inheriting the reasonable aspects of traditional Chinese legal culture, in order to reflect to the greatest extent possible, the needs of the people for dispute settlement at a particular time. Against the background of the formation of the anti-Japanese national united front, social conflicts were divided into conflicts between the enemy and ourselves and internal conflicts among the people. Civil disputes were regarded as internal conflicts among the people, which should not be solved by coercive means, but by persuasion and education in order to unite people from all walks of life in the anti-Japanese struggle. To this end, the governments of the border areas actively advocated and promoted mediation of civil disputes and promulgated many mediation regulations. For example, the *Supplementary Regulations on the Handling of Proceedings by the Judiciary at All Levels* in Shandong Province, promulgated in 1941, the *Instructions of the High Court of the Shaanxi-Gansu-Ningxia Border Area on Judicial Work in the Counties*, the *Provisional Measures on Village Mediation* in Northwest Shanxi, promulgated in 1942, and the *Regulations on Mediation in Civil and Criminal Cases* in the Shaanxi-Gansu-Ningxia Border Region, promulgated in 1943 (covering the trial implementation of the criminal settlement system), the *Letter of Instruction on Popularizing Mediation, Summarizing Jurisprudence and Cleaning Up Prisons*, issued by the Border District Government on June 6, 1944, and the *Instruction on Implementing*

Mediation Methods, Improving Judicial Work Style and Reducing People's Litigation, adopted by the Border District High Court, and the *Regulations on Civil and Criminal Mediation*, issued by the Shanxi-Hebei-Shandong-Henan Border District Government in 1945.[20]

As mediation has indeed been greatly recognized for its obvious role in resolving disputes, reducing litigation, and improving the way justice is done, the settlement of civil disputes by mediation has become an explicit work requirement in the above-mentioned legal norms or decrees. In the *Letter of Instruction on Popularizing Mediation, Summarizing Jurisprudence and Cleaning Up Prisons*, addressed to commissioners, prefects, heads of higher chambers, and heads of county judicial divisions, the Border District Government wrote:

> Governments at all levels, especially township and district governments, should not only accept requests for people's mediation, but also go looking for (sending people to mediate, appointing neighbors of both parties to mediate, staff going to the countryside and meeting the matter should be mediated) or transfer to mediation ... But mediation by the county government is not as good as by the district and township, for one thing, the people are exempt from walking more, and for another, the district and township governments know more about the situation, so the district and township governments should regard mediation as one of their main tasks.

It can be seen that at that time, public mediation in the form of government mediation was highly valued, including not only passive mediation initiated on the application of the parties, but also "seeking mediation" and "transferred mediation" carried out *ex officio* by the border administrative organs, and it is particularly noteworthy that the border government also noted the importance of resolving disputes at the grass-roots level, and particularly stressed that mediation by the county government was not as good as that by the district and township governments.

The *Letter of Instruction* also provides scientific provisions on the modalities and principles of mediation:

> Points to be noted in mediation: ... should be good at changing the mood of the parties, and the person conducting the mediation should be able to propose a solution that takes into account all aspects and is appropriate ... the outcome of the conciliation should be the complete willingness of the parties and should not be slightly forced (if the parties do not agree to the mediation and want to sue, they should not be prevented from doing so) ... In the process of promoting mediation, a bias may occur, i.e., forcing the parties to submit to the mediation in order to win the conciliation pennant. This is very unacceptable and should be prevented with care.[21]

These provisions are still pertinent and have profound practical implications even today.

Based on the contents of the *Regulations on Mediation of Civil and Criminal Cases* in the Shaanxi-Ganjiang-Ningxia Border Region, Professor Hou Xinyi divided mediation in the border area into four types of universal mediation: civil mediation, mediation by social groups, governmental mediation, and judicial mediation. Of these, government mediation is mediation conducted by staff at all levels of government and can correspond to contemporary administrative mediation. In order to implement government mediation, the border district government set up a third section within the Department of Civil Affairs, a first section within the county government, and a mediation committee at the district and township level, which was specifically responsible for mediation. At the time, there was also opposition within the Border Region to the need for a dedicated government mediation department, on the grounds that the government had limited resources and could not afford to conduct mediation, and that mediation by the first section would duplicate the work of the Judicial Division except for the lack of authority to adjudicate, which could result in long delays in disputes. However, the Border District government insisted that government mediation was necessary.[22] In terms of data, government mediation has been effective in resolving social conflicts and disputes. In 1944, for example, 1,900 disputes were mediated by the government at the district and township level in Yan'an County; 1,000 disputes were mediated by the government at the district level in Fuxian County; in 1945, 21 cases were reported in the first eight months in Tianzi District, Quzi County, of which 19 were mediated by the district government and only two were referred to the judicial division.[23]

Mediation in the border areas was performed by the government and members of society under the mobilization call of the government, reflecting the interaction between the government and the people, but the government's guidance and control over mediation were carried out throughout, reflecting both the government's determination to regulate the legacy of folk mediation and the great value it placed on the essence of folk mediation culture. In terms of the rules of mediation, emphasis is placed on changing the old method of sitting in the hall and asking questions, requiring in-depth investigation and research at the grass-roots level, i.e. doing sufficient preplanning before mediation, fighting a prepared battle and grasping the initiative of mediation. Emphasis is placed on choosing judicial officers and people with a certain status and prestige to act as mediators in order to enhance the authority of mediation; stressing that mediators should combine emotion, reason and analysis of interests and interests and maintain the necessary neutrality; adhering to the principle of parity; exerting the necessary pressure on the basis of adhering to the principle of voluntariness of the parties. Although there were unavoidable problems in the formation of the mediation system in the border areas, such as forced mediation, these problems were superficial and inevitable when the masses were mobilized and the process was implemented in an organized manner.[24] At that time and in that space, the Chinese Communist Party was tasked with transforming the political, social, and economic order of the border areas, educating the masses, and creating a new type of judicial system, and the institutionalization of mediation was from the outset markedly political and dominated by a public power mindset.

3.3 Administrative Mediation in the Modern Era (1949–2012)

After the founding of the People's Republic of China, there was an urgent need to establish a new and stable social order, and the curtain of modernization was thus raised. Making full use of mediation to resolve internal conflicts among the people became a manifestation of the distinction between the enemy and ourselves. With the gradual disintegration of traditional social structures and management methods, new social structures were formed, from provinces, cities and counties to districts, towns, and villages, with capillary grass-roots groups building up a huge social control system. Through these capillaries, the will of the ruling party and national policies and decrees were propagated and penetrated the production and life of the people at the local level, and it was in this process that the organization and institutionalization of civil mediation took place. In those circumstances, mediation not only assumed the traditional dispute resolution role, but also the role of implementing and propagating new legal concepts and policy orders, with the people's mediation and court mediation systems growing faster and administrative mediation in the strict sense being relatively weak.

The earliest institutionalized administrative mediation after 1949 arose in the field of labor disputes and marriage and family disputes. In that year, the All-China Federation of Trade Unions promulgated the *Provisional Measures on the Handling of Labor Relations*. According to Article 27 therein, if a dispute between employers and employees could not be resolved by negotiation between representatives of the "trade union and the trade association," either party could apply for mediation by the local labor bureau. This kind of mediation is the administrative conciliation for labor disputes. In 1950, the Central People's Government promulgated the Marriage Law, Article 17 of which clearly stipulated that mediation by the people's government and the judiciary was a mandatory procedure for couples to divorce, and in November 1950, the Ministry of Labor promulgated the *Provisions on the Procedure for the Settlement of Labor Disputes*, which further clarified the mediation procedure for labor disputes. Subsequently, a system of administrative conciliation of contract disputes was further established. However, the economic committees at all levels, the administrative departments for industry and commerce, the capital construction committees, and the business departments at all levels all had the authority to mediate contract disputes, and this "multi-headed mediation" model was changed in 1983 with the promulgation of the *Regulations on Arbitration of Economic Contracts*. Mediation of contract disputes was carried out by the economic contract arbitration committees set up by the administrative departments for industry and commerce at national and local levels. In April 1997, the State Administration for Industry and Commerce, in its *Report on the National Conference of Directors of Administration for Industry and Commerce*, requested that the departments responsible for contract management within the industrial and material sectors and the commercial sector, and the economic committees at all levels, be responsible for mediating and arbitrating contract disputes and inspecting and supervising the implementation of contracts. On November 3, 1997, the *Measures on Administrative Mediation of Contract Disputes* were considered and adopted by the Bureau of the State Administration for Industry and Commerce and came into force. This departmental regulation was the only specific legislation on administrative mediation applicable nationwide, which was repealed by the State Administration for Industry and Commerce on October 27, 2017 after 20 years of application. At the local level, there have been sporadic attempts at administrative mediation, for example, the *Measures on Administrative Mediation of Copyright Disputes* in the Xinjiang Uygur Autonomous Region (Xin Quan Zi [1996] No. 3) of January 24, 1996 is a normative document for the Copyright Bureau of the Autonomous Region to accept administrative mediation of copyright disputes within its jurisdiction.[25]

With the transition from a planned economy to a market economy, China has long since left the era when there was no law to follow. From the time of reform and opening-up to the time when the Central Government proposed the construction of a Grand Mediation system, the relevant legislative provisions on administrative mediation had already appeared in many laws, administrative regulations, and departmental rules. For example, the *Trial Measures on Mediation of Commercial Economic Disputes* (issued by the Ministry of Commerce on November 23, 1989), the *Measures for Handling Civil Disputes* (promulgated by the Ministry of Justice on April 19, 1990), the *Marriage Law* (amended by the Standing Committee of the Ninth National People's Congress on April 28, 2001), the *Regulations on Handling Medical Accidents* (adopted by the Standing Committee of the State Council on February 20, 2002), the *Rural Land Contract Law* (adopted by the Standing Committee of the Ninth National People's Congress on August 29, 2002, amended in 2018), the *Road Traffic Safety Law* (adopted by the Standing Committee of the Tenth National People's Congress on October 28, 2003, amended in 2011), the *Interim Measures on Mediation of Electricity Disputes* (adopted by the General Office of the Chairman of the State Electricity Regulatory Commission on March 28, 2005), the *Law on Punishment for Public Security Management* (adopted by the Standing Committee of the Tenth National People's Congress on August, 28 2005 and amended in 2012), etc. From the formulation and the issuers of these legislative documents, one can see they are of different levels of effectiveness. Some of them regulate administrative mediation of disputes in a certain field, such as administrative mediation of medical malpractice disputes and electricity disputes; others extend the scope of application to civil disputes and folk disputes, such as the *Measures for*

Handling Folk Disputes; some can be applied nationwide, while others are only applicable to rural areas. At the same time, several normative documents have been formulated in various places, such as the *Administrative Mediation Procedures for Contract Disputes in the Beijing Municipal Administration for Industry and Commerce (Provisional)* (1998).

The distinctive feature of the practice of the administrative mediation system in this period is the uneven development among the various subjects, fields, and specific mechanisms. The main subjects of administrative mediation are the administrative authorities at all levels, but not all of them have the duty to mediate disputes, and some functional departments do not carry out what is known as administrative mediation in the field of dispute resolution because of the specific nature of their work, such as the diplomatic service, the defense service, and the national security service. The circumstances in which administrative subjects with administrative mediation responsibilities under the law carry out mediation work also vary greatly. For example, grass-roots people's governments at the county, city, district, and township levels undertake most administrative mediation duties for disputes, while the State Council, provincial governments and their various line ministries are far fewer in comparison. However, among the administrative departments, judicial administration, civil affairs, public security, industrial and commercial administration, environmental protection, health, agriculture and forestry and other administrative departments have a more intense and significant role in administrative mediation work because they are responsible for managing more areas of contact with specific social members' activities. Within the scope of public security administrative mediation, traffic police mediation and public security mediation account for the vast majority of the proportion of cases.

In October 2006, the Sixth Plenary Session of the 16th Central Committee of the CPC adopted the *Decision of the Central Committee of the CPC on Some Major Issues in Building a Harmonious Socialist Society*, which clearly stated the need to "realize the organic combination of people's mediation, administrative mediation, and judicial mediation." At the same time, the State Council issued the *Opinions on Preventing and Resolving Administrative Disputes and Perfecting the Mechanism for Resolving Administrative Disputes*, which specifically proposed to focus on the use of mediation to resolve administrative disputes, and the concept of a "Grand Mediation system" was first introduced in November. These institutionalized initiatives marked the beginning of administrative mediation as one of the three major types of mediation, advocated at the national level and further regulated. Subsequently, some departments and localities began to formulate clear norms on how to use administrative mediation to resolve specific types of disputes, for example, the Ministry of Public Security adopted the *Norms on the Work of Public Security Organs in Public Security Mediation* on December 8, 2007; the Hebei Provincial Department of Labor and Social Security issued the *Notice on the Establishment of Administrative Mediation Agencies for Labor Security*

Disputes and the Establishment of Working Rules for Administrative Mediation in 2006, the *Notice on the Regulation* of *Administrative Mediation for Labor Security Disputes* in 2007, and the *Implementation Opinions on Further Strengthening Administrative Mediation* in 2008, and the Shijiazhuang Bureau of Labor and Social Security also formulated the Organization and Working Rules for *Administrative Mediation* in 2007. Since then, the administrative mediation system has turned a new page in a new historical period.

Although legislative provisions on administrative mediation have existed since the founding of the People's Republic of China, it is only recently that a large-scale and systematic standardization work dedicated to administrative mediation has really begun. Although the pace of institutionalization and development of administrative mediation is still far less developed than that of other mediation systems, such as people's mediation, it has likewise received unprecedented attention and development in the process of reforming the pluralistic dispute resolution mechanism and the administration of law and building a government based on the rule of law.

The reform of the pluralistic dispute resolution mechanism was implemented step-by-step under the impetus of the Supreme People's Court, during which a series of ADR mechanisms, including administrative mediation, were given new vigor. In 2001, the Supreme People's Court and the Ministry of Justice also reached a consensus on the development of people's mediation and decided to establish a working mechanism to link people's mediation with litigation. On January 1, 2002, the Supreme People's Court and the Ministry of Justice jointly issued the *Opinions on Further Strengthening People's Mediation* work in the New Era. On September 16, 2002, the Supreme People's Court issued the *Several Provisions on the Trial of Civil Cases Involving People's Mediation Agreements*. On February 13, 2004, the Supreme People's Court and the Ministry of Justice jointly issued the *Opinions on Further Strengthening People's Mediation Work to Effectively Maintain Social Stability*. The issuance of this series of normative documents has enabled the contractual validity of mediation agreements to be unified and clarified in the national judicial system, and has played an important guiding role in enabling the judicial organs to support the work of people's mediation and give full play to its functions.

Unfortunately, while the institutionalization and standardization of people's mediation have achieved significant results, this has "inadvertently" indirectly caused the shrinkage of administrative mediation. The introduction of the *Certain Provisions on Hearing Civil Cases Involving People's Mediation Agreements* in 2002 gave society the illusion that "only people's mediation agreements have contractual effect, while other mediation agreements, including administrative mediation, do not have such an effect." In practice, many of the mediation duties originally belonging to the administrative organs have become ambiguous, and some administrative organs have refused to mediate on this basis. Some people thought that administrative conciliation was an administrative act and feared that the parties might renege or initiate administrative proceedings, and the emphasis on administration in accordance with the law at the time also prompted many administrative authorities to refuse to exercise their duty to conciliate on this basis.[26] On September 16, 2004, the Judicial Committee of the Supreme People's Court discussed and adopted the *Provisions on Certain Issues Concerning the Civil Mediation Work of the People's Courts*, according to which, the court, with the consent of the parties, may entrust the mediation of a case to an enterprise, institution, social group or other organization that has a specific relationship with the parties or a certain connection with the case, as well as to an individual with expertise, specific social experience, a specific relationship with the parties and who is conducive to facilitating the mediation, and, after reaching a mediation agreement, the court will confirm it in accordance with the law. This has led to a further deepening of the reform of the multi-dispute settlement mechanism and the initial establishment of a system of judicial confirmation of entrusted mediation agreements and settlement agreements, etc. This has further deepened the reform of the multiple dispute resolution mechanism, and the judicial confirmation system for entrusted mediation agreements and settlement agreements has been initially established.

The Second Five-Year Reform Outline of the People's Courts (2004–2008), issued by the Supreme People's Court on October 26, 2005, proposed to strengthen and improve the litigation mediation system, attach importance to the guidance of people's mediation, support and supervise arbitration activities in accordance with the law, explore new methods of dispute resolution together with other departments and organizations, and promote the establishment of a sound diversified dispute resolution mechanism. According to the central government's unified plan for judicial reform, the reform of the multi-dispute settlement mechanism should be deepened by 2008. In July 2007, the Supreme People's Court set up a project group on "Reform of the Multiple Dispute Resolution Mechanism," with the participation of more than ten units, including the Legislative Affairs Office of the State Council, to conduct research and draft reform proposals on litigation mediation, administrative mediation, and people's mediation. In 2008, the Supreme People's Court's "three-step" approach to the reform of the multi-dispute settlement mechanism was basically established: the first stage was for the Supreme People's Court to issue normative opinions on the interface between litigation and mediation; the second stage was for the central government to issue policy documents encouraging the development of various dispute settlement mechanisms; and the third stage was to solidify the results of the reform by amending and enacting the relevant laws.[27]

Since 2008, the central government has launched a new round of judicial reform, deploying the reform task of "establishing and improving a conflict and dispute resolution mechanism linking litigation and non-litigation." On March 17, 2009, the Supreme People's Court issued the *Third Five-Year Reform Outline of the People's Courts (2009–2013)*, proposing to cooperate with relevant departments to vigorously develop alternative dispute resolution mechanisms, expand the scope of mediation subjects, improve the mediation mechanism, provide the people with more alternative dispute resolution methods, and strengthen the effective interface between pre-litigation and litigation mediation, in accordance with the requirements of a multi-disciplinary dispute resolution mechanism that is "led by the party committee, supported by the government, participated by multiple parties and promoted by the judiciary."

On July 24, 2009, the Supreme People's Court issued the *Opinions on the Establishment of a Sound Mechanism for the Resolution of Disputes between Litigation and Non-Litigation* (Fafa [2009] No. 45), which regulates the working mechanism between various types of mediation, arbitration, and litigation, and clearly stipulates that

after an agreement with the nature of a civil contract reached through mediation by an administrative organ or other organization with mediation functions is signed and sealed by the mediation organization and the mediator, the parties may apply to the people's court with jurisdiction to confirm its validity,

This thus expands the scope of mediation agreements that give contractual effect and judicial confirmation of mediation agreements.

The introduction of these documents and initiatives has encouraged the development of extra-judicial dispute resolution mechanisms such as administrative mediation, and has also helped to ease the pressure on the judiciary's caseload. On June 7, 2010, the Supreme People's Court issued the *Opinions on Further Implementing the Principle of "Prioritizing Mediation and Combining Mediation and Judgment,"* which requires the courts actively to guide the parties to choose non-litigation mediation organizations to resolve their disputes in the nearest and local area after receiving the indictment or oral indictment and before the formal filing of a case that has not been mediated by people's mediation, administrative mediation, and other alternative dispute resolution methods, and to strive to resolve conflicts and disputes before filing a lawsuit. After a case has been accepted by the court and before a decision is made, the court may, with the consent of the parties concerned, entrust mediation to relevant organizations such as people's mediation, administrative mediation, industrial mediation, etc., or to deputies of the National People's Congress or members of the Chinese People's Political Consultative Conference, etc., which are conducive to the settlement of cases by mediation.

In April 2011, 16 units, including the Central Committee for Comprehensive Governance, the Supreme Court, the Supreme Prosecutor, the Legislative Affairs Office of the State Council, the Ministry of Public Security and other units jointly issued the *Guiding Opinions on Further Promoting the Great Mediation of Conflicts and Disputes* (Comprehensive Governance Committee

[2011] No. 10), a document that deployed more specific reform tasks to various departments, especially the administrative departments, and addressed some key issues in the work of various non-litigation dispute resolution mechanisms, thus basically completing the "second step" of the reform. For administrative mediation, the *Guiding Opinions on Further Promoting the Great Mediation of Conflicts and Disputes* is very clear in its point of view, and its work tasks and requirements are detailed to several major functional departments involved in areas where social conflicts are currently concentrated and frequent, as listed below:[28]

1. Disputes reported to the 110 police service desks of public security organs that can be mediated should be promptly diverted to the relevant responsible units for handling through the Grand Mediation Organization. Public security police stations participate in the mediation of conflicts and disputes in township (street) comprehensive governance work centers, and may set up resident people's mediation rooms and invite people's mediators to participate in the joint mediation of conflicts and disputes.
2. Human resources and social security departments, together with trade unions and enterprise representative organizations, should promote the construction of labor dispute mediation organizations in townships (streets), especially in labor security service offices (stations), and do a good job in the interface between labor dispute mediation, arbitration, and litigation.
3. Health administration departments should actively coordinate and cooperate with judicial administration and insurance supervision departments to promote the establishment of standardized people's mediation committees for medical disputes, promote the establishment of a sound mechanism to safeguard the work of people's mediation for medical disputes, promote medical liability insurance, standardize professional identification agencies, unify the identification procedures and standards for medical damages and medical accidents, and strengthen the resolution and handling of medical disputes.
4. The Land and Resources Department should set up a land dispute mediation working group through the Great Mediation Work Platform, train village land dispute mediators among people's mediators, and take advantage of the situation to receive and timely mediate conflicts and disputes involving land ownership, compensation, and resettlement for land requisition, etc.
5. The Administration for Industry and Commerce should strengthen the construction of the administrative law enforcement system for industry and commerce through the Great Mediation Work Platform, and bring into play the role of consumer associations to promote the construction of a consumer rights protection network.
6. Civil affairs departments should make full use of mediation methods to handle civil affairs and administrative disputes and civil disputes related

to civil affairs and administration, speed up the construction of harmonious communities, strengthen the construction of village (resident) committees, community management, elderly care services, and the construction of full-time social workers, and establish a network of mediation organizations extending to communities and village groups.
7. The housing and urban-rural construction departments should establish a daily work contact network and liaison officer system through the Great Mediation Work Platform, and implement a joint meeting system in conjunction with relevant departments, focusing on mediating conflicts and disputes arising from urban house demolition and construction.
8. The petition and visitation departments should further improve the working mechanism to interface with the Great Mediation Work Platform, and organize and coordinate and vigorously promote the use of mediation to resolve the petitioners' demands.
9. Trade unions, women's federations, and communist youth league organizations should give full play to their own advantages and actively participate in the Great Mediation Work.
10. Party committees and governments at all levels should strengthen the organizational leadership of the Great Mediation Work in conflicts and disputes. The head of the Party and government is the first person responsible for the Great Mediation Work.

It can be said that the *Guiding Opinions on Further Promoting the Work of Large-scale Mediation of Conflicts and Disputes* has set out clear policy requirements and construction tasks for the State Council, its departments, and local governments at all levels to establish and improve administrative mediation system, which has greatly mobilized the motivation and enthusiasm of administrative subjects to carry out mediation. Of course, this has also led to many of the mediations originally belonging to "people's mediation," "community mediation" and "industry mediation" being gradually transformed into *de facto* administrative mediation in practice.

In August 2010, the Standing Committee of the National People's Congress passed the *Law of the People's Republic of China on People's Mediation*, incorporating into law the contractual validity of mediation agreements and the judicial confirmation system, completing a "tentative" exploration of legislative steps. In March 2011, the Supreme People's Court issued *Several Provisions on the Procedures for Judicial Confirmation of People's Mediation Agreements*, specifically clarifying the specific procedural issues of judicial confirmation. Article 194 of the Civil Procedure Law, which was amended and adopted in 2012, provides that

> an application for judicial confirmation of a mediation agreement shall be submitted jointly by the parties to the grass-roots people's court where the mediation organization is located within 30 days from the effective date

of the mediation agreement in accordance with the People's Mediation Law and other laws.

This provision, through the expression "the People's Mediation Law and other laws," provides a basis in litigation law for the judicial confirmation procedure of administrative mediation agreements.

While the reform of the diversified dispute resolution mechanism is being vigorously promoted, the new concept of "administration according to law and government according to the rule of law" is being implemented by the administrative organs, which together give a new theoretical connotation to administrative mediation. In the period of social transition, citizens' awareness of the subject is gradually increasing, and the administrative concept of service is emerging. As a result, the traditional administrative means of resolving disputes in the form of orders and controls are no longer effective, and administrative mediation, which is consultative, authoritative, professional, and highly effective, has become the government's "new favorite" means of resolving social conflicts.

As early as April 2004, in order to implement the basic strategy of following the rule of law and the spirit of the 16th National Congress and the Third Plenary Session of the 16th Central Committee of the CPC, adhere to governance for the people, comprehensively promote administration in accordance with the law, and build a government based on the rule of law, the State Council issued the *Implementation Outline for Comprehensively Promoting Administration in accordance with the Law* (State Development [2004] No. 10), which clearly stated that "the role of mediation in resolving social conflicts should be given full play" and that

> In civil disputes, if an agreement is reached through mediation by the administrative organ, the administrative organ should produce a mediation letter; if an agreement cannot be reached through mediation, the administrative organ should promptly inform the parties of their rights and channels for redress.

On January 1, 2010, the General Office of the State Council issued the *Legislative Work Plan of the State Council for 2010*. Among the 116 "legislative projects that need to be studied urgently and proposed when conditions are ripe," the Administrative Mediation Regulations drafted by the Legislative Affairs Office was placed among the nine "draft amendments to laws and administrative regulations that need to be formulated or amended for consideration by the Standing Committee of the National People's Congress to regulate administrative acts and strengthen the government's own construction."

On November 8, 2010, the State Council issued the *Opinions on Strengthening the Construction of a Government Based on the Rule of Law* (State Development [2010] No. 33), summarizing and promoting the experience gained since the construction of a government based on the rule of law in 2004, and proposing several specific measures. The opinion proposes:

> We should improve the mediation mechanism for social conflicts and disputes, make administrative mediation an important duty of local people's governments at all levels and relevant departments, establish an administrative mediation work system under the overall responsibility of local people's governments at all levels, with government legal institutions taking the lead and functional departments as the main body, and give full play to the role of administrative organs in resolving administrative disputes and civil disputes. The administrative mediation system should be improved, the scope of mediation should be scientifically defined, and the mediation procedures should be standardized. Mediation should be conducted proactively in civil disputes over resource development, environmental pollution, public safety accidents, and other disputes involving many people, with a large impact, and which may affect social stability … should promote the establishment of a great mediation linkage mechanism linking administrative mediation with people's mediation and judicial mediation to achieve effective interaction between various types of mediation subjects and the synergy of mediation work.

At the same time, it is required to "strengthen the work of administrative reconsideration" and

> [to] pay attention to the use of mediation and conciliation to resolve disputes; if mediation or conciliation fails to reach an agreement, a reconsideration decision shall be made in a timely and fair manner in accordance with the law, and administrative acts that are illegal or improper shall be revoked, changed or confirmed as illegal.

Under the leadership of construction planning at the policy-making level, the institutionalization of administrative mediation has been carried out in various places. Hebei Province already started to strengthen the role of administrative mediation in the field of labor and social security as early as 2007–2008. From 2009 to 2011, 21 prefecture-level cities (autonomous prefectures) in Sichuan Province formulated 22 normative documents on administrative mediation. Subsequently, provinces such as Jiangxi, Henan, Shandong, and Jiangsu have also issued opinions, rules, and measures to strengthen administrative mediation. In addition to this comprehensive administrative mediation system, many special administrative mediation systems have emerged, for example, the Fangchenggang Municipal Health Bureau has issued the *Implementation Plan for Strengthening and Standardizing Health Administrative Mediation*, which applies administrative mediation not only to the resolution of medical disputes, but also focuses on the resolution of civil and administrative disputes occurring in areas such as hospital management, medical ethics, medical services, diagnosis, and identification of occupational diseases, health law enforcement, personnel treatment, and food safety. The Suzhou Education Bureau has issued the Administrative Mediation Work System (for Trial Implementation), which provides more detailed provisions on the concept, scope of application, organization, principles, and procedures of educational administrative mediation. In addition, the Wuxi Municipal Price Bureau, the Suzhou Municipal Grain Bureau, and the Nanjing Municipal Bureau of Culture, Radio, Television, Press and Publications have all formulated documents such as the *Administrative Mediation Work System* and the *Opinions on Effectively Strengthening Administrative Mediation Work*. The models of administrative mediation have shown a diversified trend, and certain progress has been made in terms of scope of application, organization, staffing, principles and procedures, and financial security.[29]

3.4 New Developments in Administrative Mediation in the "New Era" (2013–the Present)

The "new era" is a major political judgment made in the report of the 19th National Congress of the Communist Party of China on the new historical position of China's development, which is based on the historic changes and achievements in the cause of the Party and the state since the 18th National Congress and combined with the new changes in the main conflicts in Chinese society. Therefore, the "new era" administrative mediation referred to here is a link between the past and the future, and refers to the new development of administrative mediation since the 18th National Congress of the Communist Party of China.

The *Decision of the Central Committee of the Communist Party of China on Several Major Issues of Comprehensively Deepening Reform*, adopted at the Third Plenary Session of the 18th Central Committee of the Communist Party of China on November 12, 2013, proposes to "innovate an effective system for preventing and resolving social conflicts ... improve the linkage work system of people's mediation, administrative mediation, and judicial mediation, and establish a comprehensive mechanism for mediating and resolving conflicts and disputes." On October 23, 2014, the *Decision of the Central Committee of the Communist Party of China on Several Major Issues in Comprehensively Promoting the Rule of Law*, adopted at the Fourth Plenary Session of the 18th Central Committee, also proposed to "strengthen the construction of industrial and professional people's mediation organizations and improve the linkage work system of people's mediation, administrative mediation, and judicial mediation."

On October 13, 2014, General Secretary Xi Jinping presided over the 17th Meeting of the Central Leading Group for Comprehensively Deepening

Reform and delivered an important speech, emphasizing in particular the need to

> adhere to the linkage of people's mediation, administrative mediation and judicial mediation, and encourage the resolution of problems through first mediation and other means; adhere to governance by law, and apply the rule of law thinking and the rule of law to resolve all kinds of conflicts and disputes.

The meeting considered and adopted the *Opinions on Improving the Diversified Resolution Mechanism for Conflicts and Disputes*, which was jointly issued by the General Office of the CPC Central Committee and the General Office of the State Council on December 6 of the same year (Document No. 60 [2015] of the General Office of the CPC Central Committee), which provides detailed provisions on the interface and coordination between administrative mediation and the people's courts.

In December 2015, the Central Committee of the Communist Party of China and the State Council issued the *Implementation Outline for the Construction of a Government Based on the Rule of Law (2015–2020)*, which listed administrative mediation as one of the three major institutional initiatives for civil dispute resolution in building a government based on the rule of law:

> Improve the systems of administrative mediation, administrative adjudication and arbitration. Improve administrative mediation system, further clarify the scope of administrative mediation, improve the administrative mediation mechanism, and standardize administrative mediation procedures. Improve the administrative adjudication system and strengthen the function of administrative organs to resolve civil disputes closely related to administrative activities. The relevant administrative organs shall carry out administrative mediation and administrative adjudication in accordance with the law, and resolve conflicts and disputes in a timely and effective manner.

Although the *Administrative Mediation Law* or the *Administrative Mediation Regulations*, which are universally applicable nationwide, have not yet been introduced, the institutionalization of administrative mediation has progressed in some areas due to encouragement, support, and guidance from the policy. In May 2016, the State Intellectual Property Office issued the *Guidelines for Administrative Mediation of Patent Disputes* (for trial implementation). On July 31, 2018, the State Council promulgated the *Regulations on the Prevention and Handling of Medical Disputes*, which clearly stipulates that in the event of a medical dispute, the doctor and the patient may apply for administrative mediation to resolve the dispute, continuing and expanding the administrative mediation system for medical accident compensation disputes under the *Regulations on the Handling of Medical Accidents* of 2002.

In addition, on June 28, 2016, the Supreme People's Court issued the *Opinions on the People's Courts Further Deepening the Reform of the Diversified Dispute Resolution Mechanism* (Fafa [2016] No. 14), emphasizing the need to promote the improvement of the systems of administrative mediation, administrative reconciliation, and administrative adjudication; on the same day, it issued a judicial interpretation of the *Regulations of the Supreme People's Court on Specially Invited Mediation in the People's Courts* (Fa Shi [2016] No. 14), stipulating that "legally established ... administrative mediation ... organizations may apply to join the roster of specially invited mediation organizations." On September 10, 2018, the Supreme People's Court, the Ministry of Public Security, the Ministry of Justice and the China Banking and Insurance Regulatory Commission jointly issued the *Work Specifications for "Online Data Integration Processing" of Road Traffic Accident Damage Compensation Disputes (for Trial Implementation)* in the name of the General Office of the four departments, refining the online integration processing of road traffic disputes with administrative mediation by the traffic management departments of public security organs and court mediation as the main content in terms of working mechanism, division of responsibilities, information sharing, business process, and organizational guarantee.

3.5 The Dilemma of Administrative Mediation Breakthrough

Through the historical changes and development of administrative mediation, we can see that administrative mediation is a non-litigation dispute resolution mechanism with a deep historical and cultural heritage, a huge "market" and a significant role. At this crucial period of building a moderately prosperous society and starting a new journey of building a modern socialist country, administrative mediation will become an important breakthrough in innovative social governance and an important means for various administrative entities to apply the rule of law thinking and the rule of law to resolve conflicts and issues of vital interest to the public. For this reason, administrative mediation has now been institutionalized to an unprecedented degree. Despite this, there is still an illogical peculiarity in administrative mediation in practice: the importance and prominence of administrative mediation in the dispute resolution system are not commensurate with its low degree of standardization, institutionalization, and theorization.

First, compared with people's mediation and judicial mediation, there are more than 200 normative legal documents specifically regulating administrative mediation, and the institutions and personnel authorized to carry out administrative mediation have a wide range of tentacles, but the "momentum" and "effect" of administrative mediation seem to be far inferior to other mediation mechanisms. What is even more paradoxical is that a considerable number of effective administrative mediations are functioning in the name of people's mediation, such as those conducted by grass-roots judicial and administrative organizations, in the name of people's mediation, in the process of guiding people's mediation work, as well as those conducted jointly by relevant administrative departments, industrial entities, and people's mediation organizations, such as the People's Mediation Committee for Medical Disputes, to resolve industrial disputes. For this reason, some scholars have summarized the current situation of administrative mediation in China into "three mosts," namely, most administrative organs have dispute mediation functions, most mediation functions are not obligatory duties, and most administrative mediation results are not enforceable.[30]

Second, mediators engaged in administrative mediation work in public authorities at all levels, and they are mostly state employees performing public duties in accordance with the law. They usually have a higher level of professionalism and theoretical and practical skills than people's mediators, and are especially competent in resolving professional disputes. However, the mechanisms of entry, training, incentives, responsibility, and withdrawal of mediators are not sound. Many grass-roots administrative mediation workers (such as local police officers) are reluctant to engage in mediation work and lack a sense of professional value and honor in mediation.

Third, the number of disputes resolved by administrative mediation is no less than that of people's mediation and court mediation, and in the case of public order mediation alone, the number of disputes resolved has greatly exceeded that of court mediation, and the growth rate of the number of cases concluded by public order mediation even exceeds that of people's mediation.[31] The position of administrative mediation in the dispute resolution system is not insignificant. However, it is far more difficult to count the number of cases concluded by various types of administrative mediation, the number of mediators involved in mediating cases, or to investigate the experience and weaknesses of administrative mediation in practice than people's mediation or court mediation.

Finally, the scope of application of administrative mediation covers civil, administrative, and some minor criminal cases, including not only a surprising number of public security mediation, traffic accident dispute mediation, and other general civil dispute handling, but also being widely used in civil and administrative crossover cases, group disputes and more complex or specialized dispute areas, such as patent infringement, environmental infringement, medical malpractice infringement, etc. Therefore, administrative mediation shows stronger professional advantages and high efficiency compared to other types of mediation. However, there are two controversies in the theoretical community regarding the scope of application of administrative mediation: first, whether it is only to resolve administrative disputes or civil disputes, or both; and, second, whether the disputes to be mediated must be directly related to the statutory duties of the administrative organ to which the mediation body belongs. In this regard, there are not only different academic views, but also different local legislative examples.

These problems have affected the ability of administrative mediation mechanisms to play the social governance role they were intended to play. The reason for this is that administrative mediation differs from people's mediation and court mediation in two main elements: first, there is no relatively systematic or unified legislative regulation for administrative mediation, which leads to various levels, places, and types of administrative subjects going their own way and making it difficult to unify them; second, there is no unified focal point for administrative mediation for coordination, management, statistics, and evaluation. This means that a unified administrative mediation system is necessary and that the rule of law in administrative mediation needs to be further improved.

At the local level, local legislative experiments have gradually been formed based on the practical exploration of administrative mediation in various places. For example, on June 1, 2015, the Beijing Municipal People's Government issued the *Measures on Administrative Mediation in Beijing*; on July 8, the Xiamen Municipal Government issued the *Xiamen Municipal Administrative Mediation Procedures Provisions*; on October 23, the Liaoning Provincial People's Government issued the *Liaoning Provincial Administrative Mediation Provisions*; on December 30, 2016, the General Office of the Zhejiang Provincial People's Government issued the *Measures on Administrative Mediation in Zhejiang Province*. On November 22, 2017, the *Interim Measures on Administrative Mediation in Wuhan City* was issued; etc. In addition to the *Provisional Measures on Administrative Mediation*, *Provisional Provisions on Administrative Mediation*, and *Measures on the Implementation of Administrative Mediation*, which were introduced as local legislation, there are also many *Opinions on the Implementation of Administrative Mediation* issued by local governments or their working departments at all levels. In terms of the annual number of local normative documents issued for administrative mediation, 34 were issued in 2010, 57 in 2011, reaching 99 in 2012, 23 in 2013, 18 in 2014, 14 in 2015, 9 in 2016, 4 in 2017 and 10 in 2018.[32]

At the national level, unified legislation on administrative mediation has also been put on the legislative agenda. In 2015–2016, the *Administrative Mediation Regulations*, drafted by the Legislative Affairs Office of the State Council, were included in the *Legislative Projects on Deepening Administrative System Reform and Strengthening Government Self-Building* and *Legislative Projects on Continuously Promoting Simplification* and *Decentralization of Government and Strengthening Government Self-Building*, respectively, but in 2017–2018, the *Administrative Mediation Regulations* did not appear in the legislative work plan of the State Council. In March 2018, the State Council institutional reform program approved at the first session of the 13th National People's Congress to integrate the responsibilities of the State Council Legislative Affairs Office and re-established the Ministry of Justice, which no longer retains the State Council Legislative Affairs Office. The *Administrative Mediation Regulations*, which were previously planned to be drafted by the State Council Legislative Affairs Office, may be completed in other forms by the re-established Ministry of Justice. In the future, there may be three forms of unified administrative mediation legislation: first, the Standing Committee of the National People's Congress will enact a separate *Administrative Mediation Law*, similar to the *People's Mediation Law*; second, administrative mediation will be placed in a codified Mediation Law and regulated as a part; third, the approach of sub-departmental or sub-local legislation will continue to be maintained, with appropriate unification and improvement of the existing administrative mediation mechanism.

Notes

1 Edward L. Rabin: Law and Legislation of Administrative State, trans. Wang Baomin and Tang Xueliang, *Tsinghua Rule of Law*, 2013 (2).
2 He Wenyan and Liao Yong'an: *Monographs on Civil Litigation Law* (Xiangtan: Xiangtan University Press, 2011), pp. 360–361.
3 Yuan Gang: *The Evolution of Governmental Institutions in Ancient China* (Harbin: Heilongjiang People's Publishing House, 2003), pp. 20–21. See also Song Caifa and Liu Yumin: *General Theory of Mediation Points and Techniques* (Beijing: People's Court Publishing House, 2007).
4 Zhang Jinfan: *A History of the Chinese Civil Litigation System* (Chengdu: Ba Shu Shu Shu, 1999), p. 16.
5 Yan Qingxia: *A Study of the Court Mediation System* (Beijing: Publishing House of China People's Security University, 2008), p. 9.
6 Zhang Jinfan: *A History of the Chinese Civil Litigation System*, p. 157.
7 He Wenyan and Liao Yong'an: *Monographs on Civil Litigation Law*, p. 362.
8 J. Cohen: Chinese Mediation on the Eve of Modernization, trans. Wang Xiaohong, in Qiang Shigong (Ed.): *Mediation, Legal System and Modernity: A Study of China's Mediation System* (Beijing: China Legal Publishing House, 2001), pp. 97–98.
9 Chang Yi: *Mediation System in China* (Beijing: Law Publishing House, 2013), p. 4.
10 Hu Xusheng: *Jail and Litigation: A Study of Traditional Chinese Litigation Culture* (Beijing: Chinese University Press, 2012), p. 108.
11 Chen Guangzhong and Shen Guofeng: *Ancient Chinese Judicial System* (Beijing: Mass Publishing House, 1984), p. 215.
12 Gong Rufu: A Brief Discussion of the Civil Mediation System in the Republic of China and Its Gains and Losses, *Guangming Daily*, May 26, 2009. This article examined administrative mediation in the Republic of China in some detail, and many of the texts and practices of the administrative mediation system in the Republic of China cited by him are difficult to find out in other ways. This chapter refers to this.
13 He Wenyan and Liao Yong'an: *Monographs on Civil Litigation Law*, p. 364.
14 Lu Xingshun, Liu Bo, and Zhao Zhanwu: *The Roster of First-Class Admirals of the Kuomintang* (Beijing: China Literature and History Press, 2013), p. 126.
15 Gong Rufu: A Brief Discussion on the Civil Mediation System in the Republic of China and Its Gains and Losses, p. 12.

16 Tianjin Local History Compilation and Repair Commission Office, Tianjin Municipal Bureau of Justice: *Tianjin General History – Judicial Administration* (Tianjin: Tianjin Academy of Social Sciences Press, 2008), p. 286.
17 Xu Xin: Mediation, in *China and the World* (Beijing: China University of Political Science and Law Press, 2013), pp. 135–136.
18 Gong Rufu: A Brief Discussion on the Civil Mediation System in the Republic of China and Its Gains and Losses, *Guangming Daily*, May 26, 2009, Edition 12.
19 Ibid.
20 He Wenyan and Liao Yong'an: *Monographs on Civil Litigation Law*, p. 365.
21 *Letter of Instructions from the Government of the Border Region on Popularizing Mediation, Summarizing Jurisprudence, and Cleaning Up Prisons*, June 6, 1933, Wu Yanping, Liu Genju, et al.: *Compilation of Reference Materials on Criminal Procedure Jurisprudence (Part I)* (Beijing: Peking University Press, 2005), pp. 156–157.
22 Hou Xinyi: *From Justice for the People to People's Justice: A Study on the Popularized Judicial System in the Shaanxi-Gansu-Ningxia Border Region* (Beijing: China University of Political Science and Law Press, 2007), pp. 280–282.
23 Yang Yonghua and Fang Keqin: *Draft History of the Legal System in the Shaanxi-Gansu-Ningxia Border Region (Litigation and Prison Administration)* (Beijing: Law Press, 1987), p. 217.
24 Guo Chengwei and Si Yuan: *Selected Papers and Writings of Professor Guo Chengwei* (Beijing: China Procuratorial Press, 2011), pp. 292–293.
25 See the *Decision of the State Administration for Industry and Commerce on the Repealing* and *Amending Some Regulations* (State Administration for Industry and Commerce Decree No. 92), October 27, 2017.
26 Fan Yu, Some Issues in the Interface of Litigation and Non-Litigation Procedures, in School of Lawyers, Renmin University of China. Available at: http://lawyer.ruc.edu.cn/; html/msfc/5088.html, 2011-09-27/2014-08-31. In the speech by Cao Jianming, Executive Vice-President of the Supreme People's Court, at the National Conference on People's Mediation, it is mentioned that: First, the mediation must be conducted by a people's mediation committee. According to the provisions of Article 16 of the Civil Procedure Law and other laws, the judicial interpretation clearly stipulates that the People's Mediation Committee must be the one to preside over the mediation. Only the mediation agreement reached under the auspices of the People's Mediation Committee will be subject to this judicial interpretation. Mediation agreements reached under the auspices of administrative organs, other organizations, or other mediation institutions will not be subject to this provision.
27 Jiang Huiling: The Reform Process of China's Pluralistic Dispute Resolution Mechanism, *People's Court News*, September 7, 2011, p. 8.
28 Although some elements of the work were dominated by people's mediation, the substance of administrative mediation gradually emerged in the subsequent operation of the practice.
29 Zhang Zhiyuan and Liu Lipeng: The Current Situation and Development of China's Administrative Mediation System, *Journal of Seeking Knowledge*, 2013 (5).
30 Zhao Xudong: *Disputes and Dispute Resolution: An In-depth Analysis from Causes to Concepts* (Beijing: Law Press, 2009), p. 125.
31 Official documents show that in 2006, the total number of disputes mediated by people's mediation organizations nationwide was 4,628,000, while the total

number of cases mediated by public security organs was 1,378,000, less than one-third of people's mediation, and 1,333,000 civil cases were mediated by courts nationwide during the same period; While the number of people's mediation cases reached 7,776,000 in 2009, the number of public security mediation cases reached 3,720,000, with the total number of the latter reaching about one-half of the former, and 3,593,000 cases were settled through mediation and dismissal by the courts in the same period. In the whole administrative mediation system, public security administrative mediation is only one part, and public security mediation is only one part under public security administrative mediation. See Zhang Qinglin: A Study of China's Administrative Mediation System in the New Era: A Perspective on the Resolution of Civil Disputes, PhD thesis, Xiangtan University, 2014, p. 101. Other scholars have pointed out that in urban areas, the number of disputes resolved by the 110 police alone in recent years may have exceeded the number of disputes resolved by litigation and people's mediation. "The disputes absorbed and resolved by 110 policing are so large that to some extent they can be regarded as the base of the pyramid of the contemporary Chinese urban dispute resolution system." Zuo Weimin: Dispute Resolution Mechanism in the 110 Policing System, *Jurisprudence*, 2006 (11).

32 Wolters Kluwer Prior Regulations Database, with data as of December 31, 2018. In the database of Peking University's magic treasures, there are two central regulations and judicial interpretations entitled "Administrative Mediation," one of which is the defunct *Measures on Administrative Mediation of Contract Disputes and the Guidelines on Administrative Mediation of Patent Disputes (for Trial Implementation)*, which came into effect in 2017. The other is 266 local regulations and rules, of which 6 are local government regulations, 181 are other local regulatory documents, and 79 are local working documents.

References

Chang Yi: *Mediation System in China*, Beijing: Law Publishing House, 2013.
Chen Guangzhong and Shen Guofeng: *Ancient Chinese Judicial System*, Beijing: Mass Publishing House, 1984.
Cohen, J.: Chinese Mediation on the Eve of Modernization, trans. Wang Xiaohong, in Qiang Shigong (Ed.): *Mediation, Legal System and Modernity: A Study of China's Mediation System*, Beijing: China Legal Publishing House, 2001, pp. 97–98.
Gong Rufu: A Brief Discussion on the Civil Mediation System in the Republic of China and Its Gains and Losses, Guangming Daily, May 26, 2009, p. 12.
Guo Chengwei and Si Yuan: *Selected Papers and Writings of Professor Guo Chengwei*, Beijing: China Procuratorial Press, 2011.
He Wenyan and Liao Yong'an: *Monographs on Civil Litigation Law*, Xiangtan: Xiangtan University Press, 2011.
Hou Xinyi: *From Justice for the People to People's Justice: A Study on the Popularized Judicial System in the Shaanxi-Gansu-Ningxia Border Region*, Beijing: China University of Political Science and Law Press, 2007.
Hu Xusheng: *Jail and Litigation: A Study of Traditional Chinese Litigation Culture*, Beijing: Chinese University Press, 2012.
Jiang Huiling: The Reform Process of China's Pluralistic Dispute Resolution Mechanism, People's Court News, September 7, 2011, p. 8.

Lu Xingshun, Liu Bo, and Zhao Zhanwu: *The Roster of First-Class Admirals of the Kuomintang*, Beijing: China Literature and History Press, 2013.
Rabin, Edward L.: Law and Legislation of Administrative State, trans. Wang Baomin and Tang Xueliang, *Tsinghua Rule of Law*, 2013 (2): 235–302.
Song Caifa and Liu Yumin: *General Theory of Mediation Points and Techniques*, Beijing: People's Court Publishing House, 2007.
Wu Yanping, Liu Genju, et al.: *Compilation of Reference Materials on Criminal Procedure Jurisprudence (Part I)*, Beijing: Peking University Press, 2005.
Xu Xin: *Mediation: China and the World*, Beijing: China University of Political Science and Law Press, 2013.
Yan Qingxia: *A Study of the Court Mediation System*, Beijing: Publishing House of China People's Security University, 2008.
Yang Yonghua and Fang Keqin: *Draft History of the Legal System in the Shaanxi-Gansu-Ningxia Border Region (Litigation and Prison Administration)*, Beijing: Law Press, 1987.
Yuan Gang: *The Evolution of Governmental Institutions in Ancient China*, Harbin: Heilongjiang People's Publishing House, 2003.
Zhang Jinfan: *A History of the Chinese Civil Litigation System*, Chengdu: Ba Shu Shu Shu, 1999.
Zhang Qinglin: A Study of China's Administrative Mediation System in the New Era – A Perspective on the Resolution of Civil Disputes, PhD thesis, Xiangtan University, 2014.
Zhang Zhiyuan and Liu Lipeng: The Current Situation and Development of China's Administrative Mediation System, *Journal of Seeking Knowledge*, 2013 (5): 78–84.
Zhao Xudong: *Disputes and Dispute Resolution: An In-depth Analysis from Causes to Concepts*, Beijing: Law Press, 2009.
Zuo Weimin: Dispute Resolution Mechanism in the 110 Policing System, *Jurisprudence*, 2006 (11): 51–56.

4 The Dilemma and the Way Forward for Industry Mediation

Generally speaking, industrial mediation refers to the activities of mediation organizations set up within legally established industrial organizations to mediate civil disputes related to their industries. Modern industrial mediation gradually emerged during the in-depth development of the reform and opening-up, the gradual maturation of the market economy, and the full-scale social transformation. Moreover, with the development of trade organizations or unions, they have gradually become a third sector that is relatively independent from the state system and the market system, but at the same time are interdependent, interpenetrating, and co-developing. The development of trade mediation has also ushered in new historical opportunities. Since the Fifth Plenary Session of the 18th Party Central Committee proposed building a social governance system for all people to share, industry organizations have increasingly become the mainstay in resolving social conflicts and disputes by relying on their mediation function. Unfortunately, the development of industry mediation in China is still plagued by conceptual, institutional and systemic difficulties, and there is an urgent need to design and plan the development of industry mediation from the top level of the diversified dispute resolution mechanism.

4.1 Historical Development of Industry Mediation

Industry mediation has existed since ancient times, with some guilds already mediating internal disputes in the Shang and Zhou Dynasties, which can be said to be the prototype of industry mediation in China. Throughout the feudal period, mediation existed in various forms. Particularly after the Ming and Qing Dynasties, industry mediation became increasingly popular with the development of the commodity economy at that time.

4.1.1 Historical Practice of Industry Mediation in the Ming and Qing Dynasties

From the sixteenth century onwards, as a result of increasing demographic pressure, as well as the increase in social productivity and the refinement of the

DOI: 10.4324/9781003385776-4

division of labor, production for exchange became more common during the Ming and Qing Dynasties, and the development of the commodity economy was able to surpass previous historical periods, even to the point of the emergence of capitalism.[1] Thereafter, the Ming and Qing governments, especially the local governments, changed their tradition of "suppressing merchants" and became actively involved in the management of commercial order. In response to the need for order and profit, the Ming and Qing Dynasties also saw the increasing organization of merchant groups, with the flourishing of trade associations, guilds, and guild halls. It is increasingly common to rely on professional businessmen's groups to settle intra-industry commercial disputes, resulting in a more mature form of industrial mediation that has become a useful complement to national dispute resolution.

During the Ming and Qing Dynasties, China's commodity economy began to flourish, the ranks of merchants gradually grew and the system of commerce and trade expanded. Along with this came an increasing number of commercial disputes between merchants, such as disputes over peer-to-peer competition, disputes over trade names, disputes over partnerships and over the transportation of goods, which would affect the state's maintenance of the commercial order. Based on the practical need to resolve commercial disputes, protect the interests of merchants, and maintain commercial order, merchant groups set up professional merchant groups[2] to mediate commercial disputes between members or between members and outsiders according to internal rules, regulations, by-laws, and customs, and to maintain order in the market. Historical data show that these trade merchant groups not only excelled in cultural transmission, commercial development, and social governance, but also played an important role in mediating civil commercial disputes. Statistics from the Selected Archives of the Qianjia Dao Ba of the Qing Dynasty reveal that about 20 percent of the 112 commercial litigation cases recorded in Ba County, Chongqing, had to be first mediated by the guilds.[3] According to the records of the Chamber of Commerce in Suzhou, kept in its archives, from its establishment in January 1905 to February of the following year, the Chamber of Commerce in Suzhou received about 70 cases from various industries, of which more than 70 percent were successfully concluded, and less than 30 percent were delayed and referred to the government.[4] Industry-based businessmen's groups have been widely recognized and praised by businessmen and the government for their outstanding performance in mediating commercial disputes.

As an important means of resolving commercial disputes during the Ming and Qing Dynasties, the contribution of trade mediation to the maintenance of commercial order was unanimously recognized by merchants and officials alike. However, due to specific historical conditions, trade mediation in those days faced many difficulties in its actual operation, which prevented it from becoming a permanent institution. The achievements and limitations of the past trade mediation may not be of much relevance to the present, but the historical experience of the success of mediation in the Ming and Qing Dynasties,

112 *The Dilemma and the Way Forward for Industry Mediation*

and how to avoid the identified limitations in the present, are more revealing for the current reform of the pluralistic dispute resolution mechanism.

4.1.2 Specific Practices in the Development of Modern Industrial Mediation

After entering the new period, reform began a period of hard work and deep water, social stability entered a period of risk, and various conflicts and disputes were prone to occur, affecting social harmony and stability. All this requires the social governance model to change from one-way social management in the past to open social governance. Social governance places greater emphasis on the cooperative management of social affairs through consultation and collaboration among a plurality of subjects; it emphasizes the continuous process of consultation and coordination between people and rejects the command and control of society. It emphasizes respect for the social and political rights of members of society and advocates their empowerment so that they can have a voice and influence in the process of social governance.[5] The Third Plenary Session of the 18th CPC Central Committee proposed that the overall goal of the comprehensive deepening reform should be the modernization of governance capacity and the governance system, and also put forward higher requirements for the mechanism of resolving social conflicts and disputes.

4.1.2.1 Policy and Legal Support for Industry Mediation

The change in the mode of social governance has given impetus to the participation of trade organizations in resolving disputes in the industry, and through top-down policy encouragement and bottom-up practical exploration, mediation in the professions has taken on a "thriving" appearance. With the promulgation of the *People's Mediation Law* in 2010, the Ministry of Justice immediately issued the *Opinions on Strengthening the Construction of Industry and Professional People's Mediation Committees*, proposing to give full play to the advantages of industry mediation and resolve industry disputes in a targeted manner, according to the nature and difficulty of the conflicts and disputes and the specific circumstances of the parties involved. This was followed by the *Opinions on Further Strengthening Industry-based and Professional People's Mediation Work* in 2014. After the decision of the Fourth Plenary Session of the 18th Central Committee of the CPC on *Several Major Issues in Comprehensively Promoting the Rule of Law*, which proposed to "strengthen the construction of industry-based and professional people's mediation organizations," the Ministry of Justice, the Central Office of Comprehensive Governance, the Supreme People's Court and the Ministry of Civil Affairs formulated and issued the *Guidelines on Promoting Industry-based and Professional People's Mediation* in 2016. The guidance emphasizes that judicial administrative organs at all levels, comprehensive governance organizations, people's courts, civil affairs, and relevant industry authorities should attach great importance to mediation in the industry, actively seek to incorporate it into the overall plan of the Party Committee and government to enhance social governance capacity and further promote peace building and rule of law, and provide policy safeguards for the smooth implementation of mediation in the industry. In 2016, the *Opinions on the People's Courts Further Deepening the Reform of the Diversified Dispute Resolution Mechanism*, issued by the Supreme People's Court made it clearer that it should actively promote the establishment of commercial industry mediation organizations by qualified chambers of commerce, industry associations, mediation associations, and private non-enterprise units to provide industry mediation services in areas such as investment, finance, securities and futures, insurance, real estate, engineering contracting, technology transfer, environmental protection, e-commerce, intellectual property and international trade. A series of policy encouragements at the national level have created an unprecedented policy environment for the development of industry mediation in China. In 2018, the Supreme People's Court and the China Securities Regulatory Commission jointly issued the *Opinions on Comprehensively Promoting the Construction of a Diversified Dispute Resolution Mechanism for Securities and Futures*, which emphasized the need to strengthen the construction of securities industry mediation organizations and develop securities industry mediation. In 2019, the Supreme People's Court, the People's Bank of China, and the China Banking and Insurance Regulatory Commission jointly issued the *Opinions on Comprehensively Promoting the Construction of a Diversified Settlement Mechanism for Financial Disputes*, which proposed to establish a sound system of industry mediation for financial disputes with wide coverage, adaptability, efficiency, and convenience.

4.1.3 Overview of Industry Mediation Organizations and Their Development

Driven in both directions by national advocacy and local exploration, various industry organizations have started to actively carry out the practice of industry mediation. In terms of the organizational form of industry mediation, it generally involves the establishment of professional mediation committees or mediation centers within industry associations, which then direct the operation of specific mediation platforms and mediation studios. The following will mainly introduce the useful experiences of industry mediation in the securities industry, the real estate industry, property management, and the insurance industry.

1. *Securities industry mediation.* The China Securities Association, for example, established the China Securities Association Securities Dispute Mediation Center in 2012 with the aim of properly resolving securities business disputes, protecting the legitimate rights and interests of investors, safeguarding the overall interests of the securities industry and promoting the standardized and harmonious development of the securities market.

To this end, the China Securities Association has formulated two mediation rules, namely the "Administrative Measures for Securities Dispute Mediation Work of the China Securities Association" and the "Rules for Securities Dispute Mediation of the China Securities Association," as a means of regulating the mediation procedures for securities industry disputes. In addition, the China Securities Association has given full play to the role of local associations in regional industry autonomy and has established a collaborative mechanism for securities dispute mediation with 36 local associations across the country, so that the mediation of securities disputes led by the China Securities Association can be carried out in all regions of the country. By handling securities disputes through local associations, securities disputes can be resolved locally, nearby, and quickly, reducing the cost of mediation work and improving its efficiency. In order to meet the economic development and market demands in different regions, the China Securities Association supports local associations that are in a position to establish mediation bodies and appoint their own mediators, and provides guidance to local associations to carry out mediation work in securities disputes. The China Securities Association has also established an Internet-based mediation system for securities disputes, which enables the interface and information sharing of mediation work between the mediation center and local associations, and provides timely statistics on the progress of the mediation work of each local association in securities disputes. The Mediation Center of the China Securities Association is mainly composed of professionals from securities associations, securities companies, universities, and law firms, and currently has 289 full-time and part-time mediators. At present, it mainly handles securities business disputes between members and investors, between members and members, and between members and other stakeholders. After years of practice, the industry mediation of securities disputes, led by the China Securities Association, with the cooperation of local securities associations and the active participation of members, has been gradually improved and has achieved positive results in the practice of dispute resolution. From 2013 to the end of August 2016, the securities dispute mediation centers of the Securities Industry Association and local associations received a total of 4,479 applications for securities dispute mediation and successfully resolved 3,695 securities disputes.

In addition, the Shenzhen Securities Industry Association, and the Shenzhen Futures Industry Association and a few other organizations have jointly established the Shenzhen Securities and Futures Industry Dispute Mediation Center, which is also one of the representative organizations currently engaged in mediation in the securities industry in China. The Center encourages capital market participants to use mediation to resolve securities, futures and fund disputes and other types of disputes in the capital market, following the principles of independence, voluntary will, fairness, convenience, and effectiveness, advocating integrity and friendly morality, and promoting industry self-discipline and social harmony. The scope of its mediation business is mainly: civil disputes between natural persons, legal persons, and other organizations of equal status arising from securities, futures, funds, venture capital, and other capital market businesses, and has covered disputes over financial entrustment contracts, equity transfer disputes, stock trading disputes, financing and financing disputes, securities custody disputes, and securities investment advisory disputes. According to the person in charge of the Center, since its establishment, the Mediation Center has received more than 3,000 consultations of all kinds, received, and concluded more than 600 mediation cases, with a total settlement amount of more than $3 billion.

2 *Mediation in the real estate industry.* The China Real Estate Association (CREA), for example, deliberated on and established a mediation center at its Third General Meeting of the Seventh Session in 2015. The China Real Estate Association Mediation Center has formulated special rules for mediation, a code for mediators, and charging standards. Appointment and dismissal of the Center's mediators are decided by the General Office of the President of the China Real Estate Association. In addition to being familiar with real estate business, the mediators should also be familiar with real estate-related laws and regulations and enjoy a high reputation in the industry. The Center currently has over 100 professionally trained and certified mediators, mainly consisting of retired judges, arbitrators, senior lawyers, corporate executives, and university experts. The scope of the Center is nationwide civil and commercial disputes relating to real estate, including: economic disputes between natural persons, legal persons, and other organizations of equal status relating to real estate, construction works, procurement of components, expropriation compensation, real estate finance, etc.

3 *Mediation in the property management industry.* The Property Dispute Mediation Center of Beijing Property Management Industry Association, for example, was established in 2013 and is an internal body of the Beijing Property Management Industry Association. The Beijing Property Management Industry Association has formulated the following management systems: "Management Measures for Mediators of the Mediation Center of the Beijing Property Management Industry Association (for trial implementation)," "Management Measures for Mediation of Property Disputes of the Beijing Property Management Industry Association (for trial implementation)," and "Rules for Mediation of Property Disputes of the Beijing Property Management Industry Association (for Trial Implementation)." The group of mediators includes staff of the Association Secretariat, industry experts recommended by member units, and public interest lawyers. The Mediation Center's scope of mediation includes: (1) disputes over property service contracts; (2) disputes related

to property management in bidding disputes; (3) disputes over security and cleaning contracts related to property management; (4) disputes over tort (compensation for personal or property damage) related to property management; (5) disputes over unfair competition between property service enterprises; (6) disputes over equity in property enterprises; (7) disputes over the right to information between property enterprise and owners' committees or owners; and (8) disputes over cooperation agreements between property enterprises and other enterprises.

4 *Insurance industry mediation.* Let us take the Insurance Contract Dispute Mediation Committee of the Beijing Insurance Industry Association as an example. The industry mediation organization was established in 2008 to build a communication bridge between consumers and insurance companies to facilitate the resolution of insurance contract disputes. The advantage of an insurance industry mediation organization is that it is familiar with the rules of the insurance industry, and has a professional and precise grasp of insurance law and the rights and obligations of personal accident insurance claims in the insurance contract, just like the old Chinese doctor who can effectively diagnose the cause of the disease through a few steps of "looking, listening, asking, and feeling the pulse." The mediation organization of the industry now has a professional mediation team of 200 people who are able to mediate various insurance conflicts and disputes flexibly and effectively. The Mediation Committee regularly conducts training for mediators, specifically on law, mediation practice, mediation skills, and general competence, inviting judges with extensive experience in hearing insurance cases, experts from inside and outside the industry who are well versed in insurance business and psychologists to give lectures. Through diversified mediation training, the professional quality of mediators in the insurance industry has been effectively improved, enabling them to efficiently deal with various types of insurance disputes.

4.1.4 Key Features of Industry Mediation and Its Advantages

In comparison with people's mediation, administrative mediation, judicial mediation, and other types of mediation, industry mediation is characterized by two main aspects: (1) the homogeneity of disputes; and (2) the professionalism of mediation. The homogeneity of disputes means that most of the disputes faced by industry mediation are peer-to-peer disputes, and for industry mediation organizations, there are many commonalities in these disputes. In addition, there are both cooperative and competitive relationships between peers, so it is appropriate for an industry mediator who is familiar with the knowledge and rules of the industry to conduct the mediation, which can be twice as effective.

In terms of the specialist nature of mediation, disputes between peers will often involve specialist issues within the industry and therefore require a specific specialist in industry mediation. As the saying goes, "The insider looks at the doorway, and the layman looks at the bustle." There are many disputes that cannot be mediated by lay people, so they can only be mediated by industry insiders, thus avoiding the impression that the parties do not know what they are doing. For example, the resolution of disputes in the insurance and securities sectors requires mediators to be familiar with both the content of insurance and securities transactions, as well as with the relevant legal rules, which is a specialist issue that not all mediators are capable of handling.

The main advantages of industry mediation over other types of mediation are: the advantage of purpose and resources. In terms of purpose, the purpose of industry mediation is not only to resolve conflicts and disputes within the industry, but it also has the public interest purpose of maintaining and promoting the healthy development of the industry, so it is easier to gain the trust of the disputing parties and easier to resolve disputes between industry personnel as a package. From the perspective of resource advantages, industry mediation has the advantages of information resources and human resources. The advantage of information resources refers to the fact that industry mediation organizations are more familiar with the types and characteristics of industry disputes and their causes, so it is easier to solve disputes with the right remedy. The advantage of human resources refers to the fact that industry organizations have many industry authorities within them, so mediation organized by them can often have a better mediation effect.

4.2 The Practical Basis of Industry Mediation

4.2.1 Realizing the Autonomous Function of Industry Organizations

As is well known, the reform and opening-up have led to the withdrawal of the state from its total monopoly over all social resources, thus creating more social space between the state system and the market system, and have led to the rapid development of various forms of social organizations.[6] At the same time, social organizations are better than the market through their non-profit, voluntary, and neutral nature, and better than the government in their autonomy, mutual assistance, democratic participation, and pluralistic representation. As a result, social organizations are gradually taking over those matters which are urgently needed for social and economic development but which it is difficult or impossible for the market to provide, and which the government is unable to do, They perform certain duties, such as providing public goods, performing government functions, and promoting social justice, and to a certain extent overcoming market failures and government failures.[7] This has led to the growth of social organizations and the emergence of their advantageous functions in resolving social conflicts, assisting state administration, and promoting self-regulation and order in society.

As an important member of social organizations, trade organizations, such as industry associations and trade unions are also increasingly emerging. The basis for the creation of trade associations is the "special market need," i.e., the collective formation, expression, and satisfaction of the common needs of the members of the industry through the establishment of trade associations. The specific functions of trade associations can be analyzed on two levels: internally and externally. Externally, trade associations, by virtue of their status as representative trade organizations, bring together the various resources, including expertise and professional skills, available in the industry, and, by pooling and channeling the expressions and demands of trade members, shape the demands of the industry regarding the development of the industry and other management and political aspects. Thereby, they influence government policy. Internally, trade associations are responsible for self-management and self-regulation through the formulation of trade rules, promoting the formation of a self-governing and spontaneous order within the industry, and facilitating the self-governance and development of the industry.[8] The most important functions of industry organizations, in terms of industry autonomy and maintenance of industry order, is to balance internal conflicts and resolve internal disputes within the industry, and industry mediation is an important mechanism to achieve this function. Mediation can be used to effectively resolve disputes within the industry and, more importantly, to maintain peace and goodwill within the industry. Conversely, if litigation or arbitration is used, for example, there is a risk that the adversarial nature of these two mechanisms in resolving disputes will affect the relationship between members of the industry. Therefore, given the multiple advantages of industry mediation, it can be considered an important way to resolve industry disputes and maintain order in the industry.

The resolution of disputes within the industry through industry mediation is one of the manifestations of self-governance by industry organizations. A more important manifestation of this is that the outcome of industry mediation is often exemplary and instructive within the industry. On the one hand, members of the industry can anticipate and judge the consequences of similar behavior, so that they can review and regulate their own behavior and avoid adverse consequences; On the other hand, trade associations can also improve the industry system by elevating the consensus and experience generated by the parties in dispute resolution into a code of conduct.[9] From the perspective of institutional economics, this is due to the repeated games and multiple equilibria of mediation subjects and parties to disputes that "formalized internal rules" with self-sustaining and adjusting functions.[10] In short, mediation facilitates the formation of rules for the profession and thus increases the autonomy of the profession. Thus, on the one hand, mediation contributes to industry autonomy by directly resolving industry disputes, and on the other, it shapes the rules that guide industry toward autonomy.

4.2.2 The Need for Social Forces to Participate in Dispute Resolution

Modern social governance focuses on multi-party participation, rational consultation, and constructive resolution of social problems, and is a process of constantly constructing and accumulating positive elements, such as friendliness, respect, tolerance, and trust.[11] Cooperative governance based on tolerance and trust is the path to good governance[12] and a well-ordered society.[13] The Third Plenary Session of the 18th CPC Central Committee proposed a shift from social management to social governance, which emphasized the integration of various types of social resources and the full mobilization of the enthusiasm of various subjects, thereby realizing the joint participation, collaboration, and governance of the state, society, and individuals.

Encouraging social forces to participate in dispute mediation is not only a basic requirement for building a social governance system that is shared by all, but also a practical need to cope with the increase in social conflicts and disputes and to alleviate the shortage of national resources for dispute resolution. Social forces mainly include social organizations, trade bodies, and other social forces, such as deputies to the National People's Congress, lawyers, professional technicians, and psychological counsellors. As far as trade organizations are concerned, they have special attributes, such as being non-profit, non-governmental, and social, and are in the middle between the state and citizens, and are created in the midst of diversified interest patterns and complex social contradictions, so they have the advantageous functions of expressing interest demands, coordinating social relations, reaching social consensus, and resolving social conflicts.[14] To put it more figuratively, trade organizations in modern society are a "buffer" for conflicts of interest and a "valve to reduce pressure" for conflicts and disputes. Especially in the current period of social transformation, the willingness and ability of trade organizations to participate in dispute resolution are increasing, and encouraging their participation in dispute resolution is bound to become a future trend in the reform of the diversified dispute resolution mechanism.

Encouraging social forces to participate in dispute resolution means actively promoting the establishment of internal mediation organizations by industry associations, trade bodies, and other trade organizations, and developing trade mediation mechanisms as a means of resolving conflicts and disputes arising within the particular industry. Unlike other dispute mediation mechanisms, the mediation of disputes through trade organizations has a specific professional nature. In the case of trade associations, for example, their mediators usually have a deep industry background, professional strengths, and practical experience, and are well versed in the growth experiences of the parties and the rules of the industry, so that they can grasp the root cause of complex conflicts and balance interests, thus resolving disputes quickly and effectively.[15]

4.3 The Real-Life Dilemma of Industry Mediation

Although there is a basic consensus at both the national policy-making level and the grass-roots level of governance to accelerate the development of professional mediation, unfortunately, due to a few factors, there are still many difficulties in developing industry mediation in China.

4.3.1 Inadequate Autonomy of Trade Organizations

In terms of development, trade organizations have gained tremendous momentum in Chinese society. However, it is undeniable that trade organizations still face many problems in terms of their capacity for self-governance, and the existence of these problems is a central factor affecting the smooth development of trade mediation. It is no exaggeration to say that the strength of the autonomy of a trade organization determines the level of development of trade mediation. Specifically, the following dilemmas exist in relation to the autonomy capacity of trade organizations: (1) insufficient independence and neutrality. The commonest trade associations, for example, despite being outside the system, are either diversionary reservoirs for administrative reforms or buffer valves for power exit mechanisms, making it difficult for them to be independent of state and government control and penetration. Moreover, as non-material production sectors, the scarcity of internal resources of trade associations leads to a high degree of dependence on external resources, which in turn leads them to actively request state involvement, especially in terms of establishment, resources, and material support such as office space and funding.[16] According to statistics, the survival of trade associations in practice has been mixed, with one-third of them struggling to survive, one-third barely surviving, and one-third developing relatively well.[17] (2) Lack of proper governance. The lack of proper governance of trade organizations is mainly manifested in two aspects: first, their internal governance is interfered with or influenced by external administrative forces, including institutional attachment and personal relationships based on the status of officials; second, the phenomenon of "elite governance," i.e. the heads of trade associations and chambers of commerce dominate the decision-making and implementation of the internal affairs by virtue of their own resources, prestige, or charisma, and are mainly attached to the leading enterprises or leaders of the industry. It is the inherent lack of independence, neutrality, and civic engagement of trade organizations that has led the public to question their neutrality and impartiality in resolving disputes, and to fear that trade organizations may be biased in favor of individual members, and therefore the public are reluctant to submit disputes to mediation within the industry.

4.3.2 Shortage of Professional Mediators in Industry Mediation

The late start of the development of industry mediation in China means it has yet to establish a specialized and professional team of industry mediators, which is an important factor affecting industry mediation. On the one hand, most industry mediators within industry organizations are currently part-time members of the industry organizations, who lack professional competence in mediation, and have scarce understanding and application of laws and regulations, and familiarity with industry norms. In some cases, the governmental supervisory departments of the trade organizations even treat the trade mediation organizations as retirement homes, and specifically send their elderly comrades to the trade mediation organizations.[18] On the other hand, the imperfect training system of the industry mediation team also directly contributes to the difficulties of industry mediators to acquire professional mediation skills. As a result, for a long time, some industry mediators have been unable to mediate in specific disputes, which has undermined the influence and attractiveness of industry mediation. With regard to some overseas trade organizations, most of their trade mediators are elites in the industry, who are experienced in their trade, skilled in mediation, and dedicated to the public good, so they are skilled in mediating trade disputes and can resolve them efficiently and effectively.

4.3.3 Inadequate Regulation of Industry Mediation Procedures

Adequate procedural norms are a fundamental prerequisite for achieving substantive justice. Although it is argued that if too many procedural requirements are imposed on professional mediation, it may weaken its advantages as an informal dispute resolution method, it is conceivable that without corresponding procedural safeguards, professional mediation may become alienated and its effectiveness in resolving disputes will be undermined. Therefore, considerable procedural regulation of professional mediation is a basic prerequisite for its development. Unfortunately, due to the late start of industry mediation in China, the current procedural regulation of industry mediation mainly refers to the *People's Mediation Law* and its judicial interpretation, including the application and acceptance of mediation, the selection of mediators, and the rights and obligations of mediation subjects. In terms of the degree of completeness of the procedural regulations, these articles are still too simple, and core issues such as the manner of mediation, the disclosure of confidential information, the time limit for mediation, and the rules of evidence have not yet been covered, which leaves a large gap in terms of both the number of provisions and the degree of refinement of the content compared to the mediation legislation in developed countries.[19] As a form of mediation with industrial characteristics, it is obvious that the procedural regulation of industrial mediation can no longer follow the procedures of people's mediation, otherwise the industrial and professional nature of industrial mediation will not be manifest.

4.3.4 The Validity of Industry Mediation Agreements Is Lacking

Whether a mediation agreement resulting from industry mediation can be effectively enforced is a matter of the frequency and viability of industry mediation in industry dispute resolution. The question of whether a mediation agreement reached by industry mediation should be binding and enforceable involves the degree of acceptance of industry mediation as a form of dispute resolution in various countries. At present, Chinese law does not provide for the validity of mediation agreements reached through industrial mediation and, in practice, their legal effect does not differ much from that of mediation agreements formed through people's mediation, i.e., they only have the effect of a civil contract. Obviously, having only the effect of a civil contract in an industry mediation agreement is hardly effective in binding the parties in industry mediation and cannot adapt to the needs of the development of industry mediation. If industry mediation agreements are not given a stronger binding force than people's mediation agreements, industry mediation may be reduced to wasted efforts of "using a wicker basket to draw water," and the consequences of this futile effort will affect whether or not the subject of the dispute chooses industry mediation as the dispute resolution method. Therefore, the lack of legal validity of industry mediation agreements leads to great uncertainty as to whether they can be enforced, which to a certain extent affects the scope of the role of industry mediation in practice.

4.4 The Future of Industry Mediation

As mentioned above, there are currently many shortcomings in China's industry mediation system, from the professional teams of industry organizations to industry mediation, procedural norms and legal effectiveness, which have greatly affected the promotion and development of industry mediation in China. In order to overcome these difficulties, we suggest the following aspects.

4.4.1 Enhancing the Autonomy of Trade Organizations

The Decision of the Third Plenary Session of the 18th Central Committee of the Communist Party of China on *Several Major Issues of Comprehensively Deepening Reform* proposed that "public services and matters that are suitable to be provided and resolved by social organizations should be entrusted to social organizations." In November 2018, Guo Shengkun, Secretary of the Central Committee of Political and Legal Affairs, once again emphasized the need to strengthen the construction of incubation bases for social organizations at a conference in commemoration of the 55th anniversary of Comrade Mao Zedong's instruction to learn and promote the "Fengqiao Experience" and the 15th anniversary of General Secretary Xi Jinping's instruction to adhere to the development of the "Fengqiao Experience," focusing on "empowerment and capacity enhancement," with emphasis on supporting the development of social organizations such as urban and rural grass-roots living services, public welfare, charity and mutual assistance, and professional mediation, so as to better use their important role in safeguarding public interests, providing assistance to people in need, resolving conflicts and disputes, and maintaining social stability. The policy pronouncements from the central policy-making level will provide even greater scope for social organizations to participate in social governance, and create a more favorable policy environment for industry organizations to participate in the mediation of industry disputes.

From an external perspective, it is even more crucial to enhance the autonomy of trade organizations by truly empowering them and boosting their capacity. Empowerment can be divided into direct empowerment, in which the government delegates some of its powers to trade organizations, and indirect empowerment, in which the government replaces its powers and responsibilities by purchasing the services of social organizations, while retaining the same powers.[20] Capacity enhancement means making them more capable, emphasizing tapping or stimulating their potentials to help them self-actualize or increase an impact.[21] Specifically for social organizations, it means enhancing their capacity so that they can better perform their social governance functions. The government's empowerment and capacity enhancement of trade organizations can be done in the following ways.

1. Reform and improve the dual management system of trade organizations. Since the implementation of the *Regulations on the Registration and Management of Social Organizations* in 1988, all social organizations, including trade organizations, have been registered and supervised by the registration authorities, while the competent business departments have been responsible for business guidance and daily management. This management model is known as the "dual management system," However, the dual management system is, after all, a preventative and control model. As the number of trade organizations continues to grow and their functions are enhanced, especially the urgent need for their functions to build a social conflict resolution system that is shared by all people, the constraints of this system on the development of trade organizations are increasingly evident.[22] Moreover, due to the conservatism or inaction of the registration and management authorities, a large number of industries formed by enterprises and merchants on their own initiative cannot obtain legal registration in time, thus are labeled "black (unlicensed)." The inefficient management system of trade organizations is obviously no longer able to meet the urgent need for self-governance and self-development of trade organizations in the new era. Therefore, the controlling legislative strategy should be abandoned, the dual management system of trade organizations should be changed to a registration system, and the supervision in and after the event should be strengthened to thoroughly stimulate the development of trade organizations.

2. Various ways to guarantee the funding of mediation in the industry. "Before the troops move, fodder and provisions go first," so a complete funding guarantee is the basic prerequisite for industry organizations to carry out industry mediation work, otherwise industry mediation will

become water without a source and wood without a root. On the one hand, the government can increase its financial support for industry organizations to carry out industry mediation through the purchase of services, as has been emphasized in the *Implementation Opinions on Strengthening the Construction of the People's Mediator Team*, jointly issued by six ministries and commissions in April 2018, to promote the development of industry mediation through the purchase of services. Therefore, judicial administrative organs at all levels should work together with industry authorities and finance departments to do a good job of government purchasing of industry mediation services, improve the purchase methods and procedures, actively foster industry mediation organizations, encourage them to hire full-time mediators, and actively participate in undertaking government purchase of industry mediation services. On the other hand, the legislation should support the charging of appropriate fees for industry mediation as an incentive for industry organizations and industry mediators to carry out industry mediation. Due to the non-profit orientation of trade organizations, fees for industry mediation should be based on the principle of public interest, and can only be appropriately charged according to the cost of mediation.

4.4.2 Accelerating Building a Professional Mediation Workforce

Enriching industry mediation talents is one of the main issues facing the development of industry mediation at present. Only if industry organizations can attract outstanding mediation talents into the industry field can they promote the sustainable development of industry mediation. The construction of a complete team of industry mediators can be started from the following three aspects:

1. Improve the selection and appointment mechanism of industry mediators. Industry mediators can be selected by industry organizations or by their members, to ensure the breadth and representativeness of the selection of industry mediators.
2. In addition to establishing full-time mediators, industry mediation organizations can also employ professionals from their own industry to serve as part-time mediators, thus forming an industry mediation team with a combination of full-time and part-time expertise and complementary professions and capabilities.
3. Establish a roster of industry mediators, delineate the qualifications of industry mediators, and conduct rigorous screening to restrict government staff and trade association executives from serving as mediators, thereby ensuring the professionalism, authority, and high quality of industry mediation.[23]

4. Industry mediation training should rely on qualified universities and training institutions to develop training courses and teaching materials. The courses should be set according to the characteristics of conflicts and disputes in the industry, focusing on social situation, legal policies, professional ethics, professional knowledge, and mediation skills, etc. Training may take the form of concentrated lectures, seminars, case reviews, field trips, on-site observation, court hearings, practical training exercises, etc., in order to improve the relevance and effectiveness of the training, and to establish a perfect quality assessment system for industry mediator training.

4.4.3 Establish and Improve the Code of Practice for Industry Mediation Procedures

Both strict and flexible procedural regulations are the basic prerequisite for the development of industry mediation. The procedural rules for industrial mediation should not be as strict as those for litigation mediation, nor as loose as those for people's mediation, because only with appropriate and flexible procedural rules can we achieve a mediation result that is both substantively fair and procedurally proper. Therefore, industry mediation must also follow a set of procedural requirements that are in line with the rules of industry dispute resolution:

1. With regard to the initiation of mediation, the autonomy of the parties to an industry dispute must be respected and the principle of voluntary mediation must be implemented. It is possible for both parties to a dispute to jointly apply for mediation by an industry mediation organization, or for an industry mediation organization to provide guidance on industry mediation after a dispute has arisen in the industry. The core procedural requirement for the initiation of mediation is to respect the will of the parties to the dispute and not to force mediation upon them.
2. When selecting mediators, the parties to an industry dispute may jointly select from a roster of industry mediators, and if the parties cannot reach a common view, the industry mediation organization will then appoint a mediator. Industry mediation can be conducted by a single mediator or by multiple mediators. In addition, it is important to have a system of recusal of mediators to avoid favoritism to individual members of the industry.
3. In terms of the conduct of the mediation process, the duration of the mediation should be clarified to prevent prolonged delays, and the principle of confidentiality should be clarified to protect the commercial secrets and privacy of the parties. All these are areas that need to be improved in terms of procedural regulation.

4.4.4 Improving the Mechanism for Validity of Industry Mediation Agreements

At present, the validity of industry mediation agreements is basically the same as that of people's mediation agreements, i.e., they have civil contractual effect and are not enforceable. For a mediation agreement with civil contractual effect to be enforceable, it needs to be converted through mechanisms such as judicial confirmation procedures, notary procedures for empowerment, and supervisory procedures.[24] Mediation agreements reached through industrial mediation cannot have the same enforcement effect as court decisions, arbitral awards, and other bases for enforcement that have been reached after strict due process guarantees.[25] Moreover, given the current level of development and the environment of industrial mediations, there are many legal risks in giving enforcement effect to their mediation agreements. Therefore, a mediation agreement is in fact the agreement of the parties to a dispute to rearrange their conflicting interests, which is still essentially a civil agreement, i.e., a civil contract. However, it is clear that the advantages and attractiveness of industry mediation would be undermined if industry mediation agreements were simply left to have the effect of a civil contract. In order to ensure the effective implementation of industry mediation agreements and promote the development of industry mediation, consideration should be given to establishing a credit system for industry mediation within industry organizations on the basis that industry mediation agreements have civil contractual effect, as honesty and trustworthiness are important elements and values to be pursued in the industry's self-regulation.[26] The use of credit as a reputational mechanism can "deter" parties to industry disputes from "breaking" their agreements after mediation by industry mediation organizations in order to preserve their reputation and image within the industry. In the practice of industry mediation, credit records and credit constraints may be imposed on parties who violate credit by unreasonably delaying participation in mediation, violating the duty of confidentiality of information during mediation, and refusing to honor mediation agreements, etc., to force industry members to honor mediation agreements in good faith. Undoubtedly, the use of the credit discipline, a soft law mechanism, can effectively complement the lack of effectiveness of industry mediation agreements, but the use of credit discipline must also follow the appropriate procedures and rules to protect the legitimate rights and interests of the parties and their right to redress.

Notes

1 Tang Lixing: *Merchants and Modern Chinese Society* (Beijing: The Commercial Press, 2006), p. 107.
2 Peng Zeyi: *A Collection of Historical Materials on Chinese Industrial and Commercial Guilds* (Beijing: China Book Bureau, 1995), p. 235.

3 Zhang Yu: *Commercial Rules and Order in Chongqing in the Mid-Qing Dynasty* (Beijing: China University of Political Science and Law Press, 2010), p. 175.
4 Zhang Kaiyuan: *Suzhou Chamber of Commerce Archives Series* (1st series) (Wuhan: Huazhong Normal University Press, 1991), p. 522.
5 He Zengke: From Social Management to Social Governance and Good Social Governance, *The Learning Times*, January 28, 2013, p. 6.
6 Sun Bingyao: The Problem of the Duality Between the Government and the People in Chinese Social Groups, *Chinese Social Science Quarterly*, 1994 (6l): 18.
7 Ma Changshan: *"Civil Governance" in the Rule of Law Process: A Study of the Relationship between Civil Society Organisations and the Rule of Law Order* (Beijing: Law Press, 2006), p. 56.
8 Hong Dongying: On the New Trend of People's Mediation: The Rise of Industry Association Mediation, *Academic Exchange*, 2015 (11).
9 Xiong Yuemin and Zhou Yang: The Dilemma of China's Industry Mediation and Its Breakthrough, *Political Science and Law Series*, 2016 (3).
10 Masahiko Aoki: *Comparative Institutional Analysis*, trans. Zhou Li'an (Shanghai: Shanghai Far East Publishing House, 2002), p. 11.
11 Yang L. and S. Zhao: Participation of Social Organizations in Social Governance: Theory, Problems and Policy Options, *Journal of Beijing Normal University (Social Science Edition)*, 2015 (6): 6.
12 Yu Keping: An Introduction to Governance and Good Governance, *Marxism and Reality*, 1996 (5): 39.
13 John Rawls: *A Theory of Justice*, trans. He Huaihong et al. (Beijing: China Social Science Press, 2009), p. 89.
14 Wang Ying: *The Social Middle: Reform and the Organization of Associations in China* (Beijing: China Development Press, 1993), p. 359.
15 Xiong Yuemin and Zhou Yang: The Dilemma of Industrial Mediation in China and its Breakthrough, p. 150.
16 Ma Changshan: The Rule of Law Turn from State Construction to Shared Construction: An Examination Based on the Relationship between Social Organizations and Rule of Law Construction, *Juridical Studies*, 2017 (3).
17 Long Ningli: Modernising the Governance of Economic Associations: Status Quo, Problems and Changes: An Empirical Analysis Based on National Industry Associations, *Journal of the Party School of the CPC Ningbo Municipal Committee*, 2014 (6).
18 Nai Chunchao: A Study of China's Industry Mediation System, Master's thesis, Henan University, 2017, p. 26.
19 Xiong Yuemin and Zhou Yang: The Dilemma of Industrial Mediation in China and its Breakthrough.
20 Wang Yi: Empowerment and Empowerment: A Logical Analysis of the Growth Path of Social Organisations, *Administrative Forum*, 2016 (6).
21 Gao Wanhong: Exploring the Practice of Social Work with Migrant Population from the Perspective of Empowerment, *Journal of East China University of Science and Technology (Social Science Edition)*, 2011 (1).
22 Ma Changshan, Examination and Reflection on the Legislation of Associations: From the Draft Regulations on the Registration and Administration of Social Organizations (Revised Draft for Public Comments), *Legal System and Social Development*, 2017 (1).

23 Xiong Yuemin and Zhou Yang: The Dilemma of Industrial Mediation in China and Its Breakthrough.
24 Xiao Jianguo and Huang Zhongshun: A Study on the Mechanism for Transforming Mediation Agreements into Enforcement Nominal, *Journal of Law*, 2011 (4).
25 Some scholars also believe that it is more realistic to give enforcement power to industry mediation agreements directly. The main reasons are: (1) most of the disputes in industry mediation are commercial disputes, and the parties to the disputes tend to clarify their rights and obligations within a short period of time to resolve the disputes; (2) industry mediation is a closed system of self-absorption of industry disputes, and the professionalism of industry mediation organizations and the obedience of individuals in conflict are sufficient to ensure the smooth circulation within the system. However, I believe that the above reasons are not sufficient to prove the enforceability of industry mediation agreements. See Xiong Yuemin and Zhou Yang: The Dilemma of Industrial Mediation in China and Its Breakthrough.
26 The State Council's Outline of the Social Credit System Construction Plan (2014–2020) clearly emphasizes the need for industry associations, chambers of commerce, and other industry organizations to play a beneficial role in the construction of the social credit system. The essence of industry credit construction is the self-regulatory nature of the activities of industry associations and chambers of commerce in organizing enterprises to formulate and supervise the implementation of industry credit commitments, norms, and standards.

References

Aoki, Masahiko: *Comparative Institutional Analysis*, trans. Zhou Li'an, Shanghai: Shanghai Far East Publishing House, 2002.

Gao Wanhong: Exploring the Practice of Social Work with Migrant Population from the Perspective of Empowerment, *Journal of East China University of Science and Technology (Social Science Edition)*, 2011 (1): 30–36.

He Zengke, From Social Management to Social Governance and Good Social Governance, *The Learning Times*, January 18, 2013 .p. 6.

Hong Dongying: On the New Trend of People's Mediation: The Rise of Industry Association Mediation, *Academic Exchange*, 2015 (11): 123–128.

Long Ningli: Modernising the Governance of Economic Associations: Status Quo, Problems and Changes: An Empirical Analysis Based on National Industry Associations, Journal of the Party School of the CPC Ningbo Municipal Committee, 2014 (6): 83–95.

Ma Changshan: *"Civil Governance" in the Rule of Law Process: A Study of the Relationship between Civil Society Organisations and the Rule of Law Order*, Beijing: Law Press, 2006.

Ma Changshan: Examination and Reflection on the Legislation of Associations: From the Draft Regulations on the Registration and Administration of Social Organizations (Revised Draft for Public Comments), Legal System and Social Development, 2017a (1): 14–25.

Ma Changshan: The Rule of Law Turn from State Construction to Shared Construction: An Examination Based on the Relationship between Social Organizations and Rule of Law Construction, *Juridical Studies*, 2017b (3): 24–43.

Nai Chunchao: A Study of China's Industry Mediation System, Master's thesis, Henan University, 2017.

Peng Zeyi: *A Collection of Historical Materials on Chinese Industrial and Commercial Guilds*, Beijing: China Book Bureau, 1995.

Rawls, John: *A Theory of Justice*, trans. He Huaihong et al., Beijing, China Social Science Press, 2009.

Sun Bingyao: The Problem of the Duality Between the Government and the People in Chinese Social Groups, *Chinese Social Science Quarterly*, 1994 (6): 18.

Tang Lixing: *Merchants and Modern Chinese Society*, Beijing: The Commercial Press, 2006.

Wang Yi: Empowerment and Empowerment: A Logical Analysis of the Growth Path of Social Organisations, Administrative *Forum*, 2016 (6): 61–65.

Wang Ying: *The Social Middle: Reform and the Organization of Associations in China*, Beijing: China Development Press, 1993.

Xiao Jianguo and Huang Zhongshun: A Study on the Mechanism for Transforming Mediation Agreements into Enforcement Nominal, *Journal of Law*, 2011 (4): 93–97.

Xiong Yuemin and Zhou Yang: The Dilemma of China's Industry Mediation and Its Breakthrough, *Political Science and Law Series*, 2016 (3): 147–153.

Yang L. and Zhao S.: Participation of Social Organizations in Social Governance: Theory, Problems and Policy Options, *Journal of Beijing Normal University (Social Science Edition)*, 2015 (6): 6.

Yu Keping: An Introduction to Governance and Good Governance, Marxism and Reality, 1996 (5): 39.

Zhang Kaiyuan: *Suzhou Chamber of Commerce Archives Series* (1st series), Wuhan: Huazhong Normal University Press, 1991.

Zhang Yu: *Commercial Rules and Order in Chongqing in the Mid-Qing Dynasty*, Beijing: China University of Political Science and Law Press, 2010.

5 The International Challenges of Commercial Mediation

Analysis Based on the Singapore Convention on Mediation

The globalization of law and the globalization of the economy are like twins. Throughout the history of international law, the globalization of law has always been reinforced and accentuated by the process of economic globalization. The entry into force of the United Nations Convention on International Settlement Agreements Resulting from Mediation (the Singapore Convention on Mediation)[1] has once again demonstrated to the world the leading role of economic globalization in the globalization of law. As a model of multilateralism and international cooperation, the Singapore Convention on Mediation is the most significant event in the international commercial arena in recent years and has been hailed as a milestone in the development of international commercial mediation. As Singapore's Prime Minister Lee Hsien Loong has said, the Singapore Convention on Mediation fills in the "missing third piece" of the enforcement framework for international commercial dispute resolution. Henceforth, the Singapore Convention on Mediation will form a "troika" in the field of international commercial dispute resolution, together with the Convention on the Recognition and Enforcement of Foreign Arbitral Awards and The Hague Convention on Choice of Court Agreements.[2] The preamble to the Singapore Convention on Mediation begins with the clear statement that the ultimate purpose of the Convention is to promote the harmonious development of international economic relations. A key provision in achieving this aim is that the Convention establishes a generally acceptable enforcement mechanism for international commercial settlement agreements resulting from mediation in different countries. This means that "settlement agreements" reached through international commercial conciliation are henceforth transnationally enforceable and can be effectively enforced within a contracting State. The granting of transnational enforceability to settlement agreements will undoubtedly have a revolutionary impact on the development of international commercial conciliation.

The Chinese delegation participated in the drafting and consultation of the Singapore Convention on Mediation throughout the process, and formally signed the Singapore Convention on Mediation on August 7, 2019. As a founding member and one of the first signatories of the Convention, it is particularly meaningful to a country like China, which believes in mediation.

DOI: 10.4324/9781003385776-5

In accordance with the provisions of the *Law of the People's Republic of China on the Procedure for the Conclusion of Treaties*, although the Chinese government has signed the Singapore Mediation Convention, it will only become legally binding on China once the State Council has submitted it to the Standing Committee of the National People's Congress for ratification.[3] It is for this reason that China will also face the real question of whether and when to ratify. To answer these questions, we must first analyze and assess the impact and implications of China's accession to the Singapore Convention on Mediation, and how to respond to these impacts and challenges. These difficult questions are currently troubling our policy-makers, as well as the legal practice sector. Although some scholars in China have made preliminary discussions on these issues, many of them are still mainly at the macro level, and it is difficult to respond to these questions precisely. In view of this, this chapter intends to objectively analyze the positive significance of the Singapore Convention on Mediation for China, assess the impact and influence of the Convention on the Chinese legal system, rationally respond to the queries of the academic community regarding the accession to the Convention, and then propose corresponding countermeasures to cope with the impact of the Singapore Convention on Mediation, so as to promote the application and implementation of the Convention in China.

5.1 The Positive Significance of China's Accession to the Singapore Convention on Mediation

The Singapore Convention on Mediation contains 16 articles, the main contents of which include the scope of application of the Convention, the definition of a settlement agreement, the requirements for applying for enforcement of a settlement agreement and the circumstances in which enforcement of a settlement agreement may be refused. Under the Convention, an international commercial settlement agreement is enforceable before the competent authorities of a Contracting State, if it complies with the provisions of the Convention. This makes settlement agreements, which were previously not enforceable across borders, a law with "teeth," which will greatly facilitate the use and promotion of international commercial mediation in the field of international commercial dispute resolution. The Chinese government delegation participated in the formulation of the Convention and proposed a few amendments which were accepted, providing "Chinese wisdom" to the formulation of the Convention. Objectively speaking, accession to the Singapore Convention on Mediation will have the following positive implications.

5.1.1 Promotion of Commercial Mediation

The most immediate positive significance for China of its formal accession to the Convention is the promotion of the development of China's commercial mediation system. Although mediation has long played an extremely important role in resolving social conflicts and disputes in China, the most important role is played by people's mediation. Compared to people's mediation, the development of commercial mediation in China still seems to be lagging behind. Compared with the development of commercial mediation in developed countries in Europe and the United States, the development of commercial mediation in China is still at a nascent stage. The accession to the Convention will undoubtedly be an important opportunity for the development of commercial mediation in China, which will inevitably force the development and improvement of commercial mediation in China.

The promotion effect is mainly reflected in the following: first, to push the establishment and improvement of the basic legal system of commercial mediation in China as soon as possible, and to promote the legislative process and institutional construction of commercial mediation. Second, it will promote the training of international commercial mediation talents in China to fill the current talent gap. Third, it will lead the construction of commercial mediation organizations in China and accelerate the formation of a domestic commercial mediation. Fourth, it will update the basic concept of domestic commercial mediation and promote the formation of procedural rules and technical standards for domestic commercial mediation. As such, accession to the Singapore Convention on Mediation is timely for China to actively promote the development of commercial mediation.

5.1.2 Optimizing China's Business Environment

The optimization of the business environment has therefore become an issue to which the central government has attached great importance in recent years, and the State Council considered and adopted the *Regulations on Optimizing the Business Environment* in October 2019. For a long time, the lack of efficiency in the judicial settlement of commercial disputes, coupled with the lack of transparency in the judicial process, has not only led to a rather negative evaluation of China's business environment, but also made the Chinese civil and commercial judicial system often criticized by foreign public opinion. Therefore, improving the commercial dispute resolution mechanism has not only become an important element in optimizing China's business environment, but also an important task in the construction of the rule of law and judicial reform in China.

According to the evaluation indicators of the World Bank's *Doing Business* report, the Dispute Resolution Index is one of the basic indicators for measuring the business environment of each economy.[4] The accession to the Singapore Convention on Mediation will undoubtedly effectively improve the Dispute Mediation Index in the field of commercial dispute resolution in China, thus effectively improving the business environment in China. The impact is mainly in two areas: first, accession to the Convention means that the use of commercial mediation to resolve commercial disputes will be more certain than before, and that settlement agreements will have the guarantee of enforceability, thus giving commercial entities a greater sense of security. Commercial parties will naturally be more willing to choose commercial mediation to resolve their disputes, which will undoubtedly increase the Dispute Mediation Index in the domestic commercial sector. On the other hand, the core advantage of commercial mediation over litigation or arbitration is that it can effectively resolve disputes while maintaining a friendly and cooperative relationship between the parties. The use of litigation or arbitration in resolving commercial disputes is characterized by a strong sense of right and wrong, with the parties often confronting each other in a "tit-for-tat" manner, which can easily damage the amicable relationship between the parties and lead to a break in their cooperation. Unlike commercial mediation, which seeks to maximize the interests of both parties and upholds the "win-win mindset" of harmony and prosperity, it is more conducive to maintaining and bridging the friendly relationship between the parties. Therefore, commercial mediation is known as "justice between friends." In this way, it will also help to optimize the overall business environment and facilitate business transactions. Thus, accession to the Convention will promote the use of commercial mediation in domestic commercial dispute resolution, while optimizing the domestic business environment and enhancing China's economic competitiveness.

5.1.3 Promoting "One Belt One Road" Construction

The "One Belt One Road" is an important initiative of the Chinese government to expand all-round opening-up in the new situation, and a practical platform for more countries to share development opportunities and achievements and to promote the building of a community of human destiny. A complete and effective dispute settlement mechanism is an important guarantee for the smooth implementation of the "One Belt One Road" construction, for which the Chinese government has issued the *Opinions on the Establishment of International Commercial Dispute Settlement Mechanisms and Institutions for the Belt and Road*. This opinion proposes to improve the relevant organizations, procedures, and rules, and to give full play to the positive role of commercial mediation in the international commercial dispute settlement of the "Belt and Road."

Among the 46 countries that have signed the Singapore Convention on Mediation, 43 of them belong to countries along the "Belt and Road" construction, which shows the importance of the Convention to the "Belt and Road." As the countries along the "Belt and Road" vary greatly in political, economic, cultural, religious, and legal aspects, it is inevitable that commercial disputes will arise as a result of business transactions in such a complex regional environment. At the same time, the use of litigation and arbitration to resolve international commercial disputes arising in countries along the route will also face significant differences in legal systems, judicial systems, and enforcement procedures, which will affect the effectiveness and certainty of commercial dispute resolution.[5] Therefore, "flexible" mediation may better meet the needs of the "Belt and Road" commercial dispute resolution than "rigid" litigation or arbitration. The reason why China is one of the first to sign the Singapore Convention on Mediation is also an implicit strategic plan to promote the "Belt and Road" construction. The effective implementation of the e Convention will certainly promote the use of international commercial mediation in the settlement of commercial disputes along the "Belt and Road," thus ensuring that the construction of the "Belt and Road" will go deeper, be more stable, and extend farther for the benefit of all people.

5.1.4 Enhancing the Discourse on Dispute Resolution

China has traditionally focused on mediation to resolve conflicts and disputes, both as a result of two thousand years of Confucianism and the need to maintain the normal functioning of a large population. The practice of mediation over the past two millennia has given China a rich and long-standing mediation culture and historical experience, and mediation in China is therefore known as the unique "flower of the East." Unfortunately, due to the long-standing neglect of mediation systematization, specialization, professionalization, and standardization, mediation in China has gradually lost its first-mover advantage and discourse influence in the field of international mediation. In recent times, developed Western countries have made leaps and bounds in mediation, and they have made great strides in the professionalization, discipline, and marketization of mediation. More importantly, the discourse on mediation research and rule-making has gradually come to be in the hands of developed countries such as the United Kingdom and the United States.[6] This is undoubtedly an important wake-up call for China, which has had a mediation culture for thousands of years.

The field of international relations is the main platform for the expression of discourse, which is expressed in the right to set international standards and rules of the game, as well as the right to comment on and adjudicate the merits. As the world's second largest economy, China is gradually moving closer to the center of the world stage, which requires China to change from being a "spectator" and "recipient" to a "participant" and "leader" in the formulation of international rules. On this occasion, China actively supported and participated in the negotiation, drafting and finalization of the Singapore Convention on Mediation from the very beginning, and contributed its oriental wisdom in the process, which played an important and unique role in the finalization of the Convention.[7] At the same time, it is also an important manifestation of the Chinese government's efforts to demonstrate its influence in the field of international commercial rules and to enhance the discourse on dispute resolution. In the modern international community, a well-developed and competitive dispute resolution mechanism has become an important factor in maintaining economic development and demonstrating comprehensive national power.[8] At present, a number of countries around the world, represented by Singapore, are actively developing international commercial mediation in an attempt to make their country a center for international commercial settlement, thereby enhancing the attractiveness and competitiveness of their dispute resolution mechanisms.[9] As a traditional mediation power, it is important for China to make full use of the opportunity to participate in the whole process and be among the first to sign the Singapore Convention on Mediation, accelerate the improvement of China's commercial mediation system, strive to catch up with the influence of Western countries in international commercial dispute resolution, and thus enhance China's voice in international commercial dispute resolution.

5.2 Some Challenges to China's Accession to the Singapore Convention on Mediation

The preceding paragraphs provide a more objective assessment of the positive implications for China of acceding to the Singapore Convention on Mediation. There are pros and cons to everything, and the Convention is also a "double-edged sword." Although the Convention is generally viewed positively in China, there is no shortage of disagreement among the domestic legal profession as to whether to accede to the Convention or not: lawyers and arbitrators engaged in international commercial dispute resolution, as well as the commercial sector, actively advocate accession to the Convention, while the judiciary and some academics are more conservative in their approach to accession.

5.2.1 Inadequate Preparation for Commercial Mediation in China

Is Chinese commercial mediation ready for the Convention? This is a common question among domestic legal practitioners who are conservative about joining the Singapore Convention on Mediation. Those who question it point out that there are many negative consequences if we venture to join when we are not yet fully prepared. Such doubts do not come out of nowhere, as China's commercial mediation is indeed not yet well prepared. According to scholars, the development of commercial mediation in China is still in its infancy, although it is still on the rise.[10] Both the policy regime at the macro level, the commercial environment at the meso level, and the procedural rules at the micro level suggest that the development of commercial mediation in China is lagging behind.[11] This lagging development can be seen in the following aspects.

First, there is a lack of basic commercial mediation laws in China. Compared with developed Western countries which have enacted relevant mediation laws to promote the development of commercial mediation, China is obviously lagging behind in mediation legislation, especially commercial mediation legislation. For example, the United States enacted the *Uniform Mediation Act* in 2001; the European Union promulgated the *Directive on*

Certain Issues Relating to Civil and Commercial Mediation in May 2008, and Germany enacted the *Act on the Promotion of Mediation and Other Extrajudicial Conflict Resolution Procedures* in 2012 in order to realize the domestic translation of the Directive.[12] In addition, countries such as Italy (2010), Russia (2011), Spain (2012), Portugal (2013), and Singapore (2017) have also enacted their own mediation laws.

In contrast to the above-mentioned countries, although China also adopted the *People's Mediation Law* in August 2010, filling the gap in mediation legislation in China, the Law is not closely related to commercial mediation. The reason is that the *People's Mediation Law* mainly regulates the practical operation of people's mediation, which differs from commercial mediation in many aspects, such as value orientation and procedural rules. For example, people's mediation is a mass organization, which has a "semi-official" character, while commercial mediation is an independent commercial organization; people's mediation focuses on the public interest and does not charge mediation fees, while commercial mediation is market-based and charges mediation fees; people's mediators have a popular character, while commercial mediators are professional and highly specialized. It is due to these differences that the *People's Mediation Law* cannot be applied to commercial mediation, and therefore the development of commercial mediation in China is still in a state of "having no law to rely on." Although the judicial interpretations or normative documents issued by the Supreme People's Court and the Ministry of Justice, such as the *Opinions on the Establishment of a Sound Mechanism for the Settlement of Disputes between Litigation and Non-Litigation* and the *Opinions on the People's Courts' Further Deepening of the Reform of the Diversified Dispute Settlement Mechanism*, are all related to commercial mediation. However, these "broad" provisions can hardly promote the development of commercial mediation in a substantive manner. There is still much confusion in practice as to how commercial mediation should operate. Therefore, after the signing of the Singapore Convention on Mediation, it is imperative to speed up the domestic legislation on commercial mediation in order to better align it with the Convention.

Second, domestic commercial mediation organizations are not very competitive. Commercial mediation organizations are the main force in promoting the development of commercial mediation. In recent years, a few commercial mediation organizations have been newly established in China as a result of national policies and the budding of the commercial mediation market. Domestic commercial mediation organizations have been established in a variety of forms, including non-enterprise commercial mediation organizations, such as the Shanghai Economic and Trade Commercial Mediation Center (2011) and the Beijing Belt and Road International Commercial Mediation Center (2016), and commercial mediation organizations set up within arbitration institutions, such as the Mediation Center of Beijing Arbitration Commission (2011) and the China International Economic and Trade Arbitration Commission (CIETAC) Mediation Center (2018). There are also mediation organizations set up by international chambers of commerce and trade promotion committees, such as the Shenzhen Trade Promotion Commission Commercial Legal Services Mediation Center (2016) and the China (Chongqing) Pilot Free Trade Zone Commercial Mediation Center (2018). Through the practice and exploration of these commercial mediation organizations, the procedures and rules of domestic commercial mediation have initially taken shape, laying a better foundation for the development of commercial mediation.

Unfortunately, due to the late start of the development of commercial mediation in China, the newly established commercial mediation organizations are not perfect in many aspects, such as organizational structure, design of rules, personnel composition, mechanism operation and publicity and promotion, and there are problems such as a small number of cases accepted, a small business distribution, and a lack of internationalization and openness. In addition, the current market environment has not yet created an incentive mechanism to drive the development of commercial mediation organizations, resulting in a lack of market-oriented commercial mediation and thus a lack of fundamental motivation for the development of commercial mediation organizations. It is due to these imperfections that the attractiveness, credibility, and competitiveness of Chinese commercial mediation organizations are not yet comparable to those of their foreign counterparts. Take the Singapore International Mediation Center (SIMC), established in 2014, for example, its president, Quan Huimin, said that in 2019, the center mediated more than 80 commercial disputes, with a success rate of 80 percent, and the value of mediated disputes amounting to S$2.4 billion (approximately RMB12.4 billion). As the largest independent alternative dispute resolution service provider in Europe, the UK Centre for Dispute Effective Resolution (CDER) Annual Report of 2018 shows that it mediated a total of 12,000 commercial disputes in the year, with a subject matter value of £11.5 billion, saving business entities £3 billion in time costs, relationship repair, business revenue, and legal fees, as well as generating over £30 million in revenue. This shows that the development of domestic commercial mediation organizations still has a long way to go in terms of marketization, procedures, and standardization.

Third, the training of domestic commercial mediation personnel is inadequate. International commercial disputes are highly complex, professional, and international in nature, and not something those ordinary mediators are capable of handling. Therefore, it is extremely important to train professional commercial mediators. According to statistics from the Ministry of Justice, there are currently 3,669,000 people's mediators nationwide, of which only 497,000 are full-time mediators. Most of these mediators are grass-roots legal service workers, who mainly mediate general family disputes, disputes between neighbors and other civil disputes, and whose professionalism is hardly suited to the needs of international commercial mediation. In fact, at present, those engaged in international commercial mediation are mainly foreign-related lawyers and mediators from the CCPIT, and there is a lack of specialized commercial mediation personnel. In general, the training of domestic commercial mediation personnel is currently inadequate in terms of specialization and internationalization, and there is a lack of a specialized professional education and a training system and a qualification system for practice. Therefore, objectively speaking, the construction of domestic commercial mediation talents is still unable to meet the challenges of the Singapore Convention on Mediation, and there is an urgent need to strengthen the cultivation of local international commercial mediation talents.

From the above, we can see that domestic commercial mediation is lagging behind in terms of legal system, organization, and personnel training, and is objectively not yet fully prepared to meet the needs of the Singapore Convention on Mediation. However, we cannot deny the need to accede to the Convention. Just as China acceded to the New York Convention in December 1986, the development of domestic commercial arbitration was hardly complete at that time, and the first domestic *Arbitration Law* was not promulgated until August 1994. Moreover, domestic commercial mediation is currently better developed than commercial arbitration was at the time of accession to the New York Convention. Therefore, although domestic commercial mediation is not yet fully prepared, we should not oppose accession to the Singapore Convention on Mediation for this reason, but should see it as an opportunity to develop and accelerate the development and improvement of domestic commercial mediation.

5.2.2 Impact of Fraudulent Mediation on the Judiciary

Another key issue that has been questioned by academics is the potential for fraudulent mediations to take advantage of the Singapore Convention on Mediation, thereby affecting the credibility of the domestic judicial system. This is because, prior to accession to the Convention, settlement agreements reached in international commercial matters were not enforceable in domestic courts, and therefore it is unlikely that fraudulent mediations would occur, a concern that would only arise after accession to the Convention. A fraudulent mediation in the international commercial arena is usually a settlement agreement reached by the parties (or even with the mediator) through malicious collusion to falsify the commercial legal relationship or legal facts in order to obtain an illegal benefit. A fraudulent settlement agreement, if enforced, will not only harm the interests of third parties and even the public interest, but may also undermine a country's judicial credibility. The main reason why the Singapore Convention on Mediation has aroused the concern of scholars about fraudulent mediation is due to the special setting of the scope of application of the Convention.

Unlike the New York Convention, which emphasizes the "place of arbitration," the Singapore Convention on Mediation does not contain provisions relating to the "place of mediation" and the "Contracting States."[13] Under

Article 1 of the New York Convention, an arbitral award that is sought to be recognized and enforced by the parties must be made in a country other than the country of enforcement (or be a non-domestic award), whereas under Article 1 of the Singapore Convention on Mediation, a settlement agreement is international at the time of its conclusion in that: (a) At least two parties to the settlement agreement have their places of business in different States; or (b) The State in which the parties to the settlement agreement have their places of business is different from either: (i) The State in which a substantial part of the obligations under the settlement agreement is performed; or (ii) The State with which the subject matter of the settlement agreement is most closely connected. This "internationality" may be reflected in: (1) the internationality of a settlement agreement between Company A, which has its place of business in Country A, and Company B, which has its place of business in Country B; and (2) the internationality of a settlement agreement between two companies, Company A and Company B, which have their places of business in Country A, in relation to their commercial matters in Country B. In summary, the Convention can be invoked for enforcement if the subject matter of the settlement agreement or the subject matter of the commercial dispute is "international," which greatly expands the scope of application of the Convention and fully reflects the inclusive and open nature of mediation. At the same time, as the Singapore Convention on Mediation does not allow countries to make "reciprocal reservations," settlement agreements are not restricted to "contracting parties" and any international commercial settlement agreement made by any country in the world can be applied to the Chinese courts to enforce the property of the other party in China.

It is due to this special scope of application that commercial settlement agreements reached both at home and abroad that comply with the Convention can be enforced in Chinese courts, which inevitably leads to the risk of fraudulent mediation. At the same time, the Singapore Convention on Mediation does not provide for the qualifications and procedures of mediators, which make it also prone to the risk of fraudulent mediation. While mediators in countries with developed mediation systems such as Europe and the United States value the credibility of mediators and are unlikely to make so-called fraudulent settlement agreements, there is no guarantee that mediators in countries around the world place such a high value on the credibility of settlement agreements. For example, nationals of remote, under-developed "non-contracting states" where mediation is not developed may be able to apply for enforcement with a fraudulent settlement agreement and, without strict scrutiny, may be able to obtain enforcement by Chinese courts. Some may even use this mechanism to commit criminal activities such as transnational money laundering. This is extremely detrimental to an emerging market country like China, which is both an investor and an investee country. In addition, under the Convention, international commercial settlement agreements reached through domestic mediation can also be enforced by domestic courts, which also carries the risk of fraudulent mediation. This is because the current immaturity of the mediation system in China, coupled with the incomplete construction of the social credit system, makes it difficult to avoid a small number of speculative individuals applying for enforcement of fraudulent settlement agreements in domestic courts.

The existence of these problems is the key to the strong doubts expressed by the domestic academic circles, and the judiciary about joining the Singapore Convention on Mediation. Admittedly, fraudulent mediation is an important issue facing the domestic judiciary. Nevertheless, we should not choke on it and reject the Convention. Fraudulent mediation, like fraudulent litigation and arbitration, is not a beast and can be effectively dealt with if the domestic mediation system is improved and a sound prevention and review mechanism is put in place.

5.2.3 More Pressure on Judicial Enforcement in the Courts

As an interested party, domestic judicial enforcement agencies are more concerned that accession to the Singapore Convention on Mediation will inevitably bring more cases of enforcement of international commercial settlement agreements into the courts, crowding out judicial resources and greatly increasing the pressure on their own enforcement. This is unacceptable to the courts, which are in the midst of an ongoing battle to "basically resolve the difficulties of enforcement" and are under pressure to enforce the law. As Chinese companies are actively "going global," domestic courts will have to face enforcement applications from all over the world once China joins the Convention. Given the informal and unusual nature of commercial mediation, and the wide variety of settlement agreements that may be mediated abroad, it is doubtful whether the courts will have sufficient judicial resources to deal with these enforcement applications against the property of domestic parties.[14] As a result, domestic academics and the judiciary have generally questioned the legitimacy and necessity of acceding to the Convention on the grounds that it would "increase the pressure on judicial enforcement."

> The principle of *pacta sunt servanda* (agreements must be kept) is a fundamental principle of international law, which means that a lawfully concluded treaty entails an obligation on the part of the parties to perform in good faith during the period of its validity.[15]

As a responsible power, it is China's obligation to honor the international treaties to which it has acceded. Since it has acceded to the Convention, it means that Chinese courts must fulfill their obligation to review and enforce international commercial settlement agreements. Under Article 4 of the Convention, the domestic enforcement court is required to examine whether the signatures of the mediator in the international commercial settlement agreement are genuine and valid, and whether the mediator has genuinely conducted the mediation. Under Article 5 of the Convention, the domestic enforcement courts are required to examine matters such as whether the settlement agreement is contrary to the public policy of the country and whether the dispute can be resolved through mediation under domestic law. These matters will undoubtedly add significantly to the burden of judicial review on domestic courts and increased pressure on judicial enforcement may seem inevitable! However, if we look closer, accession to the Singapore Convention on Mediation does not necessarily lead to a significant increase in judicial enforcement pressure on the domestic courts.

First, the Convention gives cross-border enforceability to international commercial settlement agreements, which will greatly increase the chances of automatic performance of settlement agreements by the parties, with a relatively low percentage of settlement agreements being applied for court enforcement. Prior to this, statistics from a few well-known international commercial mediation centers show that the rate of automatic performance of settlement agreements is also relatively high. For example, the Singapore International Mediation Center (SIMC) has mediated over 80 commercial disputes since its establishment in 2014, with a success rate of 80 percent and essentially 100 percent of the parties have self-executed the mediated settlement agreements. Of the 143 disputes handled by the Hong Kong Mediation Center (HKMC) in 2018, only two were successful in mediation and the parties did not honor their agreement. The Judicial Arbitration Mediation Services of America (JAMS) also indicated that there were very few cases where parties did not perform on their own after reaching a settlement agreement under mediation conducted by the institution. This shows that even before the Singapore Convention on Mediation came into force, the rate of voluntary performance of settlement agreements was relatively high, and it was relatively rare for a settlement agreement to be enforced in court. This is testament to the fact that commercial mediation can indeed lead to a substantive resolution of disputes, with parties willingly and voluntarily honoring settlement agreements. Accession to the Convention will give settlement agreements cross-border enforceability, which will have a stronger deterrent effect on the parties to the settlement agreement, and will result in a higher rate of self-fulfillment of the settlement agreement than before. As the legal environment for domestic civil enforcement becomes increasingly stringent, domestic parties should be more reluctant to have international commercial settlement agreements relating to them enter enforcement. Therefore, judging from the relatively high rate of self-execution of international commercial settlement agreements, domestic courts should not be overly concerned that the number of settlement agreements filed for enforcement will skyrocket, thereby increasing the pressure on their own judicial enforcement.

Second, in terms of the overall number of commercial disputes, accession to the Convention does not necessarily lead to increased enforcement pressure on the domestic courts. Under the Convention, parties may apply to the Chinese courts to enforce a settlement agreement provided that the location of the person against whom enforcement is sought and the location of the property to be enforced are in China. In other words, one of the disputing parties to the commercial dispute that is the basis of the settlement agreement must be a Chinese commercial subject in order to be able to apply to a Chinese court for enforcement. The total number of these international commercial disputes involving Chinese commercial subjects is relatively constant and can only be resolved through commercial litigation or arbitration if not resolved through mediation. In comparison, resolving commercial disputes through mediation is certainly less stressful than litigation and arbitration in terms of judicial enforcement. For one thing, commercial mediation is more efficient in resolving disputes, whereas litigation is likely to cost the courts a lot of judicial resources; for another, a settlement agreement reached through mediation is more likely to be honored by the parties themselves, especially under the deterrent of the Singapore Convention on Mediation. Litigation and arbitration, on the other hand, are more adversarial and have a lower rate of self-execution of their awards, making them more likely to be enforced by the courts. It is clear from this that with a relatively fixed number of foreign-related commercial disputes, accession to the Convention will more fully exploit the functions and advantages of mediation in resolving commercial disputes, thereby reducing judicial and enforcement pressure on the courts. Thus, while there may be an increase in the number of international commercial settlement agreements filed with the courts for enforcement in the short term, it will not result in an increase in the load on the domestic courts in the long run.

5.3 Basic Responses to the Impact of the Convention

The foregoing is a more rational response to academic and judicial doubts and concerns about accession to the Convention. Of course, these responses cannot eliminate the doubts about accession to the Convention, and the Convention will indeed have a certain degree of impact on domestic commercial mediation and trial enforcement. Therefore, China should improve its domestic laws and systems as soon as possible after the signing of the Singapore Convention on Mediation and before its ratification, in order to achieve a smooth interface with the Convention at an early date, and thus effectively respond to the impact of the Convention. With regard to the actual situation in China, the following aspects should be considered.

5.3.1 Development of Commercial Mediation Legislation

Since the accession to the Convention, the formulation of a specific "commercial mediation law" has gradually been agreed by academics and practitioners, and it is imperative to study and prove the specific legislative proposal and content. In terms of legislation, according to the Legislative Plan of the Standing Committee of the 13th National People's Congress promulgated in September 2018, there is no legislative plan involving "mediation," so the chances of enacting and adopting a "commercial mediation law" in a short period of time are relatively low. In view of this, we may consider that the State Council should first enact "Commercial Mediation Regulations" at the level of administrative regulations, and then request the National People's Congress to formulate the "Commercial Mediation Law" when the conditions are ripe. In addition, commercial mediation is like arbitration in that it falls within the scope of public legal services. The administrative department in charge of public legal services is the Ministry of Justice, which also happens to have the authority to "draft or organize the drafting of relevant administrative regulations," so the Ministry of Justice has an inherent advantage in formulating the draft regulations on commercial mediation first. In conclusion, the formulation of a commercial mediation law can be preceded by the formulation of a "commercial mediation regulation" at the level of administrative regulations.

Based on international comparisons and local practices, we believe that the main contents of the proposed "Commercial Mediation Law" should include the following aspects: the purpose of legislation, basic principles, commercial mediation organizations, commercial mediators, commercial mediation procedures, commercial settlement agreements, etc. The following conditions should also apply:

1. The purpose of the "Commercial Mediation Law" should be to regulate the procedures of commercial mediation, promote the development of the commercial mediation industry, facilitate the settlement of commercial disputes, and ensure the healthy development of the market economy.
2. The basic principles of equality and voluntary will, lawfulness, honesty and trustworthiness, maintenance of friendship and confidentiality should be adhered to throughout the process of enacting the "Commercial Mediation Law." Only under the premise of adhering to these basic principles can commercial disputes be resolved in a substantive manner while maintaining friendly cooperation.
3. A commercial mediation organization should be established, to follow a market-oriented approach, which should be the same as that of a law firm. At the same time, the establishment of a commercial mediation organization should also comply with certain conditions. For example, the person establishing the commercial mediation organization should have a certain number of years of experience in commercial mediation practice; the commercial mediation organization should have its own office space and assets in the amount prescribed by law.
4. Commercial mediators should be fair and honest citizens who are enthusiastic about commercial mediation and have a certain level of education and legal skills. At the same time, corresponding training and examination requirements should be stipulated. For example, commercial mediators should receive professional training of a prescribed length at a qualified training institution before practicing, and should be subject to a regular

assessment before they can continue to work as commercial mediators. Most importantly, the law should also specifically provide for the professional ethics and conduct of commercial mediators to ensure that they are able to resolve commercial disputes in a fair, impartial, timely, and effective manner.
5. With regard to the procedures of commercial mediation, it is important to reflect the flexibility of commercial mediation while respecting the basic norms of mediation, so that commercial mediators can seek a balance between flexibility and procedure. It is also important to note that commercial mediation procedures must be set up in such a way as to avoid a tendency toward litigation, as is the case with international commercial arbitration.[16] Otherwise, it will be difficult to give full play to the unique advantages of commercial mediation and will not be conducive to its sustainable development.
6. Commercial settlement agreements should provide for specific matters such as the matters to be set out in the agreement, the time of entry into force, the remedial procedures, and the procedures for interface with the courts. At the same time, both domestic and international commercial settlement agreements should be regulated. The question of whether domestic commercial settlement agreements have the same enforcement effect as international ones needs to be treated with caution in the legislation. In view of the current lag in the development of domestic commercial mediation, we do not consider it appropriate to give it enforcement effect for the time being.

The above are some basic thoughts on the formulation of a "Commercial Mediation Law" in China, while the specific legal provisions need to be carefully considered with reference to the experience of foreign commercial mediation legislation.

5.3.2 Activating the Commercial Mediation Market

At present, due to the constraints of various factors, domestic commercial mediation has always struggled to achieve significant development, and regional imbalance is very prominent. For example, the commercial mediation market has sprouted in the developed areas along the southeast coast while it remains dormant in the central and western regions. Therefore, in the context of the Singapore Convention on Mediation, how to activate the domestic commercial mediation market has become an important challenge after signing the Convention. In view of the current development dilemma, the following aspects can be attempted to activate the domestic commercial mediation market:

1. Improve the charging standards for commercial mediation. Fees drive the process, and they can sometimes determine the "life or death" of a

system or process.¹⁷ As a product of the market economy, the importance of commercial mediation fees cannot be underestimated. Without appropriate fee incentives, commercial mediation organizations and commercial mediators, as "rational economic agents," will naturally lack the motivation to mediate, and the market for commercial mediation will not be formed. At present, there is no unified standard for commercial mediation fees in China, and in practice, there are problems of low fees and chaotic fees, which affect the development of commercial mediation. Therefore, the establishment of a scientific and reasonable fee standard is a necessary step to activate the domestic commercial mediation market.

All overseas mediation institutions have set their own fees in line with the actual situation in their countries. The UK Centre for Effective Dispute Resolution has set separate fees for commercial mediation according to three types of mediation, including project mediation, customized mediation, and fixed price mediation. According to the statistics of the UK Centre for Effective Dispute Resolution, in 2018, mediators who mediated 20–30 disputes earned an average of £68,000, mediators who mediated 30–50 disputes earned an average of £175,000. and mediators who mediated more than 50 disputes earned an average of £330,000 in that year, with the highest-paid mediator in that year earning £780,000. The Singapore International Mediation Center does not charge a fee based on the amount in dispute, but is divided into an administration fee and a mediator fee. Each party pays a separate administration fee, which consists of an application fee of S$1,000, selection and appointment of a mediator of S$1,000 (per mediator), booking and setting up of venue and refreshments of S$1,000, pre-mediation case management of S$2,000, actual working day case management fee ($9:30–17:30 daily) of S$1,000, overtime case management fee (S$500 per hour after 18:00 on weekdays and/or weekends and/or public holidays); mediator fees are calculated separately for each mediator on a per mediator basis (hourly or daily). Also in the US, mediator rates for good mediators have reached up to US$10,000 a day, with some mediators specializing in national and global practices earning in excess of US$1 million a year.¹⁸ As can be seen from the above, countries such as the UK, the US, and Singapore have a high degree of flexibility and openness in setting mediation fees, and their commercial mediation organizations and mediators are able to earn a relatively high income, which is why the commercial mediation market in these countries is more mature and flourishing.

Therefore, in the future, commercial mediation in China should be guided by "diversification" in terms of fees, which may be proportional to the amount of the subject matter, piece rate, time rate, period rate, etc. The setting of fees should also be a market-based mechanism, with the commercial mediation organization or mediator negotiating the fees with the parties to the dispute, considering factors such as the time spent on the work, the ease of resolving the dispute, the affordability of the parties, and the credibility and ability of the mediator. Only in this way can the development of commercial mediation be thoroughly stimulated and the commercial mediation market be promoted to flourish.

2. Explore the development of individual commercial mediation. According to the definition of mediation in Article 2 of the Singapore Convention on Mediation, "Mediation" means a process, irrespective of the expression used or the basis upon which the process is carried out, whereby parties attempt to reach an amicable settlement of their dispute with the assistance of a third person or persons ("the mediator") lacking the authority to impose a solution upon the parties to the dispute. This means that mediation can be carried out by either one person or several persons and is not clearly defined by law. Commercial mediation abroad has been distinguished between institutional mediation and individual mediation, each with its own advantages and disadvantages, depending mainly on the subjective choice of the commercial mediator. At present, individual mediation exists only in the field of people's mediation in China, while there is no individual mediation in the field of commercial mediation. For the future development of commercial mediation, a parallel model of institutional mediation and individual mediation should be established, and commercial mediators should be encouraged to practice independently, which will help enrich the practice options of commercial mediators and contribute to the diversified development of commercial mediation. Specifically, the conditions for the establishment, remuneration standards, and procedural norms of individual mediation should be designed in a somewhat different way from institutional mediation.

3. Accelerate the training of commercial mediation talents. Objectively speaking, the shortage of commercial mediation talents is an important factor limiting the development of China's commercial mediation market at present. Therefore, the key to breaking the bottleneck in the development of the commercial mediation market lies in accelerating the training of commercial mediation talents. The goal of training commercial mediation talents should be to cultivate specialized, international, and professional mediation talents in practice. Specialization requires students to have a comprehensive grasp of multidisciplinary knowledge and skills such as law, negotiation, psychology, and management, so that they can handle various complex and difficult commercial disputes/ Internationalization requires students to be proficient in more than one foreign language, have an open international perspective, and be able to follow the cutting-edge developments in international commercial mediation. Professionalization means making commercial mediation a profession and establishing a corresponding professional qualification and certification system,[19] so that its practitioners have a high sense of professional respect. While highlighting these three aspects, there is a particular need to focus on "practical" training, which requires students to be involved in the process of training and to appreciate practice,[20] rather

than stopping at theoretical education. A practical training model also requires a collaborative effort between the legal education sector and the legal practice sector, such as trade promotion councils, commercial mediation organizations, and arbitration commissions, to bring their unique strengths into play in the training of commercial mediation personnel.

5.3.3 Improving the Enforcement Mechanism of Agreements

According to Article 4(5) of the Singapore Convention on Mediation, "the competent authorities shall act expeditiously in considering requests for relief," which requires States Parties, when reviewing and enforcing international commercial settlement agreements, to establish appropriate mechanisms to facilitate the timely enforcement of the agreements. Therefore, the domestic judiciary should, prior to the formal ratification of the Convention, expeditiously study and establish a corresponding mechanism for the enforcement of agreements, to dispel the doubts and concerns that the Convention will increase the pressure of judicial enforcement on domestic courts. At present, the review and enforcement of international commercial settlement agreements in China still suffer from a legal and institutional gap, and good experience in the recognition and enforcement of foreign arbitral awards over the past 30 years can be drawn upon in this regard. The most urgent task now is to amend domestic laws and introduce corresponding judicial interpretations. For example, the current *Civil Procedure Law* should add a provision on the "enforcement of international commercial settlement agreements" to Chapter 27 on judicial assistance, such as, in principle, assigning the review and enforcement of international commercial settlement agreements to the jurisdiction of the intermediate people's court of the domicile of the executee or the place where his or her property is located. In addition, the *Law on Civil Enforcement*, which is currently being drafted, must also reflect the enforcement of international commercial settlement agreements. In terms of judicial interpretation, the Supreme People's Court may draw on the practice of recognition and enforcement of foreign arbitral awards and issue *Regulations on Certain Issues Concerning the Examination and Enforcement of International Commercial Settlement Agreements* to provide uniform guidance on the enforcement of agreements in China. Specifically, by amending domestic laws and issuing judicial interpretations, the following mechanisms for the enforcement of agreements should be put in place.

First, a mechanism for the review of reconciliation agreement cases under one roof. It refers to the review of international commercial settlement agreements by a specific section of the court. At present, China has adopted a centralized mechanism for the judicial review of foreign-related commercial trials and foreign-related arbitrations,[21] which is also suitable for judicial review of international commercial settlement agreements. That is, the trial divisions of courts at all levels (intermediate people's courts or above) hearing foreign-related commercial cases should be responsible for the judicial review of international commercial settlement agreements as specialized business divisions, and then hand over to the enforcement department for specific enforcement after their review and approval. It should be noted that the review should be based on the principle of a formal review, but when the parties raise the grounds for non-enforcement, the specialized division will then conduct a substantive review.[22] In addition, a centralized data and information management platform for judicial review of cases of international commercial settlement agreements can be established with the help of the centralized handling mechanism, to strengthen the information management and data analysis of such cases. In this way, the quality and efficiency of the review can be balanced, while at the same time ensuring the correctness of the application of the law and the uniformity of the scale of adjudication.

Second, the reporting mechanism for a review of the settlement agreement cases. This originated in the judicial review of foreign arbitral awards by domestic courts in order to overcome operational shortcomings and local protectionism.[23] The reporting mechanism may prevent courts at all levels from arbitrarily refusing to recognize and enforce foreign arbitral awards, and minimize the number of cases where recognition and enforcement of foreign arbitral awards are refused, and this has received much praise from the international commercial arbitration community.[24] Therefore, we propose that it be applied to the review and enforcement of international commercial settlement agreement cases, i.e. when handling the review and enforcement of international commercial settlement agreement cases, if the intermediate courts decide that they will not enforce the international commercial settlement agreement after review, they should report to the high people's court under their jurisdiction. Where the high people's court intends to approve after review, it should report to the Supreme People's Court for verification. Only after the Supreme People's Court has reviewed it, can a ruling be made. This will facilitate the unification of the grounds and standards for review of international commercial settlement agreements and reflect the openness of Chinese courts to international commercial mediation.

Third, a pre-enforcement property preservation mechanism for settlement agreements. How does the enforcement court review an application for property preservation before or while a party applies for enforcement of an international commercial settlement agreement? Will it be granted? The Singapore Convention on Mediation does not provide for this, nor does domestic law. In order to protect the legitimate rights and interests of the parties, we believe that a pre-enforcement property preservation mechanism for international commercial settlement agreements should be established. In other words, if a party applies for preservation of property before or at the same time as the application for enforcement of an international commercial settlement agreement, the court should issue a ruling on preservation of property within a specific period if it considers that there is a genuine emergency such as the transfer of property by the debtor, and if the parties provide security. By establishing a pre-enforcement property preservation mechanism for international commercial settlement agreements, the lawful rights, and interests of the applicant for enforcement can be effectively protected and the smooth execution of international commercial settlement agreements can be promoted, thereby enhancing the trust and satisfaction of foreign parties in the judicial enforcement in China.

Notes

1 The Convention originated from a proposal by the United States to the United Nations Commission on International Trade Law (UNCITRAL) in May 2014 for a multilateral convention aimed at providing a systematic or simplified regime for the cross-border enforcement of settlement agreements arising from conciliation. Subsequently, some four years of extensive discussions among 85 Member States and 35 international organizations culminated in the adoption of the UN Convention on International Conciliation Agreements Arising from mediation at the UN General Assembly on December 20, 2018, and a signing ceremony in Singapore on August 7, 2019, where 52 countries have now signed the Convention, including five ratifications of the Singapore Convention on Mediation, which also marks the entry into force of the Singapore Convention on Mediation on September 12, 2020.
2 Wen Xiantao: The Singapore Convention and Commercial Mediation in China: A Comparison with the New York Convention and the Convention on Choice of Court Agreements, *China Law Review*, 2019 (1).
3 In the case of The Hague Convention on Choice of Court Agreements, for example, although the Chinese government formally signed the Convention as early as September 12, 2017, it is not yet legally binding for China as the Standing Committee of the National People's Congress has not yet decided to ratify it.
4 Luo Peixin: An Analysis of the "Protection of Minority Investors" Indicator in the World Bank's Doing Business Assessment, *Tsinghua Law*, 2019 (1).
5 Liao Yong'an and Duan Ming: Opportunities, Challenges and Path Choices for Developing Commercial Mediation in China's "Belt and Road," *Journal of South China University (Social Science Edition)*, 2018 (4).
6 Liao Yong'an et al.: *Conceptual Innovation and Institutional Reinvention of Mediation in China* (Beijing: Renmin University of China Press, 2019), p. 327.
7 Liu Jingdong: The Significance and Impact of the Singapore Mediation Convention on China, *Legal Daily*, September 17, 2019, p. 10.
8 He Qisheng: The Concept of Great Power Justice and the Development of China's International Civil Litigation System, *Chinese Social Sciences*, 2017 (5).
9 Singapore has undertaken a number of efforts to establish itself as a global center for commercial mediation. For example, on November 5, 2014, the Singapore International Mediation Center (SIMC) was launched by Chief Justice Sundaresh Menon and Singapore's Minister for Law, Mr K. Shanmugam SC, to effectively complement the Singapore International Arbitration Center (SIAC) and the Singapore International Commercial Court; and this was followed by the passage of the Mediation Act in 2017. These initiatives have provided a solid foundation for Singapore to become a center for international commercial mediation, and have led to the Singapore Convention on Mediation becoming the first international convention to bear the name "Singapore."

10 Qi Shujie and Li Yedan: The Extraterritorial Development of Commercial Mediation and its Reference Significance, *China Maritime Law Yearbook*, 2011 (2).
11 Wu Jun: China Commercial Mediation Annual Observation (2013), *Beijing Arbitration*, 2013 (1).
12 Cai Huixia: A Review of New Developments in the German Mediation System, *People's Court Daily*, July 12, 2013, p. 8.
13 Sun Wei: *Legislative Background and Interpretation of the Provisions of "The United Nations Convention on International Conciliation Agreements resulting from Mediation"* (Beijing: Law Press, 2018), p. 132.
14 Ge Huangbin: The Universal Dividend of the Singapore Convention is a Double-Edged Sword, *Legal Daily*, February 19. 2019.
15 Li Haopei: *An Introduction to the Law of Treaties* (Beijing: Law Press, 2003), p. 272.
16 Cong Xuelian and Luo Chuxiang: Exploring Some Issues in the Litigation of Arbitration, *Juridical Review*, 2007 (6).
17 Wang Fuhua: Costs Drive the Process, *The Jurist*, 2010 (6).
18 Geoffrey Cleeves and Naomi Lux: *Pre/meet the Lawman of the Future*, trans. Xu Jie (Beijing; Law Press, 20180, p. 143.
19 Tang Qiongqiong: The Improvement of China's Commercial Mediation System in the Context of the Singapore Convention on Mediation, *Journal of Shanghai University (Social Science Edition)*, 2019 (4): 126.
20 Hu Xiaoxia: Study on Dispute Settlement Mechanism in the Construction of "One Belt One Road," *Law Forum*, 2018 (4): 43.
21 Song Lianbin: New Developments in the Judicial Supervision System of Arbitration and its Significance, *People's Rule of Law*, 2018 (5).
22 Zhao Ping: The Interface between the Singapore Convention on Mediation and the Chinese Mediation Legal System, *China Lawyer*, 2019 (9).
23 Shen Wei: A Normative Analysis of China's Judicial Review System for Arbitration, *Juridical Forum*, 2019 (1).
24 Gao Xiaoli: The Active Practice of Chinese Courts in the Recognition and Enforcement of Foreign Arbitral Awards, *Application of Law*, 2018 (5).

References

Cai Huixia: A Review of New Developments in the German Mediation System, People's Court Daily, July 12, 2013, p. 8.

Cleeves, Geoffrey and Naomi Lux: *Pre/meet the Lawman of the Future*, trans. Xu Jie, Beijing: Law Press, 2018.

Cong Xuelian and Luo Chuxiang: Exploring Some Issues in the Litigation of Arbitration, *Juridical Review*, 2007 (6): 87–93.

Gao Xiaoli: The Active Practice of Chinese Courts in the Recognition and Enforcement of Foreign Arbitral Awards, *Application of Law*, 2018 (5): 2–8.

Ge Huangbin: The Universal Dividend of the Singapore Convention is a Double-Edged Sword, Legal Daily, February 19, 2019.

He Qisheng: The Concept of Great Power Justice and the Development of China's International Civil Litigation System, *Chinese Social Sciences*, 2017 (5): 123–146+208.

Hu Xiaoxia: Study on Dispute Settlement Mechanism in the Construction of "One Belt, One Road," *Law Forum*, 2018 (4): 43.

Li Haopei: *An Introduction to the Law of Treaties*, Beijing: Law Press, 2003.
Liao Yong'an et al.: *Conceptual Innovation and Institutional Reinvention of Mediation in China*, Beijing: Renmin University of China Press, 2019.
Liao Yong'an and Duan Ming: Opportunities, Challenges and Path Choices for Developing Commercial Mediation in China's "Belt and Road," Journal of South China University (Social Science Edition), 2018 (4): 27–34.
Liu Jingdong: The Significance and Impact of the Singapore Mediation Convention on China, Legal Daily, September 17, 2019, p. 10.
Luo Peixin: An Analysis of the "Protection of Minority Investors" Indicator in the World Bank's Doing Business Assessment, *Tsinghua Law*, 2019 (1): 151–174.
Qi Shujie and Li Yedan: The Extraterritorial Development of Commercial Mediation and its Reference Significance, *China Maritime Law Yearbook*, 2011 (2): 97–103.
Shen Wei: A Normative Analysis of China's Judicial Review System for Arbitration, Juridical Forum, 2019 (1): 34–56.
Song Lianbin: New Developments in the Judicial Supervision System of Arbitration and its Significance, *People's Rule of Law*, 2018 (5): 21–25.
Sun Wei: *Legislative Background and Interpretation of the Provisions of "The United Nations Convention on International Conciliation Agreements resulting from Mediation,"* Beijing: Law Press, 2018.
Tang Qiongqiong: The Improvement of China's Commercial Mediation System in the Context of the Singapore Convention on Mediation, *Journal of Shanghai University (Social Science Edition)*, 2019,(4): 126.
Wang Fuhua: Costs Drive the Process, The Jurist, 2010 (6): 83–98+176–177.
Wen Xiantao: The Singapore Convention and Commercial Mediation in China – A Comparison with the New York Convention and the Convention on Choice of Court Agreements, *China Law Review*, 2019 (1): 198–208.
Wu Jun: China Commercial Mediation Annual Observation (2013), *Beijing Arbitration*, 2013 (1): 29–51.
Zhao Ping: The Interface between the Singapore Convention on Mediation and the Chinese Mediation Legal System, *China Lawyer*, 2019 (9): 44–46.

6 Paradoxes and Crackdowns in Lawyer Mediation

6.1 The Problem: The Promotion of Lawyer Mediation Is "Hot" and the Implementation Is "Cold"

The development of modern mediation in China belongs to the "improvement model." i.e., a "top-down" partial improvement of traditional mediation under the leadership of the government.[1] With the modernization of the rule of law in China, the problems of a large but unevenly qualified pool of mediators, a variety of benchmarks for mediation but a lack of legal elements, flexible mediation procedures but little necessary regulation, and a wealth of mediation reform initiatives but little effectiveness in terms of benefits have become key bottlenecks to the further development of mediation in China. As a result, the modernization of the rule of law in China has led to a decline in the efficiency of mediation caused by the over-investment of labor, resulting in problems, such as the involvement of labor.[2] Therefore, given the limited resources of mediation itself, it is surely appropriate to introduce the participation of lawyers as legal professionals and thus develop lawyer mediation.

China's top-level design is also keenly aware of lawyer mediation as an important nitiative for the innovative development of mediation. From laws, regulations, judicial interpretations, and policy documents, the emergence and development of lawyer mediation in China have gone through an initial, an exploration, and a refinement stages.[3] In October 2017, the Supreme People's Court and the Ministry of Justice jointly issued the *Opinions on Conducting Pilot Work on Lawyer Mediation* (hereinafter referred to as the Pilot Opinions) with a view to promoting the practice of lawyer mediation by means of pilot projects in 11 provinces and cities to provide strong support and guarantee for the further improvement of lawyer mediation. In January 2019, the *Notice of the Supreme People's Court and the Ministry of Justice on Expanding the Pilot Work of Lawyer Mediation* required that by the end of 2019, all prefectural and municipal administrative regions should conduct pilot work of lawyer mediation, and every county-level administrative region should strive to have a lawyer mediation studio. It is easy to see that lawyer mediation has become a government-led "top-down" promotion boom.

DOI: 10.4324/9781003385776-6

However, the following two points can be noted from the practical status of lawyer mediation. One is that only a few lawyers are involved in lawyer mediation work, such as the 584 lawyer mediators employed by the two levels of courts in Hangzhou, accounting for only 8 percent of the number of practicing lawyers in the city;[4] the second is that the number of cases mediated by lawyers is relatively small. As of November 2018, the pilot provinces have now set up a total of 2,357 lawyer mediation studios (centers), with more than 37,000 cases mediated by lawyers. With more than 16,000 mediation agreements reached.[5] each lawyer mediation studio (center) had an average of only 15 mediation cases and only 7 successful mediation cases in the pilot work in more than one year. It can be found that the "hot" promotion of lawyer mediation has met with a "cold" treatment in practice. Most of the relevant research findings have discussed the overseas experience, legitimacy, advantages, and role of lawyer mediation,[6] but less in-depth analysis has been conducted on the phenomenon of "cold" implementation of lawyer mediation. In view of this, we have conducted research on the operation of lawyer mediation through seminars, in-depth interviews, and documentary review.[7] On the premise of clarifying the essence of lawyer mediation, this chapter attempts to reveal the endogenous conflict of lawyer mediation and analyze the practical problems arising from this conflict and the ways to resolve them, to examine the "hot" and "cold" of lawyer mediation on a rational platform.

6.2 The Essence of Lawyer Mediation in China Pursued

The Pilot Opinions set out the meaning, characteristics, and modes of lawyer mediation. The document defines lawyer mediation as the activity of a lawyer, a lawyer mediation studio established by law or a lawyer mediation center as a neutral third party to conduct mediation and assist parties to a dispute to reach an agreement to resolve the dispute through voluntary negotiation. Based on this definition, the Pilot Opinions provide for four working modes of lawyer mediation: (1) the People's Court Lawyer Mediation Studio Mode; (2) the Public Legal Service Center (Station) Lawyer Mediation Studio Mode; (3) the Bar Association Lawyer Mediation Center Mode; and (4) the Lawyer Firm Mediation Studio Mode. What is the essence of lawyer mediation as reflected in the above provisions? Is lawyer mediation an independent type of mediation? What is the relationship between lawyer mediation and judicial mediation, people's mediation, administrative mediation, professional mediation, commercial mediation, etc.? The answers to these questions are the basis for exploring lawyer mediation and require a clear understanding.

The current mediation system in China can be divided into the following three categories, depending on the presiding authority of the mediation: First, judicial mediation, i.e., extra-judicial dispute resolution procedures with the court as the presiding authority, or under the guidance of the court, but distinct from litigation proceedings, mainly refers to court-attached mediation. Second, administrative mediation, which refers mainly to mediation established by or attached to the administrative or quasi-administrative organs of the state. Third, civil mediation, which is generally not part of the formal judicial system or the state administrative establishment, mainly includes specialized agencies operating in the form of a consortium of legal persons or funds, as well as legal bodies of spontaneously established civil groups or associations, and also includes quasi-administrative organizations under the guidance and funding of the state, such as the People's Mediation Organization in China, and also includes loose mediation organizations that exist in various forms in the civil community.[8]

At present, there are two main views on the nature of lawyer mediation in the Pilot Opinions: the first view is that lawyer mediation is an independent type of mediation classified according to the subject of mediation. For example, the relevant comrades of the Supreme People's Court and the Ministry of Justice pointed out in their answer to a reporter's question on the Pilot Opinions that

> The establishment of a working mechanism of mediation conducted by lawyers as a neutral third party, the improvement of a lawyer mediation system that is both relatively independent and interconnected with people's mediation, administrative mediation, litigation mediation and commercial mediation ... is conducive to promoting the formation of a diversified dispute resolution system with Chinese characteristics.[9]

The second view is that lawyer mediation does not belong to the independent type of mediation classified according to mediation subjects. Some scholars suggest that lawyer mediation does not belong to the types of mediation such as people's mediation, administrative mediation, industrial mediation, and commercial mediation classified according to the attributes (subjects) of mediation, and that lawyers, as mediators, can participate in the above types of mediation organizations.[10]

In fact, according to the four working models of lawyer mediation in the Pilot Opinions, the structure of lawyer mediation can be broken down into four forms, and the essence of lawyer mediation can be dissected from them. The first model is the establishment of lawyers' mediation studios in the people's courts, which in essence are lawyers mediating cases under the entrustment of the courts, subject to court management and review, and belonging to court-attached mediation. The second model is to set up a lawyer mediation studio in a public legal service center (station). The public legal service center (station) is an effective vehicle for the collection of judicial and administrative legal services of all kinds and the provision of a wide range of public legal service products, and is the window through which the judicial administrative organs provide services directly to the people. The public legal service center (station) is an administrative body and therefore the mediation services provided by lawyers there are administrative mediation. The third model is the establishment of mediation centers in bar associations. A bar

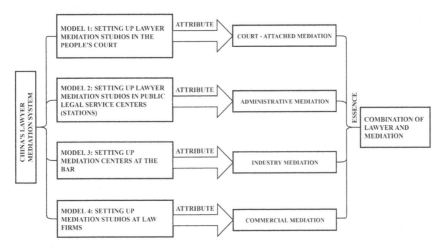

Figure 6.1 Chinese lawyers' mediation.

association is a social group of legal person and a professional self-regulatory organization for lawyers. Therefore, the mediation service provided by the Lawyers' Mediation Center established by the bar association has the nature of civil mediation, specifically, it belongs to the professional mediation in civil mediation. The fourth model is the establishment of mediation studios in law firms. The law firm can accept the parties' application for mediation as part of a lawyer's business, and charge mediation fees to both parties. This model is close to the market and is in essence a commercial mediation within civil mediation.

In short, Chinese lawyers' mediation can be broken down into four working models, the essence of which are court-attached mediation, administrative mediation, industrial mediation, and commercial mediation. Therefore, Chinese lawyers' mediation does not belong to the independent type of mediation according to the subject of dispute resolution. The essence of lawyer mediation is the participation of lawyers as mediators in judicial mediation, administrative mediation, and civil mediation, which is a product of the combination of lawyers and mediation (see Figure 6.1).

6.3 The Endogenous Conflicts of Lawyer Mediation in China

The term "lawyer" refers to the person who has obtained qualifications in accordance with the statutory conditions and procedures, and who can may lawfully be entrusted with parties or the court's designation to provide legal assistance to the parties and represent them in the relevant legal affairs activities.[11] Mediation is an activity in which the parties to a dispute are mediated and persuaded to understand each other, negotiate and voluntarily reach an agreement to eliminate the dispute, under the auspices of a third party mediator and on the basis of national laws, policies, and social ethics.[12] Lawyer mediation is a product of the combination of lawyers and mediation, that is, the lawyers as the subject of lawyer mediation, mix the "agent role" of the lawyer's essence with the "mediator role" when the lawyer presides over the mediation. Roles are the rights and obligations, code of conduct, and behavioral patterns that arise around status, and are the behaviors expected of people in a certain position.[13] Therefore, whether the mixture of the "agent's role" and the "mediator's role" is contradictory can be analyzed in terms of the status, philosophy, code of conduct, and behavioral patterns of the role.

6.3.1 Status of the Roles: Unilateral Position vs. Neutral Position

Some scholars believe that the special conflict inherent in the lawyer system is the conflict between lawyers and their clients, and the fundamental external feature of the lawyer system determined by that special conflict is the protection of the legal rights and interests of the clients.[14] Similarly, according to foreign scholars, a lawyer's role is divided into being a counselor, who helps the client to plan for the future, and an agent, who acts as a representative of the client in dialogue with others (judges, opposing parties, government officials, etc.). The essence of the lawyer's role is essentially the same in both activities, and can be described as a warrior chosen to protect the interests of the client.[15] The lawyer's position as an agent is unilateral, as in the "isosceles triangle" structure of civil litigation, where the lawyer is in opposition to the other party and its agent together with the client. In mediation, neutrality is the basic principle, so the status of the lawyer's "mediator role" is a neutral position. In the "linear" structure of mediation, the parties to the dispute are at either end of the line and the mediator is in the middle. Based on the differences in the status of lawyers' "agent role" and "mediator role," differences in philosophy, code of conduct, and behavioral patterns will be further developed.

6.3.2 Philosophy of Roles: The Litigation Concept and Behavior vs. the Mediation Concept and Behavior

In the formation of China's civil litigation service from an *ex officio* litigation model to a hybrid litigation model,[16] lawyers have, on the one hand, been influenced by clientelism, which has increased their status; but on the other hand, they have not been free from the influence of *ex officio* litigation, and work mainly around the judge's trial ideas. As a result, the "agent role" of lawyers mainly starts from a "litigation mindset." With the use of static interests, slice-and-dice thinking and backward-looking thinking. In this mindset, the lawyer will stand between the client and the court to maximize the legal rights and interests of the client without having to determine the rights and obligations of the parties to the dispute. In modern mediation, the lawyer's role as mediator should be based on community interest thinking, a dynamic interest perspective, comprehensive thinking, and a forward-looking mindset.[17] In this mindset, the lawyer mediator needs to face both parties to the dispute alone, initiate the mediation process independently, and use a combination of the three strategies of "mediation," "judgment," and "coercion" in the mediation,[18] in order to bring the parties to a dispute to a consensus. Therefore, the concept and behavior of the lawyer's "agent role" and the "mediator role" are distinctly opposed.

6.3.3 Norms of Conduct of the Role: Isolation from the Court vs. Proximity to the Court

Norms of conduct refer to the rules and guidelines followed by the role in participating in social activities, and are a generally binding standard of conduct recognized by society and generally accepted by people. An important part of the code of conduct for lawyers is the code governing the relationship between lawyers and judges. Lawyers and judges belong to the legal community of "sharing common knowledge, beliefs, and meaning,"[19] and the relationship between judges and lawyers should include mutual trust, good cooperation, and continuous supervision, but in practice, lawyers and judges lack mutual supervision, forming a community of interest and a serious improper relationship.[20] Therefore, the code of conduct of the lawyer's "agent role" must require them to keep a certain distance from the judge, and "the regularity of contact between and proximity to them can only reach a certain level, otherwise the professional majesty cannot be formed."[21] Xiao Yang, President of the Supreme People's Court, has proposed that a "separation zone" be established between judges and lawyers to safeguard judicial impartiality.[22] However, the Pilot Opinions call for the establishment of lawyer mediation studios in people's court litigation service centers, litigation and mediation docking centers or qualified people's courtrooms, equipped with necessary work facilities and workplaces. This will make the mediator more authoritative, facilitate the judge's guidance and management of mediation work, and achieve a seamless docking between mediation and judicial confirmation and other procedures. Therefore, in contrast to the lawyer's "agent role," the code of conduct of the lawyer's "mediator role" requires that they are close to the court.

6.3.4 Behavioral Patterns of Actors: Market-Led vs. Public Interest-Led

The nature of a lawyer's job determines the behavioral pattern of the lawyer's "agent role." The 2007 *Law on Lawyers* changed the macro service object of lawyers from society to clients, which can be seen as a change in Chinese lawyers from "state legal workers" to "legal workers for society" to "freelancers." Most developed countries in the world have clearly defined lawyers are freelancers, treating lawyer services as personal labor, and state that lawyers providing services to their clients should be paid. Therefore, lawyers have their own inherent pursuit of interests, which are fundamentally different from those of public interest defenders such as judges, arbitrators, or government officials, and the behavior of the lawyer's "agent role" is market-driven. However, according to the four working models of lawyer mediation in the Pilot Opinions, the first three models do not charge the parties for mediation and are pro bono mediation; only the fourth model is market-based mediation, but still can only charge the parties a fee for mediation at a low rate.

In summary, due to the differences and opposition between the "agent role" and the "mediator role" of lawyers in terms of status, philosophy, code of conduct, and behavior, lawyer mediation will produce an endogenous conflict in which the "agent role" and the "mediator role" are mixed. As some scholars put forward: "The lawyers' defense of the interests of the parties will often become a discordant voice in the mediation process, so the lawyers in the mediation process will often be marginalized."[23]

6.4 Practical Issues Arising from the Endogenous Conflicts of Mediation by Lawyers in China

6.4.1 Difficulties for Lawyers to Adapt to Lawyer Mediation

There are many differences between the "agent role" and the "mediator role" of lawyers in terms of status and philosophy, so most lawyers will have certain difficulties in adapting to the new role of mediator in a short period of time, and the specific practice is as follows.

6.4.1.1 Lawyers Have a Bias Against Lawyer Mediation

At present, there is no widespread recognition of mediation among lawyers, who believe that mediation seems to be at the lower end of the spectrum, preferring instead to engage in the higher end type of business, such as litigation representation.[24] As scholars have argued, lawyers are concerned about financial loss and a lack of understanding of the nature of mediation, and may prefer the active presence in litigation to the passive and advisory role they play in mediation.[25] The low number of lawyers involved in mediation in practice is also evidence of a bias toward lawyer mediation, as shown by the fact that of the 263 questionnaires distributed to the lawyers' community in Hangzhou, nearly 150, or over 50 percent, had not yet participated in lawyer mediation.[26]

6.4.1.2 Lawyers' Neutrality in Mediation Is Vulnerable

There is a distinction between neutrality in the narrow sense and in the broad sense. Neutrality in the narrow sense is disinterested neutrality, meaning that the mediator has no *de facto* or *de jure* interest in any of the parties to the dispute. The principle of neutrality in the broad sense also includes neutrality in the sense of fairness, meaning that the mediator must treat both parties fairly and objectively in the mediation process, without favoring either of the parties.[27] The lawyer's "agent role" is to fight for the legal rights and interests of the client to the maximum extent possible, and to stand on the same footing as the client, but not on a neutral footing. In the practice of lawyer mediation, the following cases have emerged which are worth considering.

Ren is a lawyer at T Law Firm and carries out lawyer mediation work at the mediation studio of District Court F. On April 11, 2018, 11 workers pursued claims for labor remuneration involving a total amount of more than RMB 400,000 (Case A) and, following a referral by the judge, 11 people agreed to lawyer mediation. On April 25, the defendant Company A came as promised. Considering the large number of parties, Ren and four other lawyers mediated the case. After the successful mediation, both parties jointly applied for judicial confirmation from the District Court F. In fact, Ren was the agent of the workers in another labor remuneration case (Case B) of Company A. The case went through labor arbitration proceedings and litigation proceedings, and the workers are currently in the process of applying for court enforcement.[28]

A careful analysis of the case reveals the following caveats: Ren was the agent of the workers in Case B and was in an opposing position to Company A, whereas in Case A, Ren was required to take a neutral position as a lawyer-mediator to deal with the relationship between Company A and the workers in a neutral and fair manner. The conflict between these two positions will likely result in lawyers being unable to mediate disputes neutrally and fairly when acting in their role as mediators, because in the absence of corporate assets, the lawyer may mediate to make Company A pay less labor remuneration in Case A, and the workers in Case B will then be more likely to receive more, thereby obtaining more agency fees. as a way of obtaining a larger representation fee. As a result, the lawyer's neutrality in mediation is easily affected by the conflation of the lawyer's "agent role" and the "mediator role."

6.4.1.3 Lawyers Are Not Familiar with the Thinking and Methods Required for Mediation

In practice, some lawyers often use the same thinking and methods in mediation as in litigation, which makes it difficult for them to adapt to mediation and the success rate of mediation is not high. For example, a lawyer said in an interview, "We will say to the parties that this is a mediation court, and although it is different from a trial court, the process is the same, such as we ask the plaintiff and the defendant to bring all the original evidence."[29] Some judges also reflect that lawyers who have been practicing for many years also have difficulties in adapting to mediation work:

> There was a senior lawyer who specialized in family cases, he initially felt that participating in mediation work, especially mediation divorce cases

must be handy, but as a result, after participating in several mediations, he reflected to me that: "I don't think I can do this mediation work. I thought I had represented so many divorce cases that I would be able to mediate here, but it turned out not to be the case, so I won't come." So, it's not the case that if you have a lot of experience as a lawyer, you can do a good job in mediation.[30]

From the research data (as shown in Table 6.1), the average number of mediations conducted by lawyers in the four sample courts in six months was 0.9, with a 38 percent success rate in mediation. The number of lawyers involved in mediation is low and the success rate of mediation is not high.[31]

6.4.2 The Ethical Risks of Lawyer Mediation

The lawyer's role as an agent requires the lawyer to maintain an isolated relationship, distant from the court, while the lawyer's role as a mediator requires the lawyer to be proximate to the court. This conflict will give rise to moral hazard in practice, including the risk of an unethical lawyer-judge relationship and the risk of being abused by lawyers to expand the source of cases.

6.4.2.1 The Risk of an Unethical Lawyer-Judge Relationship

First, some judges indicated in interviews that there was a phenomenon of lawyers using their status as lawyer-mediators in the courts to "worm their way into a relationship" with judges. An interview presents a case study.

> The first time this sort of thing came up was in our Court S. One of the lawyer-mediators in Court S was also involved in litigation as a representative in Court S. Once, before the case he was representing went to court, he ran up to the judge and said: "Judge, I am the mediator in our court." The judge heard these words from the lawyer-mediator and said nothing at the time, but said in court, "This agent is the lawyer-mediator of this court, please recuse yourself." In fact, it is reasonable to say that all the lawyer-mediators in our court are selected by the Bar Association from the lawyers in District C. If they cannot represent cases in District C court, it will be difficult for these lawyers to earn income by representing cases and they will not come to participate in lawyer mediation work, therefore, lawyers involved in mediation should not be recused in general. But why did the judge in Court S ask this lawyer to recuse himself? Because the judge was wondering what the lawyer meant when he deliberately emphasized that he was the court's lawyer-mediator before the hearing? What was the lawyer's purpose? The judge then reasonably doubted whether the lawyer was trying to worm his way into a relationship with the judge or whether he was going to engage in other deals,

Table 6.1 Data on mediation work by lawyers in the sample courts, December 2017–June 2018 (in units)

The court	Lawyer mediators	Delegation: number of cases	Lawyer-mediated average	Mediation: number of successes	Mediation: success rate (%)
Shaoxing City Central Court	34	5	0.15	3	60†
Yue Cheng Court	46	28	0.6	7	25
Zhuji City Court	100	269	2.7	47	17
Shangyu Court	43	2	0.05	1	50
Average	56	76	0.9	58	38

which would affect his fair trial of the case, so he asked the lawyer to recuse himself.[32]

Second, judges may offer counsel convenience based on their motivation to mobilize lawyers to participate in lawyer mediation work. The existence of this risk can be confirmed by the author's interviews with judges:

> As the lawyers come over to help us do so much mediation work, as a reciprocation you have to grant some convenience in the future when they come to represent cases. As our court president said, if the lawyer-mediator came to our court to file a case, he would open a green channel, that is, he would file the case first without keeping it on the waiting list. I think this is within the scope of the law to provide them with convenience. However, the president also mentioned that "as long as the parties want to hire a lawyer, we can register it and assign it to the lawyers who come to the court to participate in lawyer mediation work." I don't agree with this, I think it's too risky. The president wants to provide more convenience to the lawyers participating in mediation, so that they would be more willing to mediate cases for the court. But, in fact, these facilitation practices are not being implemented in the court now.[33]

As a matter of fact, the court lawyers' mediation studios are mostly set up in the filing divisions, litigation service centers, or litigation and mediation docking centers, where lawyers have more contact with judges and judicial support staff in the filing divisions and less contact with trial judges in the business divisions. As a result, it is generally difficult for lawyers to contact trial judges through lawyer mediation, creating risks that may affect the fairness of trials. However, there are exceptions that should not be overlooked: first, some courts have set up expedited tribunals in the case filing division, and the judges in the filing divisions have the right to try cases that enter the expedited trial process; second, lawyers' mediation workshops are set up in the people's courts, and lawyers may have direct contact with the trial judges.

6.4.2.2 The Risk of Alienation in the Expansion of the Lawyers' Caseload

Due to the proximity of lawyer mediation to the court, lawyers may be able to expand their representation through direct access to court cases. The first possibility is that a lawyer represents a client in a case in which he or she was involved in mediation suing under another legal relationship after the case has been withdrawn. The reason for this phenomenon in practice is that although the Pilot Opinions explicitly stipulate that lawyer serving as mediators may not serve as agents in the same case, they do not clearly define the term "same case."

The second possibility is that a lawyer refers a case that he or she has failed to mediate to other lawyers for representation. Usually, through face-to-face or back-to-back mediation etc., lawyers can get a handle on the claims, evidence, and bottom line of both parties. Although the Pilot Opinions, as well as the implementation rules of each region, stipulate that a lawyer who has presided over or participated in a mediation of a disputed matter, or even other lawyers in that lawyer's law firm, are no longer allowed to participate in the subsequent resolution process of that disputed matter and related disputes by acting as litigation agents, etc. However, a lawyer's social circle is not limited to his or her own law firm, and the above rule does not prevent a lawyer from referring a failed mediation case to his or her non-firm friends and informing them of the "private information" obtained in the mediation. There will be profit-sharing between lawyers for referrals and these profit factors will sway the lawyer-mediator not to be fair and impartial in conducting the mediation.[34]

A third possible risk is that the lawyer, through lawyer mediation, establishes contact with the parties to the dispute, gains their trust and creates opportunities to represent them in other disputes, which would be contrary to the original purpose of lawyer mediation, i.e., to advocate mediation as a means of resolving disputes. The existence of this risk can be found in the following interview:

> Our courts don't subsidize lawyers who participate in mediation work, so when I pick cases to assign to lawyers for mediation, I wonder what types of cases the lawyers like to mediate. Lawyers are busy so they will certainly not be willing to mediate some trivial disputes such as fights. This is not so with commercial cases, which usually involve the purchase and sale between enterprises. I send the information of these commercial cases to the lawyer mediation WeChat group, and ask the lawyers in the group to mediate. They often act like "rush orders," and a few cases are snatched up in less than a minute. Some lawyers even chat with me privately to say they want to mediate these cases.[35]

In terms of the enthusiasm and regularity of the lawyers to "grab orders," mediation by lawyers can increase their access to the subjects of commercial disputes, forming an indirect way of expanding their caseload.

A fourth possibility is that lawyers may advertise their status as court attorney mediators and flaunt their good relationship with the court in a variety of ways as a way of obtaining more cases. For example, a judge expressed the following concern in an interview: "The court's public announcement of lawyers involved in mediation work is to a certain extent equivalent to the court 'advertising' these lawyers, which will have an impact on lawyers developing their caseload."[36]

6.4.3 Insufficient Incentive for Lawyers to Participate in Lawyer Mediation

The conflict between the lawyer's "agent role" of the market-oriented behavior model and the public interest-led behavior model of the lawyer's "mediator role." In practice, will lead to insufficient motivation for lawyers to participate in mediation. In other words, lawyers tend to behave in a perfunctory and passive manner toward mediation work due to factors such as the cost of private time or loss of interest; second, it is difficult to participate in lawyer mediation work in a sustained and long-term manner.

6.4.3.1 Low Motivation of Lawyers to Participate in Pro Bono Lawyer Mediation

First, we analyze the motivation of lawyers to participate in mediation based on the mediation allowance. According to the author's research, courts in different regions have different criteria for subsidizing lawyers' participation in mediation in the courts. The first category is the granting of a fixed subsidy, such as the Hangzhou Intermediate People's Court, which subsidizes lawyer mediators with RMB 1,000 for each successful mediation. The second category is the granting of non-fixed subsidies, such as the Chaoyang District Court in Beijing, where the allowance is divided into four levels, usually RMB 450, depending on the complexity of the case, with the allowance reduced by half if mediation fails. The third category is the absence of subsidies, such as the free labor provided by most of the lawyer-mediators in some grass-roots courts in Hangzhou. What is clear is that these subsidies only cover the cost of transport, accommodation, and food for lawyers participating in mediation, and are usually not financially profitable, to the extent that some lawyers are concerned with representation at the expense of mediation. For example, in the research, it was found that some lawyers would have their assistants come to court to participate in lawyer mediation work when the time for representation conflicted with mediation work.

Second, we analyze the motivation of lawyers to participate in mediation in the light of the purpose of participation. Through interviews with lawyers involved in pro bono mediation, it can be concluded that the main purposes of their participation in lawyer mediation are: (1) to realize their social value and serve the public interest;[37] (2) to improve their professional skills;[38] and (3) to establish a good relationship with the court (judge).[39] However, the first reason is mainly for lawyers with a strong sense of social responsibility, while lawyers who do not have a strong sense of social responsibility may be reluctant to participate in lawyer mediation. As some judges have reflected, even for lawyers who are on the court's roster of lawyer-mediators, only a small number of them actually participate in mediation.[40] Although Article 18 of the Pilot Opinions provides for the exploration of the establishment of an assessment and recognition incentive mechanism for lawyers to participate in public interest mediation, the benefit of such an administrative incentive is limited to lawyers who are enthusiastic about engaging in public interest, and cannot fully stimulate the majority of lawyers to enthusiastically engage in lawyer mediation work.[41] The second and third reasons are motivated by the short-term needs of lawyers, who are less motivated to participate in lawyer mediation when they believe that they have largely achieved their objectives through lawyer mediation work, a phenomenon that is evidenced by the interviews with judges:

> Some of the earliest lawyers who came to court to participate in lawyer mediation were already familiar with our judges, so they didn't have the same excitement as at the beginning and slowly reduced their own involvement in mediation, i.e., they weren't as active as at the beginning.[42]

6.4.3.2 Market-Based Lawyer Mediation in Its Infancy

Market-based lawyer mediation refers to the establishment of mediation studios by law firms, which in essence belongs to commercial mediation. At present, market-based lawyer mediation is still in its infancy in China, and only a small number of law firms have set up mediation studios. In addition, there are also mediation organizations with lawyers as the main mediators and with the nature of private non-enterprises, which charge mediation fees from the parties. We use the mediation organizations in Table 6.2 as a sample for our analysis.

As can be seen from Table 6.2, the following problems exist in market-oriented lawyer mediation: First, most of the cases in lawyer mediation workshops originate from the assignment of the court, and the proportion of parties applying for lawyer mediation on their own is relatively small, and the market-oriented characteristics of lawyer mediation are not obvious. Second, the fees charged by lawyers for mediation are low. On the one hand, lawyers' fees for mediation are lower than those for lawyers' representation, for example, the mediation fee in the Beijing Diversified Mediation Development Promotion Association is half of the litigation fee, which is much lower than the representation fee charged by lawyers. Even the Beijing Rongshang Belt and Road International Commercial Mediation Center, which charges a relatively high fee for mediation, charges RMB 8,750 for a case with a subject matter of RMB 500,000, while according to the Administrative Measures for Lawyers' Service Fees, the lawyer's representation fee for the same subject matter is RMB 31,000, which is 3.5 times the mediation fee. On the other hand, if the mediation is not successful, the mediation fee will be partially refunded to the client, which leads to a significant reduction in the effectiveness of the lawyer's mediation fee. The Pilot Opinions positioned market-based lawyer mediation at a low price, while lawyers, as market players, are naturally profit-seeking and cannot be fully motivated to participate in mediation if they do not get the "price" they want.

Table 6.2 A sample of market-based lawyer mediation practice in China

Institutional profile	Source of the cases	Charging rules
Shanghai Xinmin Mediation Office, established in 2005, is part of Shanghai Xinmin law firm	Mainly from various sources such as the petitions office, people's mediation organizations, courts, social organizations and individuals	Mainly from the purchase of legal services by the Government and charged on a case-by-case basis
The Shanghai Economic and Commercial Mediation Center, established in 2014, majority of mediators composed of lawyers	Party-led application versus court or other organizations-appointed, mainly appointed by courts	The registration fee is RMB 300 per party. Two ways to calculate the fee: the parties to the dispute can choose to pay a percentage of the subject amount, or they can choose to pay the mediation fee at an hourly rate based on the time spent in mediation.[1]
Beijing Rongshang "One Belt, One Road" International Commercial Mediation Center, established in 2017, belongs to Beijing Deheng law firm	Party-led application versus court or other organizations-appointed, mainly appointed by courts. As of August 2018, there have been no cases of party-led applications for mediation and only four court-appointed cases.	The registration fee is RMB 200 per party. Mediation fee is based on the amount of the subject matter of the dispute.[2] If the mediation is unsuccessful, the Mediation Center will charge the necessary costs, provided that the costs do not exceed 20% of the fees paid and the balance is refunded to the parties.
The Beijing Association for the Development of Pluralistic Mediation, established in 2015, majority of mediators composed of lawyers	Mediation is delegated by organizations such as the courts	The mediation fee is half of the litigation costs, and will be refunded if the mediation is unsuccessful

Notes:
1 Charges according to the subject matter: below RMB 500,000, 4 percent of the amount in dispute, at least RMB 3,000; RMB 500,000–1,000,000, 2.5 percent of the amount in dispute, at least RMB 5,000; above RMB 1,000,000, 1.75 percent of the amount in dispute, at least RMB 10,000. Hourly rate, below RMB 500,000, RMB 3,000/hour; RMB 500,000–1,000,000, RMB 4,000/hour; above RMB 1,000,000, RMB 5,000/hour.
2 The mediation fee is RMB 8,750 for the amount below RMB 500,000 (inclusive); for the amount above RMB 500,000–5,000,000 (inclusive), 1 percent of the disputed amount; for the amount above RMB 5,000,000–20,000,000 (inclusive), 0.8 percent of the disputed amount; for the amount above RMB 20,000,000–500,00,000 (inclusive), 0.5 percent of the disputed amount; for the amount above RMB 500,000,000, 0.2 percent of the amount in dispute.

6.5 The Path to Resolving Endogenous Conflicts in Chinese Lawyer Mediation

From a comparative perspective, the development of mediation by lawyers in the UK, the US, and other developed Western countries has followed a "market-based path," whereby the profession, influenced by the "third wave" of the pro-justice movement, has decided to move away from the role of advisor and agent and began to act as a non-aligned interventionist,[43] so that mediation gradually became a specialized business for some law firms and lawyers, earning as much as legal representation. This path of development will effectively avoid the creation of conflicts in the role of lawyers in mediation.

However, the development of lawyer mediation in China has followed the "judicial path." That is, in the process of modernizing the rule of law, the courts and other institutions, based on the lack of resources available for mediation and the lack of legal factors for mediation, have issued laws and regulations, judicial interpretations, and policy documents to guide lawyers, as legal professionals, to participate in mediation work from top to bottom. However, China's lawyer mediation service is still facing many difficulties in order to realize the transformation from the "judicial path" to the "market path" and to establish and cultivate law firms and lawyers specializing in mediation. First, the development of China's lawyer profession still needs to be strengthened. Some data show that the number of lawyers per 10,000 people in China is 2.17, while the number in the United States is 37.[44] As the number of lawyers in China cannot meet the demands of the traditional litigation business, it is difficult to separate some lawyers to specialize in mediation business. Second, commercial mediation in China is still in its infancy. The "market-based" lawyer mediation path must be built in the context of the significant development of commercial mediation, which in China still suffers from the difficulty of establishing corporate commercial mediation organizations and the lack of a market for commercial mediation. Therefore, at this stage, the practical problems arising from the endogenous conflicts in lawyer mediation can be alleviated mainly at the level of institutional improvement.

6.5.1 Changing the Philosophy and Behavior of Lawyers Engaged in Mediation Work

First, the lawyers' perceptions of lawyer mediation should be changed. Lawyers in many countries around the world must go through a rigorous qualification process to pursue a career as a mediator and, as a result, many are proud to hold a mediator's qualification. For example, the Scottish Regional Law Society has set up the Centre for the General Accreditation of Lawyer Mediators (CALM), which qualifies lawyers to conduct such family mediation proceedings only if they have been accredited after training in a specialized program under its auspices.[45] In Switzerland, the lawyer community was initially not very enthusiastic about mediation, but there has been a dramatic change in the attitude of lawyers who are now lobbying their clients in favor of mediation, with the aim of ensuring that they retain their fair share of the future alternative dispute resolution market.[46] The Chinese lawyer community should also change its one-sided view of mediation and consider it as an extension of the lawyer's scope of practice, so as to provide better legal services to their clients and play an active role in promoting social construction.

Second, the recusal of lawyers from mediation should be improved to address the problem of confusion in the position of lawyers. The Pilot Opinions provide for three types of recusals: (1) "being a close relative of a party or its representative;" (2) "having an interest in the dispute;" and (3) "having other relations with the parties to the dispute or the representative that may affect impartial mediation." On this basis, the opinions on the implementation of the pilot work on lawyer mediation in Fujian, Zhejiang Province, and other regions added "the law firm where the lawyer mediator is located has accepted the entrustment of one party to the dispute" as a recusal situation.

This provision will provide greater clarity as to the circumstances in which lawyers may recuse themselves from mediation. The Pilot Opinions stipulate that the recusal of a lawyer-mediator includes two situations: (1) the lawyer's voluntary recusal; and (2) the party's application for recusal. In order to monitor and ensure that lawyers stand on neutral and impartial ground, the courts, public legal service centers, bar associations, law firms, and other entities may review whether the lawyer's situation falls under the circumstances for recusal.

Third, a scientific qualification requirements and training system should be set up. First, scientific qualification requirements should be set for lawyers to participate in mediation. Rule makers need to understand the difference between the role of lawyers in mediation and the role of lawyers in representation, and set basic requirements for the role of a lawyer in mediation when setting the qualifications for lawyer-mediators. At present, some regions have made preliminary explorations for reference, such as Fujian Province, which requires lawyers participating in mediation to have certain experience in mediation work.[47] Shandong Province stipulates that mediation lawyers must love mediation work, voluntarily accept the assignment or commission of the people's court to mediate disputes, and be able to devote time and energy to mediation, etc.[48] Second, conduct systematic mediation training for lawyers. Training can be divided into pre-service training, which focuses on the basic norms of mediation, mediation practice skills and professional ethics of mediation, and on-the-job training, which focuses on improving mediation skills and exchanging mediation experiences.[49]

6.5.2 Improving the Discipline Practice of Mediation by Lawyers in Related Supporting Mechanisms

For one thing, provisions regarding the discipline of lawyers in mediation practice should be added to the legal norms. At present, the rules on the discipline of judges and lawyers are scattered among numerous laws, judicial interpretations, administrative regulations, and professional codes,[50] such as the discipline of lawyers in their work institutions, the discipline of lawyers in litigation and arbitration activities, the discipline of the relationship between lawyers and their clients and opposing parties, and the discipline of the relationship between lawyers and their peers, but few of them are directly related to the discipline of lawyers in mediation, so there is a need to increase such special provisions. A review of the existing legal norms also reveals that some of the provisions can provide a reference for the discipline of lawyers in mediation practice. For example, Article 28 of the *Measures for the Administration of Lawyer Practice* and Article 50 of the *Code of Conduct for Lawyer Practice* provide rules on the prohibition of conflict of interests in lawyer practice, and on such basis, it is clarified that a lawyer who has served as a lawyer-mediator to mediate the case and his or her law firm should not establish a client relationship with the parties. Article 2, paragraph 2 of the *Several Provisions Regulating the Mutual Relationship between Judges and Lawyers to Safeguard Judicial Justice* stipulates the prohibited conduct of lawyers, to which provisions can be added that lawyers cannot declare their status as lawyer-mediator to the parties when representing them and cannot use this relationship to interfere with or influence the trial of a case. Article 27 of the *Code of Conduct for the Practice of Law* qualifies the content of a lawyer's personal advertisement, and it can be clarified on this basis that a lawyer cannot use his or her role as a lawyer-mediator in the court as a personal advertisement.

Second, a supporting mechanism related to the discipline of lawyers in mediation practice should be constructed. The first thing to do is to improve the review of conflict of interest in lawyer mediation. It should be made clear that a lawyer who has presided over or participated in the mediation of a disputed matter, neither he or she nor the lawyers of his or her law firm should be allowed to participate in the subsequent settlement procedures of the disputed matter and related disputes by acting as litigation agents, etc. At present, some large law firms have conflict of interest retrieval systems that can prevent conflicts of representation in cases of lawyers affiliated with the same law firm. Courts should strengthen the spread of information about such matters, and establish a conflict of interest review system for lawyer mediation in order to effectively prevent conflicts of interest arising from lawyer mediation.

The second is to establish a system of supervision of mediation by lawyers. The lack of supervision will lead to arbitrary behavior. Therefore, in lawyer mediation, the activities of judges and lawyers need to be supervised, and a supervision system including professional supervision, judicial and administrative supervision, and social supervision should be gradually established.

Third, to establish a disciplinary mechanism for lawyers in lawyer mediation. The *Law on Lawyers* provides for the types, causes, institution, and procedures of lawyer discipline, which may include lawyer-specific misconduct in lawyer mediation, but care needs to be taken to follow the principles and procedures of administrative punishment.

6.5.3 Improving the Two-Way Development Path Between Pro Bono and Market-Based Mediation by Lawyers

In order to mobilize the enthusiasm of lawyers to participate in lawyer mediation and to achieve the long-term and effective development of lawyer mediation, we should adhere to the two-way development path of public interest type and market type, with the market type development path being the main one.

First, the development path of pro bono lawyer mediation. At present, China's mediation system is mainly based on public interest mediation, with people's mediation, court mediation, and administrative mediation all being public interest in nature, supported and guaranteed by government funding, and providing pro bono mediation services to the parties. Some scholars have pointed out that "from its inception, the profession of lawyer has had a more public nature than other social professions."[51] As an important part of the legal professional community, lawyers bear the corresponding social responsibility and should actively participate in the public interest type of mediation work, giving full play to the advantages of legal professionalism to resolve disputes. This part of legal services should be subsidized by the government in some way by purchasing social services.

At the early stage of the development of pro bono lawyer mediation, first, the government should strengthen its support for pro bono lawyer mediation, and increase the subsidies for lawyers to participate in mediation to make up for the normal expenses of lawyers participating in mediation.

Second, it is also necessary to establish an assessment and incentive mechanism. The judicial administrative organs should commend lawyers who actively participate in public interest mediation, and give material or honorary awards to lawyers and related organizations for outstanding mediation performance, to increase the motivation of lawyers to participate in public interest mediation.

Third, establish a public interest mediation team with young lawyers or trainee lawyers as the mainstay. Young lawyers or trainee lawyers have problems such as low caseload, low qualifications, and low income, but when their income from participating in lawyer mediation can reach or even exceed the income level of the same period of representation, they have the advantages of high motivation and ample time to participate in lawyer mediation. At the same time, it also helps young lawyers or trainee lawyers to familiarize themselves with the situation of grass-roots disputes and to complete the transformation from book knowledge to practice of dispute resolution. However, the current involvement of young lawyers or trainee lawyers in pro bono lawyer mediation requires overcoming two dilemmas: First, many pilot regions have set relatively strict qualifications for lawyers to participate in lawyer mediation, for example, Fujian Province requires more than five years of practice as a lawyer and Beijing requires more than eight years of practice. Therefore, localities should appropriately relax the qualification requirements for lawyer mediation and allow young lawyers and trainee lawyers to participate in it. Second, young lawyers and trainee lawyers should be allowed to mediate cases that are suitable for them to mediate. Mediation in matrimonial and family cases requires a certain level of social experience on the part of the mediator and is not suitable for young lawyers or trainee lawyers. Young lawyers and trainee lawyers, most of whom are "academics," have a clear understanding of substantive and procedural rules and should be allowed to mediate commercial disputes that require clarification of legal relationships.

Finally, pursue the development path of market-based lawyer mediation. First, parties to disputes should be encouraged, through publicity and other means, to choose market-based lawyer mediation on their own. As Takeshi Kojima says: "If a lawyer has extremely strong skills in promoting reconciliation and convinces the public that he can find an autonomous solution corresponding to the incident, then the public will walk into the lawyer's office in a relaxed mood."[52] Next, a guided mediation mechanism should be established in law firms. For parties who seek legal advice or representation from a lawyer or visit a law firm, if the case is considered suitable for mediation, the lawyer or law firm may actively guide the parties to choose mediation as a means of dispute resolution. Again, the requirement that market-based lawyers be paid a low price for mediation should be changed so that lawyers receive an income equivalent to their labor in market-based mediation. The benign and sustainable development of lawyer mediation should be promoted in an interest-driven manner through equal competition, market selection, and survival of the fittest.[53] Finally, law firms and lawyers specializing in mediation should be nurtured to realize the transformation of "lawyer mediation" to "mediation lawyer," so that market-oriented lawyer mediation can be developed in the long run. One of the main creations of alternative dispute resolution in common law countries, which began in the late 1970s, was the adaptation by lawyers of their own type of legal service to provide neutral and complementary assistance.[54] Law firms specializing in mediation already exist in the United States, Germany, and the United Kingdom, where lawyers offer professional mediation with them acting as a neutral third party as part of their legal services.[55]

Notes

1 Zhao Yiyu: Paradigm Innovation in Mediation Research in the Eastern Discourse System, *People's Court Journal*, December 2,. 2017, p. 6.
2 The concept can be traced back to Gordon Weiser's study of the development of Gothic art. It has subsequently been used as an analytical tool by Giltz, Huang Zongzhi and Chen Befeng in their examination of agricultural and rural issues, by Dozanchi in his study of the modes of control of state power, by Wu Yingzhi in his critique of the dragon-slaying dilemma of theoretical research on the subject matter of litigation, and by Chen Weixing in his exploration of the external implantation of mediation resources in the courts.

3 Initial stage: In 2007, Article 28 of the *Law on Lawyers* made mediation one of the businesses that lawyers can engage in. In 2012, the "Overall Plan for the Reform of the Conflict Resolution Mechanism by Expanding the Interface between Litigation and Non-Litigation" included lawyer mediation for the first time. Exploration stage: In 2015, the *Opinions on Improving the Mechanism for the Diversified Settlement of Conflicts and Disputes* explicitly provided for the establishment of a lawyer mediation system, which gave the lawyer mediation system a higher level of policy basis and a broader space for development. Refinement stage: In 2016, the *Opinions on the People's Courts Further Deepening the Reform of the Diversified Dispute Resolution Mechanism* and the *Provisions on Invited Mediation in the People's Courts* clarified the three modes of lawyer mediation, and stipulated the obligation of recusal of lawyers as mediators, the obligation of notification as agents, and the procedure of participation as invited mediators. In 2017, the *Opinions on Conducting Pilot Work on Lawyer Mediation* specified the overall requirements, working modes, working mechanisms, and job guarantees of lawyer mediation.
4 Hangzhou Yuhang District People's Court Panel: "Exploring the Path of Market-Based Mediation with Young Lawyers as the Main Body." Available at: https://mp.weixin.qq.com/s/eL4-QBGiJnplo-g1LBXuHQ (accessed December 20, 2018).
5 https://mp.weixin.qq.com/s/vNZSLkHN3dTR3FE6FdTz9Q (accessed December 1, 2018).
6 The representative research results include: Li Ao: Study on the Professional Skills of Lawyer Mediation in the United States, *Seeking*, 2004 (4); Hong Dongying: The New Expansion of Lawyer Mediation Function: The Background of Lawyer-led Civil Mediation Service, *Law*, 2011 (2); Wang Honglian and Xie Qingping: Perfecting the Large Mediation Mechanism and Playing the Role of Lawyer Mediation Function, *China Lawyer*, 2011 (11); Wang Yaxin: Lawyer Mediation: Institutional Construction through "Pilot = Experiment." *China Lawyer*, 2011 (11). Wang Yaxin: The Role of Lawyers in Mediation, *China Lawyer*, 2011 (11); ; Liao Yongan and Wang Cong: From Litigation Agent to Professional Mediator: The New Picture of Chinese Lawyers' Profession, in A New Picture of the Chinese Lawyer Profession, *China Lawyer*, 2017 (12); Xiong Yuemin and Zhang Run: Lawyer Mediation: An Institutional Innovation of the Pluralistic Dispute Resolution Mechanism, *China Justice*, 2017 (11); Wang Shirong: Lawyer Mediation: Expanding the Channels for the Construction of a Rule of Law Society, *China Justice*, 2017 (11).
7 From July 2018 to August 2018, Deng Chunmei, Shao Hua, Wu Xinyin, Zhao Yiyu, and Lu Zongcheng, researchers of the Diversified Dispute Resolution Mechanism Research Base of Xiangtan University, conducted summer research in Beijing, Shanghai, Hangzhou, Shaoxing, Nanping, and Dezhou, collecting and collating a large amount of first-hand information.
8 Fan Yu: *A Study of Alternative Dispute Resolution Mechanisms* (Beijing: People's University of China Press, 2000), p. 383.
9 www.moj.gov.cn/news/content/2017-10/16/zcjd_9039.html (accessed November 22, 2018).
10 Long Fei: The Exploration Innovation and Perfection Path of Lawyer Mediation System, *China Lawyer*, 2018 (5).
11 Xia Zhengnong: *The Great Dictionary (Jurisprudence Volume)* (Shanghai: Shanghai Dictionary Publishing House, 2003), p. 37.

12 Fan Yu: *A Study of Alternative Dispute Resolution Mechanisms*, p. 176.
13 Qin Qiwen and Zhou Yongkang: *Introduction to Roleology* (Beijing: China Social Science Press, 2011), p. 34.
14 Qing Feng: *An Outline of the Chinese Lawyer System* (Beijing: China Legal Publishing House, 1997), pp. 67–68.
15 Ansonia T. Croman: *The Lost Lawyer: The Decline of the Ideal of the Legal Profession*, trans. Tian Fengchang (Beijing: Law Press, 2010), pp. 123–148.
16 As Professor Tian Pingan argues:

> The Chinese model of civil litigation is neither an extreme "ex officio" nor an extreme "partyist" model; it blends partyism and ex officio into one, embodying and reflecting both the organizing and directing functions of the judge – the court – and the status of the parties as subjects of litigation.

Tian Pingan: A Preliminary Study on the Construction of China's Civil Litigation Model, *Chinese and Foreign Law*, 1994 (5).

17 Liao Yong'an: New Concepts and New Thinking in Contemporary Mediation, *People's Court Journal*, June 16, 2017, p. 2.
18 "Intermediation" is reflected in bridging the parties in order to facilitate their dialogue. "Judgment" is reflected in evaluating the parties' claims and advising them of the authority's own judgment, for example, by proposing a solution to the dispute. "Coercion" is a situation in which the dispute authority constantly uses the resources at its disposal, directly or indirectly, to force the parties to accept a solution in order to form a consensus. See Takahiro Sagara: *Dispute Resolution and the Judicial System*, trans. Wang Yaxin (Beijing: China University of Political Science and Law Press, 1994), p. 54; Zhang Wusheng et al.: *Judicial Modernization and the Construction of the Civil Litigation System* (Beijing: Law Press, 2000), p. 317.
19 Qiang Shigong: Declaration of the Legal Community, *Chinese and Foreign Jurisprudence*, 2001 (3): 332.
20 Zhang Shanshuo: *A Study on the Chinese Lawyer System* (Changsha: Hunan People's Publishing House, 2007), pp. 131–134.
21 Zhang Wenxian and Lu Xueying: An Introduction to the Legal Professional Community, *Legal System and Social Development*, 2002 (6).
22 Liu Guiming: The Relationship Between Judges and Lawyers in My Eyes, *China Lawyer*, 1999 (9).
23 Ji Weidong et al.: *Judicial Reform in China* (Beijing: Law Press, 2016), pp. 319–320.
24 Long Fei: The Exploration Innovation and Perfection Path of Lawyer Mediation System.
25 Nadja Alexander: *Global Trends in Mediation*, trans. Wang Fuhua et al. (Beijing: China Legal Publishing House, 2011), p. 306.
26 Hangzhou Yuhang District People's Court Panel: Analysis of the Market-Oriented Mediation Path with Young Lawyers as the Subjects. Available at: https://mp.weixin.qq.com/s/eL4-QBGiJnplo-g1LBXuHQ (accessed December 20, 2018).
27 Shen Zhixian (Ed.): *Mediation in Litigation* (Beijing: Law Press, 2009), p. 62.
28 https://m.thepaper.cn/newsDetail_forward_2409832?from=groupmessage&isappinstalled=0 (accessed December 6, 2018).
29 Interview date: August 15, 2018; interview location: City Court C, City B; interviewee: Du, mediation lawyer, City Court C, City B.

30 Interview date: August 15, 2018; interview location: Court of City B, District C; interviewee: Xu, Judge of Court of District C, City B.
31 Similarly, a study shows that since July 2017, when a law firm in Hangzhou was invited to become a mediation organization at the Yuhang District Court in Hangzhou, as of early June 2018, the organization's 10 mediation lawyers mediated a total of 27 cases, an average of 2.7 cases per person per year, while full-time people's mediators mediated an average of 30 successful cases per month, resulting in 360 cases per year. See Hangzhou Yuhang District People's Court Project Group: Exploring the Path of Market-Based Mediation with Young Lawyers as the Subjects.
32 Interview date: August 15, 2018; interview location: Court of City B, District C; interviewee: Xu, Judge of Court of District C, City B.
33 Ibid.
34 Chen Unity: Lawyer Mediation: Realistic Dilemmas and Ways to Cope with Them, *China Justice*, 2018 (8): 51–54.
35 Interview date: August 9, 2018; interview location: Z City People's Court; interviewee: Chen, Judge, Z City Court.
36 Interview date: August 14, 2018; interview location: F District Court, City B; interviewee: Wang Mou, Judge, F District Court, City B.
37 As a lawyer said in the interview: "After the mediation is successful, when you receive a heartfelt thank-you from both parties, the value of participating in lawyer mediation comes out, which cannot be measured by money." Interview date: August 15, 2018; interview location: C District Court, City B; interviewee: Pang, lawyer mediator, District Court C, City B.
38 For example, a lawyer said in the interview:

> Working as a lawyer-mediator in the court, you can learn to see the case from the judge's perspective, which is very helpful to the way of thinking of the lawyer in handling the case, as well as the way of communication with the client, the opposing party and the judge.

Interview date: August 15, 2018; interview location: City B, District Court C; interviewee: Wu, lawyer mediator, District Court C, City B,
39 As a lawyer said in the interview:

> I hope to make very normal friends with the judge through lawyer mediation, friends who do not affect the fair trial of the case in this way, or friends who communicate in business, and this is the reason why I am willing to come to the court to do mediation.

Interview date: August 15, 2018; interview location: C District Court, City B; interviewee: Wu, lawyer-mediator at District Court C, City B.
40 Interview date: August 15, 2018; interview location: Court of City B, District C; interviewee: Xu, Judge of District Court C, City B.
41 Chen Tuanjie: Lawyer Mediation: Realistic Dilemmas and Ways to Cope with and Comments on Opinions on Carrying Out Pilot Work on Lawyer Mediation, *China Justice*, 2018 (8).
42 Interview date: August 15, 2018; interview location: District Court C, City B; interviewee: Xu, Deputy Head of the Filing Division, District Court C, City B.

43 Simon Roberts and Peng Wenhao: *The Dispute Resolution Process: ADR and the Main Forms of Decision Formation*, trans. Liu Zhewei et al. (Beijing: Peking University Press, 2011).
44 www.sohu.com/a/211458416_99897344 (accessed December 20, 2018).
45 Nadja Alexander: *Global Trends in Mediation*, p. 304.
46 Ibid., p. 358.
47 www.ptsf.gov.cn/xxgk/flfg/flfg_32822/201801/t20180103_934808.htm (accessed December 5, 2018).
48 www.0551law.cn/wapdisplay.asp?ID=15012 (accessed December 5, 2018).
49 The Austrian Rules for the Training of Mediators in Civil Cases, for example, set out different requirements for mediator applicants from different disciplinary backgrounds, requiring 220–365 hours of vocational training. The training is usually divided into two parts: first, it focuses on the theoretical foundations of mediation (136–165 hours), including communication theory, personality theory, team psychology, conflict analysis, law, economics, and mediation ethics; and second, practical skills training, supervision and coaching within the profession (84–165 hours). See Nadja Alexander: *Global Trends in Mediation*, pp. 102–107.
50 These include: the three major procedural laws and their judicial interpretations, the *Law on Judges*, the *Law on Lawyers*, the *Code of Professional Ethics and Professional Discipline* of the All-China Lawyers Association, the *Measures for the Administration of Lawyer Practice* of the Ministry of Justice, the *Code of Conduct for Lawyer Practice* of the All-China Lawyers Association, the *Basic Code of Professional Ethics for Judges of the Supreme People's Court*, the Supreme People's Court and the Ministry of Justice's *Several Provisions on Regulating the Mutual Relationship between Judges and Lawyers to Safeguard Judicial Justice*. *Measures for Punishing Lawyers and Law Firms for Violations of the Law* by the Ministry of Justice, etc.
51 He Hairen: Legal Aid: Government Responsibility and Lawyers' Obligations, *Global Law Review*, 2005 (6).
52 Kojima Takeshi: *Jurisprudence and Empirical Evidence of the Litigation System*, trans. Chen Gang et al. (Beijing: Law Press, 2001), p. 20.
53 Jia Yuhui: A Few Views on Promoting Lawyer Mediation, *People's Court Daily*, November 22. 2017, p. 8.
54 Simon Roberts and Peng Wenhao: *The Dispute Resolution Process: ADR and the Major Forms of Decision Formation*, p. 87.
55 Huang Minghe: Concept Renewal and Institutional Design – Lawyer Mediation in the New Era Starts Again. Available at: https://mp.weixin.qq.com/s/lBTZ_eBRBQ4t37oGHzMfrQ (accessed December 12, 2018).

References

Alexander, Nadja: *Global Trends in Mediation*, trans. Wang Fuhua et al., Beijing: China Legal Publishing House, 2011.
Chen Tuanjie: Lawyer Mediation: Realistic Dilemmas and Ways to Cope with and comments on Opinions on Carrying Out Pilot Work on Lawyer Mediation, *China Justice*, 2018 (8): 51–54.

Chen Unity: Lawyer Mediation: Realistic Dilemmas and Ways to Cope with Them, in *China Justice*, 2018 (8): 51–54.

Croman, Ansonia T.: *The Lost Lawyer: The Decline of the Ideal of the Legal Profession*, trans. Tian Fengchang, Beijing: Law Press, 2010, pp. 123–148.

Fan Yu: *A Study of Alternative Dispute Resolution Mechanisms*, Beijing: People's University of China Press, 2000.

He Hairen: Legal Aid: Government Responsibility and Lawyers' Obligations, *Global Law Review*, 2005 (6): 665–671.

Hong Dongying: The New Expansion of Lawyer Mediation Function: The Background of Lawyer-led Civil Mediation Service, *Law*, 2011 (2): 109–117.

Ji Weidong et al.: *Judicial Reform in China*, Beijing: Law Press, 2016.

Jia Yuhui: A Few Views on Promoting Lawyer Mediation, People's Court Daily, November 22, 2017, p. 8.

Kojima, Takeshi: *Jurisprudence and Empirical Evidence of the Litigation System*, trans. Chen Gang et al., Beijing: Law Press, 2001.

Li Ao: Study on the Professional Skills of Lawyer Mediation in the United States, *Seeking*, 2004 (4): 92–94.

Liao Yong'an: New Concepts and New Thinking in Contemporary Mediation, *People's Court Journal*, June 16, 2017, p. 2.

Liu Guiming: The Relationship Between Judges and Lawyers in My Eyes, China Lawyer, 1999 (9): 12–14.

Long Fei: The Exploration Innovation and Perfection Path of Lawyer Mediation System, China Lawyer, 2018 (5): 22–25.

Qiang Shigong: Declaration of the Legal Community, *Chinese and Foreign Jurisprudence*, 2001 (3): 332.

Qin Qiwen and Zhou Yongkang: *Introduction to Roleology*, Beijing: China Social Science Press, 2011.

Qing Feng: *An Outline of the Chinese Lawyer System*, Beijing: China Legal Publishing House, 1997.

Roberts, Simon and Peng Wenhao: *The Dispute Resolution Process: ADR and the Main Forms of Decision Formation*, trans. Liu Zhewei et al., Beijing: Peking University Press, 2011.

Sagara, Takahiro: *Dispute Resolution and the Judicial System*, trans. Wang Yaxin, Beijing: China University of Political Science and Law Press, 1994.

Shen Zhixian (Ed.): *Mediation in Litigation*, Beijing: Law Press, 2009.

Tian Pingan: A Preliminary Study on the Construction of China's Civil Litigation Model, Chinese and Foreign Law, 1994 (5): 41–45.

Wang Honglian and Xie Qingping: Perfecting the Large Mediation Mechanism and Playing the Role of Lawyer Mediation Function, China Lawyer, 2011 (11): 66–67.

Wang Yaxin: Lawyer Mediation: Institutional Construction through "Pilot = Experiment," China Lawyer, 2011a (11): 65–66.

Wang Yaxin: The Role of Lawyers in Mediation, China Lawyer, 2011b (11): 34–39.

Xia Zhengnong: *The Great Dictionary (Jurisprudence Volume)*, Shanghai: Shanghai Dictionary Publishing House, 2003.

Zhang Shanshuo: *A Study on the Chinese Lawyer System*, Changsha: Hunan People's Publishing House, 2007.

Zhang Wenxian and Lu Xueying: An Introduction to the Legal Professional Community, Legal System and Social Development, 2002 (6): 13–23.

Zhang Wusheng et al.: *Judicial Modernization and the Construction of the Civil Litigation System*, Beijing: Law Press, 2000.

Zhao Yiyu: Paradigm Innovation in Mediation Research in the Eastern Discourse System, *People's Court Journal*, December 29, 2017.

7 The Rise and Regulation of Online Mediation

7.1 Overview of the Development of Online Mediation

With the full spread of modern communication technology, the internet in China has continued to penetrate and combine with traditional industries, forming the "internet+."[1] During the rapid development of "internet+," online mediation has also emerged in China. Specifically, online mediation refers to the activity in which the subject with the authority to mediate disputes (including the relevant government functionaries, courts, relevant organizations and individuals) uses internet facilities (computers, mobile phones, Wi-Fi, etc.) and communication technologies and means (e.g. email, electronic bulletin boards, voice and video chat rooms, information management systems, etc.) to mediate disputes between parties with a view to reaching a mediation agreement.[2] In recent years, China has completed its initial attempts and practices of online mediation, creating the practice and innovation of online mediation with Chinese characteristics, which is increasingly being used in dispute resolution and has been unanimously recognized and widely publicized by the official media. Online mediation in China has made leaps and bounds since the outbreak of COVID-19 in December 2019. Statistics from Xinhua show that the number of online mediations from January to June 2020 increased by 245 percent year-on-year, and the number of online court sessions increased by nine times year-on-year. Statistics from the Zhejiang ODR platform for diversified conflict resolution show that the number of new user visits between January and June 2020 was 1,072,249, and the number of newly registered users was 181,985. These figures show that there has been an upsurge in the number of cases handled and mediated online during the epidemic.

7.1.1 Background to and Reasons for the Rise of Online Mediation

The rapid advance of information technology represented by the internet has led to new changes in social production, created a new space for human life, expanded new areas of national governance, and greatly improved mankind's ability to understand and transform the world.[3] Against the backdrop of the

DOI: 10.4324/9781003385776-7

internet as a distinctive feature of the times, the original social, economic, geopolitical and cultural structures of China today have changed, and society has taken on revolutionary and disruptive trends.[4] The rise of online mediation is in line with the trend of the times, the requirements of social development, and the needs of the people, and is the result of the combination of various influencing factors in the context of the internet era.

First, the development of internet technology and universal access are the basic prerequisites for the rise of online mediation. "The mobile phone is the electric light bulb of its day, and what we can imagine in the future is that almost all devices will be connected to the internet," is the vision of Ericsson's president Hans Vestberg's for the development of the internet.[5] According to a report by the China Internet Network Information Center (CNNIC), the social life pattern shaped by the mobile internet has been further strengthened, and the "internet+" action plan has promoted the diversification and mobile development of government and enterprise services.[6] Currently, the "Broadband China" strategy is being implemented and internet broadband will be further popularized in China. "It is expected that by 2020, China's broadband network will basically cover all administrative villages and open up the 'last mile' of network infrastructure."[7] As a production tool, one of the elements of productivity, internet technology has a direct impact on the productivity of online mediation. Combined with the widespread use of the internet by people, another element of productivity, the two combine to lay the basic prospects for the development of "internet + mediation."

Second, the change in public perception and increased awareness of the internet are the endogenous driving forces behind the rise of online mediation. "Democracy," "openness," and "participation" are the key words of internet thinking, and their intuitive manifestation in the internet is sharing and interaction. With the popularity of the internet, access to the internet has become a way of life and a habit that more and more people cannot do without. People interact with each other in the communities created by the internet, such as participating in politics, voting, and commenting on public issues, and so on. Under the "silent" influence of the internet, people's perceptions and awareness have quietly changed, public awareness of participation has begun to grow, and the will of citizens is increasingly being reflected. In Sina's Online People's Mediation Committee, the concept of "netizen autonomy" is being implemented. Based on this, a community committee made up of netizens adjudicates disputes on Weibo, and on this basis, a low-cost and highly efficient model of rights redress is created, with disputes on Weibo on the left and online mediation on the right.[8]

Third, the emergence and growth of new types of disputes have provided market demand for the rise of online mediation. As the numbers of internet users increase, online disputes are also growing in diversity. The emergence and growth of new types of disputes not only require new dispute resolution methods to match them, but also provide an area for online mediation to play a role. For example, the rise of online courts and online mediation in

Zhejiang is a typical example of responding to the needs of the internet and e-commerce development.[9] In Hangzhou, Zhejiang Province, almost everyone uses Alipay, and locals often say "you can go out without your wallet, but not without your mobile phone Alipay." It is the gathering place of many famous e-commerce enterprises such as Alibaba, Alipay, Taobao, Tmall, Netease, etc. E-commerce is well developed and disputes involving e-commerce are frequent. In response to the growing number of new types of online disputes, the Zhejiang High People's Court opened an e-commerce online court in April 2016, connecting online mediation with online trials, etc., and conducting pilot trials in the Hangzhou Intermediate People's Court and three grassroots courts, namely the West Lake District People's Court, Binjiang District People's Court, and Yuhang District People's Court, with online payment disputes, copyright disputes, online transaction disputes and related appeals as the main business of online trials.[10]

Fourth, the transformation of government functions and in-depth judicial reform have provided policy support for the emergence of online mediation. The Third Plenary Session of the 18th CPC Central Committee put forward a new reform idea of "innovating the social governance system," and the concept of governance has changed from "social management" to "social governance." The Fifth Plenary Session of the 18th Central Committee of the People's Republic of China put forward the development concept of innovation, coordination, green environmentalism, openness and sharing, and emphasized "strengthening and innovating social governance, promoting the refinement of social governance, and building a social governance pattern for all to build and share." Taking online mediation as an example, online court mediation combines the concepts of the internet and traditional court mediation, and its cross-border consciousness, innovation consciousness, reconstruction consciousness, humanistic consciousness, openness consciousness and connectivity consciousness are inherently in line with the country's new development concept.[11] As the judicial reform progresses, the Supreme People's Court's "Network Court," the "Sunshine Court," and the "Smart Court" projects are being implemented across the country. In June 2016, the Supreme People's Court issued the *Opinions on the People's Courts Further Deepening the Reform of the Diversified Dispute Resolution Mechanism* (hereafter referred to as the Opinions on Diversified Dispute Resolution Reform), which clearly require "innovative online dispute resolution methods," "promoting the use of modern information technology in the diversified dispute resolution mechanism" and "promoting the establishment of online mediation." In February 2017, the Supreme People's Court launched a nationwide pilot project to build an online mediation platform to further promote the construction of online mediation.[12] In 2019, the "Fifth Five-Year Reform Outline 2019–2023," issued by the Supreme People's Court, also clearly states that the parties should be guided and encouraged to choose non-litigation methods to resolve disputes, and that the establishment of a unified online platform for the diversified resolution of conflicts and disputes should be promoted. The introduction of these policies has facilitated the development of online mediation practices, and has also promoted the perfect docking of the People's Court's mediation platform with other local dispute resolution platforms to achieve data sharing and interconnection, and to promote the establishment of a unified online platform for the diversified resolution of conflicts and disputes.

7.1.2 Models, Concepts, and Features of Online Mediation

7.1.2.1 Main Models of Online Mediation in China

According to the different types of subjects promoting online mediation in China, the models of online mediation in China can be divided into: (1) government-led model; (2) court-led model; and (3) civil organization-led model.

1. *Government-led model.* The *People's Mediation Law* stipulates that the judicial administrative departments are responsible for guiding people's mediation work. Some provincial and municipal judicial administrative departments have set up online mediation platforms on their portals, such as the "Online People's Mediation Committee" in Baoji, Shaanxi Province, which is based on the "Baoji Judicial Window" portal of the Baoji Judicial Bureau. There are also other government departments that have set up online mediation platforms for specific types of disputes, such as the "Labor Personnel Dispute Mediation Service Platform" of the Human Resources and Social Security Department of Jiangsu Province. The process of running online mediation is similar across government-led models and can briefly be summarized as follows (see Figure 7.1): enter the platform website, register a username, select a mediation organization or mediator, communicate with the mediator (by phone or online). mediate online or offline, receive the outcome of the mediation.[13]
2. *Court-led model.* Court mediation is an important part of China's civil litigation system, and courts are rightfully the subject of online mediation. In practice, some courts have built mediation platforms using the internet to conduct online mediation, for example, the Beijing No. 2 Intermediate Court's WeChat mediation platform for labor dispute cases. The general process of its mediation is that the parties add the judge as a WeChat friend, the judge invites the parties into the WeChat chat room of the platform, and the judge conducts the mediation.

In the chat room, the judge consults with both parties mainly on the mediation proposal, the formulation of the main text of the mediation, and the time for the formal signing of the mediation. After both parties reach a consensus, the judge sends the drafted mediation agreement to the platform, where both parties confirm it or suggest amendments. After both

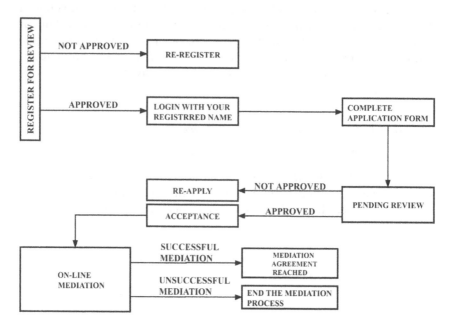

Figure 7.1 Online mediation flow chart of the Baoji Online People's Mediation Committee.

parties have jointly confirmed the mediation agreement, the judge notifies both parties through the platform to come to court for questioning, sign the interview transcript and the mediation agreement, and collect the mediation documents and hand over the money for the case.[14]

In addition, the online studio of Chen Liaomin of Hangzhou West Lake District People's Court is also quite unique. The studio is a website-style convenient litigation studio that integrates the functions of pre-litigation mediation, online case filing, case enquiry, online appointment (court or mediation), online consultation, and online mediation on the internet. The studio serves as a working platform for the court to make use of high-tech information technology and achieve governance at source, and is also a new initiative to implement the purpose of justice for the people.

3. *Civil society organization-led model.* Civil society organizations conducting online mediation mainly include the online dispute processing centers of Taobao and Tmall, the Sina People's Mediation Committee, the Sina Online Dispute Resolution Platform, the China Online Dispute Resolution Center (ChinaODR), and the Online Mediation Station of the China Consumers Association (Online315). The Sina Online Dispute Resolution Platform, for example, addresses the phenomenon that mediation information presentation and business processes vary greatly

from one court to another in practice, abstracting and outlining mediation services and forming standardized information and processes (see Figure 7.2). In terms of platform promotion, it has carried out three main types of measures: first, touch terminals are placed in court litigation service halls to deploy the internet mediation platform in order to guide mediation when parties file cases. Second, the internet mediation platform is deployed in dispute-prone areas such as communities and arbitration institutions for road traffic disputes, where quick access terminals, i.e., small PCs, are deployed. The terminals are connected to monitors or TVs for convenient operation.

Third, parties are guided to participate in mediation through the official microblog of the court. At the same time, special internet mediation platform usage cards are designed to help parties use the internet mediation platform more easily and efficiently.[15]

7.1.2.2 The Concept of Online Mediation in China

The philosophy of online mediation is the theoretical basis and the dominant value that guides the design and practical operation of this type of mediation system, which is a systematic reflection on the function, nature, and contingent model of this type of mediation based on different values (ideologies or cultural traditions). Online mediation is a product of the combination of traditional mediation and the high technology of the internet, and therefore its philosophy is inherently a mix of traditional and modern genes. The concept of online mediation is people-oriented, reflecting the ultimate concern for people, starting from the laws of human nature, respecting human rights, and considering people as substantial subjects,[16] Specifically, it consists of three aspects: (1) convenience for the people; (2) autonomy of will; and (3) sharing and co-governance.

1. *Convenience for the people.* Online mediation carries the needs of humanity and meets the requirements of convenience and benefit for the people. On the one hand, through the use of network information technology, it provides as much convenience as possible for the parties, so that mediation fully respects people, liberates them, relies on them and is meant for them. On the other hand, it pays attention to people's hearts and minds, attaches importance to the psychological feelings of the participants in mediation, especially the psychology of the parties, so that the parties' wishes can be fully expressed, and promotes "case closure, settlement of the matter, and reconciliation of people." In addition, from the level of institutional design, the mediation process of online mediation is more humane, convenient, and operational; from the level of implementation, mediators are required to have good professional ethics and excellent professionalism to better resolve disputes and serve the parties.

184 The Rise and Regulation of Online Mediation

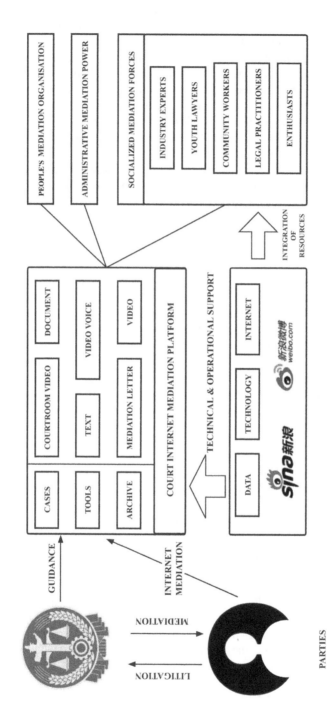

Figure 7.2 The design process of Sina's online dispute resolution platform.

2. *Autonomy of will.* Mediation is a process whereby the parties voluntarily reach an agreement on a dispute under the auspices of the relevant unit, organization, or individual and after equal consultation. Equality and voluntariness, free negotiation and protection of rights are present throughout the mediation process. The same applies to online mediation: before the mediation begins, the parties can decide on their own whether to choose a mediation tool (whether to use network communication technology) and whether to choose a mediation institution, organization or individual. After the mediation begins, the parties can freely negotiate on specific disputes, rights, and obligations, etc., decide whether to interrupt, terminate or reopen the mediation, and decide on their own the outcome of the mediation. At the end of the mediation, if the mediation is unsuccessful or the parties still dispute the mediation agreement reached, they may continue to choose other dispute resolution methods, such as arbitration or litigation to protect their rights and interests.
3. *Sharing and co-governance.* "If the mystery of the industrial era is the division of labor, then the mystery of the internet era is integration, information exchange, resource sharing and social cooperation."[17] Working together to build an open and cooperative cyberspace and a democratic and transparent internet governance system is a common call of the contemporary public. Online mediation enables more timely, convenient, and adequate communication and cooperation between the governments, the courts, and other subjects of power and the parties, and between the parties, and offers the efficient use of administrative, judicial, and other public resources, which in turn enables respect for individual rights and subject pluralism, the development of freedom and the safeguarding of order, independence, and autonomy, and openness and cooperation to be realized in the interconnection.

7.1.2.3 Features of Online Mediation

"Cross-border integration, innovation-driven, reshaped structure, respect for humanity, open ecology, and connection to everything" are the characteristics of the "internet+" era,[18] which is also the DNA of online mediation. Compared to litigation, online mediation offers the respective advantages of network communication technology and traditional mediation, and the use of the internet frees the subjects of mediation from the shackles of time, space, and cost. Mediation can remove the shackles of the costly and complicated procedures of litigation, thus resolving social conflicts more economically and effectively. Compared with traditional mediation, online mediation adds an online, combined online and offline dispute resolution channel, giving parties more procedural options. At the same time, it reduces the cost of mediation by breaking the restrictions of time and space, allowing mediators and parties to deal with disputes in a more flexible and convenient manner. Specifically, online mediation exhibits the following features.

1. *Convenience.* Convenience is the main advantage of online mediation and an important reason for the rise of online mediation. With more and more disputes flooding into the courts, on the one hand, the conflict between the courts being overloaded with cases and under-staffed is becoming increasingly prominent; on the other hand, parties are constantly being bogged down by complex and tedious proceedings. As a result, mediation has very often become the preferred option for both parties and judges. As for court mediation, some judges believe that:

   Face-to-face court mediation, due to factors such as rushed time and heavy antagonism of the parties, can easily lead to poor mediation results, while repeated single-line communication with the parties after the court for mediation is inefficient and also prone to misunderstanding and questioning of mediation work by the parties.

   Compared to litigation and traditional mediation, online mediation is simple in procedure, flexible in form, fast, and efficient. For example, the judge of the Beijing Second Intermediate People's Court used the WeChat platform to finish a labor dispute case in just five minutes. The court judge exclaimed, "A case was mediated in less than 10 sentences in WeChat. If we had to mediate in the traditional way, we don't know how many more phone calls we would have had to make."[19] Another example is the "half-day acceptance and 10-day completion" system of the Jiangsu Labor and Personnel Dispute Mediation Service Platform, which means that the mediation experts, upon receiving the case information pushed by the platform, strive to contact the applicant within half an hour, accept the application within half a day, and complete the case within 10 days.

2. *Virtuality.* Online mediation is a product of the combination of the virtual world built by the internet and traditional mediation practice, which inherits the gene of "virtuality" of the internet. The virtual nature of online mediation makes it possible to break the shackles of time and space on traditional mediation, eliminating the costs of transport, time, and lost work, and making it easier for parties to make appointments with each other and with the mediator. American scholar Ethan Katsh refers to the ODR dispute resolution environment created using web-based information technology tools as a "fourth party." At the second United Nations ODR Forum in 2003, scholars discussed the theme of the "fourth party." They argued that:

   The dispute resolution environment created by web-based information technology tools acts as a "fourth party" in addition to the dispute resolver (third party), providing a multi-layered system of communication and pluralistic information that can rapidly improve the efficiency and reduce the cost of dispute resolution.[20]

Of course, the virtuality of online mediation is also a double-edged sword. While it reduces costs and provides convenience, it also brings about problems such as insufficient user experience and lack of trust in the mediation subject. According to some scholars, the main drawback of online mediation is that:

> There is no direct communication between the parties ... and it is difficult to guess the tone or reaction of the other party through online mediation. It is also impossible to guide the behavior of the parties through visual cues.[21]

In addition, the lack of trust between mediation subjects due to the communication barriers of online mediation is also a problem that cannot be ignored.

3. *Technical system.* The technical system of online mediation is mainly reflected in two aspects: (1) the technical features of online mediation hardware, which refers to the internet technology needed to build an online mediation platform; and (2) the technical features of online mediation software, which refers to the technology (competence) needed by mediators and parties to carry out the practice of online mediation. The technical nature of online mediation hardware is self-explanatory, with contemporary high technology such as internet communication technology, big data, and cloud computing forming the basic hardware for the rise and development of online mediation. In contrast to traditional mediation, online mediation requires mediators and parties to have the basic ability to use computers, the internet, and other devices. As far as the parties are concerned, online mediation not only requires their access to computers, the internet, and other devices, but also requires the parties to be able to communicate and interact more smoothly in an internet environment, and requires them to have better text communication skills in a non-video and voice environment. For mediators, online mediation is more demanding, requiring a considerable degree of online communication skills, the ability to access and express information, and control over the mediation process.

The technical nature of online mediation raises the bar for online mediation and poses a few problems, such as the fact that internet technology usually leaves a permanent trail, making mediation less confidential; and the limited use of online mediation by parties due to the reliance on physical devices, etc.[22]

7.2 Reflections on Online Mediation in Practice

As a "fourth party," web-based information technology forms a virtual "field" in mediation, becoming a force to be reckoned with and is increasingly important in the modernization of mediation. According to the field theory of social psychology, in this "field" built by the internet, every human action can be influenced by it, and the influencing factors are multidimensional. Due to the unique field, online mediation faces some difficulties and conflicts while offering an advantage in dispute resolution.

7.2.1 The Double-Edged Sword: The Main Conflicts in Online Mediation Practice

7.2.1.1 The Conflicts Between Reality and Virtuality

Online mediation integrates the real and the virtual, and is the mediation and handling of real disputes in a virtual space. Traversing the real and the virtual, the dilemmas faced by online mediation are mainly manifested in three conflicting pairs: (1) one-way and parallelism; (2) preservation and confidentiality; and (3) trust and convenience.

1. *One-way vs. parallelism*. The two different types of communication, one-way and parallel, reflect the difference between traditional and online mediation and the tension between the real and the virtual faced by online mediation. The traditional mediation model is one-way, with participants having to attend joint meetings and single-party sessions in chronological order. In online mediation, however, participants can attend both joint meetings and single-party meetings in parallel. For example, if the online communication is in the form of an email or discussion room or dialogue box, then the mediator and a party, or between the parties, or between the mediator and the parties, can communicate individually or in a group email, or in a joint or separate discussion room (or dialogue box). Joint meetings and ex-parte meetings can be held simultaneously or sequentially, and can be crossed or staggered, allowing parties and mediators more flexibility to choose according to actual needs. The mediator can more comfortably control the mediation process:

   He can even hold an ex parte meeting with one party while a joint meeting is taking place on another site. In this way, the mediator can talk privately with both parties at the same time, without the parties having to wait, let alone being troubled by the suspicion that the ongoing ex parte meeting is passing on any secrets.[23]

   However, while concurrent mediation brings convenience, it also poses new tests for mediators and parties. For mediators, "having multiple concurrent discussions at the same time presents a challenge to mediators and requires them to effectively manage different lines of dialogue." For the parties, the ability to process textual information instantly and efficiently (including the ability to read, comprehend, type, etc.) is required, and these are clearly more demanding than in traditional mediation.

These "new hassles" brought about by parallel mediation can make mediators and parties more apprehensive and doubtful when choosing online mediation.

2. *Preservation vs. confidentiality*. In the virtual environment of the internet, preservation of data and confidentiality sometimes form a paradox: to preserve is to risk declassification, because the best way to keep a secret is not to keep it. Since online mediation is very often text-based, an accurate record of the interaction can be archived and the complete communication can be preserved. Text-based communication can narrow the differences in expression between the interlocutors and emotions can be better controlled. If the parties choose to save the minutes of the meeting, they can save the conversation records locally or log on to the relevant website directly. If they choose not to save their discussions after the meeting, their interaction records can also be completely deleted. However, while easy to preserve, the question arises as to how the duty of confidentiality of the mediation can be fulfilled in the absence of on-site supervision by the mediator. At the same time, the network is more vulnerable to hackers. Computer viruses, network attacks, spam, system vulnerabilities, network theft, and other network security issues make its confidentiality questionable.

3. *Trust vs. convenience*. How to find the best balance between trust and convenience is a challenge for online mediation in resolving real and virtual conflicts. US scholars, such as Ethan Katsh, suggest that for any dispute resolution mechanism to survive, it must have the three elements of professional value advantage (of the dispute resolution process), cheapness and trust, with a triangular relationship between these three elements. Professional value advantage, cheapness, and trust form the three sides of a triangle, and they are in a reciprocal relationship: a change in the length of one side inevitably affects the length of the other. For example, SmartSettle employs a few information and communication tools that give it a unique advantage in dispute resolution and a high level of user trust, but its convenience is also greatly reduced due to the use of information technology and the introduction of a large amount of complex software.[24]

According to our research, parties generally have doubts and concerns when they first start using online mediation. For example, the initial process of the Hangzhou West Lake District People's Court's online court is that the court sends an SMS directly to the parties through the e-commerce online court's system, informing them of information such as case acceptance and the registration requirements for online court sessions. Because the messages are sent by the system, most people who receive them at first dismiss them as spam or fraudulent messages and ignore them. In practice, the judge or clerk in charge of the case is required to make a special phone call to inform the parties of the online court session, which needs to be served together with the paperwork. Usually at the beginning, it takes about half an hour of telephone instructions for the judge or clerk to dissuade the person and get them to sign up for an online court account, and the telephone communication often takes many, many iterations. The difficulty of building trust is a common problem with online mediation "internet + trial," while bringing some convenience.

7.2.1.2 The Conflict Between Promotion and Use

The tension between promotion and use of online mediation is manifested in three pairs of relationships: (1) high technology vs. low use; (2) verbal language use vs. text language use; and (3) synchronous immediate vs. asynchronous interaction.

1. *High technology vs. low usage.* The tension between the promotion and use of online mediation is mainly reflected in the high technology and low use. In online mediation, the technical and equipment requirements vary greatly depending on the subject that is driving the mediation, for example. Mediators can use popular software such as QQ and WeChat, or they can use special systems such as the E-Commerce Online Court of the Zhejiang High People's Court. The high requirements for computers and other hardware equipment obviously restrict the use and promotion of online mediation. For example, the online courtroom of the West Lake District People's Court had used a system developed by Microsoft. Although Microsoft's system had the advantages of high clarity, fast transmission, high quality, and stability, the system was eventually not continued because it needed to run in an operating system of Windows 7 or above, and the computer configuration of the court at that time did not meet that requirement (the operating system of Windows XP was commonly used by the public at that time). On the whole, the level of application of online mediation lags behind the actual demand. Apart from specially developed systems, most of the online mediation is still stuck in the Online Mediation 1.0 era of using popular instant communication tools such as QQ and WeChat, and the potential of the relevant information technology has not been fully developed and explored, and its application in some areas and regions is not effective enough.
2. *Verbal language use vs. text language use.*[25] The use of text language can sometimes affect the conduct of online mediation. Whereas traditional mediation takes place in face-to-face oral communication, text language is widely used in online mediation. In an email environment, as text language is more formal compared to verbal and body language, the parties usually take more time to deliberate and are more composed than in face-to-face communication. However, at the same time, the language of the text, because of the way it is expressed in words, loses the vivid, intuitive,

and sensual flow of spoken and body language, and tends to be cryptic and concise in its expression of meaning, which in many cases is also prone to ambiguity and misunderstanding. As a result, many mediators, out of an abundance of caution and responsibility, often use text language followed by confirmation by telephone and video. Some mediators, with the empirical understanding that "it is best to say what can be said in person," prefer to mediate on the spot and in person.

3. *Synchronous instant vs. asynchronous interaction.* The relationship between synchronous instant and asynchronous interaction presents another paradox in the promotion and use of online mediation. In traditional mediation, communication occurs instantly and both parties and mediators need to respond immediately to new situations or processes. In online mediation, on the other hand, because of the online environment and the need to use asynchronous tools, the parties can communicate at intervals, such as text messages from QQ, voice messages from WeChat, emails, etc. They do not need to respond instantly to other participants in the process and can speak after thoughtful consideration, so there will be relatively less emotional responses from all parties to new developments. At the same time, asynchronous interaction makes it more difficult for the mediator to control the process, and the mediator is unable to respond in the first instance by meeting the parties face-to-face and visualizing the process and the various states that the parties are exhibiting.

According to a senior counselor mediator, when mediating marriage and family cases, he would not choose online mediation because it does not allow him to grasp the expressions and movements of the parties and prevents him from using body language to have an impact on the parties, compared to traditional face-to-face mediation instantly and quickly. In addition, asynchronous interactions can cause him to feel miscommunicated and interrupted. For example, in WeChat, voice messages require a click and then to listen, which not only takes more than twice as long as in-person communication, but also does not allow him to respond to certain views and emotions of the parties in the first instance.

7.2.1.3 The Conflict Between Form and Substance

The conflict between form and substance in online mediation is concentrated in the fact that the various functions of online mediation are inadequately performed in practice. Logically speaking, the obvious advantages of online mediation are that it saves the parties' transport and time costs, especially for those who cannot be present, saves judicial resources, and alleviates the conflict of "too many cases and too few staff." In contrast, in some of the current pilot courts there is a contradiction between formal convenience and substantive burden. In terms of form, there are indeed conveniences; however, they are often not reflected and sometimes create additional burdens.

Space communication costs are reduced, but time communication costs (at least in the pilot phase) need more investment. For example, for reasons of prudence and security, etc., the Westlake People's Court e-commerce online court currently has all cases going online and offline at the same time, and in addition to holding court online, all paperwork online needs to be kept in writing for filing.[26] At this stage, the workload of judges and clerks has increased significantly. For online mediation, the practice is generally "online appointment, offline mediation," except for the appointment online, the mediation is conducted offline, as a result, online mediation is only a formality, almost the same as traditional mediation.

In addition, the types of cases accepted by online mediation are limited, and most of the cases are small in terms of subject matter and relatively clear and simple in terms of rights and obligations. The lack of relevant legal constraints also makes the implementation of online mediation ineffective. These make the substantive use of online mediation subject to many restrictions, and the many formal advantages are greatly reduced by the lack of practical use.

7.2.2 Practical Features of Online Mediation in Chinese Courts

The court-led model of online mediation is the fastest-growing and most widely used of the major models of online mediation. The following will introduce the specific practice of online mediation in Chinese courts, taking online court mediation as an example.

Looking at the development of online court mediation in China over the past decade or so, we can see that the construction of online court mediation, especially after 2016, has made greater progress. Specifically, the work has been carried out from initial experiments in individual regions to comprehensive pilot projects and in-depth promotion; the subjects of dispute resolution have moved from the court alone to the joint construction of multiple bodies, such as courts, government departments, enterprises, and institutions, industrial organizations and social groups; the resources for dispute resolution have moved from a single judicial resource to diversified resources, such as public resources, social resources, and market resources; the method of dispute resolution has moved from a single and individual approach to the joint construction of platforms and sharing of resources; and the technology for dispute resolution has moved from a single internet remote communication technology to the comprehensive use of technologies such as the internet, cloud computing, big data, and artificial intelligence. The dispute resolution force is moving from being single to specialized, professionalized, and internationalized.

7.2.3 The Main Functions of Online Court Mediation

First, to link online and offline forces to resolve conflicts and disputes efficiently. The efficiency of resolving conflicts and disputes is an important indicator of

The Rise and Regulation of Online Mediation 193

the level of modernization of a country's governance system and ability to govern. In the construction of online court mediation, technologies such as the internet, cloud computing, big data, and artificial intelligence are applied to dispute resolution, through which online mediation, online filing, online judicial confirmation, and online trial are connected on the online platform and linked to offline filing, pre-litigation assigned mediation, litigation-commissioned mediation, and trial. The court can grasp the dynamics of disputes in real time, reasonably mobilize online and offline dispute resolution forces and resources, scientifically assess the current status of disputes and solutions, and predict the future development trend of disputes. Conflicts and disputes can be handled flexibly through multiple channels, including online, offline, and a combination of online and offline, and the efficiency of dispute resolution is improved.

Second, to integrate the internal and external resources of the court to solve the problem of "too many cases and too few staff." The combined forces of economic development, social transformation, and judicial reform have, on the one hand, generated many conflicts and disputes; on the other hand, judicial reform has led to lower thresholds for the courts to accept cases and reduced litigation costs. As a result, many conflicts and disputes have flooded into the courts, while the state's investment in judicial resources has lagged behind the growth rate of conflicts and disputes, and the courts have been overburdened with cases. Online court mediation, while using the docking of litigation cases to effectively divert them, can play the function of invited mediation, connecting public resources, social resources, market resources, and other diversified dispute resolution resources across the country through the internet platform, "realizing the rational allocation and resource sharing of legal and non-legal resources, official resources and private resources."[27]

Finally, it meets the actual needs of cases and provides convenient services for the people. The rapid development of e-commerce has also spawned new types of disputes, such as online transaction disputes, online domain name disputes, online game disputes, online copyright disputes and virtual property disputes, and with the development of transportation, telecommunications, globalization, and the conclusion of transnational legal consensus, transnational and cross-border commercial disputes are also increasing. The emergence and growth of these disputes have become a new demand for the development of online mediation.. The main advantages of online mediation over litigation and traditional mediation are its convenience, efficiency, low cost, and flexibility. Parties have the flexibility to choose the mediation organization and mediator, the time, place, and manner of mediation, and to file, mediate, and conduct other procedures online, reducing the need for cumbersome litigation procedures and saving costs such as time, transport, and energy.

7.2.4 *Key Features of Online Court Mediation*

First, it is increasingly informative and technological. Under the guidance of the *Outline of the Reform of the People's Courts* and the *Opinions on the*

Reform of Pluralistic Dispute Resolution, and with the promotion of the construction of "smart courts" nationwide, modern technological tools such as internet tools are increasingly being used in online mediation practice in various regions, and the trend of information and technology-based mediation is becoming more prominent. For example, the Huanggu District People's Court in Shenyang City has launched the "internet + Q&A and Mediation," with six senior judges conducting 24/7 online consultation and video mediation. The West Lake District People's Court in Hangzhou has set up the "Chen Liaomin Online Studio," which integrates functions such as online case filing, case enquiry, online mediation, online appointment, and message consultation, providing the public with website-based, convenient litigation services. The West Lake District Court has also iteratively updated its online mediation system through cooperation with internet companies such as Microsoft, Alibaba, and Sina.

Second, it is increasingly platform-based and intensive. Through the internet platform built by the courts themselves or through cooperation, the court can unify and dispatch mediation organizations, mediators, and other dispute resolution forces, effectively dovetail with people's mediation, administrative mediation, and commercial mediation mechanisms, make full use of social resources, and efficiently deal with disputes. For example, the Anhui High Court has set up six major platforms, including docking of litigation and mediation, expedited case adjudication, professional dispute resolution, online mediation, petition resolution, and overcoming difficulties in enforcement. The Sichuan High Court has launched an upgraded version of the "Sichuan Court Online Litigation Service Center," which completely integrates the docking of litigation and mediation with the internet, builds a platform for the docking of litigation and mediation and online mediation, to realize online circulation of conflicts and disputes. The largest online court mediation platform in the country is the "Online Court Mediation Platform," built by the court in collaboration with Sina.com, which links online mediation, judicial confirmation, online filing, and online trial, providing a one-stop multi-disciplinary service to resolve disputes. Since the launch of its trial run in October 2016, 421 courts, 637 professional mediation organizations, and 2,455 mediators from 15 provincial administrative units have been accredited to the mediation platform nationwide.[28] According to statistics for 2017, the platform handled 1,697 disputes, with 775 successful mediations and another 10 percent of disputes entering the judicial confirmation process. The Supreme People's Court has recently explicitly requested the six pilot High Courts in Beijing, Hebei, Shanghai, Zhejiang, Anhui, and Sichuan to take the lead in establishing a unified online mediation platform at the provincial level.[29]

Third, it is gradually being standardized and institutionalized. "Strengthening top-level design and encouraging local exploration and practice"[30] is the basic principle for deepening the reform of the courts at present.

In recent years, the central and local governments have made provisions for online mediation in the form of policy documents, guiding rules, local regulation, and internal working rules to guide the practice of online court mediation, and online mediation in courts has gradually developed toward standardization and institutionalization. At the national level, the Meishan Conference, held by the Supreme People's Court in 2015, established a new "three-step" strategy for the reform of the diversified dispute resolution mechanism: "the state formulates development strategies, the judiciary plays a safeguarding role, and promotes the national legislative process." The *Outline of the Reform of the People's Courts* proposes to "promote remote mediation" under the heading "Improve the system of litigation service centers." The *Opinions on the Reform of Pluralistic Dispute Resolution* call for "promoting the establishment of online mediation" in "innovation of online dispute resolution." At the local level, the local regulations on pluralistic dispute resolution issued by Shandong Province and Xiamen City provide for "online mediation" in principle.[31] The first specific regulation on online mediation in China is the *Rules for Online Mediation in Anhui Courts (for Trial Implementation)* (hereinafter referred to as the Anhui Online Mediation Rules) formulated and issued by the Anhui High People's Court in October 2016, which makes more specific provisions on the basic concepts and principles of online mediation, rights and obligations, mediation process, supervision and management, etc.

Fourth, it is oriented toward diversity and multidimensionality. With economic development, social transformation, in-depth reform and adjustment of interests, various types of conflicts and disputes are becoming more frequent, and the people's needs for dispute resolution have become more urgent and diversified. In the era of "internet+," the internet just gives people more space and freedom of choice. The range of online court mediation can meet the diversified judicial needs of the people and is reflected in three aspects: (1) the diversity of subjects. The subjects of online court mediation are not only courts and judges, but also invited mediation organizations and mediators from all walks of life; (2) the diversity of resources. The internet not only connects the internal resources of the court system, but also connects the public resources of society, such as governmental functionaries, industrial organizations, and social groups outside the court system; (3) the diversity of methods. The parties can choose the mediation method flexibly according to their own needs and actual situation, and can either mediate online throughout the process or combine online and offline mediation. The multidimensionality of online court mediation is manifested in two main aspects: (1) multidimensional handling of disputes. This breaks the fetters of time and space and allows for multidimensional handling of disputes in real and virtual space, online and offline; and (2) it can accept multidimensional disputes, both online disputes that are unique to cyberspace and offline disputes that occur in real space, as well as comprehensive disputes where online and offline intersect.

7.2.5 Practical Issues of Online Mediation in Chinese Courts

7.2.5.1 Uneven Regional Development and Wide Variation in Local Conditions

The development of online mediation in courts in all regions of the country shows a general pattern of faster development in the eastern coastal regions than in the central and western inland regions, and faster development in economically developed regions than in less economically developed regions. For example, Shandong and Xiamen, located in the eastern coastal region, have taken the lead in formulating local regulations on diversified dispute resolution, Zhejiang, a major birthplace of e-commerce and the internet economy, has created the first online court for e-commerce, and the West Lake District People's Court in Hangzhou has taken the lead in online court mediation. At the National Conference of Courts to Promote the Reform of the Diversified Dispute Resolution Mechanism and the Exchange of Experiences of Model Courts (later referred to as the Maanshan Conference), the five model grassroots courts came from Shanghai Pudong New Area, Zhejiang Hangzhou, Liaoning Shenyang, Yunnan Kunming, and Chongqing Rongchang District, all of which are national or regional economic centers or major towns with obvious economic, technological, and other advantages.

There are three main reasons for the regional differences: the first is economic conditions; the development of online mediation is inextricably linked to local economic development. Economically developed regions have higher financial revenues, and courts have more funds to invest in information technology construction; the internet and other infrastructure are better built, and access to the internet is convenient and inexpensive; the quality of the education of the population is higher, and internet use has become a normal part of life; and the growing development of the internet economy has led to an increasing number of online disputes. These factors form the premise and foundation for the development of online mediation.

The second is ideological awareness. The importance that each region attaches to the diversified resolution of online disputes is crucial to the development of online mediation. The fact that Anhui, located in the central inland region, was able to take the lead in introducing special rules for online mediation work is clearly the result of the high priority and active promotion by the local courts. However, there are also many courts that lack internet thinking and "have insufficient understanding of the necessity and urgency of 'going online' for diversified dispute resolution," "although they have 'touched the internet' in a small scale, they have not yet 'gone online' in depth on a large scale," and "hardware equipment has completed the transformation of information technology, but the work of diversified dispute resolution has stopped at offline."[32] If the level of economic development determines the starting point and threshold for the development of online mediation everywhere, then the level of subjective awareness of the courts everywhere determines, to some extent, the potential and momentum for the development of online mediation. The difference in the court's ideology has exacerbated the "Matthew effect" in the development of online court mediation, while also creating an opportunity for "overtaking."

The third is the source of motivation. The long-term development of online mediation requires multiple motivations from both inside and outside the courts. At present, the pressure of many court cases and inadequate staff is forcing courts to develop a diversified dispute resolution mechanism. Online court mediation may seem to be a matter for the court alone, but in fact it involves relevant government functionaries, enterprises and institutions, trade organizations, social groups, and other units outside the court. Therefore, it is not enough to rely solely on the courts themselves to promote online court mediation. At present, outside the court system, there is insufficient synergy between online court mediation and other units, nor is there a higher level of administrative or operational authority (e.g., the same level of government, the Political and Legal Affairs Commission) to oversee the overall situation and carry out unified coordination and linkage, and the online triple mediation linkage function is inadequate. Within the court system, many courts have not included online dispute resolution, including online mediation, in their work assessment objectives, and as a result, online mediation lacks incentives and guidance mechanisms.

7.2.5.2 Inconvenient Practice and Low Actual Usage

In theory, online court mediation can break the fetters of time and space, as parties can submit their conflicts and disputes via the internet, freely choose a mediator, make appointments for mediation at flexible times and in flexible ways, and participate in mediation anytime and anywhere, and judges and mediators can also follow up on mediation cases and handle disputes online at any time, thus saving time and transport costs for all parties and improving the efficiency of dispute resolution. However, online court mediation is currently not as easy to use as one might think, and usage is low in practice. Even though many disputes are accepted online, the fact remains that "online appointments are made and mediation is done offline," and online mediation is just a formality.

During our research at the West Lake District People's Court in Hangzhou,[33] we found that it was not common for the court's mediation center to receive online mediation cases, and no parties applied for online mediation for about a month before or after the research period. In addition, in the online e-commerce court in Zhejiang, where the court is located, there is an online mediation process before the online hearing, and essentially no parties have opted for online mediation. The factors affecting the use of online mediation are multiple and multidimensional, and they are intertwined and complex:

1. *Limitations on the type of dispute.* The specific type of dispute largely determines the appropriate way to resolve the dispute. Currently, the types of cases accepted for online dispute resolution are relatively limited, most of which are concentrated in some cases with relatively simple facts, clear facts and clear rights and obligations. In addition, there are other types of cases that fall into the categories of inconvenient party appearances and e-commerce disputes.
2. *Influence of participating entities.* Such factors such as judges, mediators, parties, and other subjects also affect the use of online mediation. As far as judges are concerned, there is no doubt that under the influence of the concept of trial as the core, some judges have a prejudice against mediation and do not attach any importance to mediation, let alone online mediation. In addition, in the case of the online dispute resolution mechanism, which is in the experimental stage, for prudential and security reasons, the court will also go through the process again offline for online cases and create the corresponding file documents, plus the time and effort spent on repeatedly communicating with the parties and guiding the use of online mediation, as a result, the workload of judges and clerks has not been reduced, but rather multiplied.[34] As far as mediators are concerned, many prefer face-to-face mediation as it is easier to exercise control over the process and make a timely and favorable impact on the mediated case through the ambience, words ,and behavior. As far as the parties are concerned, the lack of trust in the internet and unfamiliarity with online operations are the main factors affecting online mediation. Today, telecommunication and internet frauds are frequent, while the internet is more vulnerable to hackers, viruses, and other attacks, so its stability and security are questioned.[35] In an era when trust is already lacking, the public is even more suspicious of the internet. It is worth mentioning that in the disclaimer of the online court mediation platform released by the Sina Court Channel, the user is liable for the losses caused by network security problems and the instability of internet technology. This statement undoubtedly adds to the hidden worries and psychological burden of parties choosing online mediation.
3. *The impact of the system's operational design.* Whether the online mediation system is simple, convenient, fast, and user-friendly in its operational design affects the use of online mediation. In addition, the unfamiliarity of online operation can also affect the convenience and user experience of online mediation. For example, the first time I tried the Online Court Mediation Platform, I had a problem. I used my computer to access the Online Court Mediation Platform and followed the website's instructions to download the client software for my mobile phone. After entering the software download page by scanning the code on my mobile phone, I clicked on the "Download" button more than ten times, but there was no response and I was unable to download the software. At the same time, I found that the software has only been downloaded 1,000 times (which

should also include the number of times the staff downloaded it for testing purposes). I tried to call the website service number for help, only to find that the service hotline is available from Monday to Friday (9:00–17:30), not 24/7 (of course, the time is generally consistent with the general working hours of the court, which is somewhat reasonable). I tried to consult through online messages, only to find that the website's homepage does not have an "online consultation" section on the homepage.

7.2.5.3 Inadequate Legal Rules and Low Level of Normative Effectiveness

At present, provisions on online mediation only sporadically appear in the *Outline of People's Court Reform* and the *Opinions on the Reform of Multiple Dispute Resolution* issued by the Supreme People's Court, which are judicial documents and cannot be used as a basis for adjudicating cases. At the level of local regulations, only two regions, Shandong Province, and Xiamen City, have made principled provisions on "online mediation." The Anhui Online Mediation Rules are a special provision for online mediation pioneered by the local courts, while it is only an internal working regulation of the provincial courts and does not have normative effect. Overall, the court rules on online mediation are imperfect and have a low level of normative effect.

The Anhui Online Mediation Rules, for example, fill in the gaps in the concepts, principles, scope of application, rights and obligations, mediation process, supervision and management and other provisions related to online mediation, but the specific provisions still need to be refined, and it is necessary to issue implementation rules or explanations to further clarify and implement them. For example, the rules leave certain conceptual definitions open to dispute. The rules define the subject of "online mediation" as "invited mediation organizations and invited mediators" and exclude the courts and judges who are the subject of online mediation in practice.[36] The concept of an "online mediation platform" does not distinguish between online mediation platforms set up by courts on their own websites and online mediation platforms set up by courts on other entities (e.g., Sina Court Channel).[37] Furthermore, some provisions of the rules are not very operational in practice. For example, Article 33 of the rules provides in principle for the liability of the website operator of the online mediation platform, but lacks guidance on how to determine the specific circumstances (e.g., how to deal with the leakage of confidential information of mediation cases and loss of property of the parties due to human factors such as mismanagement or negligence of on the part of the operator).[38]

7.2.5.4 Inadequate Safeguard Mechanism and Insufficient Investment in Human, Financial, and Other Resources

The inadequacy of the court's online mediation guarantee mechanism is mainly reflected in the lack of human, financial, and material resources and support systems. In terms of staffing, there is a general shortage of court online mediation staff (including judges, clerks, mediators, technicians, etc.). For example, in the West Lake District Court's Chen Liaomin Online Studio, the entire studio was initially run by only two permanent staff, Judge Chen Liaomin and her clerk, who often used their lunch breaks, evenings, or weekends to complete the work related to the online studio as they also had to undertake the daily trials and other work of the court. In terms of funding, online mediation platforms are costly in terms of time and money to build, with millions of yuan for initial start-up funds and significant costs for later maintenance and management. As many local party committees and governments do not attach enough importance to online mediation platforms, it is difficult to set up projects for platform construction, the approval cycle is long, and funding is not available in time and in full. In terms of hardware settings, online mediation has certain requirements for computer operating systems, internet equipment and so on. In the early days, due to the lagging information technology construction of the courts, the hardware facilities of the courts in many areas could not meet the basic requirements of online mediation. With the further development of information technology construction and technological progress, the situation has now fundamentally improved, but there are still a few courts located in the old revolutionary base areas, areas inhabited by ethnic minorities, remote areas, and impoverished areas whose hardware facilities have not yet met the requirements for online mediation. As for the support system, the incentive mechanism, assessment and evaluation mechanism and talent training mechanism for online mediation have not yet been formed, and many mechanisms are still only at the conceptual stage. Therefore, the practice of online mediation is in urgent need of a set of systematic and scientific long-term support mechanisms.

7.3 The Normative Path of Online Mediation

According to Nadjia Alexander: "With the development of transport, telecommunications, globalization and transnational legal consensus, there is an increasing trend towards the globalization of mediation; and the spread of internet technology has made the role of electronic mediation increasingly important."[39] In the "E Era," the globalization and electronic turn of mediation are interwoven into the international trend for the development of online mediation, while the specific national conditions, such as the full implementation of the "internet+" strategy and the modernization of mediation constitute domestic opportunities for the development of online mediation in China. Faced with international trends and opportunities in China, how can Chinese online mediation respond to international trends, catch up with the developed countries, and converge with international standards to cope with the complex and changing international situation? Further, for a civilized country like China, it is not enough to simply follow the trends, but how to create and lead the international trends based on local resources, play to its own strengths, and balance local characteristics with foreign references? These will be inescapable issues for the development of online mediation in China.

7.3.1 Improving the Regulatory System for Online Mediation

In the development of online mediation, a scientific top-level design will further leverage the benefits of the system and promote further improvements in the productivity of online mediation. At present, among the major types of online mediation, the one with the most legislative basis and conditions is court online mediation. Take online court mediation as an example, to improve the construction of online court mediation system, we should adopt the working idea of "pilot first, learn lessons, lead by models, and promote comprehensively,"[40] encourage pilot regions to carry out bold practices, promote the achievement and experiences formed nationwide, and formulate national-level policy and regulations when conditions permit and the time is ripe.

On the one hand, provincial courts or municipal courts in urban areas that can do so may formulate the relevant rules on their own. The courts may work with relevant government functionaries (such as public security departments, judicial administrative departments, business administration departments, petitioning departments, etc.), social groups (trade unions, women's federations, etc.), enterprise organizations (internet enterprises, insurance companies, etc.) and other units and institutions to jointly formulate work rules, such as online mediation and online litigation and mediation docking, further forming a joint force for dispute resolution, and promoting the standardization and refinement of the system. The court must actively seek the support of the party committee, the government, and the National People's Congress to actively participate in and promote local legislation for the reform of the online diversified dispute resolution mechanism.

On the other hand, the Supreme People's Court should formulate regulations on the work of online mediation in courts. Based on summing up the experience of various regions, the Supreme People's Court should issue unified working regulations when the conditions are ripe. Depending on the needs of future social development, it will then be decided whether to elevate the multi-dispute resolution mechanism to national legislation.

7.3.2 Building Diversified Online Mediation Subjects

Currently, the government, courts, and other public authorities dominate the development of online mediation through administrative means, while private forces such as enterprises, social groups, and organizations are not sufficiently involved, and the "invisible hand" of the market has insufficient momentum in promoting the development of online mediation. Therefore, on the domestic side, the state should open the dispute resolution market, guide, and encourage the participation of private forces through macro-economic regulations, change the situation where public authorities dominate online mediation, build an online dispute resolution platform with the participation of multiple parties, and form a diversified dispute resolution resource with the combined strength of public, social, and market resources. On the international front, international dispute resolution forces should be absorbed through the expansion of international trade and the strengthening of international cooperation, and diversified dispute resolution forces should be developed with the joint participation of all countries and regions in the world and international organizations.

First, foster a civil online mediation organization. The government can use its authority and influence to promote other mediation subjects of online mediation and increase the participation and enthusiasm of other subjects; use policy support and financial investment to encourage, guide, and support the participation of social and private forces in dispute resolution, and cultivate private online mediation organizations in accordance with the needs of the market. For example, the government can purchase public services and entrust certain types of conflicts and disputes handled by online mediation to enterprises, civil organizations, social groups, etc. While breaking the monopoly and single provision of mediation by the government, private entities and private capital can be guided to participate in a variety of ways to promote the development of social forces in online mediation and to facilitate the formation and expansion of the commercial mediation market.

Second, build an integrated online dispute resolution platform.[41] Under the existing conditions, internet enterprises, courts, and comprehensive governance organizations should first build and improve their own online dispute resolution platforms in accordance with their own functions and business needs, and based on a certain scale of their own platforms, then consider the synergy between various platforms. Take the construction of online dispute resolution platforms built by the court system as an example: the main existing problem is that "the design ideas, element modules and relief channels of these existing platforms are separate and not uniform." "In terms of feasibility, it is possible to consider first building a national unified platform for system integration, and then providing different interfaces and plug-ins by region and by area to adapt to different situations in different places."[42] One of them is to set up a unified litigation and mediation docking data interface within the platform, to effectively connect online mediation with online filing, online judicial confirmation, online trial, electronic supervisory procedures, electronic service of process, etc., to achieve the integration and coherence of filing, service, mediation, litigation, and enforcement within the court system, to ensure the smooth conduct of pre-litigation mediation, mediation in litigation, and judicial confirmation. Second, courts at all levels can use a unified platform to "connect various types of invited mediation resources, aggregate nationwide mediation resources, and achieve nationwide matching and docking of mediation resources and mediation needs through standard internet services."[43] On the basis of the Supreme People's Court's pilot construction of an online court mediation platform in some parts of the country, more local courts should be included in the construction of the online court platform in a step-by-step and phased manner according to the actual situation of each region.[44]

Third, by using and applying big data analysis and data mining technology, through the collection and analysis of data obtained from the platform (such as dispute case, user feedback, user behavior and platform operation data), it is possible to track in real time information on the status of disputes, data on the docking of litigations and mediations, the effectiveness of dispute resolution work and typical cases of dispute resolution in various places, evaluate the workload and effectiveness of mediators, analyze the functional hotspots, operation trends, and user needs of the online dispute resolution platform, and predict the overall situation and development trend of conflicts and disputes.[45]

Finally, involving international dispute resolution forces to resolve international trade disputes. Trade globalization and world economic integration, coupled with the catalysis of "internet+," have led to the burgeoning of online dispute resolution mechanisms (ODRs) around the world, and have also made it possible and realistic to interoperate and share dispute resolution services between countries. By incorporating the power of international dispute resolution, on the one hand, international mediation organizations and talents can be introduced into foreign-related commercial disputes. On the other hand, by establishing a long-term mechanism for international commercial mediation exchange and cooperation, the commercial mediation industry, dispute resolution talents, and experience around the world can be linked together.

7.3.3 Establishing an Interconnected Online and Offline Mediation System

Online mediation in China is fragmented and ill-structured, and the mechanism for sharing resources and communicating information is not sound. The development of online mediation is also constrained by the fact that:

> For a long time, the work of resolving social conflicts and disputes in China has suffered from incomplete mechanisms, scattered forces, overlapping functions, and poor articulation, which have led to such outstanding problems as low efficiency in resolving disputes and serious waste of resources.[46]

By organically combining the actual mediation organization with the virtual space of the internet, linking and connecting online and offline mediation (online to offline), the "sharing" of dispute resolution resources can be achieved and the utilization of dispute resolution resources and the efficiency of dispute resolution can be improved. To this end, the following tasks are required.

First, to establish an online mediation organization that matches the administrative divisions. The entity organizations of people's mediation in

China already have covered all administrative divisions at all levels, therefore, with the relatively well-established organizational system of people's mediation, online mediation organizational bodies (such as online mediation committees and online mediation offices) can be set up in a systematic and planned manner in judicial and administrative departments at the provincial, municipal, and county levels or in certain administrative functions, and gradually cover administrative divisions at all levels as well as relevant industries and enterprises.

Second, to set up online mediation institutions within the court system. Online mediation offices can be set up in the Higher People's Court, the Intermediate People's Court, and the Basic People's Court to receive cases within their respective jurisdictions. The Online Mediation Office of the Higher People's Court is responsible for the operational guidance of online mediation in provincial courts. In addition, the court's unified online platform should be used to extend the nerve endings for the court to accept online mediation disputes, and to strengthen the connection with the online acceptance websites of mediation organizations and insurance company dispute acceptance websites, as well as to set up online green channels for dispute acceptance in areas where conflicts and disputes gather, such as mediation organizations and community centers, and online dispute prone areas, such as e-commerce websites and microblogs, in order to "achieve the rapid transfer of dispute information and online processing."[47]

Third, to establish an "online three-mediation linkage" system. The Comprehensive Governance Committee at each administrative level can take the lead in setting up an "online triple mediation system" to match the offline triple mediation system on the conflict prevention and resolution platform established by the Comprehensive Governance Organization. Each unit has a clear division of labor and responsibility in the "online three-instrument linkage" system, accepting unified command and coordination, which will break the status quo of "fragmentation" and "information silos" in the dispute resolution work of each unit, and achieve the organic combination of people's mediation, judicial mediation, and administrative mediation through online mediation.

7.3.4 Promoting the Professionalization of Mediation

In the wave of globalization of mediation, international organizations, countries, or regions such as the European Union, the United States, Australia, and Scotland have introduced norms for mediators and are gradually embarking on the path of professionalization of mediators. With the comprehensive transformation of Chinese society, the increasing refinement of the division of labor and the rapid development of the market economy, social conflicts and disputes are becoming increasingly pluralized, diversified, new and complex, and the requirements for resolving conflicts and disputes are becoming increasingly professional, technological, and information-based. The professionalization of mediators is not only in line with the global development trend of mediation, but is also a realistic need to match China's current national conditions. As an emerging model of mediation, online mediation requires a higher degree of professionalism in mediation compared to traditional mediation. At present, the professionalization of mediators in China suffers from unreasonable team structure and selection mechanisms, weak financial security, inadequate training mechanisms, lack of assessment and supervision, and lack of incentive mechanisms.[48] In order to promote the professionalization of mediation and create a high-level online mediation workforce, we can start by setting professional entry qualifications, improving the job security system, and fostering a professional code of ethics.

1. *Setting strict professional entry qualifications.* In terms of the source of mediators, it is important to absorb outstanding talents from all walks of life. By further expanding the database of online mediator experts to include NPC deputies, CPPCC members, lawyers, legal practitioners, and experts from various industries and fields to participate in dispute resolution in technical and professional fields, the structural transformation of mediators from monolithic to diversified and from popular to professional will be achieved, thereby enhancing the authority and credibility of dispute resolution. In terms of the conditions for the selection of mediators, certain requirements should be set not only in terms of age, education, years of experience and professional skills, but also systematic provisions should be made in terms of computer skills, online communication and coordination skills and text and information processing skills. In terms of the way mediators are selected and appointed, reference can be made to civil service examinations and national examinations for the legal profession, by means of open recruitment, unified examinations, and certification.
2. *Improving the job security system.* In terms of financial security, the state should alleviate the disparity in mediation funding across the country through central transfers, and local governments should support the cause of mediation with special budgets, such as the West Lake District Government in Hangzhou, which has set up special funds to support the construction of an online mediation studio at the West Lake District People's Court. In terms of talent training, universities, governments, and civil society and social organizations such as enterprises should carry out collaborative innovation to achieve two-way interaction between the theoretical and practical communities in mediating resources, such as teachers, talents, skills, and information. For example, universities should offer mediation majors or mediation orientation classes, develop curriculum materials in cooperation with government and enterprises, and train mediation undergraduates, master's students, and doctoral students. Universities can set up mediation theory research centers, and

governments, as well as civil society and social organizations such as enterprises, can set up mediation practice bases and mediation practice training centers, with both sides sending each other personnel for further studies. The government may set a mediator qualification examination to assess mediators, considering the standards of the national legal professional examination. In terms of assessment and evaluation, career promotion and development pathways should be scientifically set up and a ranking system for mediators should be implemented. Mediators can be graded based on their length of service, caseload, success rate, satisfaction rate, and rate of voluntary compliance, in order to give them different rights, obligations and salaries, thereby enhancing their professional recognition, and motivation.[49]

3. *Fostering a professional code of ethics.* Professional ethics and a professional spirit are important prerequisites for a professional team to maintain its vitality. A professional code of conduct for mediators can be formulated with reference to the professional code of lawyers, while an association of mediators can be set up to exercise professional autonomy. In addition, the professionalism of mediators can be cultivated through professional studies, internship visits, induction training, on-the-job training, and promotion assessment.

7.3.5 Strengthening the Culture of Mediation

The long-term development of online mediation is rooted in the corresponding cultural soil, which needs time to develop, as "Rome was not built in a day." Compared to traditional mediation, which is rooted in Chinese culture, online mediation is still new and will take some time and process to be accepted by the general public. To this end, the following should be done:

1. *Integrate the concept of online mediation into school education.* "Education starts with children." The younger generation is quick to accept and adapt to new things. If the thinking of online mediation is properly integrated into the education of primary schools, secondary schools, and universities, and enters the vision of the younger generation through school classes and extra-curricular life, the idea of online mediation will take root in the youth group like a dandelion seed and gradually spread to other age groups in the long run.

2. *Promote it throughout the community.* Just as Alipay and other electronic payment methods have swept through China's major cities in recent years, online mediation also requires publicity and promotion in order to be recognized by millions of households. At this stage, as far as the promotion body is concerned, the government, courts, and other state organs are the main force in promoting online mediation, while private forces such as enterprises and institutions, social organization, and individual citizens are also essential and important participants. In terms of the

target audience for promotion, the audience of online mediation mainly includes parties and mediation subjects. On the premise of fully respecting the autonomy of the parties and safeguarding their rights and interests, they can be guided and encouraged to use online mediation depending on the type of dispute and its specific characteristics. For mediation subjects, the specific types, procedures, methods and means of online mediation should be clarified, a specific and feasible publicity system should be introduced, and a long-term mechanism for the promotion of online mediation should be established. Mediators should be gradually trained in "internet+" thinking and skills, and the use of online mediation should be promoted among mediators.

7.3.6 Speeding Up Product Technology Development and Innovation

An important reason for the overall low level of online mediation in China and the limited application and service areas is the lagging development and use of information technology in online mediation and the low level of sharing. If we compare the development of online mediation to the popularity of mobile phones, then the reliability, affordability, convenience, practicality, and usability of high-technology will determine whether online mediation can reach millions of households. Among the many factors that limit the popularity of online mediation, the user-friendliness and ease of use, as well as the low cost of use, are particularly important. The user-friendly experience includes elements such as whether the interface is easy to operate, simple to configure and use, low risk in using it, and whether it takes too much effort and time for the user to master. At present, online mediation in China commonly uses internet mass communication tools such as QQ, WeChat, and email, using basically text, voice, and video. The technical shortcomings of screen-to-screen communication on the internet are relatively obvious, and there is still a large gap between it and traditional "face-to-face" communication. There will be a growing demand for online mediation that is closer to real life, live, and realistic. The development and innovation of product technology, the upgrading of hardware facilities, the upgrading of internet equipment and technology, and the lowering of barriers to entry can solve the contradiction between the real demand for online mediation and the supply of technology. Of course, technology development and diffusion are a complex and systematic project that requires a complete and effective mechanism from input to output as well as corresponding supporting policies. With the rapid development of technology, it is foreseeable that a super-enhanced version of online mediation, which is more realistic and even similar to "face-to-face" mediation, is just around the corner.

In addition, the establishment of a credit mark system is an effective initiative to popularize online mediation. Therefore, it is possible to indicate a credit mark for mediation subjects on local authorities or public platforms with high credibility, to enhance the trust of the parties in the subjects of civil mediation. At the same time, online mediation needs to be regulated and supervised to simplify procedures and improve efficiency, to ensure that online mediation is convenient, safe, fair, and just.

Notes

1 In March 2015, at the third session of the 12th National People's Congress, the term "internet+" appeared for the first time in the Premier's government work report. According to the report of the China Internet Information Center (CNNIC), the number of Chinese internet users reached 710 million in June 2016, and the internet penetration rate reached 51.7 percent. At the same time, the social life pattern shaped by the mobile internet has been further strengthened, and the "internet+" action plan has promoted the diversification and mobile development of government and enterprise services. As of December 2017, the number of Chinese internet users reached 772 million, with 753 million mobile phone users, and the number of users of online government services reached 485 million, accounting for 62.9 percent of the total number of internet users. In one and a half years, the number of internet users increased by nearly 10 percent.
2 Both ADR and ODR may use both online and offline technological tools to resolve disputes, so some scholars have distinguished between the two in terms of "the extent of the role of online technology in dispute resolution – whether the main procedures of dispute resolution make use of online information technology." See Zheng Shibao: ODR Research, PhD thesis, Southwest University of Political Science and Law, 2010. The concept of online mediation referred to in this chapter is broader, and includes both online mediation in ODR and mediation using network communication technology in ADR. In our opinion, if one or several stages of the whole process of mediation are conducted through the internet, it can be called online mediation in a broad sense.
3 Xi Jinping's opening speech at the internet conference (full text) is available at: www.edu.cn/rd/zi_xun/201512/t20151216_1348529.shtml (accessed May 5, 2016).
4 Long Fei: The Development Trend of Online Dispute Resolution Mechanism in China. Available at: http://finance.sina.com.cn/sf/news/2016-06-28/ 144335120.html (accessed June 29, 2016).
5 Ericsson: "Almost all devices will access the net in the future." Available at: www.chniot.cn/news/YJDT/2010/529/105299392983.html (accessed May 1, 2016).
6 See the *38th Statistical Report on the Development of the Internet in China*. Available at: www.cnnic.net.cn/hlwfzyj/hlwxzbg/hlwtjbg/201608/t20160803_54392.html (accessed October 8, 2016). According to the China Internet Network Information Center (CNNIC), that released the *42nd Statistical Report on the Development of China's Internet*: As of June 2018, the size of China's internet users reached 802 million, with an internet penetration rate of 57.7 percent; 29.68 million new internet users were added in the first half of 2018, an increase of 3.8 percent over the end of 2017; the size of China's mobile phone users reached 788 million, with the proportion of internet users accessing the internet through mobile phones reaching 98.3 percent. Available at: www.fx678.com/C/20180820/201808201529052280.html (accessed December 1, 2018).
7 Xi Jinping's opening speech at the internet conference (full text). Available at: www.edu.cn/rd/zixun/201512/t201512161348529.shtml (accessed May 5, 2016).

8 The adjudication mechanism of the Sina Weibo Community Committee is similar to that of a common law jury system, with the following process: a community committee is formed by publicly recruited Weibo users—the members of the community committee vote on whether a specific act is a violation of the law—and the site follows the convention and administrative rules. The executive committee decides on the outcome. See First Network People's Mediation Committee: The Left Hand Is the Microblogging Dispute, the Right Hand Is the Network Mediation. Available at: www.legaldaily.com.cn/index_article/content/2014-12/06/content_5876664.htm (accessed April 18, 2016).
9 In our field research in Hangzhou City West Lake District People's Court, the court's e-commerce online court judges believe that the e-commerce online court in Zhejiang is "self-generated," and is in the unique environment of Zhejiang naturally.
10 See Anon: Using the "Trial Cloud" Platform to Deepen the "Zhejiang Court Internet + Trial": Zhejiang Court E-Commerce Online Court Session, *People's Court Daily*, May 31, 2015, p. 1.
11 Cheng Xun: Promoting the Improvement of China's Diversified Dispute Resolution Mechanism with "Internet+," *People's Rule of Law*, 2015 (12).
12 See Anon: Supreme Court Launches Pilot Online Mediation Platform Construction. Available at: www.chinacourt.org/article/detail/2017/02/id/2546606.shtml (accessed February 2, 2017).
13 See Anon: Internet + Labor Dispute Mediation Innovates A New Platform for Resolving Conflicts and Disputes, *Xinhua Daily*, November 9, 2015, p. 4.
14 Beijing Court's First "WeChat Room" Online and Offline Mediation. Available at: http://report.qianlong.com/33378/2014/07/08/225@ 9724825.htm (accessed January 18, 2016).
15 See Zhang Changhao: Exploration and Practice of Sina's Internet Mediation Platform. Available at: http://finance.sina.comcn/sf/news/2016-05-05/ 093629215.html (accessed May 26, 2016).
16 Liao Yong'an and Wei Xiaofan: People-Oriented and the Revision of China's Civil Procedure Law, *Hebei Jurisprudence*, 2006 (11).
17 Meng Jianzhu: Strengthening and Innovating Social Governance to Build a Social Governance Pattern Built and Shared by All People, *People's Daily*, October 9, 2015, p. 2.
18 Ma Huateng et al.: *Internet+: A National Strategic Action Line* (Beijing: CITIC Publishing Group, 2015), pp. 19–21.
19 Gao Zhihai: Skillfully Use WeChat to Do Mediation, *Guangming Daily*, June 6, 2015, p. 6.
20 Zheng Shibao: ODR Research, PhD thesis, Southwest University of Political Science and Law, 2010.
21 Nadja Alexander: *Global Trends in Mediation*, trans. Wang Fuhua et al. (Beijing: China Legal Publishing House, 2011), p. 386.
22 Wang Wei: Types of Trust and Institutional Construction of Online Mediation in the United States, *Rule of Law Studies*, 2013 (9): 83–92.
23 Li Jianlei: Research on Non-Adjudicative Online Dispute Resolution Mechanism, Master's thesis, Beijing University of Posts and Telecommunications, 2015.
24 Zheng Shibao: ODR Research.
25 Text language is used here rather than written language, as there is a distinction between text language and written language in this case, and the text language used in online mediation can be either colloquial or written.

210 *The Rise and Regulation of Online Mediation*

26 The West Lake District People's Court in Hangzhou uses the e-commerce online court system developed by the Zhejiang High Court, which has an online mediation section. The system is set up so that 15 days before the court hearing, the parties can engage in online mediation, which is conducted in text form, with each party communicating with the mediator (unilateral meeting), who analyzes the claims of both parties and proposes a solution to the dispute based on the content of the communication. In addition, mediation can also be conducted during the online court hearing. If the parties reach agreement through mediation, the clerk will immediately create a mediation transcript and upload it to the system for the parties to click to confirm, and the click to confirm is considered a signature. The judge in charge of the case told us that in the cases he has handled, there has not been any online mediation between the parties before the online court hearing.

27 Long Fei: The Development Trend of Online Dispute Resolution Mechanism in China.

28 This set of data is real-time statistics from the online court mediation platform as of March 4, 2017.

29 See Supreme Court Launches Pilot Project to Build Online Mediation Platform. Available at: www.court.gov.cn/zixun-xiangqing-36282.html (accessed March 1, 2017).

30 *Opinions of the Supreme People's Court on Comprehensively Deepening the Reform of the People's Courts: Outline of the Fourth Five-Year Reform of the People's Courts (2014–2018)*.

31 Article 31 of the *Regulations on the Promotion of Diversified Dispute Resolution in Shandong Province* stipulates: "The use of the internet and other new technologies is encouraged to achieve online dispute resolution through online consultation, online negotiation and online mediation." Article 55 of the *Regulations on the Promotion of Diversified Dispute Resolution Mechanism of Xiamen Special Economic Zone* provides that "Agencies established in accordance with the law such as consultation, evaluation, appraisal and online mediation may charge fees if they participate in dispute resolution services."

32 Chen Guomeng: Vigorously Promoting the Construction of Online Dispute Resolution Mechanisms: Innovative Development of the "Fengqiao Experience" in the Internet Era, *Opinions on the Reform of the Diversified Dispute Resolution Mechanism of the Supreme People's Court and the Understanding and Application of the Provisions on Specially Invited Mediation* (Beijing,: People's Court Press, 2017), pp. 509–514.

33 The Court started online mediation as early as 2007 and is one of the first units in the national court system to practice online mediation.

34 One of the case clerks told us that because of the frequent occurrence of telecoms fraud, nine times out of ten when a person is initially notified to sign up for online mediation, they are mistaken for a fraud and it often takes patience to call the person and communicate with them several times.

35 The online court mediation platform disclaimer issued by Sina Court Channel states:

> The online court website service, like most internet products, is vulnerable to a variety of security issues, including but not limited to: (1) disclosure of detailed personal information, which can be used by unscrupulous individuals to cause real-life harassment; (2) trickery and password decryption;

(3) downloading and installing other software containing viruses such as "Trojan horses" that threaten the safety of information and data on personal computers and, consequently, the use of the Service. The user is responsible for any of the above.

Available at: www.fayuan.com/statement (accessed March 1, 2017).
36 Article 1 of the *Rules for Online Mediation in Anhui Courts (for Trial Implementation)* stipulates that online mediation refers to a mediation method in which invited mediation organizations and invited mediators are selected by the people's courts, registered, and certified by the online mediation platform, and are assigned by the people's courts to mediate disputes through the online mediation platform, combining online and offline mediation work to resolve disputes in an efficient and flexible manner.
37 Article 2 of the *Rules for Online Mediation in Anhui Courts (for Trial Implementation)* stipulates that an online mediation platform refers to an online dispute resolution platform with functions such as guidance of adjudication rules, case study of disputes, integration of mediation resources, online remote video mediation, online judicial confirmation, and docking of litigations and mediations.
38 Article 33 of the *Rules for Online Mediation in Anhui Courts (for Trial Implementation*) stipulates that the operator of the website where the online mediation platform is located should be responsible for the daily operation and maintenance of the platform to ensure that the platform realizes the functions in accordance with the requirements of these rules. Technical failures should be repaired as soon as possible to ensure the stable and continuous operation of the online mediation platform. The website operator should provide security for the data transmission and storage on the online mediation platform, and take the form of encryption for the case information to keep the case information confidential.
39 Nadja Alexander: *Global Trends in Mediation*, pp. 6–7.
40 Li Shaoping: Demonstration-led Innovation and Development: Continuously Enhancing the Rule of Law in the Reform of the Pluralistic Dispute Resolution Mechanism, speech delivered at the "National Courts' In-depth Promotion of the Reform of the Pluralistic Dispute Resolution Mechanism and the Exchange of Experiences of Model Courts."
41 The existing online dispute resolution platforms in China include three types: (1) online dispute resolution platforms of internet enterprises themselves; (2) unified online dispute resolution platforms of the national court system; and (3) conflict prevention and dispute resolution platforms established by comprehensive governance organizations. See Li Shaoping (Ed.): *Opinions on the Reform of the Diversified Dispute Resolution Mechanism of the Supreme People's Court and the Understanding and Application of the Provisions on Specially Invited Mediation* (Beijing: People's Court Press, 2017), p. 137.
42 Chen Guomeng: Vigorously Ppromoting the Construction of Online Dispute Resolution Mechanisms, *People's Court Daily*, December 28, 2016, p. 5.
43 Long Fei: The Current Development and Future Prospects of Online Dispute Resolution Mechanisms in China, *Legal Application*, 2016 (1): 4–9.
44 See Anon: Supreme Court Launches Pilot Project to Build Online Mediation Platform. Available at: www.court.gov.cn/zixun-xiangqing-36282.html (accessed March 1, 2017).

45 Long Fei: The Current Development and Future Prospects of Online Dispute Resolution Mechanisms in China.
46 Liao Yong'an and Liu Qing: Constructing a Diversified Mechanism for Resolving Social Conflicts and Disputes Shared By All People.
47 Long Fei: The Current Development and Future Prospects of Online Dispute Resolution Mechanisms in China.
48 Liao Yong'an et al.: *A Topical and Empirical Study of the Civil Litigation System* (Beijing: People's University of China Press, 2016), pp. 343–350.
49 Ibid., pp. 359–360.

References

Alexander, Nadja: *Global Trends in Mediation*, trans. Wang Fuhua et al., Beijing: China Legal Publishing House, 2011.
Anon: Using the "Trial Cloud" Platform to Deepen the "Zhejiang Court Internet + Trial": Zhejiang Court E-Commerce Online Court Session, *People's Court Daily*, May 31, 2015, p. 1.
Anon: Internet + Labor Dispute Mediation Innovates A New Platform for Resolving Conflicts and Disputes, *Xinhua Daily*, November 9, 2015, p. 4.
Anon: Supreme Court Launches Pilot Online Mediation Platform Construction. Available at: www.chinacourt.org/article/detail/2017/02/ id/2546606.shtml (accessed February 2, 2017).
Chen Guomeng: Vigorously Promoting the Construction of Online Dispute Resolution Mechanisms, *People's Court Daily*, December 28, 2016, p. 5.
Chen Guomeng: Vigorously Promoting the Construction of Online Dispute Resolution Mechanisms – Innovative Development of the "Fengqiao Experience" in the Internet Era, in *Opinions on the Reform of the Diversified Dispute Resolution Mechanism of the Supreme People's Court and the Understanding and Application of the Provisions on Specially Invited Mediation*, Beijing: People's Court Press, 2017, pp. 509–514.
Cheng Xun: Promoting the Improvement of China's Diversified Dispute Resolution Mechanism with "Internet+," *People's Rule of Law*, 2015 (12): 13–15.
First Network People's Mediation Committee: The Left Hand Is the Microblogging Dispute, the Right Hand Is the Network Mediation. Available at: www.legaldaily.com.cn/index_article/content/2014-12/06/content_5876664.htm (accessed April 18, 2016).
Gao Zhihai: Skillfully Use WeChat to Do Mediation, *Guangming Daily*, June 6, 2015, p. 6.
Li Jianlei: Research on Non-Adjudicative Online Dispute Resolution Mechanism, Master's thesis, Beijing University of Posts and Telecommunications, 2015.
Li Shaoping (Ed.): *Opinions on the Reform of the Diversified Dispute Resolution Mechanism of the Supreme People's Court and the Understanding and Application of the Provisions on Specially Invited Mediation*, Beijing: People's Court Press, 2017.
Liao Yong'an and Liu Qing: Constructing a Diversified Mechanism for Resolving Social Conflicts and Disputes Shared by All People, Guangming Daily, April 13, 2016, p. 13.
Liao Yong'an and Wei Xiaofan: People-Oriented and the Revision of China's Civil Procedure Law, *Hebei Jurisprudence*, 2006 (11): 133–139.

Liao Yong'an et al.: *A Topical and Empirical Study of the Civil Litigation System*, Beijing: People's University of China Press, 2016.

Long Fei: The Current Development and Future Prospects of Online Dispute Resolution Mechanisms in China, *Legal Application*, 2016 (10): 4–9.

Long Fei: The Development Trend of Online Dispute Resolution Mechanism in China. Available at: http://finance.sina.com.cn/sf/news/2016-06-28/ 144335120.html (accessed June 29, 2016).

Ma Huateng et al.: *Internet+: A National Strategic Action Line*, Beijing: CITIC Publishing Group, 2015.

Meng Jianzhu: Strengthening and Innovating Social Governance to Build a Social Governance Pattern Built and Shared by All People, People's Daily, October 9, 2015, p. 2.

Wang Wei: Types of Trust and Institutional Construction of Online Mediation in the United States, *Rule of Law Studies*, 2013 (9): 83–92.

Zheng Shibao: ODR Research, PhD thesis, Southwest University of Political Science and Law, 2010.

8 The Practice and Development of the Combination of Arbitration and Mediation

8.1 Introduction: The Origins of Combining Arbitration and Mediation

From a global perspective, the combination of arbitration[1] and mediation first originated in the arbitration practice of the China International Economic and Trade Arbitration Commission (CIETAC)[2] in the 1950s and was first clarified in its *Arbitration Rules*[3] in 1988 and subsequently also adopted by the *Arbitration Law*[4] in 1995. This practice in China has attracted widespread attention worldwide and has been followed by many countries. By tracing the reasons for the combination of arbitration and mediation in China, we believe that, in addition to the influence of the Confucian culture of harmony,[5] there are also the following underlying reasons that are less explored.

First, both arbitration and mediation have a tradition of administrative compatibility. Arbitration is a foreign product in China and was seen as a foreign element since its inception. Prior to the promulgation of the *Arbitration Law*, China followed the Soviet model and had an administrative arbitration system, whereby disputes were arbitrated by administrative organs or specialized bodies attached to administrative organs under administrative authority.[6] Thus, from its inception, China's arbitration system was engraved with the stamp of administrative rule and became an appendage of the administrative authorities. Similarly, according to the "cultural rupture theory,"[7] the mediation system introduced in the new China is very different from China's historical mediation tradition in terms of nature, authority, purpose and means, and the political function of mediation overshadows its dispute resolution function as political functions strongly permeate it.[8] There is no doubt that the path of the rule of law in China is "government-driven," with the government being the main driving force behind the rule of law movement and the goal of rule of law being accomplished mainly through the political resources of the government. Thus, both arbitration and mediation have a tradition of administrative compatibility, providing the opportunity and possibility for government-led promotion of a combination of arbitration and mediation. As Mr. Hanchen Nan, the first Chairman of the China Council for the Promotion of International Trade (CCPIT), pointed out when the arbitration rules were formulated by the CIETAC, it has always been the custom in the old revolutionary regions to adopt mediation to resolve problems between people, and mediation is a tradition of our Party that we all have to attach importance to.[9] As can be seen, the top-down promotion of administrative resources has become the driving force and basis for the combination of arbitration and mediation.

Second, it is influenced by the combination of litigation and mediation. After the establishment of the People's Republic of China, the development of litigation preceded arbitration, which, while modeled on the Soviet arbitration model, also learned, and borrowed many practices from the Chinese courts. According to Professor Tang Houzhi's recollection, "Before Chinese arbitration institutions adopted the combination of arbitration and mediation, there was first the combination of court hearings and mediation, i.e., the combination of litigation and mediation first, and only later did arbitration learn it."[10] The combination of litigation and mediation in China emerged from the "Ma Xiwu style of trial," and the emphasis on mediation is seen as one of its most fundamental features and the main hallmark of this style of trial.[11] The Chinese Arbitration Commission has also been influenced by the "Ma Xiwu style of trial" and has chosen to settle arbitration cases first and foremost by means of mediation, a phenomenon that can be explained by Takao Tanase's theory of the types of dispute resolution. Dispute resolution is divided into decisional and consensual dispute resolution, depending on whether the dispute is settled by a decision binding on a third party or by free agreement between the parties.[12] Both adjudication and arbitration are typical forms of decisional dispute resolution and are similar in nature. Mediation, as a representative of consensual dispute resolution, can be combined with both. Therefore, in Chinese dispute resolution practice, both litigation and arbitration have moved toward a combination with mediation.

With the development and promotion of the arbitration practice of the CIETAC, the combination of arbitration and mediation gradually attracted widespread attention in many countries around the world. In 1996, the International Council for Commercial Arbitration (ICCA) discussed the issue of combining arbitration and mediation at its Seoul Conference under the theme "The Culture of International Commercial Arbitration." At the conference, Professor Tang Houzhi pointed out that "there is an expanding culture in the world that favors the combination of arbitration and mediation."[13] At a time when countries around the world are facing common problems such as the "litigation explosion" and a shortage of judicial resources, the combination of arbitration and mediation has been recognized by many international organizations, countries, and regions. However, due to the very different institutional soil, the models, and forms of developing the combination of arbitration and mediation differ greatly from country to country. At present, the practice of combining arbitration and mediation in China has been influenced by the models from other countries. on the one hand, and has evolved and innovated, on the other. It is therefore necessary to explore in this chapter what new developments have taken place in the practice of combining arbitration and mediation in China, what problems exist in these developments, and how these problems should be addressed.

8.2 Theoretical Foundations: Connotations, Models, and Advantages of Combining Arbitration and Mediation

8.2.1 The Connotation and Model of Combining Arbitration and Mediation

Currently, in a symbiotic culture, arbitration and mediation are combined as a complex dispute resolution mechanism[14] that integrates arbitration and mediation in a broad and narrow sense. The combination of arbitration and mediation in the narrow sense refers to the approach pioneered by CIETCA as referred to above, whereby the parties first initiate arbitration proceedings and, while the arbitration proceedings are in progress, the arbitrator mediates the case and then resumes the arbitration proceedings when the mediation is successful or unsuccessful. The broad sense of combining arbitration and mediation includes the many forms derived from the narrower form of combining arbitration and mediation in countries around the world. Some scholars have enumerated and explained the main forms of combining arbitration and mediation, and after sorting them out, the combination of arbitration and mediation can be divided into two models: "first mediation and then arbitration" and "first arbitration and then mediation."[15] These two models contain a variety of specific forms, which differ in terms of their functional orientation, procedural settings, the rights and obligations of arbitrators and mediators, the procedural competence of the parties and the values of justice and efficiency. The choice of form depends on the agreement between the parties.

8.2.1.1 The Mediation Followed by Arbitration Model and Its Specific Forms

The main function of the mediation followed by arbitration model is to make use of the finality of arbitration to resolve disputes and to compensate for the lack of enforceability of the mediation agreement. As shown in Table 8.1, the mediation followed by arbitration model consists of five main forms. The main difference between "pure mediation followed by arbitration" and the last four forms is that the arbitrator and the mediator are usually the same person, which has the advantage of maintaining the integrity and coherence of the process and saving costs in dispute resolution. This form is applicable in two situations: first, where the mediation is successful and then proceeds to arbitration, the main purpose of which is to give enforcement effect to the mediation agreement through arbitration. For example, the Arbitration Provisions of Slovenia, Croatia, and Austria determine that if the mediator is successful in mediating the parties' dispute, at the request of the parties,

Table 8.1 Mediation followed by arbitration models and their main forms

Mode	Specific forms	Meaning	Are mediators and arbitrators the same person?
Mediation followed by Arbitration	1. Pure Mediation followed by Arbitration Pure Med-Arb	The parties initiate mediation to resolve their dispute, and then proceed to arbitration after mediation fails or is successful	Yes (usually)
	2. Compound Mediation followed by Arbitration Med-Arb-Diff	The parties initiate mediation to resolve their dispute, and then proceed to arbitration after mediation fails or is successful	No
	3. Med-Arb-Diff-Recommendation	The mediator will submit a proposal for an award to the arbitrator prior to the commencement of the arbitration proceedings, based, *inter alia*, on the facts of the case known during the mediation proceedings	No
	4. Post-Mediation Substitution Arbitration Med-Arb-Opt-Out	In a pure mediation followed by arbitration model, the parties have the right to reject the conversion of the previous mediator into an arbitrator	No
	5. The final arbitration programme MEDALOA	(Mediation and Last Offer Arbitration), is a hybrid process like the original Med/Arb process, where their difference is in the "arb phase." If the parties do not reach a voluntary settlement through mediation, each party submits a "last offer" to the Med/Arbitrator who must choose between one of two final offers. This process limits the discretion of the arbitrator to decide what he believes to be the most appropriate solution since the award must be limited to one of the offers.	No (usually)

the Arbitration Court may appoint the mediator as arbitrator, who will make a decision in accordance with the terms of the settlement.[16] The second is to enter into arbitration proceedings after unsuccessful mediation, the main purpose of which is to use arbitration to bring about a final settlement of the dispute. For example, Article 14(b)1 of the WIPO Mediation Rules provides that where the mediator is of the opinion that any matter in dispute between the parties cannot be settled by mediation, he or she may, after considering the circumstances of the dispute and the business relationship between the parties, recommend arbitration for the parties' consideration.[17]

The mediator and the arbitrator are not the same person in a "composite mediation followed by arbitration." At present, one of the main theoretical challenges to the combination of arbitration and mediation is the misgivings about the same person acting as both an arbitrator and a mediator, mainly due to the infringement of the principles of natural justice and due process, the confusion between the functions of arbitration and mediation, the loss of control over access to private information in mediation, or the risk of perception or actual favoritism in arbitration, etc.[18] These problems can be avoided with the separation of mediator and arbitrator. The "recommended mediation followed by arbitration," "Post-Mediation Substitution Arbitration," and "final arbitration scheme" are variations of the composite mediation followed by arbitration. A mediator in a "recommended mediation followed by arbitration" is required to submit a proposal for an award to the arbitrator at a later stage after the mediation has failed. The proposal is made by the mediator based on the information about the case and the relevant laws and regulations learned during the mediation process, and although it does not have legal effect, it gives the arbitrator good guidance. "The right to refuse the conversion of the mediator to an arbitrator after the mediation has failed and before the conversion to arbitration takes place, and this right to refuse is exercised without reason." A "final arbitration scheme" is also a combination of mediation and subsequent arbitration to achieve a final resolution of the dispute. As stated in Article 14(b)3 of the WIPO Mediation Rules, it is for the parties to propose final solutions and, where settlement by mediation is not possible, to arbitrate based on those final solutions, with the mandate of the arbitral tribunal in the arbitration proceedings being limited to deciding which final solution to adopt.

8.2.1.2 Arbitration Followed by Mediation Model and Its Specific Forms

The main function of the arbitration-post-mediation model is to use mediation to enhance the degree of autonomy in arbitration and to compensate for the inflexibility of arbitration. As shown in Table 8.2, there are four main forms of arbitration followed by mediation model. "Mediation in Arbitration" is conducted by the same person as the mediator and arbitrator, i.e., the parties initiate the arbitration proceedings first and the arbitrator can mediate the case during the arbitration process and then resume the arbitration proceedings if

Table 8.2 Arbitration followed by mediation models and their main forms

Mode	Specific forms	Meaning	Are mediators and arbitrators the same person?
First Chung After the ruling Mediation	1. Mediation in arbitration Arb-Med	Arbitration proceedings are initiated first, with the arbitrator mediating the case and resuming the proceedings when mediation fails or is successful	Yes
	2. Shadow mediation	Arbitration proceedings are initiated first, followed by parallel mediation proceedings, and if mediation fails, the arbitration proceedings ensure the final resolution of the dispute	No
	3. Arbitration Mediation Coexistence Co-Med-Arb	The mediator is present throughout the arbitration proceedings and may mediate when appropriate	No
	4. Mediation in arbitration enforcement	It is the use of mediation proceedings to resolve issues in the enforcement of arbitral award after the arbitration proceedings have been done	No

the mediation fails or is successful. This form was pioneered by CIETAC and there are now many countries and regions where the law and arbitration rules provide for "mediation in arbitration." For example, the rules of the Japan Commercial Arbitration Association (JCAA) provide that the arbitral tribunal may, if it considers necessary and with the consent of the parties, have an arbitrator of the tribunal mediate the dispute with a view to settlement.[19] Article 17 of the *Singapore International Arbitration Act* provides for the right of an arbitrator to act as a mediator, specifying that an arbitrator or umpire may act as a mediator and may communicate with the parties to the arbitration proceedings collectively or separately.[20]

"Shadow mediation" and "co-existence of arbitration and mediation" are specific forms of arbitration followed by mediation in which different persons act as arbitrators and mediators. "Shadow mediation is the parallel initiation of the mediation process at the appropriate stage of the arbitration, with the mediator mediating the case in order to increase the degree of party autonomy in the resolution of the dispute." If the mediation is successful, the case is closed, and if it fails, the arbitration process resumes and the arbitrator decides. The co-existence of arbitration and mediation is a procedural variant of "shadow mediation" in which both the arbitrator and the mediator participate in a small court hearing and the mediator can observe the development of the arbitration process and mediate the dispute when appropriate. Unlike other forms of combination of arbitration and mediation, "mediation in arbitration" does not take place at the dispute resolution stage, but during the enforcement of the arbitral award, with the aim of achieving an enforcement settlement, like the enforcement settlement in Chinese civil litigation.[21]

8.2.2 Key Advantages of Combining Arbitration and Mediation

As can be seen from the various forms of arbitration and mediation combined above, they have the following advantages over pure commercial arbitration and commercial mediation.

8.2.2.1 More Consensual and Flexible Than Commercial Arbitration

At present, the tendency to litigate commercial arbitration has been criticized by academics, with the main view being that arbitration is becoming as much a forum for adversarial struggle between the parties as litigation, and that proceedings tend to be as detailed and complex as litigation.[22] However, negotiated justice or mutual justice in civil and commercial dispute resolution is gaining popularity, with parties to disputes seeking the justice they need and hoping to achieve an effective resolution of their disputes through dialogue, negotiation, and compromise.[23] The combination of arbitration and mediation brings a mediation element to arbitration, where the mediator will take into account the parties' competing and non-competing interests, and their immediate and long-term interests, in order to find the best solution to the dispute and obtain the agreement of the parties. As Fuller argues, "The main characteristic of mediation is its ability to reposition the parties, not by reinforcing rules, but by helping them to gain a fresh consensus about their relationship."[24] In this way, the parties can achieve a win-win outcome through consensual agreement at the final stage of dispute resolution. In addition, the combination of arbitration and mediation is more flexible than arbitration alone, as the parties can choose between various forms of the combination of arbitration and mediation according to their needs, and the arbitrator or mediator can make "private visits" to the parties. Therefore, it is believed that the combination of arbitration and mediation is the most flexible and effective alternative dispute resolution mechanism.[25]

8.2.2.2 More Possibility of Consensus and Certainty of Outcome Than Commercial Mediation

Commercial mediation is based on the principle of voluntary will, and the consent of the parties is the key to successful mediation, but the process of mediation is a game of chance between the parties, who may not be able to reach a voluntary agreement. In a combination of arbitration and mediation, when mediation fails, the mediator may act as an arbitrator or the arbitrator may make a binding arbitral award. This is, in effect, a combination of "mediation," "judgment," and "coercion" tactics[26] used by the arbitrator to facilitate the active formation of a consensual agreement between the parties, which has been described by some scholars as "mediation with a big stick."[27] In addition, the combination of arbitration and mediation has the advantage over commercial mediation in terms of the certainty of the outcome, which is mainly reflected in the enforceability of the mediation agreement. On the contingency level, the parties are supposed to voluntarily perform the mediation agreement voluntarily reached, but the stability of the mediation outcome is easily undermined by the parties' repudiation, as can be seen from the large number of mediations entering into enforcement and the high rate of repudiation of non-judicial mediation agreements. In the combination of arbitration and mediation, the arbitral mediation or award made by the arbitrator based on the mediation agreement gives the parties the effect of applying for enforcement, which ensures the stability of the mediation outcome.

8.3 Examination of the Status Quo: The New Practice of Combining Arbitration and Mediation in China

In view of the international trend and significant advantages of combining arbitration and mediation, China is also actively developing the combination of arbitration and mediation to meet the growing demand for diversified dispute resolution. By analyzing legal norms, statistics, arbitration rules of arbitration institutions and mediation rules, we can get a glimpse of the current state of practice of combining arbitration and mediation in China, both in general and on a case-by-case basis.

8.3.1 General Overview of the Combination of Arbitration and Mediation in China

8.3.1.1 Normative Level: Legal Norms on the Combination of Arbitration and Mediation

With the increase in civil and commercial disputes and the higher demand for dispute resolution mechanisms, dispute resolution mechanisms are not only becoming more diverse, but are also gradually moving toward the development of coordination and dovetailing mechanisms. Articles 51 and 52 of the 1994 *Arbitration Law* make clear provisions on the combination of arbitration and mediation, the main contents of which include: prior mediation before the award, mediation where the parties volunteer to mediate, the making of an award when mediation fails, the making of a mediation or award when mediation reaches an agreement and the requirements for its making, entry into force of a mediation, and the making of a timely award when the parties repudiate the mediation. These provisions provide support and a basis for the combination of arbitration and mediation at the legislative level. In addition, from the normative documents, the main task proposed by the 2009 *Opinions of the Supreme People's Court on Establishing and Improving the Mechanism for the Resolution of Conflicts and Disputes Linking Litigation and Non-Litigation* is that "the mechanism for bridging litigation and arbitration, administrative mediation, people's mediation, commercial mediation, industrial mediation and other non-litigation dispute resolution methods should be improved." Its Article 9 stipulates:

> If parties without an arbitration agreement apply to an arbitration committee for mediation of a civil dispute, the mediation agreement with the content of civil rights and obligations reached after mediation by a mediation organization specially established by such arbitration committee, in accordance with the rules of fair and neutral mediation, shall have the nature of a civil contract, after it has been signed or sealed by both parties.

The main objective of the 2016 *Opinions of the Supreme People's Court on the People's Courts' Further Deepening of the Reform of the Diversified Dispute Resolution Mechanism* is that "Social resources for dispute resolution should be reasonably allocated, and the diversified dispute resolution mechanism of remediation, mediation, arbitration, notarization, administrative adjudication, administrative reconsideration, and litigation should be improved in an organic and mutually coordinated manner." In 2018, the General Office of the CPC Central Committee and the General Office of the State Council proposed in the *Opinions on the Establishment of International Commercial Dispute Settlement Mechanisms and Institutions for "One Belt, One Road"* that "we should actively cultivate and improve the dispute settlement service guarantee mechanism that organically connects litigation, arbitration, and mediation, and effectively meet the needs of Chinese and foreign parties for diversified dispute settlement." These normative documents all advocate, develop, and improve the combination of arbitration and mediation.

8.3.1.2 At the Practical Level: The Proportion of Cases Settled by Mediation and Settlement in Arbitration

The Legal Affairs Office of the State Council has always strongly advocated the establishment and development of a socialist arbitration system with Chinese characteristics, and has clearly put forward the guiding principle of "increasing the rate of expeditious settlement of arbitration cases, remediation and mediation, and the rate of automatic performance," and preventing the tendency to litigate arbitration.[28] According to the statistics in Table 8.3, the average proportion of arbitration cases settled by arbitration and mediation among

Table 8.3 Settlement of arbitration cases by arbitration and mediation nationwide[1] (unit: pieces)

Year	Number of arbitration cases accepted	Number of cases settled by arbitration and mediation	Percentage of total cases
2013	104257	60112	58
2014	113660	74200	65
2015	136924	56659	41
2016	208545	121527	58
2017	239360	69450	29

Note: [1] Data from the Annual China Commercial Arbitration Monitor for previous years.

the arbitration cases received by civil and commercial arbitration institutions nationwide from 2013 to 2017 was approximately 50 percent. Among them, the highest percentage of cases settled by arbitration and mediation was 65 percent in 2014. Scholarly research shows that, in 2014, 87 arbitration institutions nationwide, or 37 percent of the total, had a mediation and settlement rate of more than 50 percent, and in terms of geographical distribution, with the exception of the South China region, the rate of mediated and settled cases concluded by arbitration institutions in other regions was close to or above 50 percent.[29] It can be seen that the number of cases settled by domestic arbitration institutions by way of arbitration and mediation is running at a high level, reflecting the important role that the combination of arbitration and mediation plays in the settlement of civil and commercial disputes in China.

8.3.2 A Case Interpretation of Combining Arbitration and Mediation in China

How has the combination of arbitration and mediation developed and operated in China's arbitration institutions? How have arbitration rules changed in response to the need for mediation? In this regard, we examine the practices of organizations, such as CIETAC, the Beijing Arbitration Commission, the China (Shanghai) Pilot Free Trade Zone Arbitration Institute, and the Xiangtan Arbitration Commission, as case studies. The combination of arbitration and mediation in these arbitration institutions is characterized by early development, good results, innovative initiatives, and a wide range of influence, and has strong sample value.

8.3.2.1 The New Practice f Combining Arbitration and Mediation at the China International Economic and Trade Arbitration Commission (CIETAC)

As one of the world's leading permanent commercial arbitral institutions, CIETAC has made a significant contribution to the development of China's

Arbitration Law and the development of arbitration in China and the world through its practical and theoretical activities over the past 50 years. The combination of arbitration and mediation was the first of its kind by CIETAC and has had a significant impact on the development of arbitration and mediation in many countries and regions around the world. The practice of combining arbitration and mediation, which began in the 1950s, was first clarified in the Arbitration Rules in 1988 and has been progressively innovated and refined in the subsequent revision of the Arbitration Rules. In 2018, CIETAC established a Mediation Center and introduced the CIETAC Mediation Rules. In the following section we will analyze the development of the combination of arbitration and mediation in the CIETAC Arbitration Rules and the Mediation Rules.

As can be seen from Table 8.4, from the 1988 version of the Arbitration Rules to the 1998 version, only the form of mediation in arbitration in the model of first arbitration followed by mediation was provided for. The 2000 version of the Arbitration Rules added a new model of first mediation followed by arbitration, providing that if the parties reach a settlement on their own outside the arbitral tribunal, they may request the arbitral tribunal to make an award to close the case based on the content of their settlement agreement, or they may apply for the case to be dismissed. In such cases, the mediator and the arbitrator are not the same person and it is a composite type of mediation followed by arbitration. The 2012 version of the Arbitration Rules introduces a new form of arbitration followed by mediation, whereby if the parties wish to mediate but do not wish to do so under the auspices of the arbitral tribunal, the Arbitration Committee may, with the consent of the parties, assist the parties to mediate in an appropriate manner and procedures. In such cases, the mediator and the arbitrator are not the same person, as in the form of shadow mediation. The 2018 Mediation Rules build on the Arbitration Rules with clear and detailed provisions on forms such as composite mediation before arbitration and shadow mediation.

According to the available data, in 2002, CIETAC Beijing concluded 408 cases, 31 cases were settled and 72 cases were withdrawn, representing a 25 percent settlement and withdrawal rate, In 2004, CIETAC Beijing concluded 346 cases, 30 cases were settled and 82 cases were withdrawn, representing a 32 percent settlement and withdrawal rate. In 2008, CIETAC settled and withdrew 35 percent of cases, and, in 2009, CIETAC settled and withdrew 40 percent of cases. Although the above figures are not complete, the combination of arbitration and mediation has grown considerably at CIETAC.

8.3.2.2 The New Practice of Combining Arbitration and Mediation at the Beijing Arbitration Commission

Since its establishment in 1995, the Beijing Arbitration Commission (BAC) has grown rapidly into an arbitration institution that enjoys a wide reputation in China and has a certain status and influence in the international

Combination of Arbitration and Mediation 225

Table 8.4 Provisions of the CIETCA Rules on the combination of arbitration and mediation

Rule name	The form and content of the combination of arbitration and mediation	Specific provisions
Arbitration Procedure Provisional Rules (1956 edition)	None	None
Arbitration Rules (1988 edition)	Mediation in arbitration (where the arbitrator is the same person as the mediator), which essentially consists of making an award based on an agreement	Article 37
Arbitration Rules (1994 edition)	Mediation in arbitration (where the arbitrator is the same person as the mediator), which covers, *inter alia*, the initiation of mediation, the manner of mediation, the termination of mediation, out-of-court settlement as mediation by the arbitral tribunal, the making of an award based on an agreement, and the obligations to follow up if mediation fails	Articles 46–51
Arbitration Rules (1995 edition)	Same as the 1994 version of the Arbitration Rules	Articles 46–51
Arbitration Rules (1998 edition)	Same as the 1994 version of the Arbitration Rules	Articles 45–50
Arbitration Rules (2000 edition)	Mediation followed by arbitration, which essentially consists of applying for an arbitral award or setting aside a case after an out-of-court settlement. Mediation in arbitration (where the arbitrator and the mediator are the same person), mainly as in the 1994 version of the Arbitration Rules	Article 44
		Articles 45–50
Arbitration Rules (2005 edition)	Mediation followed by arbitration, which essentially consists of an out-of-court settlement followed by an application for an arbitral award	Article 40, paragraph 1
	Mediation in arbitration (where the arbitrator and the mediator are the same person), mainly as in the 1994 version of the Arbitration Rules	Article 40, paragraph 2 to section 8
Arbitration Rules (2012 edition)	Mediation in arbitration (where the arbitrator and the mediator are the same person), based on the 1994 version of the Arbitration Rules: new paragraph 5, which provides that the parties may withdraw their request for arbitration if an agreement is reached; new paragraph 6, which specifies the production of the mediation	Article 45, paragraphs 1 to paragraph 7, section 9

(*continued*)

Table 8.4 Cont.

Rule name	The form and content of the combination of arbitration and mediation	Specific provisions
Mediation Center Mediation Rules (2018 edition)	Arbitration followed by mediation (like shadow mediation, where the arbitrator and the mediator are not the same person)	Article 45, paragraph 8
	Mediation followed by arbitration, the main elements of which are the same as the 2005 version of the Arbitration Rules	Article 45, paragraph 10
	Mediation followed by arbitration, the main content of which is that the parties, based on the arbitration clause in the mediation agreement, may apply for an arbitral award to be made by the CIETAC in accordance with the content of the agreement.	Article 24, paragraph 1
	Mediation in arbitration (like shadow mediation, where the arbitrator and the mediator are not the same person), the main elements of which are: if the parties request independent mediation by a person other than the arbitral tribunal during the arbitration proceedings, the Center provides the corresponding mediation services.	Article 24, paragraph 2

arena. With the values of "independence, impartiality, professionalism and efficiency," BAC is striving to become a center for multidisciplinary dispute resolution practices, including arbitration, mediation, and construction engineering evaluation.[30] The first edition of the BAC Arbitration Rules (1995 edition) contained provisions on the combination of arbitration and mediation, and the combination of arbitration and mediation has been retained in subsequent amendments to the Arbitration Rules, which have always been innovative and refined. In 2011, the Beijing Arbitration Commission's Mediation Center was established and a separate Mediation Rule was formulated, creating a mediation process independent of the arbitration process. A review of the Arbitration Rules and Mediation Rules of the Beijing Arbitration Commission reveals the development of the combination of arbitration and mediation at the Beijing Arbitration Commission (Table 8.5).

The 1995 Arbitration Rules only provide for the form of mediation in arbitration, with the arbitrator and the mediator being the same person, and divide it into two forms: mediation before and after the tribunal sits. The 1996 Arbitration Rules and the 2001 Arbitration Rules supplement this with provisions on the refund of fees upon withdrawal of the application for arbitration, the subsequent obligations of the parties after the failure of mediation, and the fact that a settlement reached outside the arbitral tribunal is deemed to be a settlement reached under the mediation of the arbitral tribunal. The 2008 Arbitration Rules introduced an innovative form of combining arbitration and mediation by providing for a form of arbitration followed by mediation where the arbitrator and the mediator are not the same person, mainly comprising separate mediation and special provisions for international commercial arbitration. Separate mediation is a form of mediation like shadow mediation, which means that during a case, the parties can either settle on their own or apply to the Council for mediation by a mediator in accordance with the BAC Mediation Rules. In addition, in the case of mediation by an arbitral tribunal in international commercial arbitration, if the failure of the mediation results in the termination of the mediation proceedings, the parties may request a change of arbitrator if they wish to avoid the possibility that the outcome of the award may be affected by the mediation. The 2015 Arbitration Rules refine the specifics of the combined form of arbitration and mediation provided for in the 2008 Arbitration Rules, and the 2011 Mediation Rules refine the model of mediation followed by arbitration.

Tables 8.6 and 8.7 provide statistics relating to the BAC's combination of arbitration and mediation in recent years. According to Table 8.6, the average percentage of cases concluded by mediation from 2013 to 2017 was 15.5 percent. In addition, most cases withdrawn by the parties were due to settlement agreements reached by the parties, with the average percentage of parties withdrawing their claims from 2013 to 2017 being 27 percent. Thus, combining the rate of cases concluded by mediation with those withdrawn by

228 Combination of Arbitration and Mediation

Table 8.5 Provisions of the BAC Rules for combining arbitration and mediation

Rule name and date	Arbitration and mediation combined form	Main content	Specific provisions
Arbitration Rule (1995 edition)	Mediation in arbitration (the arbitrator and the mediator are the same person)	Before the arbitral tribunal session: provisions for withdrawal of a claim or request for the making of an award where the parties have applied for arbitration but then reached a settlement agreement, and the treatment of withdrawal of a claim followed by an estoppel	Article 36 Article 37
		After the tribunal session: the tribunal may first mediate before making an award; if mediation fails, the award shall be made in a timely manner; if mediation is successful, the mediation or award shall be produced as well as the requirements for the production and entry into force of the mediation; and if the mediation result is reversed before signing the mediation, the award shall be made in a timely manner	Article 38 Article 39
1996	Mediation in arbitration (the arbitrator and the mediator are the same person)	Before the tribunal session: the manner of decision on withdrawal of the application has been added to the 1995 Rules; out-of-court settlement during mediation is considered as mediation by the tribunal and the award is made based on the agreement reached by the tribunal's mediation	Article 38 Article 39
		After the tribunal's session: the parties' subsequent obligations after the failure of mediation have been added to the 1995 Rules	Article 40 Article 41
1997	Mediation in arbitration (the arbitrator and the mediator are the same person)	Same as the 1996 rules	Article 41 Article 42 Article 44 Article 45
1999	Mediation in arbitration (the arbitrator and the mediator are the same person)	Same as the 1996 rules	Article 42 Article 43 Article 45 Article 46

Year	Topic	Description	Articles
2001	Mediation in arbitration (the arbitrator and the mediator are the same person)	Before the tribunal session: same as the 1996 rules	Article 53
		After the tribunal session: A new addition to the 1996 rules is that a settlement reached outside the tribunal is deemed to be a settlement reached under the mediation of the tribunal	Article 54 Rule 56 Article 58
2004	Mediation in arbitration (the arbitrator and the mediator are the same person)	Before the arbitral tribunal sits: a new situation has been added to the 1996 Rules for the refund of fees following the withdrawal of a claim for arbitration	Article 37 Paragraphs 1–3
		After the tribunal session: provides for the initiation of mediation, the production of a mediation or award if the mediation is successful, the requirements for the production and entry into force of the mediation, and the subsequent obligations if the mediation fails	Article 38 Section 1–4
2008	Mediation in arbitration (the arbitrator and the mediator are the same person)	Same as the 2004 rules	Article 38 Article 39
	Mediation in arbitration (arbitrator and mediator are not the same person)	Individual mediation: During the hearing of a case, the parties may settle the case on their own or apply to the Council for mediation by a mediator in accordance with the Beijing Arbitration Commission Mediation Rules	Article 40
		Special provisions for international commercial arbitration: If the mediation procedures are terminated as a result of the failure of the arbitral tribunal to mediate, the Director may grant a request for a change of arbitrator if the parties request it on the ground of avoiding the possibility that the outcome of the award may be affected by the mediation	Article 58 Paragraphs 1 and 2
2015	Mediation in arbitration (the arbitrator and the mediator are the same person)	Provides for: the initiation of mediation, the possibility of requesting the withdrawal of a request for arbitration if mediation is agreed, the production of a mediation or an award; the requirements for the production and entry into force of a mediation, the correction of a mediation, and the subsequent obligations of the parties if mediation fails.	Article 42, sections 1–5

(continued)

Table 8.5 Cont.

Rule name and date	Arbitration and mediation combined form	Main content	Specific provisions
2015	Mediation in arbitration (arbitrator and mediator are not the same person)	Separate mediation: New to the 2008 Arbitration Rules: If a settlement agreement is reached by mediation, the parties may jointly request the constitution of an arbitral tribunal to make a mediation or award based on the content of that settlement agreement.	Article 43, paragraphs 1 and 2
		Special provisions for international commercial arbitration, as in the 2008 Arbitration Rules	Article 26 paragraphs 1 and 2
2011 Beijing Arbitration The Committee's investigation Deconcentration Solving the rules	Mediation followed by arbitration	After mediation, a settlement agreement is signed if the parties reach an agreement. The parties may apply to the Beijing Arbitration Commission for arbitration and request the arbitral tribunal to produce a mediation or award based on the content of the settlement agreement.	Article 23
		Subsequent obligations of the parties after mediation	Article 25
		Unless otherwise agreed by the parties, a mediator shall not act as an arbitrator in subsequent arbitration proceedings in respect of the same or a related dispute	Article 26

Table 8.6 BAC's Case Closure Table, 2013–2018[1] (Number of cases; proportion in percent)

Year	Total concluded	Closed by award		Settled by mediation		Withdrawal of application		Dismissal of cases	
		Number	Proportion (%)	Number	Proportion (%)	Number	Proportion (%)	Number	Proportion (%)
2013	1614	826	51.18	271	16.79	514	31.84	3	0.19
2014	1755	857	48.83	354	20.17	543	30.94	1	0.06
2015	2425	1373	56.62	349	14.39	700	28.87	3	0.12
2016	2917	1887	64.69	375	12.86	655	22.45	0	0
2017	3520	2170	61.65	527	13.18	823	20.58	0	0
2018	4125	2547	61.75	631	15.30	947	22.96	0	0

Note: [1] The data in the table are all from the summary of the work of the Beijing Arbitration Commission 2013–2017. Available at: www.bjac.org.cn/page/gybh/introduce e_report.html (accessed November 10, 2018).

Table 8.7 Independent mediation cases since the establishment of the BAC Mediation Center[1]

Year	Number of independent mediation cases	Number of successfully mediated cases	Number of cases converted to enforcement	Proportion of successful mediation cases converted to enforcement (%)
2012	3	0	0	0
2013	10	3	1	33
2014	118	97	83	85.6
2015	44	14	11	78.6
2016	3	1	0	0
Total	184	120	97	80.8

Note: [1] All data in the table are from the BAC's 2016 summary of work, www.bjac.org.cn/news/view?id=2909 (accessed November 10, 2018).

the parties, over these five years, the BAC used a combination of arbitration and mediation to state around 40 percent of the total number of cases were concluded.

8.3.2.3 New Practice of Combining Arbitration and Mediation at the China (Shanghai) Pilot Free Trade Zone Arbitration Court

In October 2013, the China (Shanghai) Pilot Free Trade Zone Arbitration Court was established. The Court was established by the Shanghai International Economic and Trade Arbitration Commission (SIETAC) to provide parties in the zone with zero-distance access to arbitration legal services, such as arbitration consultation, filing of cases and hearings, and is an important institutional arrangement for dispute resolution and legal protection in the Shanghai Free Trade Zone (FTZ).[31] The China (Shanghai) Pilot Free Trade Zone Arbitration Rules (hereinafter referred to as the FTZ Arbitration Rules), which were implemented by the China (Shanghai) Pilot Free Trade Zone Arbitration Court in 2014, have been described by the industry as "almost completely in line with international standards." The arbitration rules provide for the "combination of arbitration and mediation" as a separate chapter (Chapter 6), as follows.

As can be seen from Table 8.8, the FTZ Arbitration Rules provide for three forms of arbitration combined with mediation: (1) mediation by a mediator; (2) mediation by the arbitral tribunal; and (3) settlement outside the arbitral institution. Mediator mediation and arbitral tribunal mediation are models of arbitration followed by mediation, where the mediator and the arbitrator are not the same person in mediator mediation, whereas in arbitral tribunal mediation, the mediator and the arbitrator are the same person. Settlements outside of arbitration institutions are part of the mediation followed by the arbitration model where the mediator-arbitrator is not the same person. The

Table 8.8 Combination of arbitration and mediation in the FTZ Arbitration Rules

Form	Content	Article
Mediation in arbitration (arbitrator and mediator are not the same person)	In respect of mediation by a mediator, provisions are made for: the initiation of mediation before the constitution of the arbitral tribunal, the appointment of a mediator, the fact that mediation does not affect the conduct of the arbitral proceedings before the constitution of the arbitral tribunal, provisions for the suspension of the constitution of the arbitral tribunal, the recusal of the mediator, the manner in which mediation may be conducted, the possibility of withdrawing the application for arbitration or requesting the arbitral tribunal thereafter constituted to make an arbitral award if agreement is reached at mediation, the circumstances in which mediation may be terminated, and the fact that the mediator who accepts the appointment shall no longer act as arbitrator in the case unless the parties agree in writing	Article 50. sections 1–7
Mediation in arbitration (the arbitrator and the mediator are the same person)	Provisions on mediation by the arbitral tribunal: initiation of mediation after the constitution of the arbitral tribunal, manner of mediation, termination of mediation and conversion to arbitral proceedings, out-of-court settlement as mediation by the arbitral tribunal, possibility of withdrawal of the application for arbitration or production of an award if agreement is reached at mediation, subsequent obligations of the parties if mediation fails	Article 51, sections 1–5 Article 53
Mediation followed by arbitration	Provisions on settlement outside the arbitration institution: If the parties reach a settlement agreement through consultation or mediation outside the arbitration committee, they may, by virtue of the arbitration agreement reached by the parties to be arbitrated by the arbitration committee and the settlement agreement, request the arbitration committee to constitute an arbitral tribunal and make an arbitral award in accordance with the contents of the settlement agreement. There are also provisions concerning the composition of the arbitral tribunal and the procedure for making an award.	Article 52

FTZ Arbitration Rules follow traditional arbitral tribunal mediation and create a provision for mediation by a mediator, a provision that also brings the FTZ Arbitration Rules closer to the position and custom of mediation in international commercial arbitration practice.

8.3.2.4 The New Practice of Combining Arbitration and Mediation at the Xiangtan Arbitration Commission

The Xiangtan Arbitration Commission (XAC) was formally established in 1996 in Xiangtan, Hunan Province, as a legal entity, and in 2002, the XAC established the Xiangtan Arbitration Commission Mediation Center and formulated the Xiangtan Arbitration Commission Mediation Center Mediation Rules. In 2005, the Xiangtan Arbitration Commission was designated as a "pilot unit for the standardization of arbitration institutions," and the harmonious arbitration work practiced by the Commission has been respected by the national arbitration community. In 2009, the person in charge of the Legal Affairs Office of the State Council approved: "The Xiangtan Arbitration Commission is in good spirits and has a good work performance, and can be a model for arbitration institutions nationwide."[32] The Xiangtan Arbitration Committee's 2013 Arbitration Rules and the 2009 Mediation Rules respectively provide for the combination of arbitration and mediation as follows.

As can be seen from Table 8.9, the Xiangtan Arbitration Commission has provided for seven forms of arbitration combined with mediation. Mediation by the Mediation Center, which has no basis for initiating arbitration proceedings, is a model of mediation followed by arbitration. Mediation by an arbitrator or mediator prior to the formation of a tribunal after the filing of an arbitration, mediation by an arbitral tribunal prior to a hearing, mediation by an arbitral tribunal during a hearing, mediation by an arbitral tribunal prior to an award, and dovetailing of arbitration and party settlement all fall under the model of arbitration before mediation. In this case, the mediation by an arbitrator or mediator before the arbitration case is formed differs from the other forms, in which the arbitrator and the mediator are not the same person. In addition, the XAC also provides for mediation in the enforcement of arbitration, i.e., mediation by the Arbitration Commission after the entry into force of the award and during its enforcement. Thus, the Xiangtan Arbitration Commission's provisions on the combination of arbitration and mediation are more comprehensive and detailed. Some data show that from 2002 to November 2010, when the XAC implemented the Mediation Rules, a total of 3,666 cases were received, of which 2,695 cases were settled by mediation and withdrawal of the arbitration application by settlement, with an average annual mediation and settlement rate of 73.5 percent.[33]

Table 8.9 Combination of arbitration and mediation in the Xiangtan Arbitration Commission Rules

Combined form of arbitration and mediation	Main content	Articles
Mediation followed by arbitration	Provides for mediation by the Mediation Center where there is no basis for initiating arbitration proceedings and for the confirmation of settlement agreements in the case of settlements (mediation) outside this Commission	Mediation Rules: Article 10–26 Arbitration Rules: Article 62: paragraph 3
Mediation in arbitration (arbitrator and mediator are not the same person)	Provides for mediation by an arbitrator or mediator before the constitution of a tribunal after the filing of an arbitration	Mediation Rules: Articles 27–31 Arbitration Rules: Article 20
Mediation in arbitration (arbitrator and mediator are the same person)	Pre-hearing tribunal mediation	Mediation Rules: Articles 32–33 Arbitration Rules: Article 32
	Mediation by the tribunal at the hearing	Mediation Rules: Articles 34–36 Arbitration Rules: Article 49
	Pre-award tribunal mediation	Mediation Rules: Article 37 Arbitration Rules: Article 52
	The interface between arbitration and party settlement	Mediation Rules: Article 38 Arbitration Rules: Article 48
Mediation in arbitration enforcement	Mediation by the Arbitration Council after the entry into force of the award and during its enforcement	Mediation Rules: Article 39–40

8.4 Practical Analysis: Effectiveness and Problems in the Development of Combined Arbitration and Mediation in China

Through an analysis of the general overview of the combination of arbitration and mediation in China, as well as a microscopic examination of the cases of the combination of arbitration and mediation in representative arbitration institutions such as the CIETAC, the Beijing Arbitration Commission, the China (Shanghai) Pilot Free Trade Zone Arbitration Institute, and the Xiangtan Arbitration Commission, it can be found that the current development of the combination of arbitration and mediation in China has the following effectiveness and problems.

8.4.1 Major Achievements in the Development of Combined Arbitration and Mediation in China

8.4.1.1 The Combination of Arbitration and Mediation Has Been Emphasized and Advocated

First, the combination of arbitration and mediation has been emphasized and advocated at the central level. The central strategic deployment of the Third Plenary Session, Fourth Plenary Session, and Fifth Plenary Session of the 18th CPC Central Committee has completed the sublimation of the status, system, and theory for the construction of a diversified dispute resolution system.[34] The combination of arbitration and mediation, as an important element of the multi-dispute resolution mechanism, has been advocated by the General Office of the Central Committee of the CPC, the General Office of the State Council, and the Supreme People's Court in several documents.

Second, local governments focus on placing arbitration and mediation within the framework of Grand Mediation, which refers to the comprehensive use of various institutional resources for dispute resolution in contemporary China, integrating and linking them. For example, the government of Guiyang City has issued "three mediation linkages," requiring the formation of a local working mechanism in which people's mediation, administrative mediation, and arbitration mediation coordinate and cooperate with each other. The Wuhan Municipal People's Government has combined arbitration mediation with administrative mediation to deal with traffic accident damage disputes.

Third, the combination of arbitration and mediation has become an important way to resolve commercial disputes in the "Belt and Road." Compared to the pagoda-type domestic order, the "Belt and Road" runs through the Eurasian continent and is a flat-type international order,[35] with the diversity of political forms, economic status, religious cultures, ethnic characteristics, legal norms, and commercial customs of countries and regions along the route. Therefore, the use of traditional or single dispute resolution methods, such as litigation, international arbitration, and commercial mediation, can hardly meet the diverse needs of dispute resolution in the "Belt and Road." As a complex dispute resolution mechanism that integrates arbitration and mediation, the combination of the two is gradually becoming an important method of international commercial dispute resolution, and is referred to by scholars as an "expanding culture" and a principle of dispute resolution in the "Belt and Road."[36]

8.4.1.2 The Combination of Arbitration and Mediation Has Been Innovated and Developed

The practice of combining arbitration and mediation is largely established in the arbitration rules of numerous arbitral institutions, and the form of combining arbitration and mediation has been innovated and developed. The combination has its roots in CIETAC arbitration practice, but at that time there was only a single model of mediation in arbitration. With the development of the combination of arbitration and mediation, arbitration institutions began to innovate the forms of combining the two, breaking away from the practice of having the same arbitrator and mediator in the combination of arbitration and mediation. In particular, the Xiangtan Arbitration Commission has set out seven forms of combining arbitration and mediation in its arbitration rules and mediation rules, including a variety of forms of mediation followed by arbitration and arbitration followed by mediation.

8.4.1.3 Some Arbitration Institutions Have Established Specialized Mediation Centers

Some arbitral institutions have established specialized mediation centers to enable the organic combination of arbitration and independent mediation. After the mediation is conducted by the mediation center, the arbitration institution will give the results of the mediation enforceability by producing a mediation certificate or an award, which will facilitate the development of the mediation before arbitration model and the separation of the mediator from the arbitrator. The CIETAC, the Beijing and the Xiangtan Arbitration Commissions have all established independent mediation centers and have formulated Mediation Rules. In addition, some arbitration institutions have established professional arbitration and mediation centers in conjunction with industries. For example, the Haikou Arbitration Commission established the Hainan Communications Arbitration and Mediation Center, which has become the first professional mediation and handling institution for communications contract disputes in China. The Zhengzhou Arbitration Commission established the Intellectual Property Liaison Office, the Corporate Securities Center, and the Federation of Industry and Commerce Arbitration and Mediation Center to expand the coverage of arbitration work and strengthen the construction of the arbitration network. The Guangzhou Arbitration Commission, in cooperation with the Guangzhou Municipal

Bureau of Industry and Commerce, the Guangzhou Municipal Bureau of Justice, and the Chamber of Commerce, established the Guangzhou Mediation Center for Contract Disputes, the Arbitration Mediation Center, and the Chamber of Commerce Mediation Center, which have achieved good social and legal results.[37]

8.4.1.4 High Rate of Arbitration Cases Settled by Mediation and Settlement

In recent years, the settlement and mediation rates of many arbitration institutions have continued to run at a high level due to the requirement of the competent authorities of arbitration institutions to attach great importance to improving the rate of expeditious settlement, mediation and settlement, and automatic performance of arbitration work. In addition to the above analyzed arbitration institutions, such as CIETAC, the Beijing Arbitration Commission, the China (Shanghai) Pilot Free Trade Zone Arbitration Institute, and the Xiangtan Arbitration Commission, the arbitration and mediation rate of arbitration cases at Wuhan Arbitration Commission has remained above 80 percent; and the settlement and mediation rate of Yancheng Arbitration Commission was above 70 percent from 2005 to 2010.[38]

8.4.2 Problems in the Development of Combined Arbitration and Mediation in China

8.4.2.1 The Combination of Statutory Arbitration and Mediation Is Relatively Homogeneous

The demand for diversity and flexibility in dispute resolution mechanisms is becoming increasingly evident, and a single form of arbitration and mediation will not be able to meet the diverse needs of different parties, and will affect the ability of arbitration institutions and mediation organizations to resolve disputes and their international influence. At present, a variety of forms of arbitration and mediation are either expressly provided for or implicitly permitted in many developed countries. For example, in the United States, the main forms of combined arbitration and mediation mentioned above, such as simple mediation followed by arbitration, composite mediation followed by arbitration and shadow mediation, can be recognized by the courts subject to statutory conditions. Countries such as Korea, Japan, and Singapore have also recognized various forms of combined arbitration and mediation through their arbitration laws and rules. In contrast, China has a single statutory form of combining arbitration and mediation, and the *Arbitration Law* only provides for "mediation in arbitration," i.e., an arbitrator will mediate the dispute after the arbitration proceedings have been initiated. Although some arbitral institutions have innovated and developed forms of combining arbitration and mediation on the basis of the *Arbitration Law*, such as the

CIETAC and the BAC, which provide for mediation before arbitration, and mediation in arbitration where the arbitrator and the mediator are not the same person, the diversity of forms of combining arbitration and mediation still needs to be recognized by legislation, so as to guide and require arbitration institutions and mediation organizations to further enrich the forms of combining arbitration and mediation.

8.4.2.2 The Organization and Personnel Combining Arbitration and Mediation Are Not Very Professional or Internationally Focused

There are two main paths for the development of the combination of arbitration and mediation at the level of dispute resolution organizations: first, the establishment of professional arbitration and mediation institutions specializing in the use of arbitration and mediation to resolve disputes; second, the strengthening of the professionalism, internationalism, and cooperation of existing arbitration and mediation organizations to make using the combination of arbitration and mediation smoother. Although the former has the advantage of professionalism, it is more feasible to strengthen the professionalism, internationalism, and cooperation of existing arbitration and mediation organizations considering the current development of the Belt and Road dispute resolution mechanism and resources.[39] At present, China's arbitration and mediation organizations are developing rapidly, but there is still a gap between them and internationally renowned arbitration and mediation organizations. For example, the proportion of foreign-related arbitrations accepted by CIETAC is approximately 20 percent, while the relevant proportion for the Arbitration Institute of the Stockholm Chamber of Commerce in Sweden is about 50 percent and that of the Singapore International Arbitration Center is over 80 percent.[40] In terms of commercial mediation organizations, the China Council for the Promotion of International Trade/International Chamber of Commerce Mediation Center, the Shanghai Economic and Trade Commercial Mediation Center, the Xiamen International Commercial Mediation Center, and the Beijing Rongshang "Belt and Road" Commercial Mediation Center are mostly in their infancy. Therefore, Chinese arbitration institutions and mediation organizations need to strengthen their dispute resolution capabilities and internationalization. The problem with the combination of arbitration and mediation is that, due to the many differences between arbitration and mediation,[41] the use of arbitration and mediation to resolve civil and commercial disputes requires two types of dispute resolution personnel: a single type of dispute resolution personnel who specializes in arbitration or mediation; and a composite type of dispute resolution personnel who specializes in both arbitration and mediation. The second type of dispute resolution personnel is a special category, mainly applicable to the combination of arbitration and mediation, but in China, there is a lack of training for this type of personnel, and the ability of dispute resolution

240   *Combination of Arbitration and Mediation*

personnel to resolve disputes in the combination of arbitration and mediation is not high.

8.4.2.3 Procedural Challenges in Combining Arbitration and Mediation Are Difficult to Overcome

Indeed, many of the procedural challenges to the combination of arbitration and mediation in academic circles can be attributed mainly to the criticism of the unity of the identity of the arbitrator and the mediator, such as the rejection by arbitration expert, Street Laurence, of the practice of having the same person who has conciliated a case playing the role of arbitrator in subsequent arbitration proceedings. He argues that such a practice would inevitably distort and hamper the mediation process and would be an affront to and an infringement of the principles of natural justice.[42] Specifically, the combination of arbitrator and mediator status may lead to the following problems: First, in the process of mediation, the arbitrator may impose his or her opinion on the parties due to the power of arbitral award they will be given in the future, ignoring the autonomy of the parties, resulting in the phenomenon of "pressing mediation with arbitration." This phenomenon arises for similar reasons as the phenomenon of "pressing mediation with adjudication" in Chinese court mediation, which has been criticized by the academic community.[43]

Second, a mediator acting as an arbitrator in subsequent arbitration proceedings may be influenced by the mediation process and have difficulties in maintaining impartiality in the arbitration proceedings. As it is difficult to avoid confrontation between the parties in a face-to-face situation, mediators often use "private visits" in mediation, i.e., separate one-sided meetings with the parties, and in practice, "private visits" often become the most common and effective way for mediators. In a "private visit," the parties often reveal their "minimum conditions"[44] to the mediator, which is difficult for the arbitrator to know during the arbitration proceedings due to, for example, information asymmetry. If the mediator is privy to private information against the parties at the mediation, he or she will inevitably be influenced by the parties' words rather than the evidence at the arbitration stage, creating a preconceived impression that may prevent a fair arbitral award from being made.

8.4.2.4 The Mechanism for Redressing the Outcome of a Wrongful Combination of Arbitration and Mediation Is Inadequate

The absence of a scientifically sound redress mechanism will make the implementation of the combination of arbitration and mediation much less effective. As discussed above, the combination of arbitration and mediation can be divided into two models: "mediation followed by arbitration" and "arbitration followed by mediation." The instruments for the successful resolution of disputes include the arbitral mediation agreement, the arbitral award based on the mediation agreement, and the arbitral award if the mediation fails. Therefore, the result of an erroneous arbitration settlement mainly refers to an erroneous arbitral mediation and arbitral award, which can mainly be manifested in the following types of errors. One type is substantive error, which arises in two situations: first, in the case of an arbitral award following unsuccessful mediation, where the arbitrator has made an erroneous arbitral award due to an error in finding the facts or applying the law; and second, in the case of an arbitral mediation and award made pursuant to an arbitral agreement after successful mediation, where the mediation agreement is contrary to the principle of voluntary will, violates the mandatory provisions of laws and regulations, or where there is a false mediation that infringes on the interests of the state, society, or third parties. At present, the Chinese *Arbitration Law* does not provide for a procedure for the arbitral tribunal to conduct a substantive review of the mediation agreement, nor does it specify that the arbitral tribunal may refuse to produce a mediation or award based on the mediation agreement reached by the parties. The second is procedural error, which mainly includes jurisdictional error, such as in international commercial disputes, if the arbitral tribunal deals with the dispute as a non-arbitrable matter according to the law of the place of arbitration or the applicable law agreed by the parties, it is a jurisdictional error. Second, process errors, including the failure of an arbitrator or mediator to recuse himself or herself when he or she should have done so, showing corruption or favoritism in the process of resolving disputes, etc. Once again, there are errors of form, such as typographical errors, textual errors, calculation errors, etc. At present, the Chinese *Arbitration Law* only sets out three remedies for erroneous arbitral awards, namely, remedial arbitration, application for setting aside the award, and refusal of recognition and enforcement, but does not provide for remedies for erroneous arbitral mediations in the combination of arbitration and mediation, etc.

8.5 The Way Forward: Refinements and Breakthroughs in Combining Arbitration and Mediation in China

8.5.1 Enriching the Form of Combining Arbitration and Mediation and Setting Specific Operating Rules

The report of the 19th Party Congress pointed out that socialism with Chinese characteristics has entered a new era and the main conflict in Chinese society has been transformed into the conflict between the people's growing need for a better life and unequal and inadequate development. The change in the main conflicts in society is reflected in the level of dispute resolution, which is the conflict between the growing and diversified needs of the people for dispute resolutions and the unequal and inadequate development of dispute resolution resources. Especially in the context of the "One Belt One Road" cooperation initiative, China should adopt legislation and rules for arbitration and mediation institutions to recognize a variety of forms of combining arbitration and mediation, thereby meeting the diverse needs of the parties. While enriching the forms of combining arbitration and mediation, it is also necessary to stipulate specific rules for different forms of combining arbitration and mediation, including: first, establishing the legal effect of the agreement to combine arbitration and mediation; if the parties agree to choose the mode of mediation before arbitration, the parties are not entitled to apply for arbitration without mediation, Second, clearly stipulating the time and form of initiating the combination of arbitration and mediation, the selection of arbitrators and mediators, the conversion and termination of mediation and arbitration, the formulation and entry into force of the instruments combining arbitration and mediation. And, third, stipulating recusal, information disclosure, and confidentiality, etc. At present, the most credible and influential international arbitration rules on mediation and arbitration are the UNCITRAL Mediation Rules and the UNCITRAL Arbitration Rules respectively, therefore, countries may refer to these rules when setting up specific rules combining arbitration and mediation.

8.5.2 Strengthening Organizational Development and Nurturing Talent for Conflict Resolution

In terms of organizational development combining arbitration and mediation, the specialization and internationalization of arbitration and mediation organizations should be strengthened to enhance their ability to resolve disputes and their international influence. First, China needs to increase its support for commercial arbitration and mediation organizations at the legal and policy levels to help them overcome the policy barriers and institutional constraints they encounter in the process of development, and should focus on nurturing a few well-qualified arbitration and mediation organizations so that they can become internationally renowned "brands." It is instructive to note that, the *Opinions on the Establishment of International Commercial Dispute Settlement Mechanisms and Institutions for the Belt and Road* (hereafter referred to as the Opinions) clearly state that they support domestic arbitration institutions and mediation institutions that are qualified and have a good international reputation to carry out international commercial arbitration and mediation involving the Belt and Road. Arbitration and mediation organizations should also learn from the arbitration rules and mediation rules of internationally renowned arbitration and mediation organizations, in order to increase their own level of compliance with international standards.

Second, arbitration institutions and mediation organizations can sign cooperation agreements to establish a long-term and stable cooperation relationship in order to enhance the interface and cooperation between the two. In the model of mediation followed by arbitration, if the mediation organization succeeds in conciliating the case, it can, after obtaining the consent of the parties, directly refer the case to an arbitral institution with which it cooperates, which will produce an arbitral award according to the mediation agreement. If mediation fails, the mediation organization can suggest the parties choose an arbitral institution with which it cooperates for arbitration, so that the dispute can finally be resolved. In addition, qualified mediators from mediation organizations can become arbitrators in cooperative arbitration institutions and can perform the corresponding arbitration work in subsequent arbitration proceedings.

In the model of arbitration followed by mediation, if the parties do not wish to be mediated by an arbitrator, the arbitration institution may produce a roster of mediators for the parties to choose from, based on the cooperative mediation organizations. In addition, in the cultivation of complex dispute resolution talents, emphasis should be placed on the training of corresponding skills, so that arbitrators can learn how to channel, persuade, convince, and negotiate with the parties in their role as mediators; and mediators can master arbitration procedures and make arbitration awards neutrally and impartially; at the same time, scientific management of dispute resolution talents is also required, including licenses to practice, rating, reward and punishment mechanisms, and withdrawal mechanisms.

8.5.3 *Full Granting of Options to the Parties to Overcome Procedural Challenges*

Although the issue of the unification of the identity of the arbitrator and the mediator has been strongly challenged, as described above, there have been many attempts by rule-makers and researchers to overcome this challenge because of its many advantages, such as efficiency and speed. However, returning to the theoretical basis for the combination of arbitration and mediation, i.e., arbitration and mediation are both forms of dispute resolution with the attribute of autonomy, the decision as to whether the arbitrator and the mediator should be the same person should be left to the consensual choice of the parties, just as the Chinese Opinions have made respect for party autonomy a principle that should be followed in international commercial dispute resolution mechanisms. Specifically, if the parties do not wish to combine the identity of the arbitrator and the mediator, a different person should act as the mediator and the arbitrator. For example, some scholars have advocated that when a combination of arbitration and mediation is chosen for "One Belt One Road" disputes, the person involved in the mediation should not act as an arbitrator afterwards.[45] Specifically, first, the arbitration or mediation organization should inform the parties of the advantages and disadvantages of having the same person acting as arbitrator and mediator by means of an information letter or a detailed oral explanation.

Second, the parties should be allowed to jointly sign an agreement agreeing to have the same person act as arbitrator and mediator.

Third, at the level of institutional safeguards, the arbitration institution may establish a review committee to monitor the neutrality and impartiality of arbitrators who have participated in the mediation in the arbitration process. For example, CIETAC has formulated the "CIETAC Arbitrator Appointment Procedures Guidelines," "Rules for the Supervision of Cases," "Measures for the Management of Arbitrators within CIETAC (for trial implementation)," and "Measures for the Management of CIETAC Leavers," in order to strengthen supervision, discipline, and accountability, resolutely prevent the occurrence of related problems, effectively strengthen the supervision and management of arbitrators, and safeguard the independence and impartiality of case handling.[46]

Fourth, at the level of personnel security, a person of high reputation and professionalism should be chosen, hence the famous proverb in arbitration circles that "an arbitration is only as good as its arbitrator."

8.5.4 Improving Mechanisms for Redress of Erroneous Results

For the three types of errors that occur in the combination of arbitration and mediation, corresponding relief mechanisms can be put in place. The first mechanism is the relief for substantive errors in the combination of arbitration and mediation. It should be provided that the arbitral tribunal should review the legality of the mediation agreement and should have the right to refuse to produce an arbitral mediation or award based on a false mediation agreement. Second, the court's supervision of the results of erroneous arbitration and mediation combinations should be improved. The court should rule against the enforcement of an arbitration mediation or award made based on a false mediation agreement, and against an arbitration award made after the failure of mediation, if the facts found or the applicable law are deemed to be erroneous.

The second mechanism is the remedy for procedural errors in the combination of arbitration and mediation. The court can review *ex officio* the jurisdictional errors that arise in the combination of arbitration and mediation and rule that they are not enforceable. In the case of procedural errors in the process of combining arbitration and mediation, if an arbitral mediation or award is required to be made according to the mediation agreement, the arbitral tribunal may not make it after examination and the court may rule that it is not enforceable after examination. If the mediation fails and arbitration follows, the court may rule that the arbitral award is not enforceable after examination.

The last is a remedy for errors of form in the combination of arbitration and mediation. Both the arbitral mediation and the arbitral award should be subject to correction, and where the parties apply for correction, the arbitral tribunal should give the opposing party an opportunity to comment.

Notes

1 Unless otherwise stated, references to arbitration in this chapter refer to civil and commercial arbitration only.
2 The name of the organization went through the following changes: According to the Decision of the State Council of the Central People's Government on the Establishment of the Foreign Trade Arbitration Commission within the China Council for the Promotion of International Trade on May 6, 1954, the China Council for the Promotion of International Trade (CCPIT) organized the establishment of the Foreign Trade Arbitration Commission. In accordance with the Circular of the State Council of February 26, 1980 on Renaming the Foreign Trade Arbitration Commission as the Foreign Economic and Trade Arbitration Commission, the Foreign Trade Arbitration Commission was renamed as the Foreign Economic and Trade Arbitration Commission. According to the State Council's Reply on the Change of the Name of the Foreign Trade Arbitration Commission to the China International Economic and Trade Arbitration Commission and the Amendment of the Arbitration Rules dated June 21, 1988, the name of the Foreign Trade Arbitration Commission was changed to the China International Economic and Trade Arbitration Commission.
3 Article 37 of the Rules provides that:

> The Arbitration Commission and the Arbitration Tribunal may conduct mediation in the cases before them. In cases where a settlement agreement is reached through mediation, the arbitral tribunal shall render an award in accordance with the content of the settlement agreement between the parties.

4 Articles 51 and 52 of the Act contain more specific provisions on the conditions, modalities, effects and termination of mediation in arbitration.
5 Wang Chang: *The Theory and Practice of Combining Arbitration and Mediation* (Beijing: Law Press, 2001), pp. 106–111; Zhou Yang: *A Study of China's Arbitration and Mediation System* (Xiangtan: Xiangtan University Press, 2017), p. 17.
6 Luo Chuxiang: The Administrative Turn of Arbitration and its Overcoming, *Jiangxi Social Sciences*, 2012 (3).
7 Professor Qiang Shigong divides the study of the mediation system in the Shaanxi-Ganjiang-Ningxia period into two propositions: the cultural extension theory and the cultural rupture theory. The cultural extension theory considers mediation to be a manifestation and extension of the Confucian-influenced idea of "no litigation" in traditional Chinese law. See Qiang Shigong: *Mediation, Legal System and Modernity: A Study of the Chinese Mediation System* (Beijing: China Legal Publishing House, 2001), pp. 205–206.
8 Ibid., p. 205.
9 Wang Chang: *The Theory and Practice of Combining Arbitration and Mediation*, p. 307.
10 Ibid., pp. 292–293.
11 Zhang Xipo: *Ma Xiwu's Way of Trial* (Beijing: Law Press, 1983), pp. 22–25.
12 Takao Tanase: *Dispute Resolution and the Trial System*, trans. Wang Yaxin (Beijing: China University of Political Science and Law Press, 1994(, pp. 7–8.
13 Tang Houzhi: Is There an Expanded Culture that Favors Combining Arbitration with Mediation or Other ADR Procedures?, ICCA Congress Series no. 8, 2004, p. 101.

14 Composite dispute resolution is a way of categorizing dispute resolution mechanisms proposed by Professor Wang Changsheng, which refers to the organic combination of two or more dispute resolution methods. See Wang Changsheng: Research on the Combined System of Arbitration and Mediation, PhD thesis, University of International Business and Economics, 2001.
15 Hu Junhui and Zhao Yiyu: On the Use of Mediation in the Settlement of Commercial Disputes in "One Belt One Road," *Journal of South China University (Social Science Edition)*, 2018 (4).
16 Tang Houzhi, An Expanding Culture: Combining Arbitration with Mediation r with Alternative Dispute Resolution (ADR), *China Foreign Trade*, 2002 (2): 51–52.
17 See the World Intellectual Property Organization Mediation Rules. Available at: www.sipo.gov.cn/zcfg/gjty/1063146.htm (accessed November 25, 2018).
18 Wang Shengchang: *A Study on the Combined System of Arbitration and Mediation* (Beijing: Law Press, 2001), pp. 158–161.
19 Tang Houzhi: An Expanding Culture: Combining Arbitration with Mediation or with Alternative Dispute Resolution (ADR).
20 Singapore International Arbitration Act. Available at: https://wenku.baidu.com/view/ce39006bfe4733687e21aa4e.html (accessed November 25 2018).
21 Some scholars have suggested that this approach is closer to stand-alone or ad hoc mediation due to the possible temporal discontinuity between the mediation in execution and the finality of the arbitration. See Wang Shengchang: *A Study on the Combined System of Arbitration and Mediation*, p. 79.
22 Taniguchi Yasuhira: *Procedural Justice and Litigation*, trans, Wang Yaxin and Liu Rongjun (Beijing: China University of Political Science and Law Press, 2002), p. 384.
23 Tang Li: *Research on the Mechanism of Inducing Consent n Litigation Mediation* (Xiamen: Xiamen University Press, 2016), pp. 53–66.
24 Simon Roberts and Peng Wenhao: *The Dispute Resolution Process: ADR and the Main Forms of Decision Formation*, trans. Liu Zhewei, Li Jiajia, and Yu Chunlu (Beijing: Peking University Press, 2011), p. 397.
25 Gerald F. Phillips: Same-Neutral Med-Arb: What Does the Future Hold?, *Disputes Resolution Journal* (2005) (60) 24, 26.
26 Takao Shedrai: *Dispute Resolution and the Trial System* (Beijing: China University of Political Science and Law Press, 2004), pp. 84–99.
27 Simon Roberts and Peng Wenhao: *The Dispute Resolution Process: ADR and the Main Forms of Decision Formation*, p. 390.
28 Zhang Liping: Arbitration and Mediation System with Chinese Characteristics: Connotation, Basis and Advantages, in *Proceedings of the China Arbitration and Justice Forum and 2010 Annual Conference, 2010*, China Academy of Arbitration Law, China International Economic and Trade Arbitration Commission, China Maritime Arbitration Commission, Civil Division 4 of the Supreme People's Court, 2010.
29 Zhou Yang: *A Study of China's Arbitration and Mediation System* (Xiangtan: Xiangtan University Press, 2017), pp. 1–2.
30 www.bjac.org.cn/page/gybh/introduce_index.html (accessed November 10, 2018).
31 https://baike.baidu.com/item/China (Shanghai) Pilot Free Trade Zone Arbitration Court/12014616 (accessed November 10, 2018).

32 www.fabao365.com/news/698719.html (accessed November 10, 2018).
33 Zhou Yang: *A Study of China's Arbitration and Mediation System*, p. 35.
34 Li Shaoping: Efforts to Build A Diversified Dispute Resolution System with Chinese Characteristics, *People's Court Daily*, July 6, 2016, p. 5.
35 Huang Jin and Song Lianbin: Some Important Issues in International Civil and Commercial Dispute Resolution Mechanisms, *Political and Legal Forum*, 2009 (4): 4.
36 Tang Houzhi: Is There an Expanded Culture that Favors Combining Arbitration with Mediation or other ADR Procedures? p. 101. Wang Guiguo: The "Belt and Road" Strategic Dispute Resolution Mechanism, *China Law Review*, 2016 (2): 33–38.
37 Zhou Yang: *A Study of China's Arbitration and Mediation System*, p. 37.
38 Ibid. pp. 36–37.
39 Chu Beiping: The Present and Future of the Construction of the Multi-Dispute Settlement Center of the "Belt and Road," *Chinese Law*, 2017 (6): 72–90. Yuan Dasong and Zhang Zhiguo: The Construction of "One Belt One Road" in Stages and the Construction of Dispute Resolution Mechanism, *Journal of China University of Mining and Technology (Social Science Edition)*, 2018 (3): 14–27.
40 Mao Xiaofei: The Innovation of China's Commercial Arbitration System in the Context of the "Belt and Road" Initiative, *People's Rule of Law*, 2018 (2): 34.
41 Han Depei: *A New Treatise on Private International Law* (Wuhan: Wuhan University Press, 2000), p. 703.
42 Street Laurence: The Language of Alternative Dispute Resolution, *Australian Law Journal*, 1992 (66): 197.
43 For an analysis of the issue of court mediation as opposed to trial, see Li Hao: Mediations to Mediation, Trials to Trial: The Separation of Mediation and Trial in Civil Trials, *Chinese Law*, 2013 93): 5–18.
44 According to the "bilateral monopoly model" proposed by Posner, the minimum conditions or reserved price between the parties is called the effective scope of mediation, and the existence of this overlapping area is a necessary condition for mediation. See Richard A. Posner: *Economic Analysis of Law*, trans. Jiang Zhaokang (Beijing: China Encyclopedia Press, 1997), pp. 723–724.
45 Wang Guiguo: The "Belt and Road" Strategic Dispute Resolution Mechanism, *China Law Review*, 2016 (2): 37.
46 CIETAC's Operational Work Summary for 2017 and Operational Work Plan for 2018. Available at: www.cietac.org.cn/index.php?m=Article&a= show&id= 15193.

References

Chu Beiping: The Present and Future of the Construction of the Multi-Dispute Settlement Center of the "Belt and Road," *Chinese Law*, 2017 (6): 72–90.
Han Depei: *A New Treatise on Private International Law*, Wuhan: Wuhan University Press, 2000.
Hu Junhui and Zhao Yiyu: On the Use of Mediation in the Settlement of Commercial Disputes in "One Belt, One Road," *Journal of South China University (Social Science Edition)*, 2018 (4): 35–42.

Huang Jin and Song Lianbin: Some Important Issues in International Civil and Commercial Dispute Resolution Mechanisms, *Political and Legal Forum*, 2009 (4): 4.
Laurence, Street: The Language of Alternative Dispute Resolution, *Australian Law Journal*, 1992 (66): 197.
Li Hao: Mediations to Mediation, Trials to Trial: The Separation of Mediation and Trial in Civil Trials, *Chinese Law*, 2013 (3): 5–18.
Li Shaoping: Efforts to Build a Diversified Dispute Resolution System with Chinese Characteristics, People's Court Daily, July 6, 2016, p. 5.
Luo Chuxiang: The Administrative Turn of Arbitration and its Overcoming, *Jiangxi Social Sciences*, 2012 (3): 146–152.
Phillips, Gerald F.: Same-Neutral Med-Arb: What Does the Future Hold?, *Disputes Resolution Journal*, 2005 (60): 24, 26.
Posner, Richard A.: *Economic Analysis of Law*, trans. Jiang Zhaokang, Beijing@ China Encyclopedia Press, 1997.
Qiang Shigong: *Mediation, Legal System and Modernity: A Study of the Chinese Mediation System*, Beijing: China Legal Publishing House, 2001.
Roberts, Simon and Peng Wenhao: *The Dispute Resolution Process: ADR and the Main Forms of Decision Formation*, trans. Liu Zhewei, Li Jiajia, and Yu Chunlu, Beijing, Peking University Press, 2011.
Takao Shedrai: *Dispute Resolution and the Trial System*, Beijing: China University of Political Science and Law Press, 2004.
Tanase, Takao: *Dispute Resolution and the Trial System*, trans. Wang Yaxin, Beijing, China University of Political Science and Law Press, 1994, pp. 7–8.
Tang Houzhi: An Expanding Culture: Combining Arbitration with Mediation or with Alternative Dispute Resolution (ADR), *China Foreign Trade*, 2002 (2): 51.
Tang Houzhi: Is There an Expanded Culture that Favors Combining Arbitration with Mediation or Other ADR Procedures? ICCA Congress Series, No. 8, 2004.
Tang Li: *Research on the Mechanism f Inducing Consent in Litigation Mediation*, Xiamen: Xiamen University Press, 2016.
Taniguchi, Yasuhira: *Procedural Justice and Litigation*, trans. Wang Yaxin and Liu Rongjun, Beijing: China University of Political Science and Law Press, 2002.
Wang Chang: *The Theory and Practice of Combining Arbitration and Mediation*, Beijing: Law Press, 2001.
Wang Changsheng: Research on the Combined System of Arbitration and Mediation, PhD thesis, University of International Business and Economics, 2001.
Wang Guiguo: The "Belt and Road" Strategic Dispute Resolution Mechanism, *China Law Review*, 2016 (2): 37.
Wang Shengchang: *A Study on the Combined System of Arbitration and Mediation*, Beijing: Law Press, 2001.
Yuan Dasong and Zhang Zhiguo: The Construction of "One Belt One Road" in Stages and the Construction of Dispute Resolution Mechanism, *Journal of China University of Mining and Technology (Social Science Edition)*, 2018 (3): 14–27.
Zhang Liping: Arbitration and Mediation System with Chinese Characteristics: Connotation, Basis and Advantages, in *Proceedings of the China Arbitration and Justice Forum and 2010 Annual Conference,* 2010, China Academy of Arbitration

Law, China International Economic and Trade Arbitration Commission, China Maritime Arbitration Commission, Civil Division 4 of the Supreme People's Court, 2010.

Zhang Xipo: *Ma Xiwu's Way of Trial*, Beijing: Law Press, 1983.

Zhou Yang: *A Study of China's Arbitration and Mediation System*, Xiangtan: Xiangtan University Press, 2017.

9 Reinventing and Integrating the Mediation System

In the third wave of the global "proximity to justice" movement, the modernization of mediation in China is gradually lagging behind the late-blooming Western countries in the rule of law. While China's mediation system is still hobbling along on the crutches of public authority, the developed countries with the rule of law, represented by the United States, have already developed market-led mediation to a considerable degree of maturity. Of course, there are many reasons for the formation of two different mediation systems in China and the West, including the inheritance of historical traditions, differences in the concept of the rule of law, and the practical needs of political, economic, and social structures. Influenced by the institutional inertia of "path dependence," China's current mediation system is in a state of "chaos," manifested by the generalization of people's mediation, the mixing of court mediation and trial, the weakening of administrative mediation, and the blurred positioning between public interest and market-oriented, and between part-time and professional mediation. This chaotic state of affairs has led to the emergence of various new types of mediation organizations in practice, all of which have been labeled as "people's mediation," thus obscuring the institutional characteristics of pluralistic forms of social mediation, such as commercial mediation, industry mediation, and lawyer mediation, resulting in the legal positioning of official and unofficial mediation being unclear, which has seriously restricted the coordinated development of pluralistic forms of mediation and is not conducive to international exchange and cooperation in dispute resolution.

For a long time, people's mediation, administrative mediation, and litigation mediation in China have belonged to the policy-led mediation model driven by public power, which has been under attack and challenged in the fast-moving commercial society. While China's top-down mediation mechanisms have found it increasingly difficult to cope with the dispute resolution needs of the new era, and many theoretical dilemmas have emerged, the United States has successfully transformed mediation, an Eastern experience, into a socialized, market-oriented, and systematic dispute resolution mechanism, and has shown a flourishing scene, even frequently "exporting" its explored mediation science, techniques, and experience to China, the birthplace of mediation. The question of how to reshape China's modern mediation system in comparison is a fundamental prerequisite in the current reform and improvement of China's mediation system, especially in the process of formulating China's mediation law and even the *Law on the Promotion of Diversified Dispute Resolution*.

Modern mediation systems are diverse. This chapter will focus on the differences between various mediation systems, such as people's mediation, commercial mediation, industry mediation, lawyer mediation, and court mediation, in terms of their scope of action, mode of operation, and legal effects, and explore how we can treat various mediation systems as a mutually complementary and organically connected whole when building a modern mediation system, forming a state of benign interaction and competition with litigation and arbitration mechanisms, so that the current mediation mechanisms operating in various forms can achieve maximum effectiveness.

9.1 The Current State of China's Mediation System: A Single Policy-Led Mediation

At present, in addition to the parties' own reconciliation, China has built up a dispute resolution system based on litigation, mediation, and arbitration, with mediation mainly consisting of people's mediation, administrative mediation, and judicial mediation. Today, with the rapid development of the market economy, in order to resolve the increasing number of conflicts and disputes, the practical departments are constantly pushing the boundaries, from the "Trinity Mediation" to the "three kinds of mediation linkage" to the "Litigation and Mediation Docking," all reflecting the wisdom of the practical and decision-making departments and the importance they attach to the advantages of mediation. Although there are many types of mediation, they all belong to the same type of mediation, namely policy-led mediation, where public authorities are deeply involved and intervene extensively. Policy-led mediation is a top-down mediation model in which the public authorities issue policies and decrees based on the needs of the state. There are historical reasons and justifications for the formation of this model of mediation, which is distinctly different from the market-led mediation predominant in the West. Although it could play an irreplaceable role in the early stages of mediation institutionalization, as China enters a period of social transformation, this policy-led mediation alone is no longer able to meet the needs of the new era.

9.1.1 Characteristics of Policy-Led Mediation

9.1.1.1 The Public Authorities Are the Promoters and Enforcers of Mediation

In China's mediation system at this stage, public authorities, including party committees, administrative and judicial authorities, play an extremely important role. Whether it is people's mediation, administrative mediation, or judicial mediation, the leaders, promoters, and callers are all local and even central administrative and judicial organs, as well as other party and government organs. This is evident from the definition of mediation or Grand Mediation.[1] People's mediation was originally supposed to be carried out by people's mediation committees in self-governing organizations, but in practice it has given rise to various "innovative models" that are effectively hollowed out by the public authorities. It is worth considering whether mediation in China, which has a long history of several thousand years, can only be carried out under the "unified leadership of the party committee and government," "leading and coordinating by the comprehensive governance department of politics and law," "operational guidance by the judicial administration department," "the specific operation of mediation centers," and "joint participation by all functional departments." At a time when the rule of law is being built up, since mediation is a mechanism for resolving disputes that is different from litigation and is aimed at civil and commercial disputes that reflect the autonomy of the parties, is the strong intervention of the public authorities in line with the law of development of mediation?

Of course, the promotion and implementation of the mediation system by the public authorities are conducive to the formation of a complete top-down organizational system and its rapid implementation at the grass-roots level, as well as the provision of stable financial security and the full support of various departments, and even the enforcement of mediation results can be guaranteed by the coercive power of the state. However, public power is infinitely expansive and can easily be abused if it is not effectively monitored and controlled. In the field of mediation, where there is a serious lack of supervision and control mechanisms, the excessive involvement of public power will inevitably result in mediators "replacing" the voice of the parties, or even affecting the exercise of their right to appeal. In fact, this is a common occurrence in the mediation of mass incidents and cases involving lawsuits and petitions.

9.1.1.2 Mediation Has a Strong Administrative Dimension

In litigation, the parties and the adjudicator are not on an equal footing; in mediation, however, the mediator and the parties should be on an equal footing, otherwise voluntary will becomes an empty phrase. However, policy-driven mediation often results in the mediator acting as an "official" and appearing as an "authority figure" in front of the parties, and sometimes there are even scenes of "cadres" from different departments coming together to "work" on "civilian" clients. Such administrative mediation scenes cannot be found in market-led commercial mediation, but can only survive in policy-led mediation. The administrative aspects of policy-led mediation are mainly manifested as follows.

First, mediation is an administrative task for mediators. At the macro level, mediation has been given a difficult political task from the outset, and the political significance is clearly more important to policy-makers than its dispute resolution role. From a micro perspective, mediation has become a specific administrative task for mediators. Under the pressure of various assessment indicators (such as the number of cases concluded and the fulfillment rate of agreements), mediators tend to focus only on the quantity of work, while inadvertently neglecting the quality of dispute resolution, making it difficult to serve the legitimate rights and interests of the parties.

Second, policies and decrees are the basis for mediators to carry out their mediation work. Based on the need to maintain social stability and resolve social conflicts, as well as their understanding of the mediation system itself, policy-makers have formulated a series of policies and issued a series of orders, which then form the basis for the various mediation explorations carried out by the practical sector, as well as the operational guidelines for grass-roots mediation practitioners. As most grass-roots mediators hold public office, they are bound to obey these policies and orders in their mediation work. However, unlike litigation, which is governed by the law, mediation is often based on ethics, morality, customs, and practices. Mediators who also hold public office are often influenced by an administrative law enforcement mindset and apply too many of the rigid elements of the law to mediation. In addition, the complexity and diversity of real cases require a flexible and adaptable mediation mechanism, while the rigidity inherent in policy decrees of general application will lead to difficulties in policy-led mediation.

Once again, forced mediation in disguise has become the norm. The bureaucratization of the mediator team and its administrative mindset put the parties in the position of being managed, while the mediator becomes a "mediation officer." In mediation, the deterrent effect of the "mediation officer" on the parties, as well as the asymmetrical legal knowledge and case information available to both parties, provide the conditions for forced or disguised forced mediation. As Takao Tanase says:

> In cases where the mediator is in the upper echelons of society in relation to the parties, or where the parties are financially dependent on the mediator, the mediation proposal put forward by the mediator carries non-negligible weight for the parties.[2]

This quote aptly describes the relational construct of policy-led mediation.

9.1.1.3 The Parties Are Reduced to the Object of the Dispute and Lack Subjectivity

Unlike litigation, mediation is strongly intersubjective in nature. The principle of voluntary will of the parties should be given primary and full respect in the mediation process, but at this stage of mediation policy, the operation of the mediation mechanism is mostly dedicated to persuading the parties to accept mediation and its outcome, rather than guiding them to spontaneously choose or seek a win-win solution to their disputes. As mentioned above, it is not uncommon for several public authorities to jointly "work" on the parties in the context of an ambitious, linked mediation mechanism.

In a policy-led mediation system, mediation is a powerful tool for policymakers to maintain social stability and resolve social conflicts, and a good diversion strategy for courts and other dispute resolution bodies to reduce the pressure on their caseloads, acting as both a "pressure-reducing valve" and a "fire extinguisher." However, what are the expectations of the parties, whose legal rights and interests are tied to the success or failure of mediation? It seems that the voice of the parties and potential parties is always so weak that their procedural subjectivity is not fully manifested and the autonomy and voluntary will of the parties are often not guaranteed. Under this model of mediation with a strong public authority, the parties and the public as potential parties to the dispute are invisibly objectified and symbolized. This also lays the groundwork for a low rate of voluntary compliance with mediation agreements and the recurrence of conflicts in the future.

9.1.1.4 Both the Cultural Transmission and Professionalization of Mediation Are Difficult

At present, the results of grass-roots mediation in China are mostly reflected in the form of indicators such as the number and proportion of cases settled, while the building of a mediation culture is nothing more than having a few separate offices or mediation courts, arranged in the layout of a trial court or a round table, with proverbs such as "Rhymes of Persuasion and Peace" posted on the walls, in order to serve the higher-ups in their research visits to the grass-roots and for press coverage and publicity. However, a real mediation culture, such as the standardized summary and transmission of mediation experience and skills, the promotion and dissemination of the superiority of mediation, and the professional research and teaching of the scientific laws and principles of mediation, has not been effective. This also reflects the fact that under policy-led mediation, mediation work is just one of the daily trivial administrative tasks. After meeting the requirements and completing the tasks, mediators lack the enthusiasm and motivation to devote themselves to the cause of mediation and to explore and study mediation culture in depth.

In addition, policy-led mediation requires the establishment of a complete top-down mediation organization system, which is spread too widely, and with limited state funding, many grass-roots people's mediation organizations are in an embarrassing situation where both mediators and funding are in short supply. There is an irreconcilable tension between the professional requirements of judges and the professional standards of mediators in court mediation. As a result, the professionalization of mediators in terms of selection, standards of practice, training, rewards and punishments, supervision, and so on, is in a difficult state.

9.1.2 Processes and Causes of Policy-Led Mediation

Mediation, as a civil dispute resolution mechanism, did not start out with a strong administrative dimension. China's policy-driven mediation system has undergone a process of an "administrative turn" of dispute resolution mechanisms. For example, in the areas where the Yi people live, there has been a shift from traditional Yi customary mediation to socialist people's mediation.[3] Before it was transformed into "people's mediation for the people," residents voluntarily chose respected "Deku" to carry out paid mediation according to custom, which was later transformed into "people's mediation" because it was considered to have "certain flaws." "Deku Mediation" is required to follow the spirit of the law and mediate according to the law; not to charge intermediate mediation fees and to implement pro bono mediation to reflect the service nature of people's mediation; to change the previous form of verbal agreement and to produce standardized mediation documents for the record of the village mediation committee after successful mediation, and to respond to cases according to the law. The "Deku Mediation" is a classic example of the "administrative turn" of the civil dispute mediation profession, which started as a crude private paid mediation and turned into a policy-led mediation. The incorporation of civil mediation has made it possible to unify primitive and unregulated mediation practices, eliminating the application of barbaric and backward customs that could easily infringe on the legal rights of the parties, and to provide members of society at different levels with a network of inexpensive and local dispute resolution methods while popularizing national laws and regulations. However, this "administrative turn" has also led to the gradual disappearance of traditional folk mediation rules, experience, and techniques, which have been handed down through history, as they are subject to the adjustment of laws and policies. The formation of a policy-driven mediation system is due to a few factors.

First, policy-led mediation is due to the state's need to implement government orders, strengthen social control, and maintain social stability. China is a large multi-ethnic country with a large population and uneven development in different regions, making it difficult to popularize and implement laws and policies. Therefore, strengthening the leadership of the Party in China is the most fundamental guarantee for the construction of the rule of law. The party committee plays a central role in overseeing the overall situation and coordinating all parties. The political advantage of central leadership and the active promotion of party committees at all levels are the key to the effectiveness of grass-roots mediation in China, especially people's mediation. Under the political system of "party-government domination," the prerequisite for the implementation of laws, regulations, and policies formulated by the state is the propagation, interpretation, and implementation of these decrees through effective channels, and the widely distributed villages, neighborhood committees and industrial and mining enterprises are precisely at the end of the net for the implementation of the decrees, so undoubtedly the best way to propagate and interpret the laws and policies formulated by the state is through the mediation organizations set up at the end of these nets and apply them to the resolution of conflicts and disputes.

At the same time, villages, neighborhood committees, and industrial and mining enterprises are the smallest units of social control, and maintaining general harmony and stability in social life at these grass-roots levels is also the basis for achieving harmony and stability in society. A policy-led mediation system can help the state to achieve timely control and handling of conflicts at the grass-roots level, and can maintain social stability at the grass-roots level to the greatest extent possible, so that conflicts and disputes can be absorbed at the very end of social management. This is most evident in people's mediation. Although people's mediation committees are mass organizations established by law to mediate civil disputes, as they are generally set up in village committees and neighborhood committees according to administrative divisions, the way they are created, their organizational structure, guiding bodies, and funding sources are all subject to obvious administrative influences and have a high degree of consistency with the administrative hierarchy.

Second, policy-led mediation adapts to the need for dispute resolution in a village-type social structure. Chinese society has been a rural-type society with a predominantly rural population for a long time, where social relations are mainly composed of acquaintances. In a society of acquaintances, mediation has a obvious advantage over other dispute resolution mechanisms because ethics and local customs constitute the source of authority for resolving conflicts and disputes, and because the personal prestige and charisma of the mediator can play an important role in the resolution of disputes. Unlike the urban society of strangers, rural societies are also more stable in terms of the type and number of conflicts and disputes, conditions that are favorable for the role of public intervention mediation, which has limited resources. However, the relative stability of the type and number of disputes may in turn lead to a lack of motivation to improve the quality of service, as mediators do not need to pursue refinement and specialization in their work.

In addition, the use of public authority is also required to promote the institutionalization and standardization of mediation. Whether it is the alternative dispute resolution (ADR) movement, that has since taken over in the United States, or the various mediation linkage mechanisms in China, it is an important function of mediation to reduce and divert the "litigation explosion" faced by the courts. However, at the early stage of institutionalization and standardization of mediation, it was only possible to bring parties and society at large, who were used to taking their disputes to court, into the mediation process rather than flocking to the courts, through macro-regulation, wide publicity, and advocacy by the state through policy decrees. In fact, even ADR in the US would hardly have gained the momentum it has today if it had been driven by social forces alone rather than supported by the courts, the federal government, and most state governments. Thus, policy-led mediation has advantages that market-led mediation does not have.

Although policy-led mediation will continue to function effectively for a long period of time, as China continues to build the rule of law and a market economy, and as society undergoes an accelerated transformation, mediation under public authority, as a "visible hand" with macroeconomic regulation, will also have to meet challenges from all sides. If the policy-oriented approach is maintained and the public authority is allowed to intervene excessively, China's mediation system will inevitably be unable to adapt to the needs of dispute resolution in the new era, and may even lose its voice in the international mediation arena.

9.2 Challenges to Policy-Led Mediation

It is commonly believed that China is in a period of social transition, but there is no common understanding of the exact definition and characteristics of the transition period. In this regard, in the writings of Chinese sociologists, there are three main understandings: (1) it refers to the transformation of the economic system; (2) it refers to the change of social structure, including structural transformation, institutional transformation, adjustment of interests, and change of concepts; and (3) it refers to the change of social form, i.e., "social change and development from traditional society to modern society, from agricultural society to industrial society, from closed society to open society."[4] Some scholars believe that it also includes the transformation from a monolithic society to a pluralistic society.[5]

We believe that social transformation is a rather general concept with different connotations in different disciplinary fields and different contexts. The political field, the economic field, the field of international relations, etc. all have their own unique formulation of social transformation and focus of research. And in the field of dispute resolution, it naturally also presents the corresponding characteristics of the transition period. The discussion of dispute resolution mechanisms during the period of social transformation should include the transformation of dispute subjects, the transformation of dispute types, the transformation of dispute resolvers, the transformation of dispute resolution concepts, and the transformation of dispute resolution work mechanisms. It can be said that all the above aspects pose serious challenges to the current single policy-driven mediation system in China.

9.2.1 Transformation of the Subject of Dispute

The challenges to the existing mediation system during the social transition period are first manifested in the subject of disputes. According to data released by the National Bureau of Statistics in 2018, the urbanization rate of China's resident population was 59.98 percent at the end of 2018. i.e., the resident population in urban areas exceeded the resident population in rural areas. This indicates that China has ended the era of being a predominantly rural society and has entered a new urban era with a predominantly urban society. Today, China's rural areas are no longer a self-sufficient smallholder economy; the lives of Chinese peasants are now connected to the cities and they have become part of the modern industrial and commercial society. Many peasants have moved into the cities, either as migrant workers or as city dwellers. Most peasants are no longer tied to the land as they were in the past, but have been swept up in the tide of China's market economy. As a result, today China has become a "market China" and the "vernacular society" has become a "society of semi-acquaintances," and interpersonal relations have become more rationalized and are even moving toward a "society of strangers." "The fate of the peasants in contemporary rural China has become more linked to the market, to the modern nation-state and even indirectly to globalization."[6] As a consequence, the relationships between the parties to disputes have changed from one of acquaintances in the rural society to one of strangers in the urban era, and the ties that bind interpersonal relationships have changed from those of kinship and ethics to those of economic interests. At the same time, the emphasis on respect for the individuals has brought about a plurality of values and conflicting needs, and the "citizenship" process of the rural population moving to the city has inevitably been accompanied by a proliferation of new types of conflicts and disputes, all of which have posed challenges to the single policy-led mediation.

First, there is a fundamental change in the basis of trust in the mediator by the parties to the dispute. In a rural society, the parties to a dispute and the mediator are often in the same relationship circle and are familiar with each other, and through years of mediation, the mediator has built up a personal prestige that is well known to the public. This personal authority is more likely to win the trust of the parties, and the basis for this trust often exists before the dispute arises. In urban societies, however, the mobility of the population and the structure of strangers in the city itself diminish the scope for such personal authority. The trust of the parties to a dispute, who are strangers to each other, can only be built up gradually as the mediation process unfolds. This places greater demands on the mediator's professional skills, psychological qualities, and general qualities.

Second, the increased legal awareness and access to information of the parties to disputes have gradually rendered disguised mandatory mediation ineffective. The "main battlefield" of policy-led mediation is located at the grass-roots level, especially in rural societies, and in the past, it was mostly aimed at parties with little legal awareness and insufficient information about their cases. As a result of the overall improvement in the level of education for all, the exchange of information brought about by population mobility and the widening of access to legal knowledge in the information age, parties have become more aware of the need to defend their legitimate rights and interests in accordance with the law after a dispute has arisen, and various forms of compulsory mediation will eventually lose their usefulness.

Third, the increase in the number of types of dispute subjects calls for a pluralistic mediation system. The subjects of cases entering various mediation mechanisms are no longer limited to natural persons versus natural persons, but disputes between natural persons and legal persons, and between legal persons and legal persons are also beginning to seek mediation solutions. In addition, disputes between foreign companies and Chinese companies, such as the Proview and Apple disputes,[7] have also begun to be resolved through mediation. The increasing number of disputes between superiors and subordinates, between students and schools, between civil servants and their units, and academic disputes also reflect the complexity and diversity of the types of subjects in dispute. In response to the different types of subjects, it should not and cannot be solved by a single administrative mediation, but should accordingly develop commercial mediation, professional mediation, and various internal mediations to meet these challenges.

9.2.2 Change in Types of Disputes

The change that occurs between the types of disputes and the types of subject matter of the dispute remains essentially the same, but the types of subject matter of the dispute emphasize the impact on the dispute resolution mechanism because the parties to the dispute are in a special position, have a special relationship with each other, or have a unique trade nature. The types of disputes emphasize the content of the subject matter of the dispute, the legal relationship. There is, however, no absolute dividing line between the two.

First, there has been a proliferation of group disputes. Group disputes are more likely to occur and more difficult to deal with during a period of social transition, and their group nature includes not only cases where one party is multiple, but also cases where both parties are multiple. In China's current judicial environment, it is more reasonable to resolve group incidents through mediation than litigation. However, as most mediators in policy-led mediation come from public authorities, and mediation is often conducted by one or more public authorities, the public, as parties, can easily turn to the government or courts represented by the mediator in the event of a deadlock or flawed mediation. At the same time, due to the lack of neutral social mediation organizations and the fact that most of the disputed matters in group disputes are related to public services, public interests, and public policies, and mostly involve public authorities, if a mediation organization set up by the same public authority and a mediator who also holds a state public office handle the dispute, even if they are not at the same level or belong to the same system, it is inevitable that the neutrality of the parties and the public will be questioned.

Second, professional mediation is needed for industrial disputes. In the process of social transformation, these cases involving professional issues are on the rise both in terms of type and number, and it has become difficult to rely on existing grass-roots people's mediation, administrative mediation, and court mediation to cope with them, and even mediation by trade organizations is often challenged for its neutrality due to its administrative overtones. Taking medical disputes as an example, Beijing took the lead in piloting medical dispute mediation as early as 2005, setting up the Beijing Health Law Society Medical Dispute Mediation Center and the Beijing Medical Education Association Medical Dispute Coordination Center. However, as the two mediation bodies are affiliated with the health system and the insurance industry respectively, their stance is often questioned by patients.[8]

Third, new types of disputes require openness in the mediation system. Another characteristic of the types of disputes in the transition period is the emergence of new types of disputes, for example, in the area of e-commerce in China, 58,613 complaints were received from e-commerce users nationwide in the first half of 2012 alone, with an average of 320 e-commerce disputes occurring every day.[9] However, these e-commerce disputes face the following problems:

> high litigation costs, geographical distances, vast differences in language and culture, difficulties in applying the law, complex jurisdictional determinations, and recognition and enforcement of judgments, with the result that traditional litigation is quite overwhelmed in the face of such complex disputes in cyberspace,[10]

This is even more so through policy-led mediation with limited resources. If these disputes are not resolved in a timely manner, the development of e-commerce will be discouraged. This is where a new type of "Online Dispute Resolution" (ODR) comes into being, and has long been used in Europe and the USA.

In addition to e-commerce disputes, online infringement disputes and public figure disputes, which have been frequently reported in the press in recent years, are also new types of disputes, and the mediation and handling of these cases are quite different from traditional types of cases. This requires China's mediation system to break away from the monolithic policy-driven mediation pattern and establish a pluralistic and open mediation system in accordance with the realities of dispute development.

9.2.3 Change in the Concept of Dispute Resolution

In a period of social transformation where the commodity economy is developing at a rapid pace and dispute resolution mechanisms are becoming increasingly diversified, in order to make mediation stand out from litigation and arbitration and become the preferred mechanism for parties to resolve disputes, it is necessary to change the concept of mediation work, which is mainly reflected in two aspects of the objectives and structure of mediation.

First, the shift from sharing the "cake" to making the "cake" bigger. Under policy-led mediation, "the case is settled" reflects the proper resolution of the dispute, and the task of mediation is thus completed. The goal of mediation is fundamentally the same as that of court litigation, in that it seeks to restore a sense of order to life and repair fractured social relations, which is also related to the rural social structure of mainly acquaintance-based relationships. As the aim of this type of mediation is to settle disputes and settle cases, its focus is on the investigation of facts that occurred in the past, with an eye on the past and looking backward, and its looking forward is limited. In the case of economic disputes, for example, the outcome of the mediation is the intermediate distribution of the available benefits, which in the end is a process of "cutting the cake." In the process of transitioning from a planned economy to a market economy, it has gradually become apparent that relying on litigation or traditional mediation to resolve disputes not only fails to ensure that the "cake" in dispute is properly divided, but also leaves little left after the limited "cake" is cut due to the costs of the dispute resolution mechanism itself, i.e., the costs of dispute resolution are not commensurate with the benefits.

By shifting the concept of mediation from simply "cutting the cake" to trying to "make the cake bigger" through mediation, i.e. by appropriately pursuing the forward-looking and win-win effects of mediation outcomes, rather than just working on resolving immediate disputes, a virtuous cycle of "dispute resolution + value-added benefits → highlighting the comparative advantages of mediation → favored by the parties → prosperous mediation profession → higher levels of dispute mediation" can be achieved. As litigation can only legally adjudicate on the legal facts and legal relationships in dispute and cannot consider the full range of interests and relationships, and arbitration is limited by arbitration agreements and the ability to arbitrate, the most feasible way to carry the concept of mutually beneficial dispute resolution is through a new type of mediation. Once again, this places new demands on the division of labor and the specialization of mediators. In this regard, the American model of mediation is an example to be followed, as will be discussed in more detail later.

Second, the change from "management" mediation to "service-oriented" mediation, with the parties being restored as the subject of mediation. As mentioned above, the existing mediation system is tasked with maintaining social stability and strengthening social control, and mediation is seen as a means of social management. Although the slogan of mediation is "serving the people," in practice, the concept of "management" permeates the entire process of mediation. Specifically, the lack of sufficient procedural discretion for the parties, the difficulty of guaranteeing the voluntary nature of the parties and the principle of confidentiality, and the proliferation of forced mediation in disguise are all phenomena that are characteristic of "managed mediation."

We believe that if the typical civil litigation construct, i.e., the status and interrelationship between the court and the parties, is an isosceles triangle (Figure 9.1, left), then the mediation construct, i.e., the status and interrelationship between the mediator and the parties, should be a straight line through three points (Figure 9.1, right).

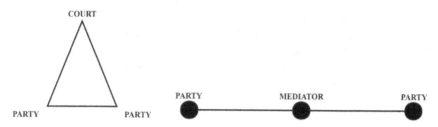

Figure 9.1 The typical civil litigation construct and the mediation construct.

In essence, mediation is a form of dispute resolution that fully reflects the autonomy of the parties' intentions, and the mediator's mediation of disputes must be conducted in accordance with the principle of the parties' voluntary will. The parties have the right to decide, of their own independent will, whether to accept, discontinue, or abandon the mediation, and to decide to accept or not to accept a certain mediation agreement option, if it does not violate the mandatory provisions of the law and does not infringe the public interest or the legitimate rights and interests of others. Reducing mediation to the dispute resolution mechanism itself, mediation is a legal service provided by society to the parties as distinct from litigation, i.e., mediation is a legal product that can be purchased, either for a fee or for free, in the same way as arbitration, notarization, and lawyers' services. Even pro bono mediation is a public legal service provided by the state for the taxpayer. The mediator's role is at best a guide, an assessor, and a servant, and should not become a controller, a manager, or even a decision-maker; otherwise, ills such as forced mediation in disguise will never be eradicated.

Contrary to the unequal status of the parties and the judge in a lawsuit, the mediator and the parties should be fully equal subjects of the proceedings and should not present themselves as "mediation officers." The respect for the individual in a period of social transformation is becoming more and more important, and accordingly, the subjectivity of the parties is becoming more urgent. Mediation should be a service-oriented mediation, rather than an administrative policy-oriented mediation, in order to highlight the subjectivity of the parties in mediation.

9.2.4 The Plight of Dispute Resolvers

First, dispute resolvers are faced with the dilemma of having too many cases, too few staff, and too little money. As seen above, the change in the subject matter of disputes, the type of disputes, and the concept of dispute resolution all point to an increase in the demands on dispute resolvers. In fact, the increase in disputes during the social transition period itself has overwhelmed the existing mediation system. Under policy-led mediation, the problem of insufficient mediation capacity is becoming more serious due to administrative staffing constraints, and the lack of financial security is also limiting the function of mediation. The shortage of manpower in township judicial offices is already a common problem in the national judicial administration system, with many judicial offices having only one judicial assistant in charge of the mediation work of the whole township all year round. The leader of one of the county judicial bureaus in our field research said frankly: "There are not enough mediators to deal with petitioners, so where is the time to study how to improve the quality of mediation work and their own quality?"

Unlike public security, procurator services, and courts, which can only be activated after conflicts have intensified, mediation can be initiated at the best time to resolve conflicts, i.e., during the budding, fermenting, and growing stages of disputes, in order to play a role in stopping disputes from escalating, but the above dilemma makes grass-roots mediation a distraction. A veteran judicial chief we interviewed was enthusiastic about grass-roots mediation work, but when talking about his working conditions, he poured out his grievances:

> Every time I receive a case, I have to ride my own scooter and pay for my own gas to go to the countryside to mediate, and it is difficult to get reimbursed afterwards; there is no recording or video equipment in the office, and the most basic forensic tools are not available, so once the dispute is unsuccessfully mediated and goes to litigation, evidence becomes a big problem. This is a big problem. This is indeed a far cry from the configuration of police stations and people's courts at the same level, and is even more incompatible with the social management role that mediation plays and is supposed to play, which will ultimately discourage the work of grass-roots mediation organizations. In recent years, many university graduates have come to work in townships. They are under enormous pressure to survive, and if even basic funding and conditions are difficult to secure, they will fall into a vicious cycle of "funding shortage – brain drain – declining performance – reduced funding."

In addition, due to the difficult conditions, newcomers are reluctant to stay, while veteran mediators are not promoted for years due to their establishment or age. Without the injection of new blood, mediators in grass-roots mediation organizations generally appear to be aging.

Second, there is a general lack of professional training for mediators. As mentioned above, the various changes that have taken place during the transition period require mediators to have not only the ability to judge legally, but also to understand the specialized field involved in the case, and they must have certain social psychological skills to be able to guide rather than order the parties to think in the same direction in a timely manner, and ultimately to try to achieve a win-win situation. In the author's view, mediators who conform to the modern concept of mediation should receive at least the following training in order to meet the needs of resolving conflicts and disputes in the new era:

- mastering basic legal expertise;
- being familiar with the principles and practices of mediation;
- understanding the laws and essentials of extra-judicial dispute resolution mechanisms;
- having good interpersonal and communication skills;
- possessing strong psychological qualities;
- having a certain understanding of sociology, psychology, economics, and other disciplines;
- being well-trained in practical operation and various dispute resolution techniques;
- having a certain grasp of dispute development trends.

This requires not only that the mediators themselves continue to enhance their learning to improve their case handling skills and quality, but also that they undergo the necessary training on a regular basis. However, the integrity of the existing pool of mediators is a major problem, not to mention the time taken to undergo training, and the question of who should be trained, what should be taught, and how should they be assessed has not yet been put on the agenda.

Third, the professionalization of mediators has been slow to take off. As s a separate profession, mediators are supposed to have their own system of professionalization standards, such as the classification of mediators into grades, selection mechanisms, examination and recruitment procedures, supervision mechanisms, exit mechanisms, association organizations, etc. However, mediators in policy-led mediation either come from the masses and are purely supernumerary, or they are public employees and are subject to the administrative personnel system, making it difficult to start the process of professionalization. In the public security, procurator courts, and court organs, there are ranks, and even though it is difficult for their staff to move up the administrative hierarchy, through hard work they can move up the ranks and receive improvements in pay and benefits, which in turn increases their sense of professional honor and motivation to work. However, for most mediators at the grass-roots level, this is a luxury because, after years of struggle, if they are not promoted to the administrative level, even their salaries stay at the same place, which shows a serious lack of incentives for mediators and a long way to go in terms of professionalism.

9.2.5 Low Confidence of Legislators in Dispute Resolution Mechanisms

The biggest problem faced by mediation is the validity of mediation agreements, which is rooted in the legislators' lack of confidence in the mediation mechanism. At this stage, there are four main dispute resolution mechanisms in China: litigation, arbitration, mediation, and conciliation (reconciliation). The adjudicative documents obtained through litigation and the arbitral awards obtained through arbitration are legally enforceable, while the agreements reached through mediation are merely contractual in nature. If judicial supervision of arbitration is "double supervision," then judicial intervention in mediation is "full supervision." This is mainly reflected in the system of judicial confirmation of mediation agreements.

Since 2009, when the Supreme People's Court began to explore judicial confirmation procedures in its *Opinions on Establishing and Improving Mechanism for the Resolution of Conflicts and Disputes between Litigation and Non-litigation*, to the *People's Mediation Law*, which came into force on 1 January 2011, which clearly stipulates that parties may apply for judicial confirmation of agreements reached through mediation, to the *Civil Procedure Law*, amended and adopted in August 2012, which provides for a special section on "Confirmation of Mediation Agreements" and clearly stipulates the procedures and legal consequences of parties applying for judicial confirmation of mediation agreements, all reflect the fact that, in the view of the legislator, it seems that mediation is not a reliable mechanism for resolving disputes, that mediators in general are not yet trusted, and that ultimately judicial review and confirmation are required to "safely" make mediation agreements enforceable. How does the judicial confirmation process work in practice at the grass-roots level? According to our field research, a popular phrase can be used to express this: "The ideal is rich, but the reality is sluggish." The judicial confirmation mechanism is not popular with the courts and mediation organizations, and is virtually "dormant" and "frozen."[11]

It is worth considering whether a mediation agreement reached by a mediator who has worked with the parties based on voluntary and legal principles must be judicially confirmed by the court in order to be considered "valid." Why not directly give the mediation agreement an enforceable effect? In our opinion, the fact that arbitral awards are given enforceability, while conciliation agreements must be judicially confirmed, reflects the legislators' distrust of the conciliation mechanism and the quality of conciliators, as if the quality of judges and arbitrators is much higher than that of conciliators, and as if the content of conciliation agreements is always unreliable. If in-depth and extensive research had been carried out, I believe that such a biased misunderstanding would easily have been dispelled. Mediation differs from litigation in that the latter is governed by law and based on facts, and ultimately upholds the public order of the state and society; whereas the scope of mediation itself excludes the types of cases that have an impact on the state and social order, and it settles disputes mainly between private parties, with the core aim of resolving conflicts through reconciliation between the two parties, with at best an additional mediator presiding over the case, compared to the reconciliation mechanism. Since the value objectives and principles of action of mediation and litigation are obviously different, and the mediation agreement itself reached through mediation, one form of dispute resolution mechanisms, has the nature of a contract, and the contract law has already provided for the circumstances in which the contract is invalid, why can't mediation agreements, that do not violate mandatory legal norms and do not infringe on public interests and the legitimate rights and interests of others, be given enforcement effect? The legislator's lack of confidence in mediation leads to its ineffectiveness, which ultimately makes it less attractive to the parties. From the standpoint of the parties, how can mediation compete with authoritative litigation and efficient and professional arbitration, and become the dispute resolution method that the parties are happy to choose on their own initiative? In other words, in a market economy where efficiency is paramount, how to "sell" mediation as a dispute resolution method to the parties in dispute and potential parties, so that the benefits of mediation are deeply rooted in people's hearts and minds, and the parties prefer mediation to resolve their conflicts after a dispute has occurred, has become an important issue in reforming the mediation system in the new era.

9.3 The Other Side of the Story: Insights from Mediation in the United States

There are several countries in the world where ADR is relatively developed and mature. The reason why we chose the American mediation system as a reference is not to deny the value of other systems in other countries and regions for China to learn from, but based on the fact that the American mediation model has formed a complete system of teaching, theory, and practice. Also, it has exported its advanced and complete system of mediation concepts and skills to China many times in recent years, to many mediation practitioners, including policy-making departments including the Supreme Court, several research institutes including the author's unit, and grass-roots people's mediators. Scholars and practitioners in China, the birthplace of mediation, are often initially skeptical and dismissive of the importing of American mediation culture, but as various training and exchanges progress, they become more certain of the experience and philosophy brought by their counterparts across the ocean and its value for China.

9.3.1 The Pluralistic Mediation System in the United States

In the United States, mediation was not accepted from the outset. The key to the recognition, support, and even advocacy of mediation in American society and justice, and its continuous development and prosperity, lies in the fact that mediation has a mechanism for the parties to resolve their own disputes, and the parties can play a more active and subjective role in dispute resolution. In the United States, mediation has gone through the following landmark stages of development: (1) in the early twentieth century, in order to resolve the social unrest caused by the labor movement, the federal government set up special labor mediators, and in 1947, the Federal Mediation and Conciliation Service (FMCS) was established to specifically mediate labor disputes, and labor mediation is the prototype of the modern American mediation system; (2) in the 1960s, drawing on the former mediation experience, mediation became an alternative way to resolve prison riots; (3) in the 1980s, the business and legal communities began to use early ADR to resolve commercial disputes, and the International Association for Dispute Resolution Center for Public Research (CPR) was formed, committing itself to prioritizing the use of ADR in disputes involving its members before litigation, while at the same time mediation became a recognized profession; (4) by the 1990s, federal legislation required federal agencies to use ADR to resolve disputes with citizens, one of the most common methods being mediation; (5) entering the twenty-first century, all state courts have some form of mediation, which parties can choose as an alternative to litigation and many different models have been developed. And for specific types of disputes, such as those involving divorce or custody cases, mediation has become a major form of dispute resolution.[12]

The American mediation system today is diverse, with a vibrant variety of governmental or private, pro bono or commercial, court-based, or court-transferred mediation programs, but there are three main types of mediation that are relatively similar in form, philosophy, and technique to those in China.[13]

The first type of mediation is community mediation. Community mediation in the United States is like people's mediation in China. It is a public service provided to citizens in the community,[14] and its mediators are mostly volunteers from law schools, lawyers, arbitration institutions, retired judges, and other professional fields who provide dispute resolution services on a pro bono basis. There are many of these non-governmental, non-profit civic community mediation agencies throughout the United States. In addition to providing dispute resolution services, community mediation can also serve as an important platform for novice mediators to train as interns, so that mediation is often conducted jointly by two mediators.

In the United States, regardless of the type of mediation, there is a strong emphasis on the principle of voluntary will and the parties can apply to stop the mediation at any time of their own free will, and can decide to change mediators or abandon the mediation at any time by challenging the neutrality of the mediator without fear of facing an adverse judgment if they do not continue with the mediation. At the same time, neutrality and confidentiality are minimum ethical requirements for mediators, and although mediators are appointed directly by the community mediation body and the parties do not generally have a choice as to who acts as mediator, they can apply for a change of mediator if they have doubts about the neutrality of a mediator. As the community mediator is neither a judge nor a government official, and has no public authority, the parties can simply request a change of mediator or refuse to mediate if they believe that the mediator is not neutral enough or is deceptive, and the reasons for this are confidential, as is the whole process of mediation, and such a change of mediator or abandonment of mediation will not have any adverse effect on the parties. It is also unlikely that a scene like the one in Chinese people's mediation, where multiple parties join forces to "work" on the parties, will be staged.

Community mediated settlements are generally not agreed upon in the form of a contract, but rather as a "Memorandum of Understanding," i.e., a non-legally binding commitment by both parties based on good faith and morality, which, in order to be legally valid, must be sought in court for civil judicial confirmation.

The second type of mediation is court-affiliated mediation. Court-affiliated mediators are either from the court staff or work with civil mediation organizations recognized by the courts. However, unlike Chinese court-affiliated mediation, the mediators in court-affiliated mediation in the United States are usually not the judges hearing the same case, mainly due to considerations of judge neutrality. In court-affiliated mediation, the court has a roster of mediators for assignment to the parties and must ensure that the mediator assigned to the parties is neutral and that there is a monitoring mechanism to ensure that the mediator does not play favorites or take sides. For example, parties can raise a complaint with the court's complaints department or the judge specializing in mediation supervision if they find that the mediator is biased, not neutral, or even apparently untrained. If a mediator is the subject of repeated complaints, he or she will be dealt with accordingly, for example, by being removed from the roster of mediators.

Many district courts also work with various private mediation organizations to refer cases that have been brought to the court but are suitable for mediation to social mediation organizations. The mediation agreement reached becomes a legally binding contract and the parties simply must comply with the terms of the signed agreement without having to return to court. However, in cases involving public interest, such as custody of minors, even if a mediation agreement is reached, the case must go back to court for judicial review. If one of the parties fails to perform the mediation agreement or performs in default, and the other party takes the case to court, the court only needs to review whether the agreement is legal in form, such as whether the parties have suffered threats and whether they are mentally impaired. Mediation agreements that have been reviewed for legality will generally be upheld by the court and the parties will be ordered to perform the agreement.

The third category is for-profit commercial private mediation agencies, such as the well-known JAMS,[15] whose main clients are companies and individuals who have the financial means to afford mediation. This type of for-profit mediation agency reduces mediation services to a commodity that competes in the marketplace and is guided by the laws of the marketplace, with the parties enjoying a high degree of subjectivity and voluntary will as clients or consumers of mediation services. As the United States is caught in a litigation explosion, the delays and high costs of litigation increasingly give commercial mediation a "comparative advantage," for example, mediation adheres to the principles of voluntary will, confidentiality, efficiency, low cost, and a win-win situation, and is highly suited to the needs of the parties, especially those in the commercial field. As a result, commercial mediation has flourished in the United States, with many mediators earning more than lawyers in the same paid legal services industry.[16]

It is worth learning that the reduction of mediation to a legal commodity or service, and the permeation of the "customer is God" credo in the provision of quality dispute resolution services to the parties, are not unique to commercial mediation, as this market-led mediation philosophy can be said to permeate the entire US mediation system, including community mediation and court-directed mediation programs, probably due to the highly developed commodity economy and contractual culture in the US. What is most lacking in China's policy-driven mediation system is precisely this spirit and philosophy of service-oriented mediation. If it is integrated with China's philosophy of service-oriented government and social management innovation, the existing shortcomings of mediation will be eradicated.

9.3.2 Characteristics of the Operation of Mediation in the United States: Market-Led

9.3.2.1 The Parties' Status as Procedural Subjects Is Fully Manifested, Making Mediation More Attractive

The United States is a society that emphasizes respect for the individual, and its mediation system has made the voluntary will of the parties a primary principle. In for-profit commercial mediation, the parties are the consumers of the mediation service, the "customers are considered God," and the recognition and respect of the parties' subjectivity in the mediation are undoubtedly the basis for winning their trust. Therefore, the parties and their lawyers can choose whether to accept the mediation, and they can also choose the specific mediator to mediate.

The most important manifestation of respect for the subjectivity of the parties is that, when faced with parties in dispute, mediators usually do not do the work of persuasion, convincing or suggesting how to solve the problem. Instead, they use various techniques including jurisprudence, psychology, and sociology from different perspectives, or even with the help of mediation venues, jokes, and games, to guide the parties to free themselves from anger and resistance and to think spontaneously in a direction conducive to dispute resolution. Most mediators do not even initiate a mediation proposal, but guide the parties step-by-step to come up with as many reasonable solutions to their disputes as possible on their own. This commitment to dialogue between the parties and their spontaneous dispute resolution, with the mediator acting as a passive and neutral "facilitator." is crucial to the subsequent implementation of the mediation agreement. The process and the agreement reflect the genuine free will of the parties to the greatest extent possible, rather than the mediator's own brainstorming of reasons and persuasive tactics..

Respect for the parties is also reflected in adherence to the principle of confidentiality. Many of the cases that come to mediation are contractual disputes between companies, or reputational or financial conflicts between individuals, and an important reason why parties choose mediation over litigation is the preservation of trade secrets, personal privacy, and good reputation. In the United States, a mediator's adherence to the principle of confidentiality is almost absolute, for example, if a party in a mediation does not wish to continue with the mediation, it is a confidential matter as to who initiates the termination of the mediation; furthermore, the mediator has a strict right to refuse to testify in any other legal proceedings involving a case after the mediator has participated in the mediation of that case. Of course, in recent years, the United States has created exceptions to the principle of confidentiality for extreme cases. Strict adherence to the principle of confidentiality builds trust in the mediator and allows the parties to feel that the mediation is "safer" than litigation in terms of protecting privacy and confidentiality. In fact, once mediation becomes a "safe haven" for the parties, it will attract more disputes to mediation than other dispute resolution mechanisms.

In many cases, therefore, rather than "accepting mediation," the parties have weighed their options and "shopped around" for a mediation service that offers better overall value for money to resolve their disputes and protect their rights.

9.3.2.2 The Driving Force Behind the Prosperity of the Mediation Market Is the Alignment of the Interests of All Parties

While China's policy-driven mediation system has been built and widely implemented mainly through the macro-regulation of the state's coercive power, the prosperity of the American "mediation market," especially commercial mediation, is mainly due to the laws of the market economy and the pursuit of economic interests by all parties to the mediation system. For the parties, the choice of mediation over litigation is itself the result of a consideration of the benefits of dispute resolution costs, as frequent delays in litigation and high financial costs are dilemmas facing justice in various countries today, and mediation is precisely a low-cost dispute resolution mechanism. Furthermore, as litigation is primarily a process of distributing existing benefits, a "cake-cutting" process, and is influenced by jury and evidentiary systems, it is often difficult to achieve substantive justice in the outcome, whereas the process of mediation usually involves many factors that may not be involved in litigation but are closely related to the creation and resolution of disputes, and it seeks to build a harmonious relationship that creates more value for both parties than just the distribution of the limited benefits that remain. As a result, mediation has the advantage of preserving or even adding value that is not possible in litigation. The pursuit of greater and more long-term benefits for both parties is obviously more attractive than insisting on immediate formal fairness, so mediation, especially commercial mediation, is attracting more and more customers, who choose mediation over litigation in the first instance after a dispute has arisen.

As mediation reduces costs for the parties and may even increase the value of the "cake," it satisfies the parties' quest for profit; in turn, because of the parties' trust and willingness to accept mediation, the mediation institution also thrives and achieves its own profit. The greater the role played by mediation, the better the dispute resolution, the less pressure on the courts to receive cases and the more orderly the country is stabilized, so that, at a macro level, the interests of the parties, the mediation body, and the state and the courts all grow.

At the same time, a competitive relationship will be formed among mediation organizations and mediators. The best mediators and mediation companies will stand out through the market law of survival of the fittest because they are able to provide better quality mediation services, and will be able to carry out more in-depth exploration and practice in the field of specialization and professionalization in mediation, which in turn will contribute to the progress of the mediation profession.

9.3.2.3 Market-Led Mediation Contributes to the Specialization and Professionalization of Mediation

Perhaps it is in the pursuit of profit that the specialization and professionalization of mediation are increasingly valued by mediation practitioners and researchers in the United States. In the United States, although there are no national norms governing the professional qualifications and training of mediators, broadly similar rules have been established in each state or each court. Some courts will require a mediator to have a relevant professional background in a particular mediation case. In family court, for example, the chief judge may require that the mediator handling these family disputes has a background in family law or experience as a social worker.

Professional licensing is not currently required to work as a mediator, and there is usually no professional certification examination or uniform training component. Generally, 40 hours of basic training are sufficient to work as a mediator, but the experience and the visibility of the individual mediator are crucial to his or her ability to conduct the practice of mediation. Although the training mechanisms for mediators are not yet well developed, there are different requirements for mediators than for other legal professional groups. For example, when retired judges join private mediation firms like JAMS as mediators, one of the first tasks of the firm is to train these senior judges in mediation and help them to switch from a judge's trial mindset to a mediator's mindset.[17] It is evident that in the United States, mediators have a strong sense of professionalism and are committed to establishing values and professional standards that are unique from those of lawyers and judges.

9.3.2.4 The Vigorous Development of Commercial Mediation Has Led to the Prosperity of the Mediation Culture

As mentioned earlier, commercial mediation has flourished in the United States. As commercial mediation is a for-profit market practice, the fluidity of the market and strong mergers allow for a high degree of mobility of mediation talent, while allowing for the transmission and proliferation of different mediation experiences and skills. In order to maximize profitability, mediation institutions need an adequate pool of mediators, which requires senior mediators to pass on their accumulated mediation experience to newly recruited mediators. Unlike the situation of learning and passing on experience under policy-led mediation in China, commercial mediation in the United States allows for the active replication and expansion of mediation experience and skills, as well as continuous improvement and enhancement.

In addition, due to the booming mediation market, mediation has become a compulsory course in some law schools and an elective in many law schools, and training courses in mediation skills are even offered in primary and secondary schools. University mediation courses are typically one semester long, with classes held once or twice a week. Mediation courses in American law schools are highly practical, and most mediation trainers have extensive hands-on experience as part-time mediators in various mediation agencies. In this teaching environment, the career orientation of many young law school students after graduation is to join a well-known mediation agency.

Unlike China, where the study of mediation is still confined to superficial issues such as why mediation, whether mediation should be conducted, and who should mediate, the study of mediation in the United States has focused on such in-depth and interdisciplinary issues as professional ethics in mediation, the principle of confidentiality and its exceptions, the neutrality of judges under court-affiliated mediation, the intersection of mediation and psychology, and the impact of brain neuroscience on mediation. The degree of refinement of mediation research in the United States has far surpassed that of China, the birthplace of mediation.

9.3.3 Implications of Market-Led Mediation for China

First, market-led mediation can provide inexhaustible impetus for the healthy and orderly development of mediation. The demands placed on dispute resolution by social transformation include not only the establishment of adequate resolution mechanisms and means, but also the healthy and orderly development of dispute resolution mechanisms. In other words, the construction of dispute resolution mechanisms must conform to their intrinsic laws and principles. Mediation is originally a social remedy mechanism distinct from litigation and is primarily designed to resolve private disputes between parties, whose subjectivity must be fully respected. Market-led mediation differs from policy-led mediation in that it emphasizes the parties' own initiative in resolving their disputes, so that disputes can be resolved to the greatest extent possible in accordance with the parties' wishes, and is a more thorough "settlement of the case." Moreover, mediation agreements reached through market-led mediation are more likely to be fulfilled and can also lead to new harmonious social relations. At the same time, depending on the market demand for the type and quantity of mediation, the development of the market for mediation services can be adjusted to avoid the waste of resources and blindness caused by excessive intervention by public power.

Second, market-led mediation can meet the diversified value demands for dispute resolution mechanisms during the social transition period. Where there is a demand, there is a market, and the degree of development and specialization of market-led mediation is basically in line with the demand for social disputes. While policy-makers have not yet seen the new situation and needs of disputes, or have not yet had time to develop universal norms, market-led mediation has already gone into action instantly and explored a mediation mechanism to meet them. For example, the ODR online dispute resolution mechanism for e-commerce disputes was initially explored by some privately owned and privately operated websites in response to the new demand for dispute resolution in the internet era.[18] I am afraid that if we rely entirely on the government to formulate policies and regulations to promote it, we will lag behind considerably. In addition, the inclusive and open nature of market-led mediation allows the courts, arbitration, and other mechanisms to interface with mediation and develop forms of mediation that can be applied to different case scenarios.

Once again, market-led mediation is in line with modern mediation concepts. The core concept of market-led mediation lies in the respect for the subjectivity of the parties, emphasizing the importance of guiding them to spontaneously seek a harmonious solution to their disputes and to play a key role in mediation of their own volition, rather than placing the responsibility of mediation on the persuasive skills and means of the mediator. As the parties are the consumers of mediation services, mediation must adhere to the principles of neutrality, voluntary will, and confidentiality, and treat the parties in dispute with an attitude of service rather than management and control, in order to gain their acceptance and trust, so that the mediation institution can increase its profitability.

Finally, market-led mediation does not exclude the necessary policy regulation. Just as the establishment and development of a market economy do not exclude the macro-regulation of the state, market-led mediation itself needs the support of the judiciary, as well as being regulated by policies and laws when necessary. For example, any mediation must not violate the mandatory provisions of the law, infringe on public interests, or the legitimate rights and interests of others; the business activities of commercial mediation institutions should comply with the relevant regulations on market competition and corporate governance; and cases involving public order and disposition of interests, such as the protection of minors and the rights and interests of vulnerable groups, should be subject to mandatory review by the courts, etc.

9.4 Reinvention and Integration of China's Mediation System

The achievements of 40 years of reform and opening-up in building a market economy and the rule of law, as well as the current pattern of mediation that has developed, have equipped China to transform and reshape the existing mediation system. Based on the above analysis of the current situation of China's mediation system and the challenges of social transformation it faces, and with reference to the advanced practices of other countries, China's mediation system can be reshaped in three ways: updating the concept of mediation, transforming policy-led people's mediation, administrative mediation, and court mediation, and vigorously developing market-led commercial mediation.

9.4.1 Renewing the Concept of Mediation

The prerequisite for transforming the mediation system mechanically is to update the existing concept of mediation, or even to innovate the concept of mediation in the light of China's national conditions and worldwide trends in mediation. In summary, the main points are as follows.

First, the subjectivity of the parties should be respected, and the concept of people-oriented should be implemented in mediation. In the author's view, the flourishing development of mediation in the United States has given us important insights, namely that in mediation, we should raise our awareness of service, respect the rights of individuals, respect pluralistic values, and aim to protect the legitimate rights and interests of the parties and satisfy the demands of both parties to the greatest extent possible, without over-emphasizing the political utility and social control effect of mediation. At the same time, it is also necessary to liberate mediators, train mediators of a high standard, and commit to fully and effectively mobilizing the initiative of the parties, guiding them to spontaneously seek appropriate solutions to disputes and replace confrontation with cooperation.

Second, it is important to focus on the forward-looking nature of mediation and create win-win mediation outcomes. Disputes are a disruption of existing social relationships, and scientific dispute resolution mechanisms not only can repair broken relationships, but also can build new and more positive social relationships. A modern mediation system should not only deal with the facts of disputes that have occurred in the past, but also help the parties to look to the future, to see both the "crisis" and the "opportunity" in the crisis of social relations; it should not only avoid the reduction of the parties' interests as a result of mediation, but also aim to preserve and increase the value of the parties' interests. It is important not only to avoid the reduction of the interests of the parties as a result of mediation, but also to preserve and increase the value of their interests.

Third, it is important to keep the mediation system open and encourage the exploration of new types of mediation. Both China in social transition and the world with its rapidly changing technology face the same problem, that is, the development of dispute resolution mechanisms can never catch up with the growth in the number and types of disputes, just as the gap between medicine and disease is ever present. This calls for letting private mediation go, breaking the administrative nature of dispute resolution mechanisms, reducing the interference of public power in mediation, and encouraging the exploration of various new types of mediation mechanisms, for example, by drawing on the US model of commercial mediation, to support the growth of the mediation market.

Fourth, mediation should be given an independent institutional status and a unique authority over the mediation system and mediators should be established. Like arbitration, the "paternalistic care" of mediation by the judiciary will not only defeat the value of mediation, but will also hinder its healthy growth and maturity. If mediation is to become an effective mechanism for social management innovation, and to truly divert and reduce the pressure on the judiciary and resolve disputes for society, its independent institutional status must be recognized and maintained, and its unique authority and effectiveness recognized from the top down, with mediation agreements being given enforceability under normal circumstances.

9.4.2 Reinventing Traditional Mediation

Although people's mediation, administrative mediation, and judicial mediation are all policy-led mediation, and in practice there are many unsatisfactory problems, they are not without value and if they can be adapted to suit its strength and weaknesses, they will be able to play an ideal role.

9.4.2.1 Consolidating People's Mediation

People's mediation is the most important part of the mediation system, carrying out the multiple missions of implementing national laws and policies, resolving conflicts and disputes at the grass-roots level, and maintaining social stability, and providing most of the society members with a local, inexpensive, and effective dispute resolution service. However, as mentioned above, people's mediation has not been given due attention for a long time. The key to transforming traditional mediation lies in solidifying people's mediation and ensuring that it gives full play to its role.

First, the team of people's mediators should be strengthened and fresh blood should be injected. The restrictions imposed on grass-roots mediators by the administrative establishment can be addressed through a ranking plan, so that mediators can concentrate on their mediation career and are no longer reluctant to take root in mediation because of the lack of "upward mobility," and can also reduce the brain drain of senior mediators and attract more young people to join the ranks of mediators.

Second, it is necessary to provide material security for people's mediation work and establish an incentive mechanism. The financial investment and material support for people's mediation work should at least correspond to the needs and effectiveness of their work, and the motivation and sense of responsibility of grass-roots mediators should be mobilized through the establishment of an incentive mechanism.

Third, the training of people's mediators should be strengthened to improve the overall quality of mediators. The limited legal expertise of people's mediators has led to major flaws in mediation agreements, which have often been denied judicial confirmation by the courts, indicating that mediators cannot be relied upon to improve the quality of their work in their spare time, but that regular training in mediation is required to meet the needs of dispute resolution in the new circumstances.

Fourth, a judicial review system of mediation agreements should replace the judicial confirmation mechanism and give legal effect to mediation agreements. The main obstacle to the work of people's mediation is the validity of mediation agreements, as agreements reached by people's mediation organizations are not enforceable and must be judicially confirmed by the courts before they can be considered "finally valid," which not only causes a waste of resources and discourages people's mediation, but also increases the burden on the parties. In fact, if the mediation conforms to the principles of voluntary will and legality, and the parties have genuinely participated in the process and approved the outcome of the mediation, it is only right to give legal effect to the agreements reached by this independent dispute resolution mechanism. On the question of how to give legal effect to mediation agreements, some scholars suggest that "the only feasible way is to submit mediation agreements directly to judicial review,"[19] i.e. after reaching a mediation agreement, the parties can apply to the court for judicial review if they have any objections, and the court can summon both parties and the mediator to verify the legality of the mediation process and the agreement, and after verification, the mediation agreement should be given the same legal effect as a judgment. In our view, judicial review and judicial confirmation of mediation agreements are different institutional designs. In terms of the effect of judicial review or confirmation on a mediation agreement, the latter is an element of validity, while the former is more of a cause of invalidity. The existing judicial confirmation mechanism is that a mediation agreement is not enforceable without judicial confirmation and can only rely on the parties' conscious performance, which gives the parties the opportunity to renege at any time; whereas if judicial review (formal review) of a mediation agreement is implemented, similar to the system of annulment of an arbitral award, the mediation agreement must be enforced as long as the parties have not filed a judicial review with the court. If the court reviews the mediation process or the content of the mediation agreement and considers it unlawful, it becomes an exception to the enforcement of the mediation agreement, thus not only giving legal effect to the people's mediation agreement, but also greatly reducing the chances of the case going back to court for trial and providing a strong monitoring mechanism for mediations that do contain errors.

In fact, internationally, the Convention on International Conciliation Agreements Arising from Mediation (which is known as the Singapore Convention on Mediation), adopted by the United Nations Commission on International Trade Law (UNCITRAL) at its 51st session in 2018, requires, for the enforcement of a settlement agreement: (1) The settlement agreement signed by the parties; (2) Evidence that the settlement agreement resulted from mediation, such as: (i) the mediator's signature on the settlement agreement; (ii) document signed by the mediator indicating that the mediation was carried out; (iii) n attestation by the institution that administered the mediation; or (iv) in the absence of (i), (ii), or (iii), any other evidence acceptable to the competent authority. In the light of the Singapore Convention on Mediation, judicial confirmation by the courts is not required to confer enforceability on a cross-border conciliation agreement.

9.4.2.2 Regulating Administrative Mediation

Compared with people's mediation and court mediation, administrative mediation is carried out by administrative organs with a wide range of legal authority and a high degree of flexibility in terms of policy, and is also in line with Chinese cultural traditions and people's psychological need for "official authority." Therefore, if it can be combined with modern administrative concepts and make full use of administrative means, proper administrative mediation will certainly become an effective dispute resolution mechanism. However, at present, there are many "chaotic" aspects of administrative mediation in China that need to be regulated.

First, the legislative norms on administrative mediation should be cleaned up and unified. According to the incomplete statistics of scholars, there are nearly 40 laws, about 60 administrative regulations, about 18 administrative rules, about 70 local regulations, about 45 local rules, and many general normative documents involving administrative mediation in China.[20] In fact, the chaotic legislative situation has also led to disorder and disproportionate implementation. Some scholars have summarized the current situation of administrative mediation in China as "three mosts": (1) most administrative organs have the function of mediating disputes; (2) most of the mediation functions of government organs are not obligatory; and (3) most of the results of administrative mediation are not enforceable.[21] This has caused a large number of cases that have been mediated administratively to flood back into the courts, and the significance of the establishment of administrative mediation has been greatly diminished. The consolidation of the effect of administrative mediation should start from the clarification of the mediation function of the administrative organs. The administration in accordance with the law and the unity of power and responsibility are the basic guidelines of administrative behavior, and the administrative organs should not be given the mediation function in a general and ambiguous manner. In the author's view, the *Administrative Mediation Law* should be formulated in a unified manner (or regulated in a unified *Mediation Law*), corresponding to the *People's Mediation Law*, to provide for the nature, tasks, and principles of administrative mediation, the organizational form of administrative mediation, and the selection, duties, and division of labor of administrative mediators, and the procedures and effectiveness of administrative mediation in the form of laws, so as to provide a unified institutional guarantee for administrative mediation and achieve standardization in the legislation.

Second, the principle of modesty of administrative mediation should be established. The principle of modesty in administrative mediation mainly lies in the restriction of the types of disputes to which it applies and the intervention procedures. In the author's view, the current administrative mediation work is not too wide and the types of disputes that can be mediated by administrative organs should be limited, and administrative organs should be more cautious in intervening in disputes as mediators. The reason is that, as a dispute resolution procedure that reflects the free will of the parties to the maximum extent possible, mediation should avoid the influence of third parties' will as far as possible, to facilitate the final and genuine resolution of conflicts. For different mediation mechanisms, the factors and degree of third-party influence are different. People's mediation, commercial mediation and other social mediation mechanisms bring in the least third-party influence factors and the least degree of influence, and the will of the parties is most fully manifested, while administrative mediation has significant third-party factors due to the unequal procedural status of the mediator and the parties, and lacks the rigid procedures and internal and external supervision mechanisms of judicial mediation, which may affect the subjectivity and voluntary will of the parties. When administrative public power encounters civil private rights, the unrestrained public power will inevitably squeeze the space of private rights. Therefore, for general civil disputes, it is not advisable to mediate through administrative organs unless both parties jointly choose to do so. At the same time, in terms of intervention procedures, if social mediation means have not been exhausted, priority should generally be given to social mediation mechanisms such as people's mediation and commercial mediation, which can save administrative resources and at the same time prevent administrative organs from interfering with civil activities by virtue of their public powers.

Once again, the principle of neutrality of administrative mediation must be ensured and a system of departmental recusal must be established. In the modern concept of mediation, the neutrality of mediators is an unquestionable "iron law," and the difficulty of guaranteeing neutrality is the main problem of administrative mediation in China at present. In practice, administrative organs often form joint mediation forces with people's mediation organizations, courts, and other public authorities to mediate group cases, such as disputes over land acquisition and relocation, medical accident disputes, property disputes, environmental pollution cases, etc. As these disputes often involve social public interests, government public policies and conflicts between administrative subjects and administrative counterparts, the administrative organ itself or other administrative subjects are already a party to the dispute or at least an interested party in these cases, and if the administrative organ, which is also the government, is to mediate, it is difficult to escape the suspicion of favoritism. In addition, many foreign companies are particularly sensitive to this in some disputes between government and business. It should be noted that different administrative departments also have different levels of neutrality, for example, public security and civil affairs departments mediate some civil disputes in accordance with the law and have relatively little at stake, while natural resources, urban construction, and health departments mediate land use, land acquisition, and demolition, and medical disputes, which often have varying degrees of interest to themselves, and their "departmental neutrality" is often questioned. Therefore, a system of departmental recusal should be established for disputes involving or having a stake in the department, and mediation should instead be carried out by a neutral, specialized mediation organization.

Finally, the practice of disguised compulsory mediation must also be eliminated. China's thousands of years of feudal society and bureaucracy have led to a fear of officials and a respect for them that are difficult to eradicate in the short term, and the administrative authorities seem to be happy to exploit this social psychology by using various disguised means of compulsory mediation. It is in the shadow of this fear or respect of officials that the parties in many cases compromise and reach a mediation agreement. The outcome of such mediation is prone to suffer a backlash, as the parties do not willingly fulfill the mediation agreement, thus making it difficult to completely resolve the dispute. Therefore, the transformation of administrative mediation requires a real change in the concept of law enforcement, respecting individuals, and parties with the requirements of a service-oriented government, mediating for those that can be mediated, not forcing mediation, and establishing a mechanism for parties to apply for relief against disguised forced mediation.

9.4.2.3 Reforming Court Mediation

Today, the implementation of mediation in China's courts is in full swing, and the 2012 amendment to the *Civil Procedure Law* has further strengthened the strength and breadth of mediation work in the courts, with systems such as prior mediation and pre-court mediation being established. However, scholars have failed to pay sufficient attention to the overheating of court mediation, and the negative impact of court mediation should not be underestimated.

The main issue to be addressed in reforming court mediation is whether to separate mediation from trial or to combine mediation with trial. We believe that mediation by the courts meets society's need for dispute resolution, and that even the US courts, which emphasize procedural fairness, have mediation attached to them, but the first problem facing court mediation is how to ensure the neutrality of the mediating judge.

In the United States, it is also a controversial issue whether a judge may mediate a case at the request of the parties when they believe that the judge knows the facts of the case best and believes that the judge can deal with the case fairly. Many civil cases in the United States are now no longer subject to jury trials, which requires the judge to both find the facts and adjudicate. Most judges and scholars agree that some of the information a judge learns during mediation can affect his or her impartiality in subsequent trials, so most American judges will not hear a case after they have mediated it. Even if a judge does manage to remain unaffected by information from the mediation, it is difficult for the parties and the public to trust that the judge will still maintain his or her previous neutrality.

Due to the inherent nature of the Chinese judicial system, the neutrality of judges is interfered with by a variety of factors. If a judge is allowed to mediate before or during a lawsuit, and continues to act as the trial judge in the case afterwards once the mediation fails, his or her inner conviction and neutrality will certainly be affected. Therefore, the transformation of court mediation is mainly the establishment of a mediation system separate from the trial.

First, there must be separation of personnel. The court may conduct mediation and may give its mediation instruments the same effect as those of judicial decisions, but the court's mediators must be separated from the adjudicators. The court should establish an independent team of mediators, and the recruitment criteria for mediators should be different from those for adjudicators. Any mediation conducted after entering the court should be conducted by the court mediator in accordance with the principles of equality, voluntary will, and confidentiality. If the parties do not accept mediation or mediation fails, it should then be referred to the adjudicator for an independent hearing. Mediators should be disciplined for disclosing confidential mediation matters to the adjudicator.

Second, it is important to achieve procedural separation. Litigation is, after all, the core work of the courts, and mediation is only an initiative to facilitate the parties and relieve the pressure of litigation, which should not be delayed and negatively affected in order to achieve the work targets of mediation. Therefore, the mediation process and the litigation process should be separated into "two lines," i.e., when the case is brought to court, before the trial, the mediation court can introduce the advantages and disadvantages of mediation and litigation to the parties and guide them to resolve their disputes through mediation. If the parties choose to mediate, the mediation will be conducted by the mediation chamber, but if the parties refuse to mediate or decide to abandon mediation in the process of mediation, the case will be heard in litigation. Once a party has opted for litigation, its options for dispute resolution mechanisms in the courts have been exhausted and it is no longer allowed to apply to return from the trial process to the mediation process, even if it realizes that the outcome may be unfavorable to it, but rather the parties can only reconcile themselves or seek mediation from social mediation organizations. Only in this way can the rigidity and authority of the proceedings be ensured, so that the quality of the trial and the administration of justice will not be affected by the prolonged mediation without resolution and pressing mediation with judgments.

Finally, there should be a higher demand for professionalism in court mediation. As the court represents the public power of the state in resolving disputes, agreements reached through court-led mediation are enforceable and, in general, court mediation is a final dispute resolution mechanism, it is necessary to establish a high standard of mediators, and the examination and recruitment, training and assessment, and supervision of mediators should be even stricter than that of judges. This is because trial judges only need to hear the facts of the case and apply the law, whereas mediators must not only be well versed in legal expertise and deal with the legal relationships involved in disputes, but also take into account other relationships that give rise to the disputes, and social factors, psychological factors, and customs and traditions, making full use of psychology, sociology, jurisprudence, and other techniques to guide the parties from confrontation to cooperation, therefore, the complexity of mediation work has largely surpassed that of trial work.

9.4.3 Integration of Mediation Systems

In China's current mediation system, people's mediation is a free, public-spirited civil mediation, which is financially supported and guaranteed by the state public treasury. If commercial mediation, industrial mediation, and mediation by lawyers are generalized to people's mediation, all regarded as a free and unpaid dispute resolution service, without establishing an incentive mechanism for mediators, this will seriously restrict the development of China's social mediation system. For this reason, the development of social mediation in China must take a differentiated path. While upholding the public interest attribute of people's mediation, the market-oriented operation of commercial mediation, industrial mediation and lawyer mediation should be supported and encouraged, as the market mechanism is an important path to nurture social mediation toward maturity. The legal relationships involved in modern commercial disputes are complex and the subject matter of litigation is large, but parties often demonstrate a high ability and willingness to pay if the mediation organization can provide high quality mediation services. Therefore, encouraging social mediation organizations to charge for mediation in specific areas is in line with the market law of "whoever uses it, pays for it,"

282 Reinventing and Integrating the Mediation System

which can attract top talents with professional knowledge to participate in the dispute resolution service industry, as well as improve the quality and effectiveness of mediation through market competition, cultivate high-quality and low-priced mediation service products, and promote a balance between supply and demand in the dispute resolution market. As the market for social mediation services in China is still in its infancy, local governments should, in accordance with local conditions, promptly introduce preferential and supportive policies such as simplified procedures and tax exemptions, encourage social forces to participate in dispute resolution by actively purchasing dispute resolution services from social mediation organizations, to promote the transformation of social mediation from a government-led to a socially autonomous one.[22] For China, where urbanization is accelerating, the development of new types of mediation is mainly through market mechanisms and vigorous development of commercial mediation and mediation in other professional fields. As the construction of China's market economy continues to progress, the rule of law environment continues to improve, conflicts and disputes are increasing, and the task of maintaining social stability remains daunting, instead of spending a large amount of public resources to promote mediation from the top down, it is better to give full play to the role of the laws of the market, to marketize and commercialize mediation, and to allow mediation to develop and grow in the same way as lawyers' services and arbitration. Only in this way can the comparative advantages and role of mediation be truly exploited.

In fact, policy-makers have also seen the inevitable trend of commercialization and socialization of mediation and have allowed pilot exploration of commercial mediation. For example, the *General Program on Expanding the Pilot Program of Reforming the Conflict Resolution Mechanism by Bridging Litigation and Non-litigation*, issued by the Supreme People's Court in 2012, has given policy support to the development of commercial mediation, proposing that "pilot courts should support commercial mediation organizations, industrial mediation organizations or other organizations with mediation functions to carry out their work," and that:

> The pilot courts should actively communicate and coordinate with relevant government departments, or through other appropriate means, to explore the implementation of paid services for mediators. Except for full-time court mediators, enrolled administrative mediators and people's mediators who do not charge mediation fees, other enrolled special invited mediation organizations or special invited mediators may provide paid services.

Although the document is only an exploratory proposal for the court's litigation-mediation docking mechanism, it is encouraging as it alludes to the trend toward the construction and development of commercial mediation.

In summary, we believe that while the development of China's mediation system is moving toward pluralism, it should also focus on the integration and development of different types of mediation. In other words, while consolidating the traditional advantages of policy-led mediation, it is also necessary to actively develop society-led mediation and market-led mediation, to realize the resonance of the three types of mediation in social governance. First, in consolidating policy-led mediation, administrative mediation should be further activated and judicial mediation regulated, bringing into play their mediation strengths in both administrative and judicial fields; second, in nurturing society-led mediation, the social transformation of people's mediation should be realized, while the active role of industrial mediation in social autonomy should also be more fully exploited; and, finally, in stimulating market-led mediation, a favorable legal environment and policy incentives should be provided for the commercialization of commercial and arbitration mediation. In terms of incentives for market-led mediation, a favorable legal environment and policy incentives should be provided for the commercialization of commercial mediation and arbitration mediation. Good social governance relies on the complementary strengths and integration of the three types of mediation. On the other hand, the procedural interface between the three types of mediation should also be emphasized and strengthened. For example, in the process of litigation, the interface between judicial mediation and people's mediation, industry mediation, and arbitration mediation can be strengthened, and in cases where judicial mediation is not effective, people's mediators, industry mediators, and arbitrators can be invited to participate in mediation in a timely manner to jointly resolve conflicts and disputes. In short, to achieve the reinvention and integration of China's mediation system, we should adhere to the people-centered approach and strive to provide the people with hierarchical, multi-channel, efficient, and low-cost dispute resolution!

9.5 Conclusion

The progress of human society has always been accompanied by the creation, development, and resolution of disputes, and the degree of sophistication of dispute resolution mechanisms has become one of the yardsticks for measuring the degree of human civilization. Today, the world is in an era of individuality and accelerated integration, and mediation, as the most promising dispute resolution mechanism, is gradually gaining the attention of countries around the world. China is both an ancient and a major country in mediation, but it is not necessarily a powerhouse in mediation compared to the United States, which has since risen to the top. Updating the concept of mediation in China, scientifically reshaping, and transforming the existing mediation system, and promoting the integration and development of the mediation system are not only of great significance in promoting the traditional mediation culture, but also a good prescription for easing social conflicts and building a harmonious society.

Notes

1. Zhang Wusheng: On the Construction of China's Grand Mediation Mechanism: An Analysis of the Relationship between Grand Mediation and ADR, *Legal and Commercial Studies*, 2007 (6).
2. Takao Tanase: *Dispute Resolution and the Trial System*, trans. Wang Yaxin and Liu Rongjun (Beijing: China University of Political Science and Law Press, 2004), p. 13.
3. Yang Jun and Yang Jiankun: "De Gu" Mediation: The Ebian Experience Spreads in the Yi Region, *Sichuan Law Journal*, November 10, 2011, p. 3.
4. Li Xiangming: *A Study of Popular Literature and Art in the Transition Period* (Changsha: Hunan People's Publishing House, 2009), p. 2.
5. Liu Mingjun and Wang Zhiyan: A Perspective on the Tendency of "Pan-utilitarianization" in Chinese Society during the Transition Period, *Jianghan Forum*, 2002 (8).
6. He Xuefeng: *The New Rural China*, preface by Su Li (Guilin: Guangxi Normal University Press, 2003), p. 6.
7. Wu Fan: Proview Apple Enters Bargaining Stage, *Shenzhen Special Zone Daily*, May 7, 2012.
8. Wang Dan: Medical Disputes Have a "Neutral" Mediation Committee, *Beijing Daily*, May 31, 2011.
9. See the 2012 China E-commerce Market Data Monitoring Report, published by the China E-commerce Research Center on August 21, 2012, p. 29.
10. Gao Weiping: ODR: Future Trends in Resolving E-Commerce Disputes in China, Master's thesis, East China University of Political Science and Law, 2008.
11. Hou Minna et al.: Realistic Dilemmas and Ways Out of the Judicial Confirmation System of People's Mediation Agreements: An Analysis of a Survey of Nine Grass-Roots Courts in Z City, H Province, in Yanling County People's Court, Hunan Province. Available at: http://ylxfy.chinacourt.org/article/detail/2016/05/id/1850697.shtml (accessed November 11, 2018).
12. James E. McGuire, Chen Zihao, and Wu Ruiqing: *Peace is Precious: Mediation and Alternative Dispute Resolution in the United States* (Beijing: Law Press, 2011), pp. 7–8.
13. Liao Yong'an: *How to Be a Good Mediator: Insights rom Mediation Training in China and the United States* (Xiangtan: Xiangtan University Press, 2012), p. 22.
14. Communities in the United States are those social relationships and social groups that are made up of a homogeneous population with shared values, that are close, in and out of friendships, that help each other out, that help each other in sickness, and that are compassionate. People do not join such groups by purposeful choice, but as a result of natural formation. People are bound together by common interests and common goals, and by ties of blood or place such as relatives, neighbors, and friends. It can be said that the American community is a social circle in which acquaintanceship predominates. See Xie Fang: *American Communities* (Beijing: China Social Press, 2004), p. 8.
15. JAMS is the largest private provider of alternative dispute resolution (ADR) services in the United States, established in 1979, with 23 dispute resolution centers throughout the country. The agency is now headed by James E. McGuire. See Li Zheng: The Process and Effectiveness of Private Mediation in the Perspective of ADR: The Case of JAMS in the United States, *Journal of Law*, 2009 (11).

16 For example, the aforementioned James E. McGuire of JAMS charges up to US$600 per hour for mediation. See Liao Yong'an: *How to Be a good mediator: Insights from Mediation Training in China and the United States*, p. 105.
17 Ibid., p. 110.
18 Zhu Lei: A Preliminary Study on Online Dispute Resolution Mechanism, *Seeking*, 2003 (1).
19 Zhao Xudong: *Disputes and Dispute Resolution: An In-Depth Analysis from Causes to Concepts* (Beijing: Peking University Press, 2009), p. 133.
20 Zhu Xinxin: Administrative Mediation System in Social Transformation, *Administrative Law Studies*, 2006 (2).
21 Zhao Xudong: *Disputes and Dispute Resolution: An In-depth Analysis from Causes to Concepts*, p. 125.
22 Liao Yong'an and Jiang Fengming: New Ideas for Developing Social Mediation in China in the New Era, *China Social Science Journal*, January 19, 2018, p. 1.

References

Gao Weiping: ODR – Future Trends in Resolving E-Commerce Disputes in China, Master's thesis, East China University of Political Science and Law, 2008.

He Xuefeng: *The New Rural China*, preface by Su Li, Guilin: Guangxi Normal University Press, 2003, p. 6.

Li Xiangming: *A Study of Popular Literature and Art in the Transition Period*, Changsha: Hunan People's Publishing House, 2009, p. 2.

Li Zheng: The Process and Effectiveness of Private Mediation in the Perspective of ADR – The Case of JAMS in the United States, *Journal of Law*, 2009 (11): 15–17.

Liao Yong'an: *How to Be a Good Mediator: Insights from Mediation Training in China and the United States*, Xiangtan: Xiangtan University Press, 2012.

Liao Yong'an and Jiang Fengming: New Ideas for Developing Social Mediation in China in the New Era, *China Social Science Journal*, January 19, 2018 p. 1.

Liu Mingjun and Wang Zhiyan: A Perspective on the Tendency of "Pan-utilitarianization" in Chinese Society during the Transition Period, Jianghan Forum, 2002 (8): 41–45.

McGuire, James E., Chen Zihao, and Wu Ruiqing: *Peace is Precious: Mediation and Alternative Dispute Resolution in the United States (English-Chinese)*, Beijing: Law Press, 2011.

Tanase, Takao: *Dispute Resolution and the Trial System*, trans. Wang Yaxin and Liu Rongjun, Beijing: China University of Political Science and Law Press, 2004.

Wang Dan: Medical Disputes Have a "Neutral" Mediation Committee, Beijing Daily, May 31, 2011.

Wu Fan: Proview Apple Enters Bargaining Stage, Shenzhen Special Zone Daily, May 7, 2012.

Xie Fang: *American Communities*, Beijing: China Social Press, 2004.

Yang Jun and Yang Jiankun: "De Gu" Mediation: The Ebian Experience Spreads in the Yi Region, *Sichuan Law Journal*, November 10, 2011, p. 3.

Zhang Wusheng: On the Construction of China's Grand Mediation Mechanism: An Analysis of the Relationship between Grand Mediation and ADR, Legal and Commercial Studies, 2007 (6): 111–115.

Zhao Xudong: *Disputes and Dispute Resolution: An In-depth Analysis from Causes to Concepts*, Beijing: Peking University Press, 2009.

Zhu Lei: A Preliminary Study on Online Dispute Resolution Mechanism, Seeking, 2003 (1): 75–77.

Zhu Xinxin: Administrative Mediation System in Social Transformation, *Administrative Law Studies*, 2006 (2): 72–77.

Index

administrative adjudication 17, 53, 81, 102, 103, 222
administrative mediation 17, 29, 33, 36, 37, 40, 49, 52, 67, 81–109, 116, 153–5, 170, 194, 204, 222, 236, 250–2, 259, 274, 275, 277–9, 283
administrative organs 9, 20, 21, 38, 81, 89, 94, 99, 100, 102, 104, 107, 112, 124, 154, 170, 214, 277–9
alternative dispute resolution mechanism (ADR) 36, 77, 79, 94, 175, 176, 208, 245–8, 256, 266, 267
ancient 10, 47, 48, 68, 75, 81, 82, 84, 85, 106, 108–10, 283
arbitration 4, 9, 10, 29, 37, 53, 91, 95–7, 102, 118, 133, 134, 136, 138, 140–4, 147–51, 159, 169, 183, 185, 214–49, 251, 260–2, 265–7, 273, 275, 282, 283
Arb-Med 219

civil disputes 2, 4, 7, 9, 11, 12, 14, 16, 19, 21, 33, 36, 41, 42, 47, 68, 72, 75, 81–5, 88, 89, 92, 97, 99, 100, 102, 104, 108–10, 115, 137, 256, 278, 279
civil mediation trials 48
Combination of Arbitration and Mediation 214–49
commercial mediation 15, 19–21, 31, 36, 37, 40, 42, 67, 77, 79, 130–55, 165–7, 194, 202, 203, 220–2, 239, 250–2, 259, 269–75, 278, 281–3
Co-Med-Arb 219
The Communist Party of China, 1, 7, 11, 12, 26, 50, 53, 76, 79, 101, 102, 122
conflicts 10, 11, 14–17, 19, 21, 23, 26–9, 31–8, 43, 45, 52, 56–9, 61, 66, 69, 74, 88–91, 96–9, 101–3, 110, 112, 116–19, 123, 125, 132, 134, 155, 158, 167, 169, 172, 180, 181, 185, 188, 189, 192–5, 197, 202–4, 209, 212, 222, 241, 251, 253, 254, 256, 258, 263–6, 270, 275, 278, 279, 282, 283
contract 82, 91–3, 96, 108, 116, 122, 126, 222, 237, 238, 266, 268
court-commissioned mediation 66, 68, 71
court-led model 181, 192
court mediation 4, 5, 36, 37, 47–80, 91, 103–6, 109, 170, 180, 181, 186, 192–8, 201, 203, 210, 240, 247, 250, 251, 254, 259, 274, 277, 279–81

dispute mediation index 132, 133
dispute resolution 1, 8, 10, 13–19, 21, 23, 24, 35–7, 39–45, 47, 48, 53, 55, 58, 60, 61, 64–70, 72–5, 77–9, 81–3, 91, 93–7, 99, 102–4, 107–14, 118, 119, 121, 122, 125, 130–5, 137, 145, 153–5, 168, 170–3, 175, 176, 178–82, 184–6, 188, 189, 192–9, 201–5, 208–16, 220–2, 227, 232, 236–9, 241, 243, 245–48, 250, 251, 253–7, 259–62, 264–7, 269–83
diversified dispute 15, 36, 53, 66–8, 77, 78, 81, 95, 103, 110, 113, 119, 136, 154, 172, 180, 193, 195–7, 201, 202, 209–12, 221, 222, 236, 247, 248, 251

entrusting mediation 68, 69, 72
empowerment 112, 122, 123, 126–9
ethical risks 160

Fengqiao experience 25–38, 43, 45, 122, 210, 212
forced mediation 64, 84, 90, 253, 261, 262, 279
Fraudulent mediation 138–40

harmony 1, 10, 11, 14, 16, 32, 33, 59, 75, 78, 82, 83, 112, 115, 133, 214, 256

Huang Zongzhi 12, 41, 42, 44, 48, 49, 68, 75, 77, 78, 171

industry mediation 20, 31, 98, 110–29, 250, 251, 283
international commercial dispute 130, 131, 133, 135, 222, 237, 242, 243
internet 29, 30, 114, 178–83, 185–90, 192–8, 200–3, 207–13, 273
internet mediation platform 183, 209

judicial mediation 29, 37, 40, 47, 52, 59, 87, 90, 93, 100–3, 116, 153, 155, 204, 221, 251, 252, 275, 278, 283

lawyer mediation 20, 37, 40, 152–78, 250, 251, 281
legislation 21, 37, 42, 59, 84, 92, 105, 106, 109, 121, 124, 127, 128, 135, 136, 142–4, 201, 239, 241, 267, 278
litigation 5–7, 12, 17, 20, 21, 23, 30, 32, 33, 35, 36, 40, 44, 47, 48, 51, 53, 55–71, 74–89, 94–7, 99, 103, 106–9, 111, 118, 125, 133, 134, 136, 140, 142, 144, 149, 150, 153–60, 162, 163, 165–7, 169, 171–3, 175–7, 180–3, 185, 186, 193–5, 201–3, 211–13, 215, 220, 222, 236, 245, 246, 248, 250–3, 256, 259–63, 265–8, 270–2, 280–3

mandatory mediation process 65
market-led 157, 250–2, 256, 269, 271–4, 283
MEDALOA 217
Med-Arb-Diff 217
Med-Arb-Opt-Out 217
mediation agreements 9, 10, 11, 37, 51, 67, 69, 94–9, 107, 121, 122, 126, 128, 129, 153, 221, 254, 264–6, 268, 273, 275, 276
mediator 2, 4, 7–10, 12, 13, 16, 19–21, 23, 25, 29, 30, 32, 34–42, 44, 45, 64, 66–8, 70, 74, 82, 88, 90, 96, 97, 104, 114–17, 119–21, 124, 125, 136–40, 143–6, 152–69, 171, 172, 174, 175, 181, 183, 185–91, 193–5, 197–200, 203–7, 210, 211, 216–21, 224–30, 232–5, 237, 239–43, 252–4, 256, 258, 259, 261–83
mediation system 1–6, 8, 14–16, 21, 22, 24, 29, 33, 34, 36, 37, 39–42, 44, 45, 47–9, 52, 58, 59, 61, 72, 75, 77, 79, 88, 90, 92–5, 98, 100, 102, 103, 105–9, 114, 122, 127, 129, 131, 135, 140, 150, 151, 153, 154, 170, 172, 173, 176, 183, 194, 198, 201, 203, 204, 214, 245–83
medical disputes 29, 97, 101, 102, 104, 260, 279

neutrality 37, 56, 64, 90, 120, 156, 158, 159, 244, 259, 267, 268, 272, 273, 278–80

ODR 178, 186, 208, 209, 213, 260, 273
offline mediation 192, 195, 203, 209, 211
one belt one road 133, 150, 241, 243, 246–8
online mediation 30, 32, 35, 178–92, 193–213
oratorical mediation 48
order 2, 10, 11, 14–16, 23, 25, 27, 70, 75, 78, 85, 87, 91, 94, 111, 117, 118, 122, 125–9, 136, 138, 142, 148, 157, 167–70, 173, 183, 185, 188, 204, 205, 206, 219, 220, 236, 242, 244, 251, 254, 260, 262–6, 268, 272, 273, 280
overstepped 2

parties 2, 7, 9, 10, 12, 14–17, 20, 22, 23, 30, 32, 36–8, 40, 41, 47, 50, 53, 55–7, 59, 60, 62–90, 94–6, 98, 99, 112, 117–19, 122, 125, 126, 128, 133, 138–42, 145–9, 153, 155–9, 162, 163, 165, 166, 168–71, 173, 180–3, 185–8, 190, 191, 193, 195, 197–9, 202, 207, 210, 215–22, 224–30, 232, 233, 238, 240–2, 243–5, 247, 251–6, 258–63, 265–81
people's mediation 1–49, 51, 52, 59, 67, 70, 72, 74, 77–9, 81, 89, 91, 93, 94–108, 112, 116, 121, 122, 125–8, 132, 136, 146, 153, 154, 166, 170, 179, 181, 182, 194, 203, 204, 209, 212, 222, 236, 250, 251, 252, 254–6, 259, 265, 267, 268, 274–9, 281, 283
People's Mediation Law 8–10, 14, 15, 17, 19, 21, 37, 41, 44, 99, 106, 112, 121, 136, 181, 265, 278
The Pilot Opinions 152–4, 157, 158, 162–5, 168
policy-led mediation 250–60, 262, 264, 272, 273, 275, 283
process 3, 10, 16, 19, 21, 23–5, 36, 47, 49, 56, 57, 60–3, 65–7, 69, 70, 72, 73, 82, 89–1, 94, 103, 104, 107, 108, 112, 119, 125–8, 130, 132, 134, 135, 143–6, 150, 151, 157–9, 162, 163, 167, 175, 176,

181, 183–5, 187–9, 191, 194, 195, 197–9, 202, 206, 208, 209, 216, 217–20, 227, 240–2, 244, 246, 248, 251, 253, 255, 256, 258, 259, 261, 264, 265, 267, 269, 270, 276, 280–3
public interest-led 157, 163
public remedies 16, 39, 70
Pure Med-Arb 217

The reform and opening-up 8, 13, 14, 24, 27, 28, 58, 72, 110, 117
reinvention 149, 151, 273, 283
rule of law 8, 11, 20, 23, 27, 29–32, 35, 36, 42, 43, 45, 53, 57, 58, 60, 63, 65, 72, 76, 77, 79, 80, 85, 88, 94, 99–103, 105, 106, 109, 112, 113, 127, 128, 132, 150–2, 167, 172, 209, 211–14, 247, 250, 252, 255, 257, 274, 282

The separation of mediation and trial 60–3, 76, 78, 247, 248
settlement in litigation 61, 65
shadow mediation 219, 220, 224, 226, 227, 238
Singapore Convention on Mediation 130, 131, 134, 135, 138, 140, 277

social autonomy 24, 38, 39, 72, 73, 77, 79, 283
social capital 37, 71–3
social governance system 31, 77, 78, 110, 119, 180
socialization 21, 31, 35, 36, 42, 45, 66–71, 73, 74, 77–9, 282
socialization of justice 66, 70
social mediation 19–25, 29, 36, 37, 39, 40, 42–5, 69, 73, 250, 259, 268, 278, 281, 282
soviet 1, 4, 88, 214, 215
subjectivity 253, 254, 262, 268, 269, 272–4, 278

trial 5, 8, 12, 14, 15, 17, 21, 34, 36, 37, 40–5, 47–69, 75, 76, 78–80, 83, 84, 88, 92–4, 96, 101–4, 108, 110–12, 115, 121, 122, 126–9, 142, 147, 154–6, 159, 162, 169, 174, 180, 185, 190, 192–5, 198, 200, 202, 209, 211, 212, 215, 222, 244–50, 254–7, 258, 259, 271, 277, 280–3
tribunal mediation 47, 232–5

unification of mediation and trial 61, 64

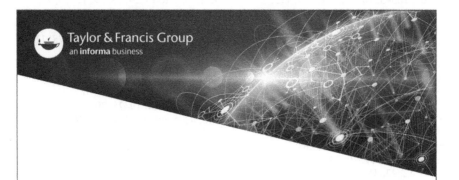